This signed edition of

2010
TAKE BACK
AMERICA

by

DICK MORRIS
AND
EILEEN McGANN

has been specially bound by the publisher.

2010
TAKE BACK AMERICA

2010

TAKE BACK AMERICA

A Battle Plan

DICK MORRIS
and EILEEN McGANN

HARPER

An Imprint of HarperCollins*Publishers*
www.harpercollins.com

Illustrations on pages: 254, 257, 258, 273, 274, 275 by John Sprengelmeyer, www.Sprengelmeyer
.com

HarperCollins books may be purchased for educational, business, or sales promotional use.
For information, please write: Special Markets Department, HarperCollins Publishers,
10 East 53rd Street, New York, NY 10022.

FIRST EDITION

Library of Congress Cataloging-in-Publication Data is available upon request.

ISBN: 978-0-06-198844-8

10   11   12   13   14   DIX/RRD   10   9   8   7   6   5   4   3   2   1

**To Eugene J. Morris,
now in his 100th year!**

CONTENTS

Introduction... 1

PART ONE: THE STAKES   7

The New Dangers 11

Obama Wants to Transform America.................................... 17

The Danger of Bureaucratism 19

Obama Is Leading Us into Socialism.................................. 20

And Europe Pays the Price of Socialism 23

The Global Bureaucratic Tyranny..................................... 27

Lincoln vs. Jefferson: The Historical Perspective.................. 29

Pessimism Is the Bodyguard of Socialism 32

There Is Still Time 33

Unemployment 33

Inflation 47

The World Loses Confidence in the Dollar 55

The Next Crash?... 59

Huge Tax Increases Ahead 62

Health Care 69

Vulnerable Democrats Who Voted for Obamacare 82

Obama Makes Us Debt Slaves 83

The IMF Takes Over Our Economy 92

The Onset of Socialism 102

Constitution? What Constitution? Obama Disregards It 112

Can We Trust Obama with This Much Power? 118

Obama's Wrath: The Fight with Fox News 119

Obama's Favor: His Largesse Toward Goldman Sachs 122

Cap and Trade: The Middle-Class Tax Increase 126

Losing the War on Terror 133

PART TWO: THE TARGETS   141

The Senate 143

The House of Representatives 204

PART THREE: THE STRATEGY   247

Debunk the Myth of the Moderate Democrat 250

Nationalize the Campaign and Make Obama the Issue 255

Don't Be Limited by Ideology 260

Do Not Move to the Center 264

Offer a Positive Alternative 265

Don't Trip Over Your Own Proposals: Stay on Offense 267

The Unemployment Issue 270

The Health-Care Issue.. 276

The Tax Issue.. 279

The Afghanistan Issue... 284

How to Answer a Negative Campaign 286

PART FOUR: THE ELECTRONIC PRECINCT   293

How You Can Help Beat Obama and the Democrats.................. 293

Acknowledgments 309

Notes 311

Index 339

INTRODUCTION

Casting your vote in the November 2010 elections may be the single most important thing you do all year.

Because these elections will be *the* critical turning point for America's future.

For the definition of what is America.

For the chance to take back America.

In 2010, in this 234th year of our astonishingly successful American democracy—at the dawn of the second decade of the new millennium—America stands on the edge of an ideological precipice.

A precipice we can't back away from or ignore.

We stand overlooking a chasm that separates those who want our values, our culture, and our economic systems to endure from those who want to change everything—regardless of the consequences.

On the one side is the familiar America that we know and love.

On the other is a very different America: the dream of Barack Obama.

His dream is a pipe dream.

His dream is our nightmare.

Make no mistake: Fulfilling Obama's quixotic vision for our future would result in the systematic ruin of just about every segment of the America we know and love.

Don't underestimate him. He's made no secret of his determination to radically alter our economic structure, to socialize our health-care system, to transform our foreign policies, and to compromise our national sovereignty.

Those are his plans. And he's deadly serious about fulfilling them.

But we can still stop him—if we act together in November.

We still have the power to prevent him from ideologically devastating and economically paralyzing this great nation. Because that's what he plans to do.

But Obama can only accomplish his frightening agenda if the Democrats maintain their majority in one or both houses of Congress. We can block him by breaking his party's monopoly on the legislative branch.

And we can do it.

The change Barack Obama believes in is not the change we believe in.

His strategic mantra is REDISTRIBUTE!

He plans to redistribute wealth, to redistribute access to health care, and to raise taxes until it no longer makes sense for productive people to keep working. He intends to increase the Death Tax so that money that's already been taxed once is taxed again—and then, yes, redistributed.

But that's not all. He envisions creating an expansive, and expensive, federal government that regulates, controls, and pays for an ever-increasing percentage of our daily lives. We repeat: His dream is truly our nightmare.

He wants to minimize the sovereignty of the U.S. government over the United States of America itself, and, instead, maximize the authority of foreign nations over U.S. economic policy. He enthusiastically embraces a One World philosophy, instead of validating the importance of individual nations—including the nation whose laws and people he swore an oath to protect.

As part of this One World strategy, he treats our longtime friends and allies with suspicion, while welcoming our enemies with naïve tolerance. He insults the British and the French and betrays the Poles, while kowtowing to the North Koreans and the Iranians.

He agrees to allow the G-20 nations to replace the lower 48, Hawaii, and Alaska in deciding how much we can pay executives in private American corporations. If he's not stopped in 2010, he'll try to place the entire American economy under the rule of the International Monetary Fund and the G-20 (including countries like Argentina, South Africa, Saudi Arabia, and Russia). It's in the works.

Here's how the *New York Times* described the G-20 agreements he endorsed in September 2009:

> The agreements . . . would lead to much tighter regulation over financial institutions, complex financial instruments and executive pay. They could also lead to big changes and more outside scrutiny over the economic strategies of individual countries, including the United States.[1]

In a characteristic understatement, Obama predicted that the G-20 agreements would make our financial system "far *different*."[2]

He might have chosen plainer words: far weaker, severely undermined, radically subverted, dangerously destabilized, and permanently damaged.

Obama believes in those kind of changes.

Changes that don't work and run counter to our best interest.

Fantasies that are extremely dangerous.

And the elections of 2010 may be our last chance to stop his plans for transforming the United States into a collectivist nanny state, a city-state of the world.

If we don't turn the tide this fall, it may well be too late. If we reelect another rubber-stamp Congress, Obama will be able to change America so fundamentally that we won't recognize it and likely won't be able to change it back.

That's how precarious things are.

If we deprive Obama of his lackeys in Congress, however, his extreme program will go nowhere. Which is just where it belongs.

It used to be that both parties in Congress had members who were well-intentioned, independent thinkers. Congressional representatives who were courageous enough to diverge from their party and stand against legislation that went against their own beliefs and the strong will of their voters. But those days are over. If there's one clear lesson we've learned from the health-care debacle, it is that the existence of a moderate democrat is now nothing but a myth.

At this moment, no more moderate Democrats exist. The species is extinct.

Now, there are only Democrats. Generic democrats. Robots. Automatons. John F. Kennedy—an independent-thinking Democrat of the old school—once said, "Sometimes party loyalty asks too much."[3] That is definitely the case today.

Today's Democrats are nothing but sheep, blindly following their shepherds, Reid and Pelosi, wherever they are driven. But unlike the biblical shepherds in Jeremiah 3:15, Reid and Pelosi do not lead their flock with knowledge and understanding.[4] No, they are ignorant wolves masquerading in shepherds' clothing, dominating their pack by dangling campaign contributions, gargantuan earmarks, and threats.

That's how legislation is passed today: by bribing the members with expensive goodies for their district. By threatening them with primaries. By forcing them to pass legislation during the middle of the night. Legislation they haven't even read. Legislation they opposed, on principle, only weeks before.

Legislation their constituents overwhelmingly oppose.

But they don't care. The Democrats in Congress have legislated with total disregard for public opinion.

The public knows that stimulus spending would not help the economy, but the Democrats passed it anyway.

The public wants less government, but the Democrats expanded it anyway.

The public opposes Obama's notion of health-care "reform," knowing it will worsen the quality of care, but the Democrats passed it anyway.

They just don't care.

It's no surprise that the public approval rating for Congress dropped to 18 percent in a recent Gallup poll, and that eight out of every ten Americans have a negative view of Congress.

This gap between what America wants and how Congress votes has grown into a profound chasm. It must be reversed. Because if we return a Democratic Congress once again in 2010, we are forfeiting our own voice in the way we're governed.

And we certainly don't want to do that. In fact, we must do just the opposite. We need to throw the Democrats and their leaders out of Congress and assert our right to a representative form of government. A Congress where our elected officials listen to their constituents, where they read and understand what they're voting on and vote based on their conscience, not their party.

Is that asking too much?

Think about it: In less than a year, Obama has pushed the national deficit to $1.2 trillion. We now borrow forty cents of every dollar that we spend. This new debt level—increased by 25 percent in one year—will so undermine confidence in the dollar that U.S. currency may well lose its primacy among the world's nations, permanently undermining America's global position.

And that's not all: If we let him continue to control Congress, Obama will use that deficit as a pretext to raise taxes so substantially that we will become, in effect, a fully European-style socialist country.

Can he do that?

YES, HE CAN!

Obama believes in these kind of changes. Obama's economic policies can only be described as colossal failures. The unemployment rate has been hovering around 10 percent—but even that masks the true rate of 17.5 percent, once you factor in the number of people who are underemployed in part-time jobs or who have given up even looking for a job. And for these Americans there's no relief in sight.

Billions of dollars later, it's clear that Barack Obama's ideas just aren't working.

November 2, 2010, is the time to take back America.

In this book, we offer a battle plan for exactly how to do it.

We describe the unparalleled stakes and what we fear may happen if Obama and the Democrats continue unchecked.

We provide specifics about the key races, the targets we need to trounce, and detail the ammunition we must use against them.

Finally, we outline how you personally—using the Internet and other resources—can contribute to the movement and make a difference.

Election Day 2010 can be the beginning of a new era—and the end of Barack Obama's dream of a socialized America.

We can win this. And we must.

Remember the call to arms that Shakespeare's Henry V made to his soldiers:

We few, we happy few, we band of brothers;
For he to-day that sheds his blood with me
Shall be my brother; be he ne'er so vile,
This day shall gentle his condition;
And gentlemen in England now-a-bed
Shall think themselves accurs'd they were not here . . .[5]

Don't curse yourself in November, brothers and sisters.
Be there with us on Election Day, and take back America.

PART ONE

THE STAKES

Barack Obama is ruining America.

He is destroying everything that makes us great.

The danger has changed . . . and grown. In our book *Fleeced*, written in February 2008, we predicted the stock market crash that came seven months later. In our most recent book, *Catastrophe*, we warned that Obama would prolong the recession and increase the national debt.

But now the stakes have become even greater. Those significant worries seem almost trivial in the face of the impending realities that confront us unless President Obama's agenda can be defeated and his compliant Congress turned out to pasture.

Envision the country Barack Obama is creating—the future we have in store if we let him continue to control Congress:

- Inflation will soar—not as a lamentable side effect of our government's policies, but because the government *wants* it and needs it . . . since that's the only way it can pay off its debt.

- An intractable budget deficit will force up interest rates, and they won't come down for many, many years. So unemployment will stay permanently high—just as it does in Europe—because the government is hogging all the funds needed to create jobs in order to pay for its deficit.

- Confidence in the dollar will ebb so badly that it will no longer be the global currency—forcing tax and interest rate hikes for all Americans.

- The government will get the power to seize and reinvent any company it deems insolvent yet "too big to fail."

- Washington will set the standards that govern who gets lifesaving treatment or surgery . . . and who is left to die. Government health-care rationers will make the fateful decisions. They will balance cost against human life, ordering health providers to follow government protocols and prohibitions—even when it means an early death for tens of thousands of helpless elderly people.

- We will become a nation in which doctors are increasingly scarce and unavailable. Instead of doctors without borders, we will have borders without doctors. With slashes in reimbursement rates, cuts in medical income, and no relief from student loans, the supply of doctors will dry up; care will have to come from nurse practitioners or physicians' assistants . . . or, in some cases, from foreign doctors with a limited command of our language and training that many medical professionals regard as suspect.

- The locus of decision making for the U.S. economy will shift from Washington to Europe, as the International Monetary Fund (IMF) and the G-20 group of nations assume command of the global economy. The United States will become just one more nation under its thumb.

- The top U.S. tax rate—combined with most states' rates—will reach more than half the income of the productive, entrepreneurial class—shriveling incentive and narcotizing ambition.

- America will lose its remaining manufacturing jobs to Asian nations that don't impose carbon taxes on their industries.   .

And, finally, we must ask whether a president who has shown himself to be highly sensitive to criticism—who blackballs Fox News for its objective news coverage—can be trusted not to abuse these enormous powers for his own political ends. Will his critics find their companies on the Obama administration's short list for seizure? Will they be denied the crucial carbon-emissions permits they need to conduct their business?

Can this president be trusted with this kind of power?

• • •

But this terrifying vision need not come to pass. We still have time to reverse the dangerous course upon which Obama has set America. There is still time to take our country back. If we return a Republican Congress in 2010-and defeat Obama in 2012—we can avert the worst. That's what this book is all about!

THE NEW DANGERS

The economy is bad and it will get worse. Former Federal Reserve chairman Paul Volcker, who rescued America in the 1980s from inflation induced by government spending during the previous decade, made this disturbing prediction in his interview with *Der Spiegel* magazine in December 2009:

> *Der Spiegel*: "The U.S. has not yet instituted any kind of reform policy. What we see is the government and the Federal Reserve pouring money into the economy. If one looks beyond that money, one sees that the economy is in fact still shrinking."

> Volcker: "What should I say? That's right. We have not yet achieved self-reinforcing recovery. We are heavily dependent upon government support so far. We are on a government support system, both in the financial markets and in the economy."[1]

Our economy is on a heart-lung machine, which pumps currency through our veins through the artificial purchasing of Treasury and mortgage-backed securities. As long as we're wired to the machine, interest rates remain low and credit stays cheap. But eventually we will have to come off the machine and borrow real money from real lenders—and Washington will have to pay higher interest rates when we do. And with those permanently higher rates will come high—and likely permanent—unemployment.

So it's no longer just a question of high cyclical unemployment. Obama's policies now threaten to create permanent joblessness—just like in Europe, where the unemployment rate never comes down and one-tenth of each nation's population accepts a life of perpetual dependency on the government. The industries that have been decimated by this recession—retail, manufacturing, publishing, and so on—were already under attack from technological change; they're not coming back and neither are their jobs. And Obama's deficits, debt, and taxes will prevent us from replacing them.

Once, we worried about budget deficits. Now we face the very real prospect that we will become a nation enslaved to debt. We may be following the same trajectory as some families that have to spend their lifetimes paying back money they borrowed during a period of great need—or, in the case of the United States, during the opening days of the Obama presidency, when his stimulus package ballooned the deficit. We may have to spend so much in paying down our debt—year in and year out—that it will consume our national treasure. Where past generations had to choose between guns and butter, we will be able to afford neither—not when each year we will have to pay $1 trillion or more in interest and principal on Obama's debt. By 2012, depending on how interest rates change, it is likely that every penny we get from the federal personal income tax will have to go to debt service!

It will be like having to spend your whole paycheck on your mortgage.

We used to fear that the Federal Reserve Board would raise interest rates and dampen economic growth. But Obama's deficits have so weakened the world's confidence in our currency that we face the prospect of permanently high interest rates if we're going to attract the money we will need in order to fund our national debt each year. Regardless of whether or not it is good economic policy, Obama has left the Fed with no option but to raise rates far into the future so that people will lend us their money.

We used to worry about whether China would continue to buy our debt. But Obama's borrowing spree will likely trigger a global run on the dollar, sending its value plummeting and inflation soaring at home. The global dominance of the dollar, established at the Bretton Woods conference in 1944, may end with the Obama administration.

We've all been worrying about inflation. But it's becoming increasingly obvious to economists that inflation is the only way to pay down our federal deficit and the resulting debt. Only by debasing and, in effect, devaluing our currency will we be able to meet our obligations. Those who lent us money, in other words, will have to be repaid in cheaper dollars than the ones they lent. Savings throughout the United States will wither as the elderly and salaried employees race to keep their wages and pensions in line with inflation.

Already we see the harbinger of coming inflation—the increase of the money supply:

PRINTING PRESS: THE INCREASE IN MONEY SUPPLY

Increase in Adjusted Monetary Base (AMB), which includes currency and required excess bank reserves.

September 10, 2008	$875 billion
January 28, 2009	$1.172 billion
December 2, 2009	$2.094 billion

Source: Federal Reserve Board[2]

Former Federal Reserve chairman Alan Greenspan put it well: "My concern is that legislation or other actions on the part of Congress may prevent [a balance sheet reduction]. Unless we sterilize or unwind the big monetary base we've built up, two, three years out inflation really begins to take hold."[3]

Eventually, this run-up of inflation will have to be checked. And the only way to do *that* is a massive recession brought on as a deliberate act of government policy as happened in the late '70s and early '80s. Interest rates will soar to the high teens, as they did in 1981–82, and economic growth will come to a crashing halt. An inflation explosion caused by a deliberate act of public policy will be cured by a recession caused by a similarly calculated federal government move.

It may be the greatest man-made disaster in history.

We have been worried that Obama's health-care proposals would create a scarcity of medical resources that would lead to the rationing of care. But it's now apparent that Obama's program may drive so many doctors into retirement, and may lead so many young people to choose other professions, that medical care for all patients in the United States—now the best in the world—may deteriorate sharply and permanently.

We may become a country virtually without doctors.

Indeed, our concerns about the impact of Obama's health-care changes may have fallen short of the mark. The real change that he wants to get under way is nothing short of a government-sponsored kind of euthanasia in which lifesaving medical procedures are balanced against their cost and the worthiness of the patient. Those too old or too sick would be excluded from treatment—even if that treatment were necessary to save their lives.

We see the first signs of this new policy in the recent government advisories about mammograms. For years the government urged women over forty to get annual screenings. Now the Department of Health and Human Services' Preventive Services Task Force has about-faced and is suggesting that women over fifty need only receive them every other year, and that they're not even necessary for women ages forty to fifty. Why? Not because annual exams wouldn't catch many early cases of cancer and save many lives. The federally appointed group says it changed its position because of "risks of overtreatment," but there's no ignoring the implication of their decision. Apparently, the bureaucrats believe that the number of lives saved by mammograms is too small to justify the cost of annual exams. Medical evidence makes it clear that mammograms for women in this age group save one life for every 1,900 screenings. With a U.S. population of 21.9 million women in their forties, that works out to 11,500 lives that will be lost if there is no annual screening.

So why did the government change its recommendation? Whatever reason they give, it's obvious that the decision saved millions of dollars. Suddenly, human life has a price tag. Euthanasia is now government policy.

In our earlier books, we wondered if Obama's policies might drive our manufacturing business offshore. But his plans now make it clear that he will tax carbon emissions so heavily—and let China and India get away without doing so—that most of our manufacturing capacity will move offshore.

All we'll have left is a service economy.

We used to worry that Obama was hopelessly naïve in his dealings with America's enemies. But it's becoming obvious that he harbors a bias against our long-term allies, even as he unsuccessfully curries favor with our adversaries. He pressures Israel to stop building settlements, yet he does little to stop Iran from making atomic bombs. He halts the deployment of missiles in Eastern Europe, leaving Poland and the rest of the region on their own in resisting Vladimir Putin's expansionism. He comes down hard on democracy advocates in Honduras, but reaches out to shake hands with the dictator in Venezuela.

Whose side is he on?

We were concerned that Obama would waste our resources trying to rescue dying companies like General Motors. Now it is clear that he intends to establish permanent industrial relics—like the state-owned factories in China—that produce products people don't want, but stay in business anyway, at taxpayer expense, because the alternative would mean laying off their employees and antagonizing politically powerful unions.

As Obama has dug us into the hole by raising federal spending from $3 trillion to $4 trillion and tripling the deficit, we have begun to suspect that he has a diabolical plan—to use the deficit to justify huge tax increases on all Americans in the coming years.

Ronald Reagan used the deficit to force liberals to cut spending.

Barack Obama is going to use it to make conservatives accept higher taxes.

We felt uneasy as Obama committed huge sums to rescue banks, insurance companies, and other financial firms. We used to worry that he was expanding government regulation of the private sector. But now it isn't regulation we fear—it's expropriation. The new legislation Obama and Treasury Secretary Timothy Geithner are seeking would give the federal government the power to seize any business, fire its management, wipe out its investors, and run it as a government company for as long as it wanted, spending unlimited taxpayer money in the process. The feds would simply have to say that, in their opinion, the company is not solvent and that they believe its failure would endanger the economy.

Fidel Castro and Hugo Chavez have no broader powers!

Even if he doesn't take control of your firm, Obama is planning to limit your salary by controlling executive compensation. And he has used the Troubled Asset Relief Program (TARP) bailout funds to take over a controlling voting interest in our major banks and financial institutions. He is increasingly telling them to whom they should lend money. Once he controls the lending, he realizes, he can control the entire economy—and use the bailout funding to bring about a socialist transformation of our way of life.

Groups such as ACORN and Moveon.org raised eyebrows with their tactics on behalf of Candidate Obama. But ever since President Obama came to Washington, his near-hysterical criticism of Fox News and anyone else who doesn't toe his line have us worrying that we may be in the first stages of an attempt to roll back our democracy and inhibit freedom of speech. Remember: All dictatorships begin with increasingly strident criticism of the news media.

Obama's internationalism rankled us. We worried that he dismissed the very idea of American exceptionalism. But now he has put the entire American economy under the rule of the G-20 nations (including countries like Argentina, Brazil, South Africa, Indonesia, Saudi Arabia, China, and Russia) and the International Monetary Fund (IMF). Increasingly, it will be these countries and the European central bankers who control the IMF that will make the fundamental decisions on how fast we should grow, how intensely we should regulate business, what taxes we should levy, and which sectors of our economy we should emphasize. The Federal Reserve Board, the Securities and Exchange Commission, and the Treasury Department threaten to become, in effect, mere implementers of a global economic strategy designed by the IMF and the G-20 countries.

We foresaw that Obama would pull back from the war on terror. But he has done so with such speed that we're now facing either of two very likely catastrophic scenarios: Either Iran will get nuclear weapons and use them to wipe out Israel, or Israel will attack the mullahs in Tehran to stop them from annihilating her, precipitating a Middle East–wide war.

But permanently high unemployment, a mounting national debt that strangles us, manufacturing jobs that leave us as fast as they can, and a health-care system that deteriorates each year—none of these are necessarily in our future.

What Congress has passed, Congress can undo.

If the Republican Party captures both houses in the 2010 elections, the Democrats and Obama will be in shock. Everyone will write off his chances in 2012. Democratic senators who aren't up for reelection in 2010—thus giving them a temporary reprieve—will scramble to change the most offensive parts of Obama's program, anxious to mollify voters before they themselves have to appear on the ballot.

There is still time!

OBAMA WANTS TO TRANSFORM AMERICA

When Barack Obama arrived in Washington, our nation fell, unknowingly, into the grip of a committed socialist. And he will continue to emasculate our economy and our way of life—if we do not stop him.

Obama's slate of radical legislation in 2009 and 2010 is only a beginning. If we let him keep control of Congress in 2011 and 2012, he will destroy our free enterprise system and replace it with government control of all aspects of our lives. He will work with the Europeans to enslave us in a global socialist system.

Obama does not represent merely an alternative ideology or a different set of substantive priorities. He wants to change the basic philosophy and guiding principles of our nation—to turn us into something we have never been, and that most of us don't want to become.

It's not just that Obama wants to strengthen political control over our economy and bureaucratic regulation of our businesses. It's not merely that he seeks to socialize medicine and make it a government monopoly. It's not just that he covets one automobile company here or a financial services corporation there. It's not just that his spending priorities are digging us into a pit of debt.

Obama's transformative presidency goes far deeper.

He is seeking to replace individualism with collectivism, and self-determination with community governance. He is seeking to dull the profit motive that now generates commerce, and the democratic impetus that animates our politics, by subjecting them to the deadening hand of bureaucratic control.

And, worst of all, Barack Obama wants to change *us*. He wants us to become dependent on government, to reduce our self-reliance, to curb our ambition, to narcotize ourselves with leisure, and to care more about the strangers we live among than the family for whom we are responsible.

He is trying to seduce us with his offers of protection from cradle to grave. And, in return, he asks only that we sign over much of our freedom, our self-reliance, our ambition, and our initiative.

He will break the covenant that lies at the basis of what it means to be an American: that if we work hard, get educated, seize opportunity, practice thrift, and play by the rules, we will get ahead in life.

He is reconfiguring our society, teaching the poor to turn to politics to take what the marketplace has denied them. Have others worked harder? Taken more risks? Prepared themselves better? Taken more advantage of opportunity? *Don't worry,* he seems to say. *Government will redress the imbalance. We are a benign bureaucracy of experts, guided by politicians who speak for you. We will make the rich give you what you want. And all you need to do is vote us into power . . . again and again.*

In Obama's world, the individual is less important than the community. In his construct, it is politics, not commerce, that will determine the distribution of resources.

Obama wants to dumb down life so that everybody gets an increasingly equal share—regardless of one's own effort, ability, risk, and contribution to society.

His mandate for us is simple: Curb your competitive instincts. Don't play to win. Work to share and collaborate with your competitor, even if it means accepting a life of mediocrity. Work less. Put in fewer hours. Accept less pay. We will provide enough jobs and pay for everybody.

Obama even asks that we take less medical care. That we die earlier than we otherwise would. To expand full medical services to the 17 percent of Americans (including legal immigrants) who currently lack coverage, he would transform the care the rest of us get from excellent to mediocre.

We all get up in the morning to make a living to provide for our families. But Obama wants to stop us from spending our hard-earned money to be sure we're doing all we can to keep them healthy.

So what are we left to work for? Why get up in the morning? To buy a yacht? A fancy restaurant dinner? A bigger house? Who cares about these if your family's good health hangs in the balance? By divorcing our work and our effort from the outcome of good health, he would rob us of the incentive to produce and mute the ambition that makes our country run.

Why work? he asks.

THE DANGER OF BUREAUCRATISM

Now, after we faced and destroyed the demons of the twentieth century, we meet the greatest threat of all to our freedom at the outset of the twenty-first. It was not the strutting dictators of the 1930s or the faceless apparatchiks of the Soviet Union who posed the greatest peril to our freedoms and our way of life. Nor are the Islamic fascists in ski masks the greatest threat to our liberty.

The most potent adversary of democracy is bureaucracy.

Bureaucracy offers us a vague promise: *Give us the power, take away our political constraints, let us rule, and we will do it right.*

It plays on the same emotion as dictatorships do. It tells those who are fed up, fearful, and fatigued by politics to let the experts take over.

Angry at the obduracy and callousness of insurance companies? Let us allocate the medical resources. You can trust us to make the best decisions. After all, we don't have a profit motive.

Furious at the shenanigans of Wall Street? Let us step in. We'll curb the excesses and stop the abuses.

Fearful of climate change? Disgusted at the apparent insensibility of polluters, utilities, and carmakers? We'll decide who gets the carbon credits. We will specify who can emit what—and we'll get it right.

Horrified at the obscene salaries of corporate CEOs? Revolted by their golden parachutes even as their companies crash around them? Calm down. Leave it to us. We'll regulate them—and we'll make sure everything is done appropriately and properly.

Afraid of global competition? Worried about your company closing down and throwing you out on the street? Don't get upset. We saved GM. We rescued Chrysler. You can trust us to take care of you. Just don't run afoul of our mandates—or you might end up broke and dead, like Lehman Brothers.

Tired of seeing photos and reading reports of abusive interrogations? Fearful for your civil liberties? Don't worry. We can protect you from terrorism without getting your—or our—hands dirty. No need for excesses. Trust us.

Early in the century—when our ancestors were still naïve about civil service and saw "merit selection" as the alternative to patronage politics—

some public policy commentators believed in the fantasy that the nation's business could best be conducted by administrators who would disregard politics and profit and make all the correct decisions for our country.

But now, as we watch bureaucracy (and its handmaiden, public employee unionization) destroy one by one the institutions of our nation—the Post Office, the Veterans Hospitals, the public schools—we see the bureaucrat for what he is: our oppressor.

We are coming to recognize the wisdom of James Harrington, the seventeenth-century British enlightenment philosopher, who wrote: "The wisdom of the few may be the light of mankind. But the interest of the few is not the profit of mankind."[4]

In his excellent and influential book *Liberty and Tyranny*, Mark Levin quotes the philosopher/theologian/novelist C. S. Lewis about the danger of the tyrant who claims to be acting in your own best interest: "Of all tyrannies, a tyranny exercised for the good of its victims may be the most oppressive. It would be better to live under robber barons than under omnipotent moral busybodies. The robber baron's cruelty may sometimes sleep, his cupidity may at some point be satiated. But those who torment us for our own good will torment us without end for they do so with the approval of their own conscience."[5]

We now appreciate that the bureaucrat usually works hand in hand with big government, big business, and big labor to dominate our lives. A handful of people gather at a table in Japan and Western Europe and decides how their people should live. We don't have that in America, with our small businesses and pluralistic government of checks and balances—not yet.

But Obama is working on it.

OBAMA IS LEADING US INTO SOCIALISM

In her poem "The New Colossus," inscribed on the base of the Statue of Liberty, Emma Lazarus wrote: "Give me your tired, your poor / Your huddled masses yearning to breathe free / The wretched refuse of your teeming shore / Send these, the homeless, tempest-tossed to me."[6]

Americans embraced that image of a nation that welcomed those who wanted to work hard and grow and build their lives. But Barack Obama has replaced this call for self-reliance with an offer of security and serenity protected, subsidized, and sheltered by the government.

Obama heralds his arrival on the battlefield of our politics not with a cacophony of confrontation, but with a lulling siren song designed to sedate and anesthetize us while he transplants our essence and replaces it with something else entirely.

His sirens—the modern equivalent of those voices that tried to lure Ulysses onto the rocks and to his death in Homer's *Odyssey*—sing the same soothing lullaby that has long since lulled Europe and Japan into a trance.

THE SIREN SINGS: *Put aside your ambition. Don't work so hard. Slow down and live a little. Don't worry. Give the government your insecurities. Let us take care of them.*

BUT REALITY ANSWERS: If we go back to being a nation of child-like dependents, relying on a parental government, we will become poorer and poorer, having to make do with less and less. Government cannot create jobs or wealth. It can only take from some and give it to others. And if people cannot keep their own money, they will stop working, innovating, taking the risks that are key to survival and growth—and we will all have less.

THE SIREN SINGS: *You're not alone in the world. You have your community to surround you and a safety net below you. We have anticipated all the vagaries of life, all of its uncertainties, and have made provision for them.*

BUT REALITY ANSWERS: It's the fear of failure, as much as the dream of success, that motivates us all to work hard, compete, and succeed. If life holds no perils, there's little to get us out of bed in the morning. While we must protect those who cannot help themselves, for most of us it's the fear of bad outcomes—as much as the lure of reward—that impels our labor.

THE SIREN SINGS: *Give up some of your sovereignty and independence. You won't need it anymore. Your leaders will show you what to* *do. You must surrender what you have to the community. We are all in this together. We are a unit, an entity. We will share the sacrifice, take care of each other, and let our government point the way.*

BUT REALITY ANSWERS: Government does almost everything *worse* than private business. The U.S. Postal Service is a joke compared to FedEx and UPS. The Veterans Administration hospitals are a disgrace to the men and women who have served us. Our government cannot control our borders. It can't even distribute flu shots to those who need them. Private and church schools educate better, for less money, than public educational institutions do. State universities are drowning in their own bureaucracy. And the list goes on. Only in the military, police, and firefighting services—with their extraordinary standards of martial discipline, self-sacrifice, unit cohesion, and morale—does the public sector excel.

THE SIREN SINGS: *Abandon the delusions of your religious faith. They are old, for a different time. You don't need them anymore. Secular humanism has made them unnecessary. Turn away from the spurious rituals and the false security they offer. Embrace the real security of a committed community led by enlightened experts.*

BUT REALITY ANSWERS: We each have a God-sized hole in our heart and soul. Without faith, some people turn to addiction; others lose themselves in narcissism. Some become workaholics, others compulsive gamblers, and still others status-seekers who make the acquisition of material goods their own yardstick in life. Where religion falters, self-involvement takes the place of child rearing, and birth rates drop. Values decline—and an increase in crime, sexually transmitted disease, and suicide are the result.

THE SIREN SINGS: *You don't really need your democracy anymore. Let us experts run things. We know better than you what you need and we have the knowledge to get it for you. Turn away from the cantankerous politics of shrill debate. Trust those who act with benign knowledge of what is best for you.*

BUT REALITY ANSWERS: The experts covet power, and power corrupts them as easily as it does anyone else. Bureaucracies become obsessed with self-perpetuation and soon lose sight of the populations they are supposed to serve. They develop cozy relationships with the power brokers in big companies to form a consortium of business and government to control our lives. It is only through democracy that we can fight their tyranny.

AND EUROPE PAYS THE PRICE OF SOCIALISM

By every indication, Europe has lagged under socialism while the United States has soared under free-market capitalism.

Bruce Stokes, the international economics columnist for the *National Journal*, points out that Western Europe today is only as wealthy as the United States was in 1989!

EUROPE VS. AMERICA: SOCIALISM VS. CAPITALISM

- Europe will not reach the level of U.S. wealth until 2024!

- In 2007, per capita GDP in the European Union (not counting eastern Europe) was $27,897. That's $100 less than the U.S. per capita GDP in 1989!

- Germany's per capita GDP is at the same level the United States reached in 1990.

- France's per capita GDP is at the level the United States reached in 1989.

- Before the current recession, Europe's unemployment rate was 50 percent higher than in the United States.

- From 2001 to 2006, Europe's economy grew at only half the rate of the U.S. economy.

Source: National Journal[7]

Stokes sums up the impact of Euro-socialism:

> The sad fact for Europeans is that the very programs they've implemented in order to create a more socialistic society—capitulation to powerful labor unions, higher taxes, more bureaucratic regulation of industries, limitations on employers' ability to hire and fire, unsustainable welfare benefits, etc.—have had the opposite effect. Because of those policies, Europe has suffered from long-term chronic unemployment, slower growth and less entrepreneurial innovation.[8]

Contrast this with Stokes's description of the fruits of American free enterprise over the same period:

> In contrast, America maintained one of the lowest tax rates of the industrialized world during the past 25 years, and pursued relatively free-market policies compared to our friends across the Atlantic. As a result, the American economy posted positive growth during 288 out of 300 months between 1982 and 2007, and GDP grew 3.4% during that span. Also during that period, America witnessed dramatic increases in median income and total wealth, while inflation and interest rates remained remarkably low.[9]

But defenders of Euro-socialism like to argue that "Europeans may be poorer, but they're happier."[10] Are they? The evidence says they aren't.

As the *Wall Street Journal* has noted, Americans work a lot harder than Europeans. So shouldn't we be less happy?

European men retire at the age of 60.5; women retire even sooner. The *Journal* points out that "the average U.S. worker takes 16 days of vacation each year, less than half that typically taken by Germans (35 days), the French (37 days) or the Italians (42 days)."[11]

Why aren't they happier? Because their economies don't work!

The "inconvenient truth" is that Europeans, compared to Americans, are quite miserable.

Pew Global, the opinion research firm, found that "two in three Americans (65%) rank themselves relatively happy with their lives. . . . Europeans tend to be somewhat less happy. Just over half the French (57%) and not quite half the Germans (48%) say they are very satisfied with their lives."[12]

HAPPINESS: THE UNITED STATES AND EUROPE COMPARED

Satisfied with Own Life

United States	65%
Great Britain	59%
France	57%
Germany	48%
Italy	48%

Satisfied with the Quality of Their Lives

United States	65%
Western Europe	53%

Satisfied with Family Income

United States	76%
Western Europe	65%

Source: PewGlobal.com[13]

A more grisly indication of unhappiness is the suicide rate—and Europe is afflicted with a decidedly larger share of men and women who take their own lives.

SUICIDE RATES IN THE UNITED STATES AND EUROPE

Nation	Suicides per 100,000
Belgium	21
Finland	20
France	18

Austria	18
Switzerland	18
Germany	14
Sweden	14
Denmark	14
United States	11
United Kingdom	7

Source: WordPress.com[14]

And Europeans drink a lot more.

ALCOHOL CONSUMPTION IN THE UNITED STATES AND EUROPE

Nation	Liters per capita, 2006
Ireland	13.4
France	13.0
Austria	12.9
Denmark	12.2
Czech Republic	11.9
United Kingdom	11.0
Switzerland	10.2
Finland	10.1
Germany	10.1
Netherlands	9.6
United States	8.6

Source: Forbes magazine[15]

The entire ethic of Western European socialism is oriented around leisure. The Institute for Quantitative Social Science at Harvard noted, "Americans work 50% harder than Germans, French, or Italians." [16]

Asked to rate the importance of "leisure" in their lives on a scale of +4 to −4, Europeans gave it a +2 in the Institute's study. Americans gave leisure a −1. But asked to rate the importance of "hard work," Americans gave it a +4 while Europeans gave it a −2. As the Institute noted, "Europeans work to live while Americans live to work." [17]

The *Wall Street Journal* (always quick to extol the virtues of work) reports that 89 percent of Americans told the General Social Survey in 2002 that they were "very satisfied or somewhat satisfied with their jobs." Asked if they would continue working if they had "enough money to live as comfortably as you would like for the rest of your life," 69 percent of Americans said they would. [18]

The *Journal* concludes:

> For most Americans, work is a rock-solid source of life happiness. Happy people work more hours each week than unhappy people, and work more in their free time as well. Even more tellingly, people with more hours per day to relax outside their jobs are not any happier than those who have less non-work time. In short, the idea that our heavy workloads are lowering our happiness is twaddle. [19]

Yet the socialists continue to sing their siren song: *Work less, play more, trust us, be happy.*

THE GLOBAL BUREAUCRATIC TYRANNY

Alone among the nations of the developed world, America resisted this siren song of socialism—until Obama sang its melody.

The rest of the industrialized world had already fallen into a stupor. We are next.

A bureaucratic empire has always ruled Japan. Though in modern times the nation has had an emperor, and now a prime minister, as its figureheads, their political control remains a thin veneer covering the massive bureaucracy giving the Japanese the illusion before World War II of a monarchy and now of a democracy.

After World War II, Europe was bone-tired and distrusted its governance. When the bureaucrats of the European Union offered hope, sustenance, shelter, and peace, it jumped to accept. All Europeans had to do to reach this utopia was to trade in their nationalism, mitigate their ambition, attenuate their individualism, and limit their democracy.

But the socialist experiment was always haunted by the example of the United States, which refused to take its bait. The utopia could not function as long as freedom, individualism, and democracy were thriving over the horizon and across the ocean. When Mitterrand's France embraced socialism in 1981, capital fled to Thatcher's Britain and Reagan's America. Now, as the United Kingdom languishes under the domination of the European Union's deadening bureaucratic rule, only the United States remains out of the mix.

In order to succeed, however, socialism requires global control. As long as free enterprise rules somewhere in the world, capital will flow there. Workers will move there. Jobs will flourish there. And the socialized businesses in other, older parts of the world will wither and die in the face of competition.

If one country requires businesses to offer eight weeks of paid vacation, limits overtime, and bans layoffs, companies will move to nations without these regulations.

If one nation taxes a disproportionate share of a person's wages and income, people will flee for lower tax havens.

Socialism can function only when all the outlets are closed and the exits sealed.

European socialism needs to conquer America in order to survive.

The radicals who founded contemporary socialism recognized this. From the earliest days of the Bolshevik Revolution, Vladimir Lenin maintained that it was impossible to have socialism in one country alone. Worldwide revolution was the only way communism could survive. When the worldwide upheaval he hoped for failed to materialize, he had to try to make it on his own. Lenin reluctantly turned back to capitalism with his New Economic Policy (NEP). After Lenin's death, his successor, Joseph

Stalin, found the solution: He could achieve socialism if he killed everyone who stood in his path. Having eliminated the profit motive as a tool to keep the people productive, Stalin employed terror as a substitute. When the terror stopped, the system fell apart. It could not compete.

But the European Union cannot use terror to hold its people in line as Stalin did. And without terror, the only way socialism can work is if there is no alternative. If the entire world is socialist, capital cannot flee and competition can't motivate work.

This is why the European socialists love President Obama. They realize that the only way they can maintain their own government-dominated economies is if Obama helps them spread the socialist revolution to America.

The socialists have already taken over most of our banks and financial institutions. They are trying to pass legislation to control our health-care system. Through the excuse of global warming, they are striving to take over our utilities and manufacturing industries. But their appetites are unrestrained. They want more power and control.

LINCOLN VS. JEFFERSON: THE HISTORICAL PERSPECTIVE

The battle between economic freedom and hierarchical controls (be they government or private) is not alien to our own shores.

From the beginning of our country, we have faced a battle between those who believe in relying on free and open markets to give ambition full range and generate upward mobility for individuals and progress for society and their opponents who would use systems of oppression and taxation to hold men and women down and to maintain hierarchical class structures.

In Lincoln and Jefferson, we see the dichotomy.

Abraham Lincoln was a devout adherent of the wage system. The transition in his life came when he left his father Thomas Lincoln's subsistence farm and took a paying job on a riverboat in the Mississippi River. Thomas's loss was Abraham's gain as he began his steady climb into the upper middle class (aided by marrying into a rich family and by his career as a railroad lawyer).

Lincoln's opposition to slavery was as much economic as idealistic. He knew all too well that the promise of working one's way up the economic or social ladder was empty as long as employers still had the option of using slaves to work for nothing. We think we have trouble competing with imports made by underpaid Chinese workers. Imagine competing with slave labor!

But our other American icon, Thomas Jefferson, took a different view. Distrusting the urban masses, he wanted an America populated by a landed aristocracy on top, their slaves on the bottom, and a class of independent yeomen farmers in the middle—self-reliant, to be sure, but without sufficient commercial clout to crowd the elbow room of the aristocracy. For all his vaunted insight that all men are created equal, this slaveholder (who, unlike George Washington, did not free all his slaves upon his death) used the system of forced labor to hold small entrepreneurs and wage earners down and keep them in their places. Wages stayed too low to allow upward mobility because employers could always turn to slave labor instead.

Jefferson prided himself on treating his slaves well—though paternalistically. He clothed and fed them, provided free health care, and even lived with one of his slaves, Sally Hemings, who bore his children. But for all of his concern and empathy, he denied them the one thing they wanted: the freedom to make their own lives and realize their own ambitions.

Slavery, in Jefferson's time, blocked upward mobility by stopping the wage system from moving families up the economic ladder. Today, taxes serve the same purpose.

Our modern plantation owners—people with unimaginable wealth, such as George Soros, Jay Rockefeller, Nancy Pelosi, Jon Corzine, the Kennedys, and the millionaires of the Senate—use taxes to keep their competitors down. By passing out paternalistic benefits to the poor and the lower middle class, while taxing the middle class to pay for them, they win the votes of the former and deny the latter the means of accumulating sufficient wealth to move into their exalted social circles. Once known as "limousine liberals," their own massive wealth makes them immune from the impact of taxation. Having already made, married, or inherited their money, they have no qualms in using the money of the middle class to buy the votes of the poor and do not worry about how these very taxes will block the middle classes' upward mobility. They kowtow to public employee unions and let them destroy our government services in return for their votes and political support. They need not worry about bad public schools. Their children go to private schools. With their own security guards, they don't care much about the quality of policing. When you're flying in private jets and being driven around in limos, why worry about public transportation?

The historic ideal of service and philanthropy is thus turned on its head.

Once, the robber barons of the past—the Carnegies, Rockefellers, Mellons, and Morgans—endowed colleges, libraries, parks, churches, and communities. The evidence of their latter-day goodwill—after decades of economic pillaging—surrounds us. Fortunately, there are still genuine philanthropists, such as Bill Gates, who use their fortunes to give others the means of economic mobility.

But the rich men and women who have now become our senators, congressmen, governors, cabinet officers, and presidents merely mouth the ideals of philanthropy—while using their wealth to get elected to public office (or, as with Soros, to control those who do). There they use the power their money has bought them to buy off the masses with programs, and to enfeeble the upper middle class with taxes. And when taxes are not enough to hobble those who want to rise to become their peers, they resort to the ultimate tax—inflation—to rob the wage- and salary-earners of the fruits of their enterprise.

This class of the politically oriented rich uses the power to tax the way Jefferson used the lash—to live alone atop their mountains, preaching justice but living lives based on oppression and slavery.

In a broader sense, these modern-day socialists would use government's monopoly on the legitimate use of force to hold down the ambitious and creative and smother their initiative. Under their system of high taxation, economic upward mobility becomes increasingly impossible. It is only through manipulating the power of government by acquiring political clout that one can advance.

The 2009 epidemic of swine flu provides a great example of how this system works. American science did its part and came up with a vaccine to protect us against the new H1N1 virus. Then government stepped in and messed it all up. Production was delayed; mistakes were made that rendered the all-important shots unavailable until well into the flu season. No matter how much you were willing to pay, you couldn't protect your family. The government, having created the scarcity in the first place by mismanaging the vaccine production, allotted where the shots should go. But then politics stepped in. Goldman Sachs, well connected to Treasury secretaries past and present, managed to wangle several thousand shots for its top employees. If you had political power, you could get the shots; if you had none, you were out of luck.

But the system of government control doesn't work. If we hobble those who generate wealth, create jobs, and catalyze growth, we cannot help the many who depend on government handouts. If no one is creating wealth, there's nothing to tax. A vicious circle sets in: Taxes go up, revenue drops, productivity evaporates, and society falls down. This is what happened in the Soviet Union, and unless we take action it will happen here.

PESSIMISM IS THE BODYGUARD OF SOCIALISM

And when things go wrong, as they always do under socialism—when the economy slows down and sputters to a halt, when unemployment increases and inflation is upon us—the socialists use fatalism and pessimism to assure us that these bad outcomes would have happened anyway. *Had it not been for us*, they say, *things would have been even worse*. President Obama, for example, no longer promises to create jobs; instead, he just tries to comfort us by claiming he's "saving" jobs.

Like Jimmy Carter, Barack Obama keeps assuring us that we're living in an era of scarcity: Smaller is better, less is more. Already, we see signs that this pessimism is taking hold in the American spirit. In November 2009, a Rasmussen Poll showed that 47 percent of Americans agree that "our best days are behind us" and only 36 percent feel they remain "ahead of us." [20]

Voters accept the bad economic news and see it as unavoidable—though some still attribute it to George W. Bush, not to Obama's misguided policies. When unemployment stays high, Obama says it would have gone even higher without his stimulus package. When consumer confidence remains at rock bottom, the socialist apologists say that things are worse than they had thought when they took power and promised change.

We need a Ronald Reagan to come along and tell us it's not so.

That we are a strong nation with a vast untapped capacity.

That our best years are ahead of us.

And that we can transcend any of the limits the fatalists would set for us.

THERE IS STILL TIME

Socialism and its principles are so alien to our national way of thinking that it is a hard sell to the American people. The assumptions of a welfare state don't rest easily in American minds; the allure of security in mediocrity rings hollow to our ears. We know better. We are, by nature, an optimistic people. That's our legacy from our immigrant forebears. Those who were pessimistic stayed in Europe and crafted their socialist paradise. But the people who valued ambition, hard work, upward mobility, the freedom to make something of themselves, came to America. And we are their progeny. We will not easily be put back into the feudal-*cum*-socialist cocoon from which our ancestors fled.

If we win the elections of 2010, we can reverse this course and hush its siren song.

Just as we all saw how well Reaganomics worked, and watched global communism come crashing down, we are all witnessing the failure of Obama's version of socialism. Repentant, grateful for the chance to escape, and determined not to make the same mistake again, we can embark as a united people to change the disastrous course onto which this socialist president has cast us. Maybe not all of us will join this movement. But enough. Enough.

That's what the election of 2010 is all about.

Let's take a closer look at what is at stake.

UNEMPLOYMENT

Everybody knows that unemployment has soared under President Barack Obama. When he took office, 7.6 percent of the American workforce was out of work. By January 2010, it was 9.7 percent.

OBAMA'S CHANGE: MORE UNEMPLOYMENT

2009 Unemployment Rate

January	7.7 percent
February	8.2
March	8.6
April	8.9
May	9.4
June	9.5
July	9.4
August	9.7
September	9.8
October	10.1
November	10.0
December	10.0
January 2010	9.7

Source: Bureau of Labor Statistics[21]

But the situation is actually *worse* than even those figures suggest. It would be foolish to think that only one American worker in ten is unemployed. The fact is that many, many people have simply given up looking for work—and those former workers, those who have given up hope, are no longer even counted as part of the labor force. In all, fewer than six Americans in ten are now employed. Only 59.2 percent of Americans are employed—the lowest level in twenty-five years.[22] (As recently as 2006, that figure was 66 percent.)[23]

In fact, the most relevant statistic is not the widely reported "unemployment rate" but rather the underemployment rate. This statistic reflects the real extent of underuse of our most precious resource: human labor and intelligence.

In November 2009, the unemployment rate stood at 10 percent. But the underemployment rate, calculated by the Bureau of Labor Statistics, was *17.5 percent.*[24]

The following chart shows the increase in the two measurements of unemployment:

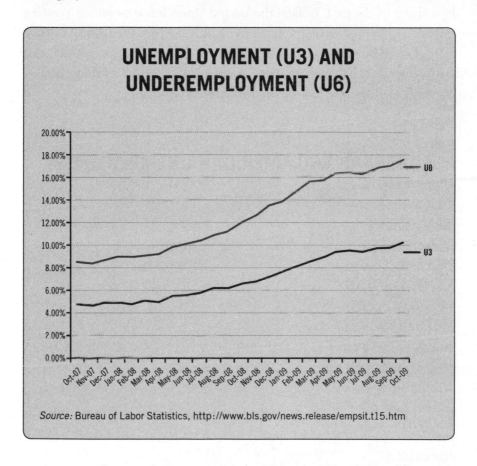

UNEMPLOYMENT (U3) AND UNEREMPLOYMENT (U6)

Source: Bureau of Labor Statistics, http://www.bls.gov/news.release/empsit.t15.htm

And unemployment today is not like it used to be. Joblessness now goes on and on and on. The *Wall Street Journal* reports that as "the long term jobless rate hits its highest point on record, more than a third of those who are out of work have been looking for more than six months, making this category of unemployed the biggest since the Bureau of Labor Statistics began tracking it in 1948."[25] And more than half of the unemployed—54 percent—do not "expect to ever regain the same job."[26] Pessimism and permanence are the distressing accompaniments of this recession.

The prospect we now face is not the intermittent up-and-down fluctuations of unemployment we have had since the end of the Great Depression. Thanks to Obama's policies, we're confronting the possibility of an unemployment rate that never comes down, just as they have in Europe.

If we stay on Obama's course, lower joblessness in the United States will be a thing of the past. In fact, the United States has now joined Western Europe as the land of high unemployment. Compare the relative rates of European nations and the United States in 2007 and now. In 2007—and for twenty years before that—the U.S. jobless rate was lower than those of the nations of Europe. Now it's higher. And likely to last.

EUROPEAN AND AMERICAN UNEMPLOYMENT

2008		2009	
France	8.6	U.S.	10.0
Germany	8.6	France	9.5
Italy	6.1	U.K.	7.8
U.K.	5.5	Italy	7.8
U.S.	4.4	Germany	7.7

Source: Financial Times[27]

Only Britain has an unemployment rate that is historically as low as that in the United States, largely because it is the least socialized of the European economies.

And even if the early signs of "economic recovery" show staying power, that doesn't mean it will extend to the underemployed workforce. The fourth quarter of 2009 saw a 5.5 percent expansion of our nation's Gross Domestic Product (GDP), but in the very same period, we saw unemployment stay up near 10 percent. The policies of the Obama administration may leave us with a permanently high level of joblessness, whatever the fate of our economic growth.

Why isn't unemployment coming down?

Allen Sinai, chief global economist at the research firm Decision Economics, argues, "It's a change in the structure of the business cycle. There appears to be a new tendency to substitute against labor. It's permanent, as long as there are alternatives like outsourcing and robotics."[28]

But a more eclectic range of causes seems to be at work.

A recent Associated Press article lists some of them:

WHY AREN'T THE JOBS COMING?

- The auto and construction industries helped lead the nation out of past recessions. But the carnage among Detroit's automakers and the surplus of new and foreclosed homes and empty commercial properties make it unlikely these two industries will be engines of growth anytime soon.
- The job market is caught in a vicious circle: Without more jobs, U.S. consumers will have a hard time increasing their spending; but without that spending, businesses might see little reason to start hiring.
- Many small and midsize businesses are still struggling to obtain bank loans, impeding their expansion plans and constraining overall economic growth.
- Higher-income households are spending less because of big losses on their homes, retirement plans, and other investments. Lower-income households are cutting back because they can't borrow like they once did.
- Even before the recession, many jobs had vanished or been shipped overseas amid a general decline of U.S. manufacturing. The severest downturn since the Great Depression has accelerated the process.

Source: USA Today[29]

What do all these factors have in common? Obama is making them all worse!

Let's examine each of the causes cited above—the difficulties of the auto and construction industries; lax consumer spending; the absence of bank financing; the reluctance of high-income households to spend; and the decline of American manufacturing—and see how Obama is making them all worse.

The auto industry is mired up to its neck in government ownership and control, which is radically reducing the attractiveness of cars made by those companies in the American market. Almost two-thirds of Americans—63 percent—say they wouldn't buy a car from a bankrupt automobile company, and 58 percent say they would "rather buy a car from a manufacturer who did not take federal money."[30] Indeed, Obama has decreed that General Motors must continue product lines that aren't profitable as he converts a market-oriented company into a federal public works project. No engine for job growth there.

Similarly, the construction industry can't get the financing it needs for home construction. Since 2008, all categories of mortgage lending are down: prime jumbo mortgage lending is down 24 percent, subprimes are off 34 percent, option ARM mortgages have decreased by 19 percent, alt-A mortgages are down 23 percent, and commercial mortgages are sagging by 10 percent.[31] With the federal government hogging all the nation's capital (federal borrowing is up 41 percent over the same period), how can the construction industry recover? Obama's spending-and-borrowing spree is hogging up all the oxygen in the system!

And what is behind the lack of consumer spending and the insecurity of higher-income households that the AP article cites? They stem, of course, directly from two key policies of the Obama White House: his huge budget deficit (and the consequent likelihood of inflation), and his support for future tax increases. Combined, these threats hold consumers at bay; they are driving up savings rates while dampening down consumption. Enlightened—and frightened—by the recession, many people are paying down their credit card balances, car loans, mortgages, and home equity lines of credit to prepare for the inflation and taxation storms that are on the horizon. Others are just stuffing money in the mattress. But spending is down—precisely because of the insecurity created by the Obama administration.

With the federal deficit tripling in size, the money supply (technically the Adjusted Monetary Base) more than doubling, and runaway inflation in the offing, is it any surprise that consumer spending, the core of the American economy, is taking a vacation? While Obama's micro-policies, like stimulus spending, may help a worker get a government job, the deficit more than offsets these gains by paralyzing the confidence of consumers whose spending is the only way to generate private sector employment.

Higher-income households, in particular, are facing huge tax increases in the future. George W. Bush had cut the rates for the top tax bracket, but Obama is committed to letting that expire in 2010, pushing the rate up to 39.6 percent. And House speaker Nancy Pelosi is pushing a millionaire surtax. Today, she says the tax is designed to pay for health care; tomorrow, however, she'll doubtless present it as a way to reduce the deficit. And Obama has advocated eliminating the ceiling on the FICA (Social Security) tax so that we would all have to pay it on our entire incomes, rather than below the $100,000 cutoff as at present. What higher-income household in its right mind would resume spending with these taxes on the horizon?

Why can't small and mid-size businesses get bank loans? Again, Obama's policies are to blame. Rather than force the banks to clean up their balance sheets and write off the dead loans, the administration printed new money and gave it to banks. Major financial institutions weren't forced to face the music and clean house. Instead, they got bailout money, which allowed them to carry on, pretending that everything is all right.

But it's not all right. The balance sheets of major financial institutions are crammed with nonperforming loans, houses awaiting foreclosure, borrowers on the verge of bankruptcy, and worthless paper securities. Hampered by this overhang, the banks aren't in a lending mood. They're not really banks anymore, just leviathans that are too big to fail—but too crippled to function.

The situation in American banking in the aftermath of the financial crisis is eerily similar to that which confronted Japan after its real estate bubble burst in the 1980s. Banks, which had been relying on inflated property values as collateral for their loans, found themselves mired in bad debt. Rather than force them to scrub their balance sheets, write off bad loans, and move forward, the Japanese government gave the banks more and more money to paper over their losses. The result was two decades of stagnation—called the "lost decades" by the Japanese.

Obama has followed the Japanese example. And now he faces the same conundrum: Unless and until the banks clear their balance sheets of bad debt—taking the hit by admitting these loans will never be repaid—they will be unable to make new loans. With infusions of federal funding, the banks won't fail, but they won't lend either. Obama's policies are likely to lead us into the same decades of stagnation that Japan has endured.

Unless we can turn things around in the next election.

Finally, the AP article cites the difficulties of American manufacturing. Once again, it's the Obama policies that are causing their decline—by the looming threat of cap-and-trade legislation, which would force manufacturers to accept crippling production limits. Despite pledging during the campaign to fight outsourcing and protect American jobs, Obama's policies have kneecapped what is left of our once-vital manufacturing economy.

Manufacturing jobs have been declining in America for a decade, even though our share of global output has retained a relatively steady first-place ranking of 24 percent (we've been making more, in other words, with fewer workers). In 1973, manufacturing accounted for 24 percent of all U.S. non-farm jobs. By 2008, it was below 10 percent.[32]

DECLINE IN MANUFACTURING JOBS

Year	Manufacturing Employment (in thousands)
2000	17,263
2001	16,441
2002	15,259
2003	14,510
2004	14,315
2005	14,226
2006	14,155
2007	13,879
2008	13,431

Source: Bureau of Labor Statistics [33]

And, during the recession, manufacturing employment has fallen by a further 2.1 million jobs.[34]

That's pretty normal.

But here's something that's not normal—and that's not a good sign for our economic recovery: American companies aren't just cutting back their production output while they wait for things to get better. They're outsourcing their work, closing factories permanently, and replacing more and more workers with robots as automation advances.

Historically, manufacturing employment has risen and fallen with the business cycle, leading the economy out of recession as consumer demand improved.

But no more. As Peter S. Goldman, author of *Past Due: The End of Easy Money and the Renewal of the American Economy*, writes:

> In the middle of the last century, a retailer in Chicago who needed goods likely had to place an order with a factory in the Midwest. Today, that retailer could well be part of a conglomerate that taps a global supply chain; it sends its orders to workers in China and elsewhere, or to domestic factories that can increase production without hiring many more people, either by further automating or by bringing in temporary workers.[35]

Allen Sinai, president and chief global economist for Primark Decision Economics, points out that "our view of the business cycle is antiquated . . . it dates to a time when manufacturing employed roughly one-third of the American workforce, well before what we now call the global economy."[36]

In the past few years, American manufacturing has enjoyed a reprieve on its way to extinction as energy prices started to rise rapidly. The advantage enjoyed by China, and other countries with lower labor costs, began to erode as the cost of shipping goods to the American market rose sharply. Before long, increased energy costs were offsetting these nations' lower worker pay.

But no more. Obama's proposed cap-and-trade legislation—little more than a tax on carbon emissions—threatens to eliminate this newfound advantage for U.S. companies. By imposing a tax on manufacturers who reside in the United States, but not on those that are in India or China (both of whom refuse to go along with the emissions taxes), Obama creates a massive incentive to move manufacturing jobs out of the country.

The result? When an American factory closes, the odds are increasing that it will move away, rather than wait for Obama's carbon-tax axe to fall.

So it is Obama's policies—many ostensibly designed to promote employment—that are creating this environment of permanently high joblessness.

And technological change is adding to the problem. According to economist Jacob Funk Kirkegaard of the Peterson Institute for International Economics, "such industries as finance, retail trade, publishing, and broadcasting are suffering from structural job losses that won't likely turn around with an expanding economy." He estimates that more than a third of the U.S. economy is suffering this kind of structural unemployment.[37]

Retailers, for example, aren't just laying off workers due to the recession; they're seeing much of their brick-and-mortar business evaporating as consumers go online. The finance industry is shrinking as the Internet facilitates direct transactions that increasingly obviate the need for high-priced brokers.

As the *Wall Street Journal* reports, "firms are continuing to cut costs even as the economy heals, meaning they are getting more from existing work forces."[38] The Labor Department noted that nonfarm productivity rose at an annual rate of 9.5 percent in the third quarter of 2009—more than four times the average rate over the past quarter century. Current employees have to work harder and produce more, as businesses are reluctant to hire back more workers.[39]

A good president would stress the importance of worker reeducation. As Kirkegaard notes, the special skills of workers from sectors facing structural unemployment "may be mismatched for higher-potential industries like healthcare and education."[40]

But instead of telling workers who have lost their jobs the truth—that the jobs aren't coming back—Obama keeps them hopeful with the palliative of federal stimulus spending. He narcotizes their pain with dollars from Washington, which sends a clear signal to those who face permanent unemployment: No need to learn new skills! Just get comfortable on our dime, and you can stay on the government dole until things get better.

In the 1990s, when President Bill Clinton faced a massive structural change in the American economy as it adjusted to global competition, he was under great pressure to do more to stop big companies from "downsizing" (in the vocabulary of the day). But he understood that when mega-companies shed middle-level workers and management, it was part of the transition to the information-based economy. Just as the British Enclosure Acts of the eighteenth and nineteenth century pushed the labor force off the land and into cities, where they became the workers for the new industrial revolution, so these former employees of firms like IBM became workers in the information age industries. Instead of trying to fashion tax and regulatory policies to keep workers at their old jobs—or to so dose them with federal spending that they did not feel the pain of their layoffs—the Clinton administration encouraged American workers to reeducate themselves to adjust and adapt to the new landscape.

All the Obama administration is doing is postponing their day of reckoning.

And the Obama stimulus package does more than just postpone the adjustment to changing market patterns. It is actually *creating* unemployment, according to Louis Woodhill of the Club for Growth. He writes that the stimulus "is in the process of turning a nasty recession into a genuine depression. The massive sales of U.S. Treasury bonds to finance 'stimulus,' bailouts, and other government spending is sucking capital out of the private sector and destroying jobs." [41]

Woodhill explains that gross domestic private investment in 2009 dropped by 25 percent as money went to the government rather than to the private sector. He points out that "the 500 largest U.S. non-financial companies now hold more than $1 trillion in Treasury bills, amounting to more than 10% of their total assets. Corporate cash flows are rising, but the money is being invested in government bonds, rather than growth." [42]

And, at the same time, credit card companies, often the best source of capital for small businesses, have cut credit card lines by 25 percent, further curbing private sector job creation. [43]

In all, Woodhill writes that it takes $313,000 of capital to create a private sector job. But each of the jobs that the administration claims the stimulus has "created or saved" costs about $1.2 million. As Woodhill explains, "this means that selling the bonds required to fund one temporary 'stimulus' job will take enough capital out of the private sector to destroy four 'real' jobs." [44]

Woodhill notes that the Obama program is not jump-starting the economy or catalyzing the private sector, as Obama claimed when he proposed it. Rather, it's giving people government jobs, which does nothing to get the private sector moving. When the president first proposed his stimulus package, he predicted that 90 percent of the jobs it would create or save would be in the private sector. Instead, the *New York Times* reports that "over half" of the jobs are in the public realm. In fact, of the 640,000 jobs the administration claimed the stimulus spending saved or created, 325,000 were in public education (including teachers, administrators, and support staff).[45]

Economist Barry Elias estimates that a dollar invested in the private sector will do twice as much good as one invested in the public realm. (In economic terms, it will have twice the velocity.)[46] Yet Obama consistently takes dollars from the private sector and gives them to the public sector.

Some of the jobs were in neither the public nor the private sector, but in what can only be described as the imagination. For example, the purchase of a $1,047 rider lawn mower for the Fayetteville National Cemetery in Arkansas was reported to have created fifty new jobs—presumably as various people traded off riding the machine![47]

And, even as Obama's misguided spending policies hurt the economy, unemployment is bound to increase in the immediate future.

Joshua Zumbrun, writing in Forbes.com, explains why the unemployment rate is "certain to climb higher" even "if job growth soon returns."

He cites four reasons:

1. The higher birthrates of the late 1980s and 1990s will raise the number of men and women seeking jobs by 100,000 per month. In October 2009, the economy lost 170,000 jobs. So even if job growth returns, unless it goes higher than 100,000 per month, the jobless rate will continue to climb.

2. Zumbrun notes that the unemployment rate "does not include people who are so discouraged they have given up searching [for work]. . . . If these discouraged and marginally attached workers all started looking for jobs today, the unemployment rate would jump to 11.6%. These workers will not return all at once. But as conditions start to improve, they'll return to job hunting, driving the rate up."

3. In addition to the 15 million Americans who are unemployed, 9.3 million Americans are working part-time but would like full-

time employment. They ought to be counted as unemployed but, instead, we call them "underemployed."

4. The Bureau of Labor Statistics is far from infallible (or impartial). In October 2009, for example, it reported the U.S. unemployment rate as 10.2 percent—when it was actually 10.7 percent. The BLS had overcounted jobs by 824,000. The revisions will show up in the data in February 2010. Such mistakes are not uncommon (and may be deliberate).[48]

How can an agency like the Bureau of Labor Statistics, whose sole assignment is to track changes in America's workforce, get things so wrong? In part because the Bureau has a blind spot, it tends to measure employment by big businesses only. Yet most of the job loss in America today is taking place among small businesses. In October 2009, for example, the BLS survey of households (people) showed a loss of 589,000 jobs for the month— the real figure. But its survey of "establishments" (businesses) found that only 190,000 jobs had disappeared.[49] And 190,000 was the figure it announced to the world.

It's not only the unemployed, or even the underemployed, who are fueling the nation's economic problems. According to an estimate by Kenneth Couch, an economist at the University of Connecticut, those workers who *do* manage to find jobs and return to the workforce are making an average of 40 percent less than they did when they were laid off. He estimates, based on past recessions, that it takes an average of six years before workers who have returned to full employment make what they did before they were laid off (in inflation-adjusted dollars). Younger workers make it faster than their older colleagues do.[50]

But whether those hit by the recession have to take part-time work, or find full-time jobs at less pay, or remain unemployed, they drain away the consumer spending the economy needs to recover.

To deflect blame for this dismal economic situation away from Obama, the pessimists contend that this high unemployment is just a symptom of the new economic era we're entering. The age of low unemployment is over, they decree; in the future, we will have to accept these higher levels of joblessness as a given. It's not Obama's fault that jobs are scarce, they would have us believe. It's just part of the new paradigm.

Kenneth S. Rogoff, a Harvard economist and coauthor of a history of financial crises, *This Time Is Different: Eight Centuries of Financial Folly*, recalls that when he was a graduate student, most economists viewed the normal level of unemployment to be about 7 percent.[51] Rogoff says that the weak hiring in recent times "is really just a return to normal." He foresees unemployment settling "in to a long-term average of about 6 percent."[52]

Others echo Rogoff's pessimism. Nobel Prize winner Edmund Phelps and Pacific Investment Management Co. CEO Mohamed El-Erian have argued that the recession will drive the "so-called natural [unemployment] rate higher, perhaps to 7 percent." El-Erian says, "we are in the midst of a large and protracted increase in both actual unemployment and its natural rate."[53]

As noted above, pessimism is the bodyguard of socialism. When ill-advised government policies make things worse, the apologists are quick to rush in and tell us this is the best we can hope for. They try to convince us that our problems aren't the result of failed big-government policies or deficits or inflationary interest rates, but of structural factors beyond our control.

Baloney!

If Obama hadn't increased the deficit by squandering our resources on a wasteful, short-term, one-shot stimulus package, we wouldn't have the current crisis of consumer confidence. If he'd insisted on making banks write off their bad debts and becoming functional again, businesses would be in a legitimate position to start raising new capital. If he hadn't threatened everyone—particularly those who can spend money—with tax increases, he would have adequate consumer demand to push down unemployment. And if he weren't threatening to impose a carbon tax, the manufacturing sector wouldn't be fleeing the country rapidly.

Our president himself admits that he was undeserving of the Nobel Prize for peace he accepted in the fall of 2009. One thing's for sure: He certainly doesn't deserve an award in economics!

However, it's critical for us all to recognize that this economic course is not set in stone. If we win the election of 2010, we can reverse each aspect of Obama's demented agenda.

We can rekindle economic growth by cutting taxes, particularly on capital gains. The resulting surge in economic growth will prove that unemployment is not permanently high. The manufacturing sector, relieved of the threat of cap-and-trade and the harassment of the federal Environmental Protection Agency, can take advantage of lower energy costs to compete and win. Housing construction will increase as federal borrowing drops, and small businesses will no longer be shoved aside at the loan window by a ravenous federal treasury. The car industry will be reprivatized, so that it can once again generate jobs by making cars that will sell—even if bureaucrats don't like them.

Each of these policies can change. If—and *only* if—we change Congress first.

INFLATION

But the unemployment Obama will cause won't be the only source of economic misery. It will be accompanied by rampant inflation.

Obama has dug us so deeply in debt that there is really only one way out: inflation. No matter how drastically he raises taxes, he has already borrowed far more than we can ever realistically hope to repay. Only by letting the dollar weaken and its value drop can he pay back those who have lent us money.

Though 5 percent of our national debt is in Treasury Inflation Protected Securities (TIPS), whose interest rate rises and falls with inflation changes, 95 percent is not. For those who hold this vast bulk of our bonds—the Chinese among them—the future is not bright. They are going to be repaid in dollars worth far less than those they originally lent. The interest rate they get will come nowhere near replacing the value their bonds will lose due to inflation.

And it's not just the Chinese. It's also your retirement pension fund! U.S. pension funds invest 22.7 percent of their total assets in bonds.[54] In an inflationary spiral, the value of that portion of their portfolios will wither rapidly.

By borrowing real money and repaying it in Monopoly money, Obama may not make our creditors happy, but he will avoid default and bankruptcy.

But this policy comes at a price. The weakened dollar will send consumer prices soaring in the United States. It will lead to massive inflation in the near future.

Oil imports offer a good example of how this inflation will come about. Since oil prices are denominated in dollars, the weaker the dollar gets, the more it will cost per barrel. Those who live in yen or euro zones won't notice the price increase because they don't deal in dollars. They'll simply be able to get more dollars for each unit of their own currency, and they'll be able to pay the higher nominal dollar price of oil with no worries.

But for the American driver or homeowner, the higher dollar price of oil will send prices soaring.

For the past few decades, American consumers haven't had to worry too much about inflation—in part because of the vast volume of foreign imports. These low-priced products deterred domestic manufacturers from raising their prices. But as the dollar weakens and imported products cost more, domestic companies will feel free to raise their prices.

If the late 1970s were characterized by "stagflation" (the combination of economic stagnation and wild inflation), the next few years may see the advent of "depressflation" (worse economic conditions combined with high inflation).

Inflation can be caused by a great demand for too few goods, or by higher costs to make the goods or deliver the services . . . or by both factors together. When prices are pushed up by greater demand, economists call it "demand pull" inflation. If they rise because costs go up, that's called "cost push" inflation.

We'll likely get hit with both barrels.

Demand pull inflation is inevitable because there's way too much money in circulation. According to the Federal Reserve, the money supply has risen from $875 billion in September 2008 to $2.094 billion on December 2, 2009—an increase of $1.2 trillion in fourteen months![55]

How did this explosion take place?

During the boom period of the early 2000s, the Federal Reserve Board kept interest rates at historic lows. With the cost of borrowing money cheap (actually free, because interest rates were below inflation), speculation flourished, laying the basis for the crash of 2008.

But once the economy fell apart, the Fed further lowered interest rates—all the way to zero. Then, unable to go lower (only Elton John can go "too low for zero"), the Fed started printing money to increase the economic stimulus.

(And here's something worth understanding: "Printing money" isn't exactly what they did. The Fed didn't literally start its printing presses. Rather, it went on a shopping spree. The Treasury went to banks that owned government bonds or mortgage-backed securities and said it wanted to buy them. The banks were happy to unload them and get the cash. Where did the Treasury get the money? It *invented* it—"printing" it metaphorically, by increasing the amount of money it was willing to supply to banks. Then the Treasury went to those same banks that had just gotten this windfall of new cash and asked to borrow some of it. "Sure," the banks said, "after all, it's your money in the first place." And so the newly minted money rolled back into the Treasury to pay for all of Obama's borrowing. And we end up paying interest on the money we borrow—which is actually the money we gave to our lenders in the first place! This is really the same kind of Ponzi scheme that landed Bernie Madoff in jail—but since this is the government doing it, it's legal.)

As a result of the government's clever scheme, the amount of money in circulation rose almost two and a half times. But as the money supply has more than doubled, consumer demand hasn't doubled. Car purchases haven't doubled. Housing sales haven't doubled. In fact, the sales figures are largely flat!

So where is the money?

It's in hiding, waiting for better economic times before it comes out to be spent. People are using the money to pay down their credit card debt, to pay off their car loans, to reduce their student loans, or to catch up on their mortgage payments. They are saving the money, not spending it. That's the smart thing to do—but it doesn't help the economy.

Just as we predicted in *Catastrophe*, Americans took the stimulus checks Bush sent out in 2008 and put them in their bank accounts. They probably did the same with the funds Obama gave away at the start of his term. According to a study by Claudia Sahm of the Federal Reserve and Joel Slemrod and Matthew Shapiro of the University of Michigan, "most Americans saved their 2008 stimulus checks and only about a third of consumers spent them."[56] So most of the $96 billion Bush spent and, likely, the almost $300 billion Obama spent is still nestled in savings accounts and money markets, or was used to pay down personal debt. It's as if Obama filled up every car in America with gas—but then all the drivers decided to stay home with their vehicles languishing in the garage, holding out for the weather to clear. Sounds sensible, right?

Maybe when it's pouring. But what will happen when the good weather comes? They're all going to feel like going out at once. They'll all come out of the garage at the same time to take the car for a spin.

The result? An economic equivalent of a god-awful traffic jam: massive inflation.

Suddenly, there'll be too much paper money chasing too few goods or services—and prices will skyrocket.

But we'll also be hit by cost push inflation, which is a lot worse. The real culprit here is the deficit and the national debt (which is really just the accumulation of each year's deficit).

Right now, the Fed is borrowing a lot of money to pay for the deficit. From whom? From those who got the free money in the first place by selling their bonds to the Treasury. This process of printing money and then borrowing it back can go on for only so long. At some point—soon—the Fed and the Treasury will have to stop playing the game. All indications are that it'll have to come to a stop in 2010. If it doesn't, the money supply may become so enlarged that we'll be risking the kind of wallpaper-your-apartment-with-money inflation that killed Weimar Germany and opened the door to Hitler.

And the larger the deficit is, the more we're risking a massive run of inflation, and the more interest lenders are going to demand in order to part with their money. After all, if they're stuck with bonds that pay only 3 or 4 percent—and inflation is at 10 or 20 percent—they'll soon lose all their money. To compensate for the loss, interest rates will have to go up. Very fast and very high.

Most businesses in America these days operate on debt. They borrow money for their cash flow, for expansion, for new product lines, and so forth. If interest rates go way up, so will the costs of delivering goods or services.

Meanwhile, however, these higher interest rates will inhibit economic activity. High interest rates will prevent, or dissuade, people from buying new cars or homes.

If all of this happens—interest rates rising and economic activity falling—businesses will sell fewer products or services but they'll still have to pay for their interest costs (their fixed costs) out of the products or services they do manage to sell.

That will mean higher prices—*much* higher prices.

And higher prices will mean higher interest rates, which will mean even higher prices in turn. That's how we get to depressflation.

With the federal government now having to borrow one-third of each dollar it spends, the need for more and more borrowing will drive interest rates ever higher. Obama's policies have seen to that!

Already, smart investors see the tsunami of inflation on the horizon. They're flocking to buy gold and copper as a hedge against rising prices. Look how the price of gold has shot upward in the first year of the Obama administration:

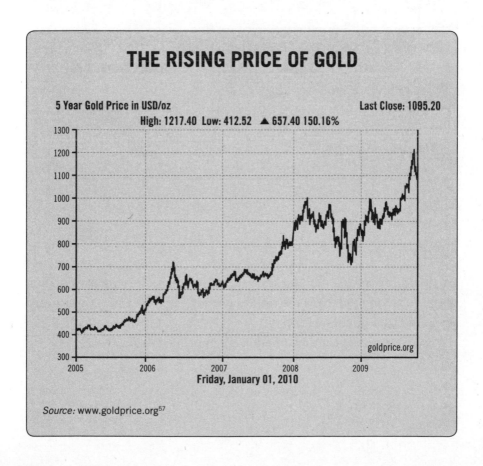

Source: www.goldprice.org[57]

Gold prices began trending sharply upward as the federal deficit began to mount in mid-2007. But the increase since Obama took office—from about $700 to more than $1,100 per ounce—is exceptional.

While Wall Street investors happily count their stock earnings, they would do well to consider the ratio between the Dow and the price of gold. The higher the ratio, the less fear of inflation there is; the lower the ratio, the greater the fear.

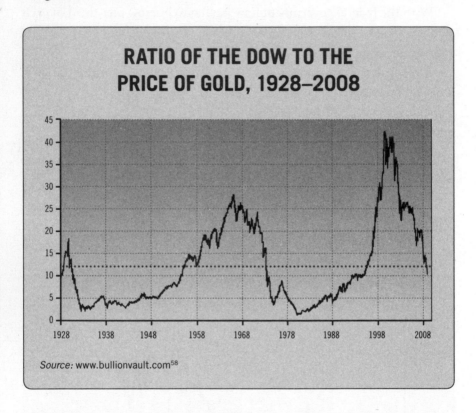

RATIO OF THE DOW TO THE PRICE OF GOLD, 1928–2008

Source: www.bullionvault.com[58]

As this chart reveals, the last time the ratio crashed, the mega-inflation of 1977–82 followed. Now the ratio is crashing again—a harbinger of the inflation that's on the horizon.

The warnings of coming inflation are pouring in from all quarters.

THE COMING INFLATION TSUNAMI

- James Ballard, the president of the Federal Reserve Bank of St. Louis, told the *Financial Times* that "uncertainty over the outlook for inflation 'is as high as it has ever been since 1980.' He said the US central banks still faced a lingering threat of deflation, but might have to pivot quickly once this danger passed to face the threat of excess inflation." [59]

- Martin Feldstein of Harvard, a former Reagan adviser and past head of the National Bureau of Economic Research, warns that "inflation will emerge as a threat to the economy . . . he says 'in the next few years inflation is going to be [a] bigger problem [than deflation].' " [60]

- Warren Buffett told CNBC that his "concerns about inflation are 'on the rise.' " [61] And he told the annual shareholders' meeting of Berkshire Hathaway, "what we are doing is borrowing from the rest of the world and building up government debt. The classic way of reducing the impact and cost of foreign debt is by reducing the value of the dollars you're going to repay them with." [62]

- Investor Marc Faber, publisher of the appropriately named Boom, Doom, and Gloom Report, told Bloomberg News that he is "100 percent sure that the U.S. will go into hyperinflation. The problem with government debt growing so much is that when the time will come and the Fed should increase interest rates, they will be very reluctant to do so and so inflation will start to accelerate." He predicts that prices will rise at levels approaching those in Zimbabwe. [63]

- Puru Saxena, editor of Money Matters, says that "once business activity picks up, our world will have to deal with high inflation. Now, given the ability of the American establishment to essentially create dollars out of thin air, I have no doubt in my mind that it be able to inflate the economy. However, this will come at a huge cost and the victim will be the American currency." [64]

The federal government has been trying to reassure us that inflation is low. According to economist Barry Elias, however, the statistics they use to bolster their claim understate the rate of inflation by 50 percent. The methodology they use, he notes, was last overhauled during the early 1990s. Things have changed since then in the real economy but not in the inflation measurement. People are buying a different mix of products and services, and the old inflation measurements have not been updated to keep up.[65]

This statistical inaccuracy is largely deliberate, both to reassure us and to hold down increases in cost-of-living adjustments built into Social Security and other pension or pay plans. According to Elias, it results in an overstatement of economic growth of 2 to 3 percent each year. Happy juice to reassure us all![66]

It's bad enough that we have to cope with rising prices while we face declining incomes and fewer jobs. But the prospects are even worse when you realize that the Federal Reserve Board won't be able to cushion the impact of this depressflation by cutting interest rates, the normal antidote to unemployment. The economy may need lower rates, but the Fed will be prevented from lowering them by various forces. First, as in 1979–82, it will need to keep rates high in order to fight inflation. Second, it will have to pay higher interest rates to attract lenders who will give government the money to pay for Obama's deficit and debt. The Fed will have to scrounge for cash, and it won't be able to bring down rates.

What does all of this mean? That we're in for a long, long haul of high unemployment and high inflation—all because Barack Obama couldn't restrain his big-spending ambitions once he took office!

But inflation is not the only way to repay the Obama debt. Economic growth is the other way. When President Clinton dueled with House speaker Newt Gingrich over how to balance the budget in 1995–97, each had his pet hobbyhorse. Gingrich wanted to cut spending. Clinton wanted to raise taxes. But eventually Clinton came around to the idea of cutting the capital gains tax (which Gingrich and Senate majority leader Trent Lott had wanted all along). So the tax was cut. And revenue poured in! The deficit, which was supposed to take eight years to eradicate, was gone in less than two years.

The results of the 2001 Bush tax cut were similar. Bush sliced the top rate from Clinton's 39.6 percent to 35 percent and cut the capital gains rate from 20 percent to 15 percent. The result? The rich paid *more* in taxes! *More?* Yes, more. Even though the rates were lower, the economic growth they kindled brought in hundreds of billions extra each year. The proportion of taxes paid by the richest one percent rose from 37 percent in 2000 to 40 percent in 2006, even though their tax rates had been cut!

If the Republicans capture Congress in 2010, we can enact just such a solution again and pay down our debt without inflation.

If we lose, however, a bleak future looms ahead.

THE WORLD LOSES CONFIDENCE IN THE DOLLAR

There are even deeper and more profound consequences to Obama's spend-borrow-tax mentality. The potentially rapid rate of inflation looming ahead is forcing the rest of the world to reconsider its dependence on the dollar as the basic international currency, revisiting a decision that has governed the world economy since the Bretton Woods Conference of 1944.

With the dollar losing 8 percent of its value in the past year (after initially gaining value in the early days of the global economic meltdown), countries are questioning whether they have confidence in our currency any longer.

For the past three decades, the United States has bought huge amounts of imports from abroad, principally from China. Then we went back to China and asked them to buy our bonds with the dollars we had given them. In effect, we paid for those imports with bonds. Beijing consented, because it wanted to sell its products in the United States and because of its faith in our currency—but also because it was awash in dollars. What better place is there to invest dollars than in U.S. government–guaranteed bonds? But if the dollar is no longer the international unit of currency, anyone wanting to buy U.S. government bonds would first have to change their currency reserves into dollars—possibly at a loss—and then buy the bond with the dollars they get. This would curb the willingness of others to lend us money, dramatically.

And now, with the dollar falling rapidly in value and the deficits mounting, China is joining the rest of the world in questioning its longtime confidence in the dollar.

Economist Eswar Prasad of Cornell University explains the dangers for the average American if the dollar should lose its privileged position as the global currency. As long as the world is "willing to accept dollars and buy dollar-denominated bonds," he explains, then the rest of the world will be willing to finance our economy and our consumption.

If the dollar loses its status, however, "it would be much harder for the U.S. government to run large deficits." Prasad adds: "If you are the average Joe, you should definitely be worried because if the U.S. dollar loses its status it is going to mean higher borrowing costs for the U.S. government, which will mean the average Joe will have to pay higher taxes, the U.S. government will spend less on services, and there will be higher interest rates—or some combination of the above." [67]

The more the dollar falls in value, the more expensive foreign imports get. This trend drives up prices and may "provide domestic producers latitude to increase prices . . . to maximize profits." [68] It means higher interest rates and higher prices.

More and more, experts are predicting a coming collapse of confidence in the dollar.

On October 23, 2009, Nobel laureate Paul Samuelson said he'd "come to fear that the inevitable disorderly run against the dollar looms earlier than I used to think." [69]

And though Federal Reserve chairman Ben Bernanke still sees challenges to the dollar's value as a "long-term" rather than a short-term problem, even he recognizes that "if we don't get our macro house in order . . . that will put the dollar in danger and that the most critical element there is long-term fiscal stability." [70]

The United Nations, too, has jumped on the anti-dollar bandwagon. Last fall, the UN Conference on Trade and Development attacked the dollar-based system of global currencies, blaming it for the financial collapse of 2008–9, and calling for a "wholesale reconsideration" of the dollar-based system. One of the authors of the UN report added that "replacing the dollar with an artificial currency would solve some of the problems related to the potential of countries running large deficits and would help stability." [71]

What will replace the dollar? Probably not the yen. Japan is mired in a stag-recession that has lasted for two decades. The euro won't work either. The euro zone includes some nations that were admitted in a burst of continental consciousness that has been harmful to the euro's status as a common currency. Greece, now flirting with bankruptcy, was the first to encounter rough sledding, and Spain, suffering almost 20 percent unemployment, probably isn't far behind. Ireland, once the *miracle du jour* of the European Union, is suffering more than the continent from the recession. (The United Kingdom, whose debt-to-GDP ratio has skyrocketed even more than ours, does not use the Euro.)

The dollar's inevitable slide may be temporarily attenuated because the euro may slide more. Churchill once said that democracy was the worst form of government except for all the others. Similarly, our currency may be the worst—except for all the others!

But the globalists aren't dismayed by any of this. They remain determined to dislodge the dollar from its position of primacy. To replace it, they have created a new global currency issued by the International Monetary Fund (IMF) called Special Drawing Rights (SDR).

SDRs made their unheralded appearance on the global stage in May 2009 at the summit meeting of the G-20 nations. Without fanfare, the leaders of the twenty nations' central banks and the IMF announced that they were going to issue $250 billion of SDRs "to increase global liquidity."[72] The amount grew, eventually reaching $283 billion.

The *Telegraph*, the British newspaper, reported that the decision to issue SDRs was buried in "a single clause in Point 19 of the communiqué issued by the G20 leaders." The paper noted that it amounted "to a revolution in the global financial order."[73]

The IMF has had the authority to issue SDRs for fifty years, but has only now chosen to do so, thereby "putting a de facto world currency into play," one that is "outside the control of any sovereign body."[74]

But the IMF is controlled, de facto, by European central bankers. And it's challenging the United States for global leadership, seeking to discipline American economic policy through the G-20 organization that it staffs. Replacing the dollar with the SDR is their ultimate goal. But replacing the dollar with SDRs would be a laughable course. Sure, some may be worried that the U.S. economy supporting the dollar is in recession—that we seem to be printing money with no basis to support it.

But is there legitimate reason for concern that the U.S. government, with all its power to tax and a vast national wealth to draw upon, might not be able to meet its obligations? And what about the IMF and the SDRs it will print? Remember, the IMF has *no* economy behind it. *No* tax base. *No* power to tax. *No* national wealth. It is simply a bureaucracy, backed up by various national governments that are under no obligation to support or sustain it. To replace a currency backed by the strongest and richest country in the world with paper that's issued by an international body—with none of the powers of sovereignty—and pretend this new currency is more secure than the dollar is absurd.

Nevertheless, a chorus of support for SDRs has sprung up—led by voices like leftist billionaire George Soros. Indeed, Soros has linked his two pet projects, SDRs and climate change, to propose that developed countries pay less-developed nations in SDRs to help them adjust to climate change.

The *Wall Street Journal* reported, "Mr. Soros suggested that rich nations finance climate subsidies for developing nations by tapping into some of the $283 billion in SDRs that the IMF issued to respond to the global financial crisis." [75]

The dollar is also under siege by the Arab Gulf states, China, Russia, Japan and France. The *Independent*, another U.K. newspaper, reported that these nations "are planning to move away from pricing oil in dollars to using an array of currencies including the Japanese yen, the Chinese yuan, the euro, gold, and a new unified currency in the Gulf Co-operation Council"—a group that includes Saudi Arabia, Abu Dhabi, Kuwait, and Qatar. [76]

There are those who feel that losing the dollar as the global currency would be a blessing, because it would limit our government's ability to be irresponsible and keep printing money and incurring debt. They argue that if we had to compete on a level playing field with other nations, and they didn't have billions of greenbacks kicking around, we would never be able to be so self-indulgent and borrow so much money.

They're right, but it would be a grueling dose of cold turkey for the American people to have to deal with another global currency. But we might have to undergo it . . .

Unless we pull off a Republican victory in 2010.

If we do, we will send the world the same message that Reagan's election sent in 1980: The United States is back! Pursuing supply-side remedies to our economic problems will help the nation grow, bringing down our deficit and our debt. The socialists of the world will be amazed: Free enterprise will have done it again. Talk of abandoning the dollar as the international currency will evaporate.

And the IMF can pay itself in the SDRs it seems to like so much.

If things carry on as they are now, on the other hand, permanently high interest rates and persistent unemployment may be the legacies of the irresponsible Obama administration.

And that's assuming we don't fall into another financial crisis.

THE NEXT CRASH?

One good definition of insanity is to do the same thing over and over again and expect a different result. That's what the Obama administration is doing these days.

Even as it picks up the pieces from the financial collapse of 2008–9, it's seeding the next collapse with its policies. The core of the financial crisis was the subprime mortgages issued to homeowners who couldn't afford to pay market interest rates. Enticed by artificially low rates, these families took the plunge and moved into homes beyond their means. When the incentive teaser rates expired and their mortgage interest went up, these families defaulted in droves. All of the investments predicated on these mortgages became suspect, and the pyramid scheme began to unravel.

But Obama is retracing Bill Clinton's footsteps: He's already allowing the subprime mortgage market to start growing again!

This time the villain is not Fannie Mae or Freddie Mac—they're in receivership—but the Federal Housing Authority (FHA) and the Federal Reserve Bank itself. FHA is busily lending mortgages to families that can't afford them, and the Federal Reserve is happily buying up mortgage-backed securities that other investors are too smart to purchase.

The FHA is playing the role once occupied by the likes of Countrywide Financial, lending money for only a 3.5 percent down payment at attractive interest rates. Its loan volume has quadrupled, rising from 425,000 loans in 2006 to 1.8 million in 2009. Half of all first-time U.S. homebuyers used FHA financing.[77]

The FHA is using many of the same con artists who made the subprime loans to poor families that triggered the last crisis. The FHA's inspector general recently warned that the agency was not requiring proper documentation before making loans, and was failing to "assure that lenders met all applicable requirements."[78] It even failed to ensure that convicted financial criminals were barred from making FHA-insured loans. As *Reason* magazine recently reported, the inspector general's spot-check of FHA-insured loans found that "just one out of twenty-two approved applications contained all the documentation needed to meet the FHA's own standards for guaranteeing a loan."[79]

Already, one loan in six is at least ninety days delinquent or in foreclosure. Gary Lacefield, a former HUD investigator, predicts that this situation will lead to an "FHA insurance Armageddon." He warns, "sometime in the next 15 to 18 months you're going to see a major hit on the FHA insurance fund."[80]

And with Obama in control of Congress, you can bet that another taxpayer-funded bailout will follow.

Meanwhile, the Federal Reserve Bank is offering itself as a buyer of last resort for mortgage-backed securities predicated on these delinquent loans. The Federal Reserve Bank has purchased $850 billion in mortgage-backed securities since the beginning of 2009 (its holdings were zero or negligible as of January 2009).[81]

And so the cycle of overly generous lending—backed by a buyer willing to purchase securities based on the loans, inevitable foreclosure, crisis, and government bailout—repeats itself without end!

And where is Obama while all of this is happening? He's cheering them on! At an Oval Office meeting on December 14, 2009, the president challenged top bankers to explore "every responsible way" to increase lending, asking them to take a "third and fourth look" at their rejected loans with a view toward extending credit more broadly. He demanded that they expand lending to pay Americans back for their bailouts. "Given the exceptional assistance banks received to get them through a difficult time," he said, "we expect them to explore every responsible way to help get our economy moving again."[82]

In other words: *We saved your bacon. Now show your gratitude by making the same mistakes you made before so we have to bail you out again!*

It gets worse. Like a man applying masking tape to a gaping wound, Obama is even pressuring mortgage lenders to cut corners in restructuring loans that are already facing default. Remember: It was just such a policy, by these same lenders, that led these same homeowners to default on these same mortgages in the first place. Now Obama is after the lenders to go back to the days of squishy repayment terms—so that people can stay in homes they can't afford.

On December 1, 2009, the *Los Angeles Times* reported that "the Obama administration today announced a renewed push to get mortgage companies to convert hundreds of thousands of temporarily restructured home loans into permanent ones by the end of the year to help keep struggling homeowners from falling into foreclosure. Obama is sending what administration officials described as three-person 'SWAT teams' to the offices of those firms to help them obtain the necessary documents from borrowers and trouble-shoot problems." [83]

The newspaper noted, "the administration is hoping to embarrass mortgage servicing companies into doing more to make trial modifications permanent by highlighting those that are not performing well. But it also could levy penalties or other sanctions against laggards based on the agreements they signed to participate in the program." Assistant Treasury Secretary Michael Barr said, "servicers that don't meet their obligations under the program are going to suffer the consequences." [84]

In other words, the administration is telling the same lenders that made the bad loans that caused the financial crisis to make more bad loans . . . or else!

Republicans opposed the expansion of Fannie Mae and Freddie Mac lending that led to the financial crisis; they can be counted on to stop the crisis from being reborn by the same stupid policies. The GOP doesn't have to help poor people stay in homes they can't afford. It doesn't need to nurture impossible dreams to get elected. It can offer the poor what it has always offered: a ready and real path to upward mobility, a path away from government dependence.

But Obama still won't own up to the fundamental fact that it was government guarantees that allowed—and government regulations that forced—Fannie Mae and Freddie Mac to make the subprime loans that led to the collapse. And his inability to understand history has serious consequences—because he's repeating the mistakes that got us here in the first place. On Christmas Eve 2009, the Obama administration announced that it was lifting the $400 billion cap on guarantees of Fannie Mae and Freddie Mac mortgage loans. The taxpayers have already put $111 billion into these two quasi-public institutions. But remember that Freddie and Fannie made, guaranteed, or bought $1.6 trillion of mortgage loans by the end of 2008. The *Washington Examiner* presciently noted that "the removal of the $400 billion cap suggests that things are about to worsen considerably." [85]

Indeed.

In a front-page story on December 30, 2009, the *New York Times* published an interview with Wellesley economist Karl E. Case, who is gravely concerned about the housing situation. "I'm worried," he said. "Everyone's worried. If prices sink 15 percent from here, which is a possibility, and the 2008 and 2009 loans go bad, then we're right back where we were before—in a nightmare." [86]

As George Santayana said, "Those who cannot remember the past are condemned to repeat it." [87]

HUGE TAX INCREASES AHEAD

Central to Obama's economic program of expanded government and income redistribution is his determination to raise taxes. Indeed, as a candidate he even made his pledge to raise taxes on the wealthy a fundamental part of his campaign.

When Obama took office, however, he realized that he couldn't pass higher taxes in the middle of a major recession. Even the Democrats in Congress realized that this was no time to take even more liquidity out of the economy. The rich would just have to wait for their tax increases.

But Obama did not intend to abandon his high-tax goals. In fact, he had a bold plan for ensuring that they wouldn't be forgotten. Instead of first raising taxes and then spending the money, he took the opposite path: He began his presidency by spending massive amounts in his stimulus package in the opening week of his administration. That way, he could rest assured that higher taxes would inevitably follow. He knew that the resulting deficit would kindle increasingly strident demands for higher taxes. And he was right.

Obama and the Democrats are bent on using the pressure their deficits are creating to force through big tax increases. Politically, they couch their campaign for higher taxation by saying that they want to tax the rich. The implicit argument is that those with high incomes can afford to pay more in taxes.

But what they're *really* proposing is to raise taxes on the top dollar a taxpayer earns—the marginal tax rate. By raising these taxes, the Democrats are creating a disincentive to making more money. They ensure that there is less and less point in working harder and producing more income. The higher marginal taxes stifle incentive and narcotize ambition.

The real issue is: Will a higher top tax bracket remove the incentive to earn more money?

It doesn't really matter how much the rich are taxed. What does matter is how much the next dollar (economists would say the marginal dollar) of income is taxed.

The question is not whether the mouse can afford the extra tax on his cheese. It is whether he won't want any more cheese if we keep taxing it more. Will a tax on ambition dry up the American profit motive?

The United States has one of the most progressive tax systems in the world. The richest one percent of our taxpayers contributes 40.4 percent of federal income tax revenues.[88] But Obama wants to increase their share drastically.

Right now, the top marginal tax rate in the United States is about 42 percent (35 percent federal, 2.9 percent Medicare, and an average of 4 percent of state and local income taxes). The Heritage Foundation reports that this puts the United States at the same level as the average top marginal tax rate (also 42 percent) for the thirty most economically developed nations in the world (members of the Organisation for Economic Co-operation and Development, or OECD).[89]

But Obama's tax plans will send our top marginal rate skyrocketing.

Obviously, Obama and Congress are going to push for increases on taxes for the wealthy. In his 2011 budget, Obama calls for going back to the pre-Bush top bracket of 39.6 percent from the current level of 35 percent. Meanwhile, House speaker Nancy Pelosi and Ways and Means committee chairman Charlie Rangel want to raise taxes on the top bracket even more by imposing an additional surtax of 5.4 percent. The House passed just such a surtax as part of their Obamacare bill in 2009. Other proposals involve increasing the Medicare tax and changing the FICA (Social Security) tax so that we have to pay it on our entire income, not just the first $100,000 as at present.

HOW OBAMA AND PELOSI WILL INCREASE THE TOP TAX RATE

Current Law

Top income tax bracket	35%
Medicare tax	2.9
Average state/local top tax	*4.0*
TOTAL TOP TAX RATE	41.9

Obama's and Pelosi's Proposals

Top income tax bracket	39.6%
Medicare tax	3.9
Surtax	5.4
Average state/local top tax	*4.0*
TOTAL TOP TAX RATE	52.9

Source: Heritage Foundation[90]

Under Obama's plan, the United States will have some of the highest taxes in the world—higher than Germany or Britain or France.

The Heritage Foundation reports that, at 52.9 percent, the top tax rate under this plan would be "higher than the top rate in all but three countries in the OECD: Denmark (60 percent), Sweden (56 percent), and Belgium (54 percent)."[91]

TOP TAX RATE BY NATION

Nation	Top Tax Rate
Denmark	60.0%
Sweden	56.4
Belgium	53.7

UNITED STATES	52.9	(*Under Obama's proposal*)
Netherlands	52.0	
Finland	50.1	
Japan	50.0	
Austria	50.0	
Germany	47.5	
Australia	46.5	
Canada	46.4	
France	45.8	
Italy	44.9	
Spain	43.0	
Portugal	42.0	
UNITED STATES	41.9	(*Current*)
Switzerland	41.7	
Ireland	41.0	
Greece	40.0	
United Kingdom	40.0	
Norway	40.0	

Source: Heritage Foundation [92]

And if Obama can control Congress after 2010, the tax increases will come fast and thick. Who knows where they will fall next?

One likely candidate for an increase is the so-called Death Tax—the inheritance tax that has fallen to zero in 2010 due to the schedule of Bush tax cuts passed in 2001. In his 2011 budget, Obama proposes to hike the tax back up to 45 percent in 2011 and apply it to all estates worth more than $3.5 million. So, if you're planning to die soon, you'd better go to your Maker in 2010—while the tax is still at zero!

The problem with the Death Tax isn't how it affects families that own the wealth so much as how it impacts those who earn money to accumulate it.

The tax itself is paid by only the top 2 percent of families. They are not especially deserving of our tears. But our unemployed men and women are. For their sake—not for the sake of the wealthy themselves—we should kill the Death Tax.

The central question for wealthy elderly Americans is what to do with their money. Should they keep it in cash or easily liquefied investments, or is it better to plow the money back into their businesses?

They don't always care. But we sure do. We want them to keep the funds in their businesses, creating jobs and growing. But the Death Tax gives these wealthy Americans an incentive to hold their assets in cash or in an investment, which allows them to get at it painlessly and easily. If a person dies with $10 million, and his estate has to pay the government 45 percent of the amount over $3.5 million, his heirs have to come up with approximately $3 million in a matter of months. If the funds of the deceased are in cash or a liquid asset, that's easy: Just sell some assets or liquidate some investments. Maybe you have to sell a little short, but it's not too bad.

But if the fortunes of the deceased are tied up in a business or a farm, it can be much harder to pry loose $3 million. You find yourself having to close factories, liquidate jobs, sell off a controlling interest of the stock, or sell land and do other things that are inimical to the long-term interests of the family, the business, and their workers.

So the Death Tax creates an incentive *not* to invest money in one's business, but to keep it in things like houses and yachts and luxury goods—or cash and gold and bonds—that are easier to liquidate.

As America's rich age, they will become less and less likely to invest their money in ways that create jobs . . . because of the inheritance tax.

There is also the matter of incentive to create wealth. Rich people may not lose much sleep over whether their kids hang on to their toys, like planes and yachts. But many care that the businesses or farms to which they devoted their lives survive after their death.

Rich people don't save money so that they can spend it down to zero before their deaths. A study by Obama adviser Larry Summers and economist Laurence Kotlikoff "showed that patterns of savings don't validate that model [that they spend down their savings]." The study found that "between 41% and 66% of capital stock was transferred by bequests at death or through trusts and lifetime gifts. A major motivation for saving and building businesses is to pass assets on so children and grandchildren have a better life." [93]

Indeed, the study showed that "intergenerational transfers" account for the vast majority of U.S. capital. Men and women make money and build businesses to pass them on to the next generation. The Death Tax makes that hard; it encourages rich people to indulge themselves with liquid assets, rather than help us all by building their businesses.

And there's a chance that Obama will not only restore the Death Tax, but that he'll hike it way up. In his 2011 budget proposal, he calls for restoring the tax to its 2009 level of 45 percent on estates of $3.5 million per person or more. But, with a liberal Congress, Obama might choose simply to let the Bush inheritance tax cut expire. That would drive the rate up to 55 percent and drop the exemption to only $1 million. Anyone with a house and cars or businesses that come to $1 million or more would have to pay more than half of their inheritance in taxes.

What an incredible incentive to encourage people to stay home, sleep late, and do nothing but golf!

WHAT WE FACE: OBAMA'S NEW TAXES

1. Marginal income tax rates are set to rise when the Bush tax cuts expire in 2011. The top rate will go from 35 percent to 39.6 percent.

2. The Social Security Tax (FICA) will likely be raised so that the total tax (6.7 percent on employees and 6.7 percent on employers or 13.5 percent on the self-employed) will apply to all income, not just to the first $100,000 as at present. Obama may scale that back, as he proposed in his campaign, so that the tax exempts income between $100,000 and $200,000, but taxes everything above that.

3. A new surtax may follow. Whether as part of the health-care bill or as a deficit reduction measure in the near future, Obama will likely propose a surtax of 5.4 percent on all incomes over $500,000 for individuals and $1 million for couples. These sums will likely not be indexed—so that, as with the Alternative Minimum Tax, the surtax hits more and more people as inflation drives up nominal incomes. That way this tax, now disguised as a tax on the super-rich, will just represent a de facto increase in the top bracket to 45 percent.

4. Capital gains and dividend taxes will go up. Both are currently taxed at 15 percent, but they are scheduled to rise in 2011 when the Bush cuts

expire. Capital gains will rise to at least 20 percent, and Obama has left the door open to increasing it to 28 percent. Obama may only raise the capital gains tax for single people earning $200,000 or more or for married couples making more than $250,000. The lower tax rate for dividends will expire, and they may end up being taxed at the same rate as regular income, although Obama says he will only raise it to 20 percent.

5. Lower personal exemptions or itemized deductions for taxpayers earning more than $250,000. He proposes to cut the amount these taxpayers can deduct for state and local taxes, charitable contributions, and home mortgage interest. Right now, these folks can deduct the entire cost from their income taxes. If the tax rate at the time is 39.6 percent, then the government pays that portion of their donation or mortgage interest or local tax payment. But Obama wants to limit the impact of the deduction so that it only is worth 28 percent of the amount, about a 30 percent reduction in the value of these deductions. This change will hurt people in high tax states, depress home construction, and slice charitable giving.

6. The estate tax will go back up to 45 or 55 percent and may apply to all inheritances over $1 million.

7. The employee and employer share of the Medicare payroll tax would rise to 1.95 percent from the current 1.45 percent. For the self-employed, it would go up from the current 2.9 percent to 3.9 percent. This tax may apply to all people, or be limited to single people with incomes above $200,000 and married couples above $250,000.

8. The Senate health bill includes a new 40 percent tax on high-value health insurance plans. The tax would cover many plans valued at more than $8,500 for an individual and $23,000 for a family. And, since these sums are only indexed for regular inflation—not medical premium inflation—more and more taxpayers will have to pay the tax. In 2013, according to the Senate Finance Committee, 14 percent of all health insurance policies will be subject to the tax. By 2016 it will rise to 25 percent, and by 2019 it will go up to 31 percent.

Source: Wall Street Journal[94]

If Obama retains control of Congress after the 2010 election, we're all in store for big tax increases. Calculate how much they would cost you and then give a portion of that to finance Republican campaigns so you won't have to pay them!

HEALTH CARE

The right-to-life debate has polarized public opinion in the United States and around the world. People of good faith disagree on when life begins: at conception, at viability, or at birth. But no one disagrees that life ends at death.

Yet it is at this end of the spectrum that Obama is eroding the right to life, by forcing a scarcity of medical resources on the United States in a bid to extend limited resources to more and more people without augmenting them.

Instead of making a universal commitment to do what it takes to extend human life as long as possible, the Obama health-care system sees geriatrics only through the prism of cost control. Time and again, it is forcing doctors and hospitals to answer the question: *Is it worth it? Is this particular patient's life of sufficient quality and likely to last sufficiently long to justify the expenditure needed to prolong it?*

Human beings have no standing to ask this question. Only God does. But Obamacare preempts divine authority, and arrogates to men and women the responsibility for deciding when life is worth preserving and when it is not.

To a certain extent, all doctors and all families have always faced this excruciating decision. Many elderly people leave living wills so that they can weigh in on the matter when the time is right. But these decisions are usually made on medical grounds, offsetting the pain and discomfort against the quality of the life being saved.

Now, Barack Obama is demanding that it be decided based on cost.

He is doing so by foisting upon us a system based on a calculation of Quality Adjusted Life Years (QALYs), in which physicians, with bureaucrats peering over their shoulders and cost accountants peering over theirs, must equate life with money and come up with an answer.

Like a bank amortizing a mortgage over the years of life remaining in the house, doctors and family members must justify the procedures they want for their patients and loved ones by citing the number of high-quality years remaining for the patient.

This terrible burden is being foisted on us by Obama's refusal to expand the number of doctors as he forces the system to accommodate more patients. As he expands the patient population, and slashes reimbursement rates of payment to doctors for treating them, he is taking a land of plenty and transforming it into one of scarcity and hard, inhuman choices.

This rationing is really a form of government-induced euthanasia, in which the cost of prolonging a human life is balanced against the worth of the patient. If his or her earning capacity is limited or nil, if there is no family, or if the patient is otherwise handicapped, the bureaucrat may decide to withhold treatment. Or, in other words, to let the patient die.

For years, health-care policymakers have wrestled with the fact that a vast amount of money can be spent at the very end of a patient's life in an often futile effort to squeeze out some extra time. Fifty billion dollars—about a tenth of Medicare spending—goes for doctor and hospital costs incurred in the final two months of a patient's life.[95] But policymakers have been understandably reluctant to face the issue, since it comes close to playing God.

Obama has no such scruples. A huge portion of his proposed Medicare cuts target precisely the money spent at the end of a person's life.

Sarah Palin took a lot of heat for saying that Obama's proposals amount to establishing "death panels" within the government. But she wasn't far wrong. Obama's plan wouldn't involve actual tribunals to hear each case and make the life-or-death decision, but it would require all doctors and insurance companies to follow cost-driven bureaucratic guidelines in making the decisions. That's even worse—because it leaves the victims with no day in court; no appeal after the decision is made.

For the government to withhold lifesaving surgery or treatment because the cost of the procedure is too rich when judged against the "quality" of a patient's "adjusted remaining years" is to violate the very basis of our civilization. It transforms the Obamacare debate from the realms of finances and health care into a moral issue: Does a human being have the right to withhold treatment and condemn an innocent person to death simply because of a third party's judgment about their quality of life?

The final version of the health-care legislation approved by the Senate in late 2009 averted the threat of universal socialized medicine. Thanks to a goal-line stand by Senator Joseph Lieberman (I-CT), provisions for a "public option" were deleted; the final bill offered no government-owned, -subsidized, and -operated health insurance company to compete with private firms, an idea that would inevitably have put them out of business. The glide-line trajectory leading to a single payer may have been interdicted. But Obama hasn't given up on the public option and may yet pass it.

But Lieberman's intervention did nothing to protect the elderly who would remain subject to the whims and dictates of bureaucrats and cost accountants as they seek the medical care they need to stay alive if Obamacare passes.

Obama's legislation threatens us all because it could usher in the day when the American practice of medicine—as we know it—may well disappear.

Why? Because there will simply be too few doctors left to maintain it.

Thanks to Obama's war on doctors, the future may be filled with nurse practitioners and physicians' assistants. Seeing a real live doctor may become an increasingly rare experience. And those who do find a doctor may confront a huge language barrier, as one in four American doctors was born abroad, and 25 percent were educated abroad.[96]

Even before Obama's health-care program takes effect, the population of primary care physicians in the United States has been dwindling dangerously.

Joseph Stubbs, president of the American College of Physicians, has called the shortage of doctors "already a catastrophic crisis."[97]

As Bloomberg News notes, "underserved areas in the U.S. currently need 16,679 more primary-care physicians to reach a medically appropriate target of 1 for every 2,000 residents."[98]

And the application of Obama's health-care proposals will only make the situation worse, by increasing the number of patients while decreasing the number of doctors available to treat them. As Stubbs points out, "now we're talking 30 million more people who will want to see a doctor. The supply of doctors just won't be there for them."[99]

In Massachusetts, where Governor Mitt Romney pushed through a universal health-care bill much like Obama's, Bloomberg News reports that "the average waiting time to see a family-medicine doctor in Boston is 63 days." In Miami, it was seven.[100] And, partially because of the Romney health-care bill, "as many as half of the doctors in the state [of Massachusetts] have closed their practices to new patients, forcing many of the newly insured to turn to emergency rooms for care." [101]

Allan Goroll, a professor of medicine at Harvard Medical School, concluded, "The primary lesson of health-care reform in Massachusetts is that you can't increase the number of insured unless you have a strong primary-care base in place to receive them. Without that foundation of primary care, Massachusetts has ended up with higher costs and people going to emergency rooms when they can't find a doctor." [102]

Atul Grover, chief advocacy officer for the Association of American Medical Colleges (AAMC), warns, "we're not going to have enough doctors, even if you don't consider expanding insurance coverage to millions of people. . . . It's just a question of time before it leads to longer waits for all of us to get in to see the doctor." [103]

Even former Senate majority leader Tom Daschle, President Obama's first choice to serve as secretary of health and human services, says, "if you expand coverage without expanding primary care, you will overwhelm emergency rooms that are already overcrowded." [104]

H. Kenneth Walker, professor of medicine at Emory University School of Medicine, puts it bluntly. "Primary care in the United States is dead," he writes. "The demise is occurring because the number of graduates entering the field . . . is undergoing a marked decline that shows no signs of reversal." [105]

Since 1997, Dr. Walker notes, the percentage of medical school graduates planning to enter primary care has plummeted from 53 percent (7,218 out of 13,567 graduates) to only 21 percent (1,777 out of 8,337 graduates) in 2005. He says that "medical school students and residents see the primary care physician as a harried, deeply troubled and unhappy individual who spends inordinate hours delivering care but who finds the time he or she is able to give patients inadequate, the quality of care delivered intolerable, the income derived too little, and the regulatory hassle unacceptable." [106]

This looming shortage of primary-care physicians is especially dangerous since, according to Dr. Donald Gordon of Danbury Hospital in Connecticut, "one must complete an Internal Medicine, Family Practice, or Osteopathy before applying for a fellowship (specialty) in GI (Gastro-Intestinal) Cardio, Endocrine, Pulmonary, Rheumatology or Nephrology." [107]

If too few doctors are entering the door of primary or family medicine, too few will pass through to become the medical care specialists we also need.

The number of U.S. medical school students going into primary care has dropped 51.8 percent since 1997, according to the American Academy of Family Physicians (AAFP).[108] According to *USA Today*, "considering it takes 10 to 11 years to educate a doctor, the drying up of the pipeline [of family care physicians] is a big concern to health-care experts. The AAFP is predicting a shortage of 40,000 family physicians in 2020, when the demand is expected to spike. The U.S. health-care system has about 100,000 family physicians and will need 139,531 in 10 years. The current environment is attracting only half the number needed to meet the demand."[109]

A big part of the problem is that family-care physicians are underpaid. The following chart compares pay for different medical specialties:

DOCTORS' STARTING SALARIES, 2007

Radiology	$350,000
Anesthesiology	$275,000
General surgery	$220,000
Otolaryngology	$220,000
Emergency	$178,000
Neurology	$177,000
Psychiatry	$160,000
Internal Medicine	$130,000
Family Medicine	$130,000
Pediatrics	$125,000

Source: Journal of the American Medical Association[110]

From 1997 through 2004, the compensation of primary-care and family-practice doctors rose from only about $130,000 to $150,000. Over the same time, the pay for radiologists rose from $260,000 to $400,000 and for orthopedists from $300,000 to $400,000. Dermatologists saw their pay rise from $175,000 to $300,000. In both 1997 and 2004, primary-care and family-practice doctors remained at the bottom end of the medical compensation scale.

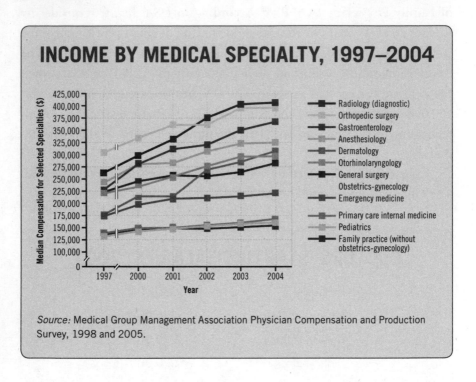

INCOME BY MEDICAL SPECIALTY, 1997–2004

Source: Medical Group Management Association Physician Compensation and Production Survey, 1998 and 2005.

And, as a direct result, fewer men and women are entering the ranks of general care or family medical providers. The number of anesthesiologists has risen by 150 percent in the past decade; the number of pathologists has gone up by 122 percent, the number of radiologists by 34 percent. But the number of new family-practice physicians *has plummeted by 51 percent* over the same period—and the crop of additional internal medicine practitioners has fallen by 18 percent.

Medical school tuition and expenses generally range from $140,000 to $200,000. Usually financed with student loans, these fees saddle young physicians with a heavy financial burden from their first day on the job— a burden that undoubtedly deters many idealistic doctors from entering primary-care practice.[111]

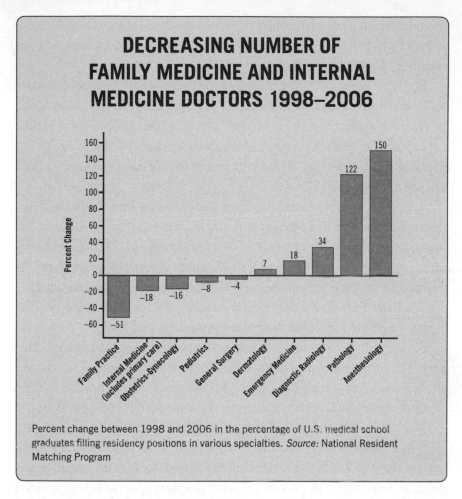

DECREASING NUMBER OF FAMILY MEDICINE AND INTERNAL MEDICINE DOCTORS 1998–2006

Percent change between 1998 and 2006 in the percentage of U.S. medical school graduates filling residency positions in various specialties. *Source:* National Resident Matching Program

While Obama's health-care legislation contains several superficial incentives for medical school graduates to enter family practice or internal medicine, the harsh fact is that his program threatens to further rob us of all kinds of doctors, including family and internal medicine practitioners.

The president's program would add two thousand new residency spots for primary-care doctors and general surgeons. The proposal originally called for fifteen thousand, but it was trimmed to hold down costs.[112] Two thousand extra doctors is a pitiful response to the problems of providing care for 30 million new patients!

The *Wall Street Journal* reports that the health-care reform legislation "increases funding for the National Health Service Corps, which helps repay student loans for doctors, nurse practitioners and dentists who work in underserved parts of the country. Primary-care doctors who participate can get up to $50,000 of loans repaid. The bill also reallocates some unused residency slots toward higher-need areas.[113]

But what good will $50,000 do? The average medical school graduate today starts out owing about $156,000 in loans, according to the AAMC. "It is utterly absurd that our graduates have that kind of debt," said Arthur S. Levine, dean of the University of Pittsburgh School of Medicine. "Every day, students tell me they'd like to be primary-care doctors, but they can't afford to." [114]

And these incentives to encourage people to go into medicine fly in the face of the fact that Obama is financing his program by slashing reimbursement rates for doctors. His overt program of $500 billion in cuts on Medicare payments to doctors and hospitals means that caregivers get less money for each patient they see, test they order, or inpatient they accommodate. Indeed, the president's system calls for breaking down the health-care field into 7,500 diagnostic groupings and requires doctors to report annually on how much they spent treating each patient in each category. The government then has to calculate which physicians are in the top 10 percent in cost of their care. These doctors must then be fined, and their reimbursement rates cut, to punish them for spending too much money.

The results for patients, of course, will be cheaper and lower-quality care. Sick patients may have a hard time finding doctors who are willing to treat them and thus risk subjecting themselves to fines for spending too much on their care. Doctors will order fewer tests to avoid being included in the category of physicians who are to be penalized. The system incentivizes low-quality and perfunctory medical care.

Yet Obama has included no real provision for tort reform in his legislation. So even as the federal bureaucrats second-guess a doctor for ordering MRIs or CT scans or other such tests, the trial lawyers will second-guess his failure to do so after the fact. And the poor doctor is caught in the middle with rising malpractice insurance premiums.

One answer would be to limit medical malpractice lawsuits. In Mississippi, which passed such legislation, malpractice insurance premiums were cut in half. But the trial lawyers who fund Obama and the Democrats won't let them pass this commonsense solution.

But if the consequences for patients of this dumbing down of medical care are dangerous, for doctors they are abysmal. Conscientious doctors will be penalized, and their incomes cut, for spending too much money treating their patients. Those who brush aside the run-of-the-mill practice to focus on those who need care the most are more likely to be punished for their idealism by incurring a fine and a reduced reimbursement rate. And doctors will constantly have bureaucrats looking over their shoulders as they make life-and-death decisions about their patients.

This bureaucratic meddling, and the dumbing down of care that will result from the cut in reimbursement rates, will combine to drive even more doctors out of the profession. Idealism, of course, is what keeps many doctors hanging on. If they are forced to compromise on patient care and to make life-and-death decisions based on dollars and cents, however, many physicians can be expected to sour on the practice—and find Obamacare inconsistent with their treasured Hippocratic Oath.

In a survey by *Investor's Business Daily*, 45 percent of physicians said they would consider retiring or closing down their practices if Obamacare passed.[115]

When 78 million baby boomers born from 1946 to 1964 start turning sixty-five in 2011, the shortage of primary-care physicians is going to become increasingly acute.

As the *New England Journal of Medicine* notes, Obama's health-care legislation, which extends coverage to "Americans who lack insurance," will make "the need for more doctors . . . escalate."[116] And *USA Today* concludes, "finding a doctor will get increasingly difficult, waits for appointments will grow longer, and more sick people will turn to crowded emergency rooms."[117]

Ted Epperly, president of the AAFP, an association that represents more than 93,000 physicians, notes that "if a patient goes to a doctor's office, he might not be treated by his doctor: One way overwhelmed family physicians have been dealing with patients is to have office visits overseen by a nurse practitioner or a physician's assistant, some of whom can dispense certain prescriptions and recommend specialists."[118]

Epperly adds, "At the time we need family-care physicians the most, we are producing the least. The nation's medical schools are failing to produce a workforce that is essential to caring for America's communities."[119]

Foreign doctors are likely to fill part of the void. In March 2009, 21 percent of the resident positions for family medicine were filled by non-U.S. citizens educated internationally. Another 18 percent went to American citizens educated abroad.[120]

A combination of Obama's war on wealth, and his particular zest to cut the compensation of doctors, will probably combine to make the American medical community a world increasingly deprived of doctors— particularly primary-care physicians.

This is what has already happened in Canada. According to the magazine of the Fraser Institute, while Canada was "once the home of the developed world's highest physician-to-population ratios," it now "ranks a miserable 26th among 28 nations that maintain universal access to health insurance."[121]

And this shortage is reflected in long waiting lists. In 1993, it took an average of 9.3 weeks—about two months—to see a specialist after a referral from a general practitioner in Canada. By 1997, the average wait was 11.9 weeks, about three months. Now it takes 17.3 weeks—four months. Just to see a specialist![122]

As he pushed for passage of his health-care program, President Obama was at great pains to set a ceiling of $900 billion on the ten-year cost of the effort and to demand that it not add to the federal deficit. Senate and House Democratic leaders made a great show of trying to meet the president's cost parameters. But the idea that this program's cost can be held to less than a trillion dollars over ten years is absurd. Michael F. Cannon, the Cato Institute's director of health policy studies, has suggested that it will really cost $6 trillion.

And average Americans are quite certain that the health-care legislation would cost much more, in fact, than Obama says it will. The Rasmussen Poll reports that:

- 78 percent believe that the health-care program will cost more than projected

- 81 percent believe it will lead to higher middle-class taxes

- 68 percent say it will add to the federal deficit[123]

Americans know what's up—even if their Congress doesn't.

Here's how the Congress hid the real cost from the American people:

HOW CONGRESS LIED ABOUT
THE COST OF HEALTH CARE

1. Congressional leaders projected the costs over six years and the revenues over ten years to make the numbers appear to balance. The money raised by measures such as cutting Medicare, slashing doctors fees, taxing health insurance plans, fining people for not buying insurance, and taxing medical devices like pacemakers all starts coming in at the beginning of 2010. But the spending on covering the uninsured doesn't start until 2013. So by counting only six years of spending, Obama told the country that his program would cost $900 billion over six years. As Senator Judd Gregg (R-NH) says, "when all this new spending occurs—from 2014 through 2023—this bill will cost $2.5 trillion over that ten-year period." [124]

2. Cannon notes that "another gimmick [to hide the real cost of the health-care bill] pushes much of the legislation's costs off the federal budget and onto the private sector by requiring individuals and employers to purchase health insurance. When the bills force somebody to pay $10,000 to the government, the Congressional Budget Office treats that as a tax. When the government then hands that $10,000 to private insurers, the CBO counts that as government spending. But when the bills achieve the exact same outcome by forcing somebody to pay $10,000 directly to a private insurance company, it appears nowhere in the official CBO cost estimates—neither as federal revenues nor federal spending. That's a sharp departure from how the CBO treated similar mandates in the Clinton health plan. And it hides maybe 60 percent of the legislation's total costs." [125]

Together, Cannon estimates that the "on- and off-budget costs over the first 10 years of implementation reaches $6.25 trillion." [126]

Perhaps the best evidence of the shortcomings of the health-care reform that Obama is foisting upon us comes from the Democratic senators who voted for it themselves, each scrambling to exempt his own state from its pernicious effects. A few senators, like Connecticut's Chris Dodd—always alive for a chance to get a payoff—got good old-fashioned pork in return for their votes ($100 million for a University of Connecticut Medical Center—the future Chris Dodd Center?). But most merely sought to stop the bill from hurting their own states as much as it hurt the other forty-nine.

Nebraska's Republican senator Mike Johanns, who voted against the bill, observed: "If the [Obama health-care bill] cannot pass without carve-outs, what further evidence is needed that it is bad policy?" [127]

The *Wall Street Journal* documents the pre-Christmas deals that individual senators got in order to exempt their own constituents from the terms of the bill they were shortly to vote to impose upon the nation as a whole:

WHAT THEY GOT: THE SENATE DEALS BEHIND OBAMA'S HEALTH-CARE "REFORM" PACKAGE

Your Senate at Work

The following are examples of special provisions added to the Senate health-care bill, some at the last minute, to win the sixty votes needed to allow the bill to proceed to debate and passage:

Connecticut: $100 million for the University of Connecticut medical center.

Florida: A grandfather clause that exempts Florida residents from losing Medicare Advantage benefits. Cost: $3 billion to $5 billion.

Louisiana: $300 million in Medicaid subsidies to "certain states recovering from a medical disaster" (i.e. Katrina).

Massachusetts, Vermont: $500 million and $600 million, respectively, in higher Medicaid reimbursements.

Michigan: Exemption from the insurance fee for Michigan Blue Cross/Blue Shield.

Michigan, Connecticut: Higher reimbursements for certain hospitals under Medicare.

Montana, North and South Dakota, Wyoming: Higher Medicare payments to "frontier" hospitals and doctors.

Montana: Medicare coverage for individuals exposed to environmental health hazards in or around Libby, an asbestos Superfund site.

Nebraska: Exemption from the insurance fee for Nebraska Blue Cross/Blue Shield and Mutual of Omaha; and 100 percent federal payment for new Medicaid coverage, at a cost of $100 million.

Vermont: $10 million for community health-care centers.

Source: Senate Finance Committee [128]

It is into this new world—of scarce doctors, lower-quality medical care, universal access to long waiting lists, and an obsessive focus not on health but on costs—that Obama welcomes us.

Will Obama's health-care legislation pass? At this writing, congressional Democrats are scrambling to find a way to pass it despite losing a Senate seat in Massachusetts in the January 2010 special election. The bill has already passed both Houses but in different forms. It could become law instantly if the House passed the Senate version and sent it to the White House. Then no further action by the Senate would be needed.

But House liberals are upset with certain provisions of the Senate bill. They don't like that it doesn't include a public insurance company. They feel that its fines for not buying insurance are too low and that its subsidies to help people buy policies are too meager. They want the program to be funded by a surtax on the wealthy rather than by taxes on health insurance premiums. And, while they're at it, they'd like to delete the prohibition on using funds for abortion that is not in the Senate bill but is in the House version.

The liberals could probably be induced to overlook these shortcomings, especially if Senate majority leader Harry Reid (D-NV) offers to correct at least some of them by passing a separate budget bill that, using a procedure called reconciliation, would require only fifty-one votes for passage.

But the conservative Democrats may block the bill in the House. At least twenty-three Democrats voted for Obamacare in the House on its first passage and came from marginal districts. These vulnerable Democrats may hold the key to killing Obamacare in 2010. They need to hear from you.

VULNERABLE DEMOCRATS WHO VOTED FOR OBAMACARE

Mike Arcuri, New York, 24th District (Utica, Syracuse)

Marion Berry, Arkansas, 1st District (Eastern Arkansas)

Christopher Carney, Pennsylvania, 10th District (Scranton)

Kathy Dahlkemper, Pennsylvania, 3rd District (Erie)

Stephen Driehaus, Ohio, 1st District (Cincinnati)

Gabrielle Giffords, Arizona, 8th District (Phoenix)

Alan Grayson, Florida, 8th District (Orlando)

John Hall, New York, 19th District (Westchester)

Baron Hill, Indiana, 9th District (southern Indiana)

Steve Kagen, Wisconsin, 8th District (Green Bay)

Paul Kanjorsky, Pennsylvania, 11th District (Scranton–
   Wilkes-Barre)

Mary Jo Kilroy, Ohio, 15th District (Columbus)

Ann Kirkpatrick, Arizona, 1st District (Phoenix)

Dan Maffei, New York, 25th District (Syracuse)

Harry Mitchell, Arizona, 5th District (Phoenix)

Allan Mollohan, West Virgina, 1st District (Clarksburg, Wheeling)

Tom Perriello, Virginia, 5th District (Roanoke)

Nick Rahall, West Virginia, 3rd District (Bluefield, Charleston)

Mark Schauer, Michigan, 7th District (Lansing)

Carol Shea-Porter, New Hampshire, 1st District (southern
   New Hampshire)

Zack Space, Ohio, 18th District (Columbus)

John Spratt, South Carolina, 5th District (Rock Hill)

Dina Titus, Nevada, 3rd District (Las Vegas)

But, even if it passes, Obama's health-care legislation is not etched in stone. Despite the fact that it—ridiculously—includes provisions that bar certain aspects from being repealed, it can and will be changed. And it can and should be repealed.

By the time the new Congress convenes in January 2011, they will face a citizenship teeming with complaints about the Obama program if it were to pass this year. The elderly will be outraged when they are being denied care after being forced to give up their Medicare Advantage benefits. The young will realize that they're no closer to getting insurance, and that all the legislation does is force them to pay a fine for not having a policy even when they can't afford the premiums. Every American family will experience sticker shock when they get their new insurance bill with the hefty premium increases Obamacare will force the insurance industry to charge.

And pressure will mount to reform the reform. If the Congress is in Republican hands, these changes may come in time to save our health-care system. The most dangerous parts of Obamacare don't take full effect until 2014–16.

There is still time . . . if we change the Congress in the 2010 election.

OBAMA MAKES US DEBT SLAVES

The story of how we got into the financial crisis is well-known. Homeowners, anxious to spend more money than they had, took out subprime mortgages for homes they couldn't afford, enticed by artificially low interest rates. Then, when the rates returned to normal, they found their mortgage payments doubling and tripling within a few months. Many defaulted, and many more have fallen far behind.

This exact story may now be applied, verbatim, to the U.S. government.

When Obama took office, he was anxious to spend more money than we had, so he ballooned the federal deficit and sent the national debt soaring. In his first year in office, this most irresponsible of all American presidents increased federal spending from $3 trillion to $4 trillion, and increased the national debt from $9.6 trillion to $12 trillion!

As with the subprime mortgage families, the effect of the increased debt has been cushioned by low interest rates. Why are they so low? First, because foreigners who were terrified by the financial crisis flocked to the safety of U.S. government–guaranteed debt. Second, because the Federal Reserve Board held interest rates at historic lows—one quarter of one percent—to try to stop the economic collapse of late 2008 and early 2009. And, third, the fed keeps rates low by buying mortgage-backed securities and Treasury notes and injecting more and more currency into circulation.

But now, just as with the subprime borrowers, interest rates will soon have to resume their normal levels—and the U.S. government will face a debt shock of monumental proportions.

The deficits Obama is racking up, and the debt we must incur to cover them, are making our free nation into a debtor slave. We are not enslaved to a master race (we defeated Hitler) or to a fraudulent ideology (we crushed communism) but to our own debt. This tsunami of red ink represents a qualitative difference from the past.

Deficits are nothing new; we've had them for decades. But what the Obama administration has done to us is beyond belief.

Nothing could show his irresponsibility better than the chart below, which shows the size of each year's federal budget deficit as a percentage of our total economy (GDP). As you can see, the percentage was relatively minor—usually 2 or 3 percent, occasionally rising above 4 percent and peaking at 5.88 percent in the recession year of 1983.

Under Obama, it has skyrocketed—to 12.93 percent!

FEDERAL DEFICIT AS PERCENTAGE OF GROSS DOMESTIC PRODUCT

Year	Percentage
1981	2.52%
1982	3.93
1983	5.88
1984	4.71
1985	5.03
1986	4.96
1987	3.16
1988	3.04
1989	2.78
1990	3.81
1991	4.49
1992	4.58
1993	3.83
1994	2.87
1995	2.22

1996	1.37
1997	0.26
1998	−0.8
1999	−1.37
2000	−2.42
2001	−1.27
2002	1.52
2003	3.47
2004	3.56
2005	2.58
2006	1.90
2007	1.17
2008	3.24
2009	12.93

Source: U.S. government [129]

Deficits have always been a headache and a claim on our children's inheritance. But never before have they grown so high that the debt we must incur to fund them becomes a serious competitor for our national funds each year.

As of September 30, 2009, the national debt was $12 trillion and the interest was $383 billion. Our total federal spending was about $4 trillion: Roughly, one dollar in ten went to pay interest on the debt.

Now, as the federal Office of Management and Budget (OMB) tell us, we face $9 trillion in new debt over the next decade. That would bring our debt to $21 trillion in ten years.

But even that hard-to-swallow estimate is foolishly optimistic. It assumes no great growth in spending and almost $14 trillion in new revenues. Congress usually fails to hold down spending or to raise taxes. But the greatest flaw in the OMB estimate is that it assumes that interest rates will stay low. Now, investor Lawrence Kadish reports that they are averaging only 3.2 percent. But, as he notes, they reached 15 percent under Carter.

"With our mounting national debt and budget deficits," Kadish writes, "it is reasonable to assume that in the near future interest rates on new and refinanced debt could double or triple." [130]

Let's say, for the sake of argument, that the costs only double (rising to 6.4 percent, a very optimistic assumption). The interest on our current debt of $12 trillion would then be $768 billion—or 19 percent of our federal budget. That's what our debt should cost and will when interest rates return to normal.

Have a look at how much we should be spending on debt payments (under normal interest rates) compared with the amount we spend on other items in the budget:

INTEREST AND OTHER FEDERAL SPENDING COMPARED

Interest

Actual interest paid (at 3.2%)	$383 billion
Interest we should be paying at normal rates (6.4%)	$768 billion

Other Spending

Social Security	$644 billion
Medicare	408 billion
Medicaid and Children's Insurance	224 billion
Defense	515 billion
Unemployment, Welfare, Other Mandates	360 billion
War on Terror	145 billion

Source: Federal Budget, 2008

You see? Even at today's low rates, our interest payments are so high that they outrank all categories of federal spending but Social Security, Medicare, and defense. But when interest rates return to normal (say about 6.4 percent), *they will exceed every other budget category*!

We collect about $900 billion from all personal income tax payments combined. The interest level we would be at today, under normal interest rates (i.e., 6.4 percent), would eat up 85 cents of every dollar we pay in personal income taxes!

The *New York Times* confirmed, in November 2009, that "the United States government is financing its more than trillion-dollar-a-year borrowing with IOUs on terms that seem too good to be true. But that happy situation, aided by low interest rates, may not last much longer." [131]

As the *Times* noted, "the government faces a payment shock similar to those that sent legions of overstretched homeowners into default on their mortgages." [132]

Robert Bixby, executive director of the fiscally conservative Concord Coalition, says, "the government is on teaser rates. We're taking out a huge mortgage right now but we won't feel the pain until later." [133]

In this case, Europe was wiser than we were. While our budget deficit grew to 10 percent of our GDP, the euro zone's shortfall was only a touch over 6 percent. Only the U.K., where deficits soared to 12 percent of GDP, was as irresponsible as the Obama administration. In France, the deficit was only 7.5 percent; in Germany, it went only as high as 5 percent. [134]

In past generations, Congress and the president often had to choose how to spend its money. During the Reagan years of spending cuts, this question dominated the national debate as he sliced discretionary social spending and let the defense budget skyrocket.

In two or three years, however, we will be able to afford neither guns nor butter. We will only be able to keep our head above water by paying the interest on our debt.

Who was the idiot who said about debt, "We owe it to ourselves, so it's no big deal if debt goes up?"

These folks argue that the debt isn't a problem because we owe it to Americans. They say that the debt service payments simply represent a redistribution of money from some Americans to others. But they are wrong. The proportion of our debt that is owed to foreigners has tripled since 1992.

Of the $10.7 trillion in total federal government debt that was outstanding at the end of 2008, about $3.1 trillion (29 percent) was owed to foreigners, about 13 percent to China, and 11 percent to Japan. So when we start paying down our debt, about one dollar in three we repay will leave the

United States, burning a big hole in our buying power and our economy.[135] Today, the annual total we pay to foreigners comes to about $115 billion a year. But when interest rates return to normal, it will rise to more than $230 billion—and will continue to grow as the debt increases.

Our trade deficit runs between $400 billion and $600 billion a year, depending on the state of our economy. We work hard to stop unfair foreign trade practices from driving the deficit even higher. And now we are preparing to hand over to foreigners between $200 billion and $300 billion in interest payments!

And this huge interest burden—bequeathed to us by Obama's outrageous spending—comes at a time when we can least afford it. Our biological clock is ticking.

The baby boomer generation, born between 1945 and 1964, will turn sixty-five between 2010 and 2029. Their accumulated, and rapidly escalating, Social Security and Medicare demands will draw ever-increasing shares of whatever money we have left after paying off the interest on our debt.

As William H. Gross, managing director of the Pimco Group, has said, "What a good country or a good squirrel should be doing is stashing away nuts for the winter. [But] the United States is not only not saving nuts, it's eating the ones left over from the last winter." [136]

Already the deficit is consuming so much of our nation's capital that there isn't room for the private sector to borrow to create new jobs and stir growth. Like the household whose entire paycheck goes to paying its mortgage and other debt, its members can't go back to school to upgrade their skills and get better jobs—because every penny must go to the howling creditor-wolves at the door.

As George Melloan, author of *The Great Money Binge: Spending Our Way to Socialism*, wrote in the *Wall Street Journal* on November 24, 2009, "the credit market has been tilted to favor a single borrower with a huge appetite for money, Washington. Private borrowers, particularly small businesses, have been sent to the end of the queue." [137]

Look at how the $27 trillion debt market has changed since the economic crisis began in 2008. While the government borrowed more and more, private lending dropped lower and lower. The government crowded out private borrowing with its huge deficit and mounting debt, leaving nothing for small businesses or consumers to borrow.

Government spending is not the solution. It is obviously the problem. Look at how government debt has shot up while personal and business borrowing has crashed. Washington is borrowing all the money!

CHANGE IN DEBT SINCE 2008

Government

Treasury bills	Up 40%
Municipal debt	Up 6%
Govt.-insured mortgage-backed securities	Up 21%

Private

Mortgages

Prime jumbo	Down 24%
Subprime	Down 34%
Option ARM	Down 19%
Alt-A	Down 23%
Commercial	Down 10%

Consumer

Auto loans	Down 33%
Credit cards	Down 12%
Home equity	Down 43%
Student loans	No change

Business

Commercial paper	Down 35%
Junk bonds	Down 7%
Investment-grade bonds	Up 5%
Institutional leveraged loans	Down 12%
Bank loans and leases	Down 8%

Source: Wall Street Journal[138]

Obama recently announced that the banks that borrowed TARP funds had paid back $200 billion. He said the money was available for "deficit reduction" or to "help small business create jobs." [139]

But then he merrily announced that he was going to use all the money to pay for a "Stimulus 2" program of additional government spending: $100 billion will go to state and local governments, $30 billion to help small businesses grow, and $30 billion for consumer credit. He announced all this new spending because he wants to be seen—politically—as fighting to create jobs.

Here's some news, Mr. President: It's only through deficit reduction that you'll be able to make any money available for small businesses to borrow to create jobs. Raising the deficit—even to finance programs designed to create jobs—actually *costs* us jobs.

Not only does the size of the deficit spending crowd out job-creating private sector borrowers, but the socialistic intervention of the federal government in the banking sector does as well. As Melloan explains, "the Federal Reserve . . . has been telling bankers that they must cut risk." The Fed even announced, "it will evaluate the salaries of bank officers on how carefully they manage risk." [140]

"By official definition," Melloan adds, "Treasury securities are risk-free, so how better to manage risk than to pad your bank's portfolio with Treasury securities, which is what bankers are now doing." [141]

The result, he writes, is that "under the new management from Washington, bankers who take a flyer on a venture that might someday become an Apple, Microsoft, or Google, will risk not only their depositors' money but a possible pay cut." [142] And they're not about to do that!

Why should banks bother with consumer or business lending? The U.S. Treasury is offering bankers the cushiest deal in town. They can borrow money from the Fed at a nearly zero interest rate—and then lend the Fed its own money back at 3 percent!

As economist Barry Elias puts it, "essentially these entities are earning free interest. The Federal Reserve Bank lends funds to an institution at a much lower rate of interest than the Federal Reserve Bank pays the same institution to borrow the same funds (by selling U.S. Treasury securities). To camouflage this relationship there may be internal fund transfers on both sides of the transaction that incorporate different ownership titles." But the deal is the same: Borrow at 0 percent and lend back at 3 percent.[143]

Nice deal. Why mess around with helping people buy cars or homes or businesses to expand or new companies to start? Obama invites them to sit back, make 3 percent, and let the good times roll—and keep the regulators off their backs in the bargain!

Except that our economy has no engine to power growth.

And it will get worse.

The Chinese have gotten skittish about buying Treasury debt, forcing more and more of the lending to come from U.S. banks and depriving our businesses of the capital they need to grow. Melloan, a former columnist and deputy editor of the *Wall Street Journal* editorial page, warns that "feeding the government and starving free enterprise looks like a prescription for long-term economic stagnation. It's not unlike what we witnessed in the depression in the 1930s." [144]

So if Washington can't afford to pay the interest on its debts, can't borrow from foreigners to pay for it, and doesn't want to edge out private borrowing in the capital markets, how do we pay back the huge debt Obama has foisted on us?

There's only one answer: huge, rampant, runaway inflation—not inflation because of an artificial psychosis that grips the economy, but inflation that's deliberately caused by the government as an instrument of policy to get out of its debts.

That's *precisely* the kind of inflation that gripped Weimar Germany in the 1920s. Unable to pay the reparations for World War I imposed by the Allies, the government inflated its currency to pay the debt with valueless marks.

Welcome to the future Obama has designed for our economy!

Of course, there's another way: economic growth, spurred by lower federal spending, reduced federal taxes, and less regulation of business. There's still time to apply Ronald Reagan's solutions to Barack Obama's problems!

(Obama likes to say that the deficit was $1.3 trillion when he "walked in the door" on Inauguration Day. Don't believe him. He's manipulating the data. In the fiscal year that ended on September 30, 2008, the deficit was $485 billion. By the time Bush was ready to leave office, increased spending and decreased revenues had pushed the deficit to about $600 billion. But, when the financial crisis hit, Bush got Congress to vote $700 billion in TARP loans to banks and insurance companies. Under federal budget rules, a loan is treated just like other spending. So, technically, the deficit was $1.3 trillion—the $600 billion plus the $700 billion in TARP funds. But the $700 billion was just a short-term loan. As of this writing, $500 billion has been paid back. Yet, instead of depositing these funds in the Treasury, Obama spent $300 billion of it on his stimulus package. This new spending—as opposed to short-term borrowing under TARP—combined with other spending and revenue shortfalls has pushed the deficit up to $1.4 trillion in fiscal 2009. The reality is that Obama virtually doubled the deficit.)

THE IMF TAKES OVER OUR ECONOMY

The economic policies Obama is enacting can be repealed when right-thinking people take back our government—in 2011, we hope!

What will be harder to reverse is the erosion of American sovereignty.

Former United Nations interim ambassador John Bolton—one of the best minds in our country—has described Obama as the "first post-American president." [145] By this he meant that President Obama has made it clear that he sees himself as a kind of global president for the United States—that is, a president with global priorities and loyalties who sees his mission as molding American policies to conform to those of other nations.

Think of the British colonial governors in pre-Revolutionary America: Their job was not to represent the people of the colony, or even to act in their interests. Nor were they, in any sense, the colonies' ambassadors to the Crown. Rather, they were there to ensure that the colonies served the best interests of the king of England and his Parliament.

President Obama is working hand in hand with the International Monetary Fund (IMF) to craft just such a sort of global dominion over the United States.

We're not normally given to conspiracy theories. But who can doubt the evidence as Obama hurtles down this course?

The IMF has long been the policeman of international finance. Offering loans backed by the world's major economies, it seeks to help countries prop up their currencies—at a price. The price is usually conformity to the IMF's policy and economic priorities. The IMF lectures nations on the importance of bringing down their external debt and balancing their national budgets, and rewards them with lines of credit to shore up their currencies against international speculators.

In the meantime, the world's economic powers gathered at regular G-7 conferences, where the United States, Canada, the United Kingdom, France, Germany, Italy, and Japan coordinated their finances and policies. In the 1990s, Russia was admitted as a sop to reformist president Boris Yeltsin, making the gathering the G-7 plus 1.

In the last year of the Bush administration, however, the G-7 expanded its membership to include nineteen nations and the European Union, and now goes by the name G-20. The members include:

OUR NEW MASTERS: THE G-20 NATIONS

Argentina	Italy
Australia	Japan
Brazil	Mexico
Canada	Russia
China	Saudi Arabia
European Union	South Africa
France	South Korea
Germany	Turkey
India	United Kingdom
Indonesia	United States

What a crowd to be part of—and subservient to!

• Argentina defaulted on its international debts at the start of the decade and she still can't borrow money internationally. Back then, her president, Nestor Kirschner, told the world to get lost and settled the nation's debt for twenty-five cents on the dollar. His wife is still running the country.

- Brazil is ruled by an elected Marxist president, Luiz Inácio Lula da Silva, who has made temporary amends with capitalism but still allies himself closely with Venezuela's Hugo Chavez.

- China has thousands of political prisoners, is governed under a totally undemocratic system, and regularly spends a fortune to censor the Internet and keep its people uninformed.

- Mexico is bravely struggling to kill off its drug trade, which still rules large parts of the country.

- Russia, an oil-rich nation, loses one million in population each year. It has a male life expectancy of fifty-nine years (seventy for women),[146] and has pulled back from democracy into an autocratic dictatorship where elections are a sham. It falls near the bottom of Transparency International's ranking of honest governments: At number 145 among the 180 nations surveyed, it's one of the forty most corrupt nations in the world.[147]

- Saudi Arabia still enforces Sharia Law, stones women for adultery, and cuts off the hands of those who are caught stealing. Apparently, the policy isn't all that effective: Saudi Arabia ranks number 81 on the TI list.[148]

- Indonesia is ranked number 144 on the TI list and, until recently, had never had a stable, democratic government.[149]

These deserving countries are our new masters. We have one vote at the G-20 and so does each of them. Does this seem fair? Not when you look at the relative sizes of our economies.

GDPs OF G-20 NATIONS

United States	$14,441 billion
Japan	4,911
China	4,327
Germany	3,673
France	2,867
United Kingdom	2,680
Italy	2,314
Russia	1,677
Brazil	1,573
Canada	1,500
India	1,206
Mexico	1,088
Australia	1,013
South Korea	929
Turkey	730
Indonesia	512
Saudi Arabia	469
Argentina	325
South Africa	277
European Union	18,388

Source: International Monetary Fund [150]

The European Union gets five votes: the U.K., France, Germany, Italy, and the EU itself. The GDP of the United States equals that of the bottom thirteen nations combined.

The nations were chosen, of course, based on political considerations. Saudi Arabia is included because of its oil. Turkey is there because it may not be admitted to the EU and needs a consolation prize. South Africa was picked because Africa needed a representative. Argentina—God knows why.

Now, you may be wondering why some other nations *aren't* represented. Here's the list of nations with GDPs larger than that of South Africa, the smallest of the G-20 nations: Spain, the Netherlands, Poland, Belgium, Switzerland, Sweden, Norway, Austria, Taiwan, Greece, Denmark, Iran, and Venezuela. We can be grateful for the last two exclusions. The rest were excluded because of global political correctness.

The reality, of course, is that so unwieldy a group as the G-20 will be dominated by the staff of the IMF. And that was its intention.

When the matrix of international organizations was established after World War II, Europe and the United States informally agreed that the head of the World Bank would be an American, and the leader of the IMF would come from Europe. The current executive director of the IMF is Dominique Strauss-Kahn, a Socialist Party leader in France whose nickname is *le grand séducteur* (need we translate?).[151]

Among his female conquests, according to the *Times* of London, was Piroska Nagy, who worked in the Africa Department of the IMF. She left the firm and now works in London at the European Bank for Reconstruction and Development.[152]

The newspaper noted that "Mr Strauss-Kahn denied that he had abused his position as managing director, either by giving Ms Nagy preferential conditions for leaving the IMF or helping her to get the job in London. The EBRD said that there was nothing irregular about the recruitment of Ms Nagy."[153]

Toute d'Europe was too polite to mention that Paul Wolfowitz, the American who headed the IMF's sister organization, the World Bank, was fired because of his relationship with an unmarried woman, Shaha Riza. Deciding that it was inappropriate for her to work for the World Bank while he was the head of the organization, he helped her to get a job at the State Department. For this he was canned. (Not really. He led a vigorous and altogether appropriate investigation of corruption at the World Bank, cancelled loans to nations that used the funds improperly, and fired staffers who had approved them. So deep was the culture of corruption at the Bank that the senior staff used the scandal as an excuse to get rid of him.)

But not only was M. Strauss-Kahn not fired—he helps run the world's economy.

At the September 2009 G-20 summit in Pittsburgh, the United States essentially agreed to relinquish a large part of its economic sovereignty to the wider world.

The G-8 (including Russia) was always a clubby, collegial grouping of the presidents and prime ministers of the world's leading nations. With only eight members, it amounted to a floating summit meeting where the key world leaders could bond, probe one another's views, and look for real consensus. It functioned quite well, and accorded appropriate primacy to the world's top elected officials: All the presidents of the original G-7 nations were democratically elected.

The G-20 is something else altogether. It was not an expansion of the G-8, but a separate group, formed during the Asian financial crisis of 1999, to "help the G-7 talk with the wider world." [154]

During the global financial meltdown of 2008, however, the big nations of the G-8, along with the big banks and companies, seemed to lose their self-confidence. They grew concerned that they had screwed up and that the economic collapse was their fault. Or, more particularly, America's fault.

CNN reports, "Europeans [are] emboldened by their belief that the credit crisis didn't originate on their soil. . . . They say that means the more tightly regulated European banking model has triumphed over the more lax laws favored in America." Accusing the United States of "cowboy capitalism," Europe now insists, in the words of French president Nicholas Sarkozy, that "self-regulation to solve all problems, it's finished. Laissez-faire, it's finished. The all-powerful market that is always right, it's finished." [155] *Fini. Fini. Fini.*

Instead, Europe's agenda is clear. As CNN summarized, it includes "greater oversight of hedge funds and investment banks; increasing how much money banks need to keep in reserve; more transparent and universal accounting standards; and limits on executive pay. . . . All that would be accompanied by a new global network of regulators—regulators that would presumably have power over U.S. banks." [156]

The experts at the IMF and the central bankers of the world sensed that the meltdown had created a policymaking void. And into it leaped the true competitor of democracy: bureaucracy in the form of the experts at the IMF.

These bureaucrats realized that, as long as the central policymaking forum was the G-8—an assemblage of leaders of big nations—they would forever be second-string players on the world stage, the hired help. But if, in the name of globalism, they could dilute the G-8 by elevating the G-20 as the supreme governing body, they could make the forum so unwieldy that the staff could actually dominate the process. And if they linked the G-20 to the IMF—a group controlled by the world's European bankers—the bureaucrats and economists could really run the show (while relegating the elected leaders to addressing the "non-economic issues").[157]

The shift in power from the G-8 to the G-20 was absurd. The old G-8 accounts for 81 percent of the GDP of the new G-20. And, if you brought in China to make it the G-9—still a manageable group—you would have 91 percent of the G-20's GDP included.

It's hard to escape the idea that the G-20 was deliberately structured to give Europe an overwhelming voice, and to dilute the power of elected officials and emphasize the leadership of the bureaucrats.

Obama, of course, endorsed this shift. But then he went further—moving to weaken U.S. voting power in the IMF and to increase the clout of the less developed nations. Under the old IMF voting rules, the developed nations cast 57 percent of the votes while the less developed ones controlled only 43 percent. That made sense: After all, developed nations put up the money for the IMF in the first place. But Obama insisted on transferring 5 percent of the votes from the richer nations to the poorer ones, making the division a more equal 52–48, and transferring power from the lenders to the deadbeat debtors!

The power the G-20 and the IMF seized at the September 2009 Pittsburgh summit was so vast that it amounts to a global economic coup d'etat. What's astonishing is that an elected president of the United States made the coup happen.

The G-20 and the IMF are now to function "as a board of directors for the global economy."[158] The body is charged with adopting goals for each country's economy and monitoring how well it moves to reach them. The goals themselves were largely good ones. But the aggregation of power the G-20 assumed in making these decisions is staggering. No longer will elected governments count for much. The key decisions will be made by the central bankers at the IMF and the G-20.

The G-20 set out at once to set priorities for the global economic future. It decreed that the United States would "have to define ways to boost savings" to close its current account deficit, and would "commit to a sharp deficit reduction by government." Meanwhile, "China, Germany, and Japan . . . would . . . reduce [their] reliance on exports." Europe would improve its competitiveness, which could mean "passing investment-friendly tax measures and re-opening the debate about making it easier to fire workers—viewed as one way to encourage employers to hire more freely." China "would face perhaps the biggest challenge: remaking its economy so it relies far less on exports to the U.S." [159]

So every country has its new marching orders.

The *Wall Street Journal* reported that the "leaders from the G-20 are working on ways to enforce commitments countries make, which would involve reviews—though no specific sanctions." [160]

As the *Journal* reported, "The U.S. is pressing for what it calls a 'peer review' process, by which G-20 countries, with the help of the IMF, would assess whether each other's policies are working." But Europe wants to have tougher enforcement. They are "pushing for a 'trigger' mechanism. If a country's current account surplus or deficit goes over a certain limit, for instance, that would require negotiations to get the country back in line." [161] So the budget negotiations between Congress and the president, or between the two political parties, would amount to no more than a warm-up for the real challenge—getting Europe, Argentina, Indonesia, Saudi Arabia, South Africa, and the like to agree on how we should run our economy.

Thankfully, the *Journal* was able to report, "none of the countries, though, are calling for specific redress, such as trade sanctions or foreign-exchange penalties for countries that don't live up to their promises." [162] But can they be far behind?

Our new G-20 rulers also agreed to "new limits on corporate compensation" and "new requirements . . . that banks hold more capital to discourage risk-taking and absorb big losses." [163]

This new assumption of power by unelected bureaucrats and central bankers is antithetical to notions of national sovereignty and democratic representation. The fact is that while economics is undoubtedly global, democracy is only national. Indeed, the biggest shortcoming of the European Union is its lack of democracy. The president and foreign minister under the new Treaty of Lisbon are not directly elected, and the European Parliament, while elected, is largely powerless. Its members, for example, may not introduce legislation; its function is purely to ratify the measures proposed by the EU bureaucracy.

And crucial members of the G-20—China, Russia, and Saudi Arabia—have no real democracy at all. In fact, the European Union reflects the continent's bad experience with democracy (e.g., Germany in the 1930s) and its suspicion of popular decision-making.

But now the United States is willingly sublimating its economy and its power to the will of the European bureaucrats who run the EU. Once we recover our senses, will we ever be able to get our sovereignty back?

Unfortunately, our new masters, the IMF and the European bankers, don't have much of a track record in encouraging economic growth. Across the last decade, the United States grew faster than the European Union euro zone by a cumulative rate of 2.9 percent.

The fact is that the European Union's growth model largely focuses on what Barry Eichengreen calls "coordinated capitalism." [164] Big government, big corporations, and big labor unions sit at the table and hammer out economic policies, and then rely on the government to implement them through regulation. While this approach worked well in the aftermath of World War II, when the priority was getting Europe back on its feet, it has produced low growth rates in the past two decades.

Why? First, the European growth consensus fails to take account of the needs of new and small businesses, which provide the bulk of the growth in the United States. In fact, the unions, big companies, and governments coordinate their policies in order to give the large corporations an advantage over their smaller competitors. Through subsidies and other regulations, the EU holds down the very small entrepreneurial companies that fuel so much of the world's economic growth.

And the Europeans are all dedicated to big government and high taxes. They do not believe in tax cuts to fuel consumer demand and economic expansion. As a result, most of their economic growth is oriented to export—particularly to the American market (where demand is stoked by lower taxes).

Eichengreen, in his marvelous book *The European Economy Since 1945*, argues that, by the 1970s, the very policies that fueled Europe's explosive recovery after World War II undermined the continent's growth. "The same institutions of coordinated capitalism that had worked to Europe's advantage in the age of extensive growth now posed obstacles to successful economic performance," [165] he writes.

HOW THE EUROPEAN MODEL STOPPED WORKING

(text from Barry Eichengreen)

- **Banks wouldn't invest in new technologies.**
  "Bank-based financial systems had been singularly effective at mobilizing resources for investment by existing enterprises using known technologies, but they were less conducive to growth in a period of heightened technological uncertainty. Now the role of finance was to take bets on competing technologies, something for which financial markets were better adapted." [166]

- **Labor unions stifled new technologies.**
  "The generous employment protections and heavy welfare-state charges that had given labor the security to accept the installation of mass-production technologies now became an obstacle to growth as new firms seeking to explore the viability of unfamiliar technologies became the agents of job creation and productivity improvement. Systems of worker co-determination, in which union representatives occupied seats on big firms' supervisory boards . . . now discouraged bosses from taking the tough measures needed to restructure in preparation for the adoption of radical new technologies." [167]

- **State-run companies protected obsolescence and hindered innovation.**
  "State holding companies that had been engines of investment and technical progress were no longer efficient mechanisms for allocating resources in this new ear of heightened technological uncertainty. They were increasingly captured by special interests and used to bail out loss-making firms and prop up declining industries." [168]

Obama should feel quite at home in such fiscal disarray!

Until the Obama administration, the United States relished the difference between its economy and Europe's. In fact, French president Nicholas

Sarkozy was elected on a platform of remaking the French economy using pro-growth policies that had succeeded in the United States. But the Obama administration seems determined to gorge itself on humble pie for America's role in triggering the global recession. The administration is going along with the European consensus—even though it obviously doesn't work.

Obama does love to apologize!

The IMF has long been a proponent of raising taxes and cutting spending to balance national budgets. Its attempts to impose a policy of austerity on developing nations have likely sparked more revolutions than Marx, Lenin, and Engels combined.

The very words of the IMF's economic recovery plan were that the financial system regulators in the G-20 countries must do more to "discourage risk-taking" [169] by banks and financial institutions. Translation: They should lend only to governments and to big, credit-rated companies. No more flyers on guys with innovative ideas they cooked up in their garage.

The Reagan-Thatcher-Bush approach to encouraging economic growth—stimulating consumer spending by cutting taxes—is definitely out of fashion at the IMF. These are the people to whom we have given control over our economy!

The one silver lining in all this is that, to date, Obama has not presented the Senate with any global economic treaty requiring its ratification. What he has set in place through presidential pronouncements can be undone by such statements in the future by a new administration. It's up to us to be sure that we monitor what Obama does, and to fight any measure that would put us in a straitjacket of global or European domination for the future. And it's up to us to take our country back by winning in 2010!

THE ONSET OF SOCIALISM

The near-collapse of America's major financial, insurance, and car companies in 2008–9 has given socialism a new intellectual life. The lessons the world learned in 1989–91 have been brushed aside. It's as if the Berlin Wall has gone back up—but this time there's no freedom peeking from beyond the barrier. The socialist consensus has swept the world!

But government regulation and taxation can only redistribute wealth.

It cannot create it. Wealth creation can only come from the private sector; it springs only from the profit motive (or its converse, fear of failure). Without incentives, there is no risk, innovation, creativity, or even much hard work. Each bracket higher the tax code climbs, it robs not only the taxpayer but the tax consumer as well, since it decreases economic growth.

President Barack Obama has been the architect of this move toward socialism. Central to his strategy is the realization that who controls the banks controls the economy. There is no need for overt government ownership of the means of production, as Karl Marx called for. Control of the banks, and the power to decide who gets credit and who doesn't, is quite enough.

With an assist from then president George W. Bush and senators Barack Obama and John McCain, here's how the socialization of the banks happened:

THE PATH TO SOCIALIST BANKING

1. In September and October 2008, the major brokerage houses in the United States teeter on the brink of bankruptcy. One of their number, Lehman Brothers, has already failed and others are at serious risk.
2. President Bush and his Treasury secretary, Henry Paulson, propose a huge bailout to inject $700 billion of capital into failing financial institutions to stabilize them and stop a run on their assets. The plan is called Troubled Assets Relief Program (TARP).
3. Republicans in the House try to stop the bill (they had the majority then) and substitute an approach masterminded by former House speaker Newt Gingrich to insure banks rather than pass out checks to them. The House defeats the Bush bailout proposal.
4. Republican presidential candidate John McCain "suspends" his campaign to return to Washington to round up Republican backing for the TARP bill. The Republicans in the House cave in at the behest of their nominee and agree to it.
5. But then, Democrats ask, what will the taxpayer get out of the TARP bailouts? Had the Republicans listened to Gingrich, the question would have had no force, since no money would

have changed hands. But in the context of the Bush TARP bill, the question demands an answer.

6. Bush and Treasury Secretary Henry Paulson agree that those getting TARP money would be obliged to turn over stock to the government. But they are careful to make clear that it must be pre-ferred stock. (These stockholders are "preferred," meaning that they receive dividends but have no voting rights in the company.)

7. The TARP bill passes. Half the money is allocated under Bush, the balance under Obama.

8. Obama and his Treasury secretary, Timothy Geithner, announce that the Treasury and the Federal Reserve Board will examine each bank that got TARP money to rate its financial strength. Some banks want to return the TARP funds, the crisis having passed, but Obama and Geithner won't let them until they pass a "stress test."

9. The stress test results come on May 8, 2009. They find that ten of the big banks do not need extra capital and can return the TARP money. They are JPMorgan Chase, Goldman Sachs, Morgan Stan-ley, US Bancorp, Capital One Financial, American Express, BB&T, Bank of New York Mellon, State Street, and Northern Trust.[170]

The Treasury tells nine other big banks—and hundreds of smaller ones—that they must raise more capital:

BIG BANKS ORDERED BY THE GOVERNMENT TO RAISE NEW CAPITAL

Bank	New Capital Required
Bank of America	$33.9 billion
Citigroup	5.5
Fifth Third	1.1
GMAC	11.5
KeyCorp	1.8
Morgan Stanley	1.8

Regions Financial	2.5
SunTrust	2.2
Wells Fargo	13.7

Source: *Los Angeles Times*[171]

10. How will these banks raise extra capital? Obama and Geithner have a plan: Transform the preferred stock the companies gave the government into common stock. Common stock would show up as an investment, not a loan, on the bank balance sheets, and *presto!* They'll have enough capital.

    Oh yes—by the way, once you do that, the government will have enough common (voting) stock to own you!

11. The banks jump at the chance and socialism comes to American banking.

The web of federal controls will grow even wider if Obama keeps his majorities in Congress. On October 22, 2009, Fox News reported that the government had ordered "pay cuts for the top 25 earners at the firms that received the most aid from the $700 billion Wall Street rescue package . . . looking to cut salaries by 90 percent from last year's levels, and to cut total pay by half."[172]

In justifying the curbs on executive pay, Treasury secretary Geithner pointed out that when top corporate employees are paid based on formulae that reward risk taking, the results could be bad for the company and the nation.

He had a case. After all, allowing Franklin Raines's compensation as the head of Fannie Mae to be based on the size of their mortgage portfolio only encouraged the subprime debacle: Raines got $90 million over six years, and the world got the subprime collapse. (See our book *Outrage*, which predicted this.)

So perhaps there is a case for some government regulation of executive compensation. But Obama and Geithner went far beyond that, appointing a "pay czar"—Kenneth Feinberg—to set actual dollar limits on executive pay.

Right now, the caps on executive compensation apply only to the largest of the banks and other financial institutions that received TARP money and have yet to pay it back: American International Group (AIG), Citigroup, Bank of America Corp., General Motors, GMAC, Chrysler, and Chrysler Financial.

But, as Fox News reported, "the move raises questions about whether the mandate will be limited to the seven firms Kenneth Feinberg is currently targeting—and whether it could trickle down to smaller companies." [173]

"He has a lot of authority with respect to not just the seven, but with respect to all TARP firms," said Stephen Bainbridge, a law professor at UCLA. "It's an enormous expansion of federal power over corporations." [174]

In all, five hundred firms got TARP funding; most still owe the federal government money. It's almost inevitable that Obama and Feinberg will eventually apply the same rules to all TARP recipients that they're now levying on the largest ones: to do otherwise would likely run afoul of the constitutional guarantee of equal application of law.

But the danger lurks that their curbs could go even further, affecting all businesses, large and small. In the fall of 2009, Obama announced plans to increase lending to small businesses and give them access to TARP money. Will the curbs on executive pay follow this federal "aid"? Will small and medium-sized businesses resist taking federal funds for fear that it may? And will smaller businesses be able to abstain from federal funding when their competitors are getting it?

We see a pattern here in Obama's path to government ownership and control over every aspect of the American economy—a steady movement toward socialism. Rather than overtly legislate these controls over all businesses, large and small, he holds out the prospect of federal aid to help them over hard economic times (which his own policies are prolonging). At least some of the firms will doubtless accept. The others will suddenly find themselves competing against the federal government—and the pressure will grow on them to accept dollars from Washington as well.

Once a firm takes a federal subsidy (or is forced to take one because its competitors are doing so), Obama's way is clear to increase government regulation, by law or by coercion.

As Fox News notes, "the Washington pay czar who's ordered steep pay cuts for executives at bailed-out firms could have practically unlimited power to regulate compensation at any company that gets federal funding, lawyers say—even if his legal authority is sketchy." [175]

Bainbridge points out that Obama and Feinberg will have an "informal" authority to regulate executive pay at any firm that gets federal aid. "Certainly he has the ability to cajole even where he doesn't have the ability to directly regulate," the UCLA law professor noted.[176]

As Fox News explains: "Since these companies owe money to the federal government, that gives the Obama administration political leverage—to exercise its ownership stake, or to embarrass the executives in the press, or to target the companies in any number of other ways." [177]

The government has shown that it's willing to play hardball to force executives of federally financed firms to accept deep pay cuts. As Fox News reports, "In early October [2009], Citigroup decided to shed energy trader Andrew Hall and his business after Feinberg threatened to go after his $100 million bonus. It didn't matter that the pay was determined last year. Plus outgoing Bank of America CEO Ken Lewis also agreed this month to forego his 2009 pay." [178]

As executive compensation attorney Robert Sedgwick notes, Feinberg does not need to be hemmed in by his strict legal authority in slashing corporate pay. "The fear by executives that their names will be dragged through the mud in the press is enough to ensure compliance." [179]

Meanwhile, the Associated Press reports, "the Federal Reserve is now proposing to police banks' pay policies—even for those that didn't receive a bailout." [180]

Guided by the decision at the G-20 Summit that nations will attempt to limit executive compensation, the Fed may now extend the regulatory umbrella so far that even banks that don't receive federal funds—or that have paid them back—may find their executive compensation policies under its thumb.

But controlling the banks wasn't enough for the Obama socialist revolution. He wanted to extend government control to *all* major financial institutions, not just those that still owed TARP money. So he and Geithner came up with a new concept: that government should regulate any financial institution (or other company) that was "too big to fail." In other words, if the company or bank were so large that its failure or bankruptcy might trigger a need for federal intervention, the government would step in and regulate it.

This policy turns the incentive-based principles of capitalism on their heads. No longer would CEOs of big companies seek to grow or to maximize profits. To do so might lead them to fall into the "too big to fail" category—and trigger regulation of their own pay! Success is no longer the objective. A little failure starts to look like a good thing.

In the meantime, the Obama-Geithner plan guarantees that the top business school graduates will run screaming in the other direction when one of the regulated "too big to fail" companies comes offering a job. The talent drain away from major companies assures years of stagnation and negative growth. It guarantees that bankers, risk-averse by temperament, will spend their waking hours looking over their shoulders to see what the regulator thinks and their sleeping ones dreaming nightmares of audits and oversight.

And so, on October 30, 2009, Geithner proposed a 253-page bill, which the Treasury had drafted with Rep. Barney Frank (D-MA), chairman of the House Financial Services Committee. As the *Los Angeles Times* reported, the bill would "give federal officials power to regulate, seize and dismantle large financial firms whose failure would pose a risk to the economy." When the government stepped in, the bill provided that "management would be fired, unsecured creditors would take losses and shareholders' investments could be wiped out. After a company's assets were sold, any taxpayer costs would be paid by other large and medium-size firms through an assessment." [181]

The proposal would "place no limit on how much money the government could spend after it stepped in," and, most importantly, "allows federal officials to use government money to enable the company to continue doing business and return to 'a sound and solvent condition.' " [182]

In other words, the government could seize a private company based solely on its belief that the firm is in danger of failing and that its bankruptcy would, in the government's unchallengeable opinion, cause national hardship. It could fire the management, wipe out the investors, and then run the company in perpetuity—with taxpayer-funded public subsidies.

Here's more detail on what this bill provides:

PROVISIONS OF THE FINANCIAL INSTITUTIONS REGULATION ACT

1. Regulators would be able to block a healthy bank from certain business practices or mergers, even order it to shrink, if its size, interconnectedness or other variables were deemed to pose a risk to the U.S. economy.

2. Financial corporations with more than $50 billion in assets would have to pay into a $150 billion fund to deal with future collapses of large financial companies.

3. The government would be able to order certain large banks to split off their commercial bank from their investment bank if regulators identify specific concerns.

4. Large banks would have to submit to consumer compliance exams from a new federal agency. Many small banks would be exempt.

Source: Wall Street Journal [183]

If this bill is not socialism, what is? Fidel Castro can only dream of having such power!

This legislation gives the president such sway over every private-sector firm that no one could possibly defy his political will. Let's say you're the CEO of a major corporation: Are you really going to donate funds to Obama's political opponent when the president has the power to seize your firm and fire you? Are you going to go public with criticisms of the administration or the Treasury Department when they can take you over?

There is no appeal in the bill from the edicts of the Treasury secretary. If you work for a living, you're under his thumb!

General Motors, already taken over by the government, is a good example of what will happen to American companies in the future if we don't curb Obama's powers.

When Obama took over General Motors, we all assumed this was a unique situation: A major employer, the lifeblood of Michigan, was teetering on the brink and Obama had to rush in to save it. But Geithner's proposals indicate that the GM seizure is really a model for how the government plans to deal with a wide range of companies.

So what's wrong with a government-run company?

It can't put profits first. It has to put politics first. If General Motors wants to close down a factory that's losing money, it will have to contend with the congressmen and senators who represent the area. The resulting political firestorm will be too much to weather. Better to just dig deeper into the taxpayers' pockets and subsidize the red ink factory.

Could GM outsource pieces of its production to a foreign company that can do it more cheaply? Even if the contract would save money and make GM more profitable, that wouldn't be an option: The stink in Congress over outsourcing would be too loud to tolerate. Better just to ask for more subsidies.

And if the consumers want larger, gas-guzzling cars, can GM afford to ignore their preference and turn out the fuel-efficient vehicles the environmentalists in Congress want? Well, in the new world, it's going to *have* to follow Congress's lead, regardless of what its consumers want. Because, in the last analysis, GM no longer has to satisfy the marketplace, its investors, or its consumers. It has only to satisfy its owners: the federal government.

The result is clear: General Motors will exist forever as a relic, a fossilized dinosaur whose employees will keep making cars people don't want, losing money in the process, and living off public subsidy. The fact that their payroll checks come from a car company, not welfare, is a sop to the pride of its workers.

Now, like a monument to failure, there is a company called the "old GM," renamed Motors Liquidation Company. This company has lost $100 million since the "new GM" emerged from bankruptcy. It remains in bankruptcy court and lists assets of $1.5 billion and liabilities of $35 billion.[184]

The "new GM" plans to keep making Buicks, Cadillacs, Chevrolets, and GMC trucks. But it will stop producing Saturns, Hummers, Saabs, and Pontiacs. The workforce will be cut to 64,000 U.S. workers (down from 91,000 at the start of 2009). The worldwide GM workforce will be 235,000.[185]

So the U.S. government has lent GM $770,000 for each job it has "protected."

But some of the bailout money will go overseas—even as GM lays off American workers. Steven J. Dubord reports, "Fritz Henderson, chief executive of GM, recently stated that the company might be using its funds to restructure its European unit, Opel. Back in August, GM China announced a $293 million venture. In October, GM South Korea received an infusion of $400 million, while operations in Mexico just initiated a $300 million transmission plant." [186] (Henderson, tired of government oversight, was replaced on an interim basis by Edward Whitacre Jr. on December 1, 2009, while a permanent replacement was sought.)

In the meantime, the Motors Liquidation Co. litigates on in bankruptcy court. China is awash in such companies: Seven of ten Chinese workers are employed by state-owned enterprises (SOEs), which consume 70 percent of the industrial capital of the country. But the SOE generates only 40 percent of the national output.[187] For more than a decade, the government in Beijing has struggled to shed this monkey from its back, but the vast number of people employed in SOEs has made it impossible. Recently, the SOEs have forced their way to the head of the line to get money from China's stimulus package, crowding out the small privately owned businesses that have fueled China's extraordinary economic growth.

While China tries to get out from under this mass of state-owned businesses, Barack Obama is busy creating them over here. General Motors is the first.

The Committee for a Responsible Federal Budget reports that the government loans to the auto industry "are very unlikely to be recouped in full. Full repayment of the $50 billion invested in General Motors, for example, would require the company's stock value to rise almost ten-fold, and it is not clear whether GM will remain viable, even without repaying these investments." [188]

If it survives at all, General Motors will be a ward of the state for a long, long time.

While the General Motors takeover is now historical fact—one that will be hard to reverse—the regulatory package Geithner and Barney Frank have cooked up is not yet passed. It can and must be stopped. After the health-care bill is resolved, this will be the new battle—and we must stand our ground! Its provisions are economically terrifying, and their potential for political coercion makes them even worse.

If there were no other reason, the importance of blocking the Geithner-Frank package (or repealing it if it becomes law) would make it urgent that we win Congress back in 2010.

(And what a delicious irony: Obama is pushing a populist proposal to end tax breaks to companies that move jobs overseas when four out of five GM jobs are offshore—and Obama runs the company!)

CONSTITUTION? WHAT CONSTITUTION? OBAMA DISREGARDS IT

In its flurry of executive action—ratified by a compliant, rubber-stamp Democratic Congress—the Obama administration has gone far afield in reinterpreting the federal Constitution. The legislators may have looked the other way at these usurpations; we can only hope the federal courts will be less agreeable.

Of course, it's the nature of such issues that the litigation—and subsequent court decisions—lag behind the pace of executive and legislative action. But, when they finally come before the courts, vast swaths of Obama's agenda may be rejected.

For example, at the core of the Obama health-care program is the "individual mandate" that requires everyone to have health insurance. Clearly, the government would have the authority to tax each person and use the money to provide insurance. But can it make everyone buy a privately provided product from a third party?

The Heritage Foundation thinks not, noting that "an individual mandate to enter into a contract with or buy a particular product from a private party, with tax penalties to enforce it, is unprecedented—not just in scope but in kind—and unconstitutional as a matter of first principles and under any reasonable reading of judicial precedents." [189]

The Foundation correctly points out that "nowhere in the Constitution is Congress given the power to mandate that an individual enter into a contract with a private party or purchase a good or service and . . . no decision or present doctrine of the Supreme Court justifies such a claim of power." [190]

The authors of the Obama Bill say that requiring people to buy health insurance is covered by the Constitution's interstate commerce clause, which allows Congress to regulate a "class of activity."[191]

But where is the interstate commerce? Congress has refused specifically and repeatedly to allow health insurance companies to compete across state lines. Republicans have been seeking this authority for years as a way to use private competition to hold down costs, but the Democrats have always refused.

And the Heritage Foundation asks a further question: What activity is being regulated? The activity of not buying health insurance? As the foundation notes, "proponents of the individual mandate are contending that, under its power to 'regulate commerce' . . . Congress may regulate the doing of nothing at all."[192] The absurdity of this is clear: "never in this nation's history has the commerce power been used to require a person who does nothing to engage in economic activity. Therefore, no decision of the Supreme Court has ever upheld such a claim of power."[193]

Liberals who try to justify the individual mandate to buy health insurance often cite state government requirements that drivers must buy automobile insurance. But this comparison misses two key points: First, that requirement extends only to those who wish to drive, not to every citizen. And, second, states *do* indeed have broad police powers to act in the interest of the public's health, safety, and welfare. But Washington doesn't. Its powers are confined to those enumerated in the Constitution—and, try as they might, it's hard to find any provision allowing the feds to impose such a requirement on all Americans.

Whether or not the health-care bill itself is constitutional, the amendments that Senate majority leader Harry Reid jammed into it to secure the votes for its passage may be a different story.

The Obama health-care bill dramatically expands Medicaid coverage, requiring states to enroll everybody who earns less than 150 percent of the federal poverty level.

This sum varies by family size. Single-person households who earn less than $16,500 (in 2009 dollars) would be covered. Two-person families would be covered up to $22,000. Families of three living together would get Medicaid coverage if they made less than $27,500, and four-person families would get coverage up to $33,000.[194]

But since Medicaid (unlike Medicare) is a federal and state program, individual states are required to contribute a portion of its costs. The amounts vary based on an objective statistical formula that counts the poverty population in each state and other indications of financial need.

As Senator Reid trolled for votes in the Senate, however, he freely dispensed federal dollars—assuring Senator Ben Nelson of Nebraska, for instance, that his state would not have to increase its contribution to the federal Medicaid program. Of course this windfall, which will save Nebraska over $100 million annually, takes no account of any objective measurement of poverty in the state.

The Constitution requires equal treatment under the law: Similarly situated persons cannot be treated differently. The idea that a state with more poor people than Nebraska will have to pay for Medicaid, while the folks in Omaha and Lincoln get off free, violates the Constitution. But, long after the courts have buried that provision, Nelson's vote will remain on the record—allowing our health-care system to be destroyed.

But the constitutional problems with Obama's program are hardly confined to health care. Fox News analyst and former judge Andrew P. Napolitano argues that the entire TARP program is unconstitutional, pointing in particular at the executive pay caps imposed on the big banks that borrowed its funds.

Here is Judge Napolitano's analysis of the problems with the TARP statute:

TARP IS UNCONSTITUTIONAL

(from the writings of Judge Andrew Napolitano)

- TARP, Napolitano argues, promotes only "short-term private benefit, rather than the general welfare, as the Constitution commands all federal spending." [195]

- It violates the equal protection clause "by saving some businesses and letting others that are similarly situated simply expire." [196] For example, it saved Goldman Sachs but not Lehman Brothers.

- And it gives the secretary of the Treasury "the power to spend taxpayer dollars as he sees fit, in violation of the express constitutional grant of the nondelegable spending power to the Congress." [197]

- Caps on executive pay at TARP-funded institutions are unconstitutional because they violate the "doctrine against unconstitutional conditions," Napolitano argues. "The government may not condition the acceptance of a governmental benefit on the non-assertion of a constitutional liberty." [198] Because the freedom of contract is constitutionally protected, the government may not "condition corporate welfare on the prohibition of contracts with employees above an arbitrary salary amount." [199]

- "The salary caps also constitute a taking. High-ranking executives are corporate assets with experience and knowledge unique to their employers' businesses. By arbitrarily reducing their salaries to serve the government's political needs, deflating their worth to their employers, incentivizing them to work less, or chasing them away, the government has stripped these individuals of their personal value and of their value to employers without just compensation. Such a taking is prohibited by the Fifth Amendment." [200]

The Constitution clearly and expressly prohibits Congress from passing a "Bill of Attainder"—that is, an act "that singles out an individual or group for punishment without a trial." [201]

Defenders of pay czar Feinberg's actions targeting specific people and companies don't deny that he's singling them out for punishment without a trial. They simply claim that his actions are constitutional because the Constitution's proscriptions apply only to Congress, not to an appointed pay czar.

But Senator Robert Byrd (D-WV) has challenged the entire practice of the presidential appointment of czars like Feinberg to oversee aspects of his program. In February 2009, Byrd wrote to Obama criticizing the appointment of these officials, who exercise broad power—as their moniker implies—but are not subject to Senate confirmation.

As Town Hall's Ken Klukowski noted, "Senator Byrd said that these appointments violate both the constitutional system of checks and balances and the constitutional separation of power, and [are] a clear attempt to evade congressional oversight." [202]

If Obama tries to justify Feinberg's use of bills of attainder to slash the pay of individual executives at specific firms by saying that the czar wasn't appointed pursuant to the constitutional process requiring Senate confirmation, isn't he like the proverbial child who kills his parents, but then pleads for mercy because he was orphaned?

Congressman John Carter (R-TX) also doubts the constitutionality of the federal takeover of General Motors and Chrysler. A former Texas state court judge, Carter argues that the federal government unconstitutionally took "possession of secured property in the form of the contracted investments of GM and Chrysler stock and bondholders . . . through a sophisticated manipulation of GM's and Chrysler's board of directors and dealers and the federal bankruptcy courts." He says, "the net result has been abrogating the contracts of the investors, and transferring their assets to the United Auto Workers and Fiat." [203]

Congressman Carter compares Obama's seizure of GM and Chrysler stock and bonds to President Harry Truman's nationalization of the steel mills during the Korean War, an act the Supreme Court ruled to be unconstitutional. As Carter writes, the "Truman Administration['s] contention—much like the Obama Administration position today—was that the aggregate powers of the Constitution and acts of Congress created new, more far-reaching powers." [204]

He points out that the "Court flatly rejected this contention, writing [in *Youngstown Sheet & Tube Company v. Sawyer*] that 'nowhere in the Constitution is the executive granted the right to seize power.' The Court continued, 'Congress has not granted the President the power to take possession of property, and the Constitution does not grant the President the power to take possession of property.' " [205]

What Obama did in the takeover was simple. He put the rights of the unsecured stakeholders—the United Auto Workers—ahead of the bondholders, whose rights were legally secured.

The Indiana state pension funds have already sued to challenge the constitutionality of the federal takeover of GM and Chrysler. CNS news reports that the "Indiana suit . . . contends that the [GM and Chrysler takeover] deal, as structured, unfairly favors the interests of the company's unsecured stakeholders ahead of the secured stakeholders, such as the Indiana pension funds. Unsecured holders are getting 59 cents on the dollar, while secured holders are getting 29 cents." [206]

Barack Obama has arrogantly described the bondholders, who had lent the company money over the years, as "speculators." As Dr. Mark W. Hendrickson, faculty member, economist, and contributing scholar with the Center for Vision and Values at Grove City College, points out, these "speculators range from retired blue-collar workers to investment firms managing the retirement accounts of state and municipal employees, school endowments, and other such suspicious characters. Yet Obama views and portrays them in class-warfare terms—as greedy capitalists whose property should be expropriated and redistributed to labor. This is textbook Marxism." [207]

Indiana's state treasurer, Richard Mourdock, who represents the Indiana State Police Pension Fund, the Indiana Teachers' Retirement Fund, and the Major Moves Construction Fund, argues that the sale of stock was illegal because the feds used TARP funds, and "Congress only approved use of that money for financial institutions such as banks, insurance firms, and credit unions." Mourdock asks a simple question: "Is Chrysler a financial institution? Clearly not." [208]

A U.S. Bankruptcy Court judge ruled that Indiana had no standing to challenge the use of TARP funds, but the U.S. Circuit Court of Appeals has since reversed the ruling and accepted the case.

The Indiana suit came after a Texas federal district court dismissed an action brought by a group called Texans Against Government Waste and Unconstitutional Conduct. While the court said that the Texas group had no standing to challenge the use of TARP funds, it did find substantive merit in the lawsuit's allegations and arguments.

The court wrote, "On its face, this definition (of 'financial institution' under TARP) would not appear to include automobile manufacturers and the terms of the act do seem to limit the use of TARP funds to assisting financial institutions." [209]

"Plaintiffs' arguments have even more persuasive force given that a bill, HR 7321, specifically designed to authorize the distribution of TARP funds to auto manufactures passed the United States House of Representatives," the U.S. District Court ruling continued. [210] "Passage of that bill by the House, even though not ultimately enacted, raises the question of why was such a bill necessary if the Act already authorized the distribution of TARP funds to the auto industry?" the court wrote.[211]

The judicial branch of our government has yet to be heard from on the issue. But the laws passed by Obama and his rubber-stamp Congress are likely to face intense scrutiny at the highest levels of our courts and a goodly proportion, one hopes, will be overturned.

CAN WE TRUST OBAMA WITH THIS MUCH POWER?

Will the broad powers Congress showers on Obama be misused? Certainly, the power to take over virtually any company his administration thinks is in danger of becoming insolvent and is thought to be too big to fail is enormous; it could be applied by an unscrupulous president to intimidate and bankrupt his foes and reward his allies. Obviously, the pay czar's power to slash the pay of anyone at any firm receiving federal funds could also be abused.

Will Obama abuse these powers?

Unfortunately, his record suggests that he will.

When Obama needed approval to take over GM and Chrysler from bondholders, he didn't hesitate to use his vast financial leverage to compel compliance, pressuring brokerage firms that got TARP money to sell out the interests of their bondholders.

The result is that 100,000 bondholders, who had lent GM $27 billion, got a return of less than ten cents on each dollar they lent—while the United Auto Workers, which was owed $20 billion, got a return of about six times that amount.[212]

How did the White House get the bondholders to agree to take such a measly return? It encouraged the organization of a "steering committee" composed of big brokerage houses and banks that had received TARP loans. Together, their investors represented 54 percent of GM's unsecured bonds. Not surprising, they cast aside the interests of their investors—the bondholders to whom they had a fiduciary duty—and did what Obama told them to do by approving the plan.[213]

Jim Martin, president of 60 Plus, an advocacy group for the elderly (many of whom are bondholders), complained, "from the beginning there's been a lack of transparency in this entire restructuring process. No one seems to have the best interests of small bondholders at heart."[214]

But when it came to weighing the needs of elderly bondholders and the UAW, which had backed Obama to the hilt, it was no contest.

The amount of power that Obama has amassed through TARP, and his increasing regulatory clout, is astonishing. When we consider how Obama nurses grudges, and the paranoia with which he treats enemies, such a power grab becomes truly frightening.

To grasp the depths of Obama's largesse on one hand, and wrath on the other, examine his relationship with two companies: one he detests, Fox News, and one he favors, Goldman Sachs.

OBAMA'S WRATH: THE FIGHT WITH FOX NEWS

The most dangerous illustration of Obama's intolerance of political opposition is his war against journalists who criticize him—and, in particular, against Fox News.

In 2009, Obama's communications director, Anita Dunn, led a White House charge against Fox News, declaring it not to be a legitimate news organization but rather "an arm of the Republican Party."[215] The Huffington Post reported that the White House has decided to "push back hard" against Fox News, citing Dunn's "lengthy and brutal denunciation" of the cable news network. Dunn called Fox News "a vehicle for Republican Party propaganda and an ideological opponent of the president."[216]

But a study by the nonpartisan and highly respected Pew Research Center belies Dunn's charges. Pew reports that, while 40 percent of Fox News stories about Obama in the last six weeks of the 2008 campaign were negative, an equal number—40 percent—of the stories about his Republican opponent John McCain were negative.[217]

As Pew reports, 39 percent of CNN's stories about Obama were negative—so their negative coverage of the Obama campaign was essentially no different from Fox's. Yet there was a difference: 61 percent of CNN's stories on John McCain were negative![218] Judging by Pew's numbers, it was CNN, not Fox, that was guilty of bias during the 2008 campaign.

Even worse was the coverage at MSNBC. There, Pew reports, only 14 percent of the stories about Obama were negative—while *73 percent of those about McCain were unfavorable.*[219]

MEDIA COVERAGE OF THE 2008 PRESIDENTIAL CAMPAIGN

Cable Network Negative Stories

Fox News

Obama	40%
McCain	40%

CNN

Obama	39%
McCain	61%

MSNBC

Obama	14%
McCain	73%

Source: Pew Research Center[220] (The Pew study appropriately distinguishes between the news and opinion segments of Fox News, CNN, and MSNBC; its studies reflect its survey of their news coverage, not opinion/commentary shows like *Hannity, Countdown with Keith Olbermann,* or *Larry King Live.*)

But Obama can't handle "fair and balanced." He wants sycophancy. So, on September 20, 2009, President Obama appeared on five Sunday morning talk shows—those of ABC, CBS, NBC, CNBC, and CNN—but refused to appear on Fox News Sunday with Chris Wallace. Anita Dunn herself blamed Fox's coverage of the administration for the snub: "Is this why he did not appear?" she asked rhetorically. "The answer is yes."[221]

In October 2009, Fox News reported that it had been "informed by the White House that Obama would grant no interviews to the channel until at least 2010."[222]

Dunn told the *New York Times* that the White House would treat Fox News "the way we would treat an opponent. As they are undertaking a war against Barack Obama and the White House, we don't need to pretend that this is the way that legitimate news organizations behave." [223]

This hyperbolic treatment of Fox News recalls nothing so much as former president Richard Nixon's enemies list—a collection of twenty journalists, columnists, commentators, and public officials the administration saw as especially biased against them. The list included nationally syndicated columnist Jack Anderson, whose reputation for exposing corruption in both parties and at all levels of government was without parallel. It also listed Pulitzer Prize winner Edwin Guthman, Daniel Schorr of *CBS*, and Mary McGrory of the *Washington Post*.[224] Those on Nixon's list found themselves audited by the IRS and harassed by the federal government. Some even were wiretapped by the FBI.

How far will Obama go in harassing those who disagree with him and have the audacity to report their opinions publicly? His powers would dwarf those of President Nixon if Obama gets his way. Unlike his predecessor, Obama could take over any of their news organizations or their corporate parents, fire their management, dismiss their boards, and reconstitute them as he wishes.

Some Democrats have even proposed extending TARP or other subsidies to struggling news organizations. Though many of these voices profess to be alarmed at the death of many of the nation's leading newspapers, one wonders if their real goal isn't to extend the reach of federal control into the mediasphere.

Leonard Downie Jr., the vice president of the *Washington Post*, is one of those who have called for government subsidies for the news business. "American society must now take some collective responsibility for supporting news reporting—as society has, at much greater expense, for public education, health care, scientific advancement and cultural preservation, through varying combinations of philanthropy, subsidy and government policy." [225]

On December 2, 2009, the *Wall Street Journal* reported that Federal Trade Commission chairman Jon Leibowitz was launching a study to determine "whether government should aid struggling news organizations which are suffering from a collapse in advertising revenues as the Internet upends their centuries-old business model." The paper noted that the FTC would "examine whether government should change the way the industry is regulated, from making news-gathering companies exempt from anti-trust laws to granting them special tax treatment to mak[ing] changes to copyright laws."[226]

One wonders if Leibowitz might have been encouraged in his deliberations by his wife, *Washington Post* columnist Ruth Marcus.

When we put together the two ends of the Obama administration—the left hand, which extends subsidies and tax goodies, and the right hand, which cites government aid as an excuse for intrusive regulation—a disturbing but haunting question surfaces: Does Barack Obama plan to extend aid to news organizations . . . and then use this assistance as leverage to regulate their coverage?

Let's say the trial balloon floated by the FTC becomes administration policy, and Congress grants special tax benefits and other regulatory favors to "news organizations." Would Obama contend, as his communications director does, that Fox News is not a legitimate news organization? Would the administration grant goodies to the other networks but withhold them from Fox News to punish it?

Or would the administration's hand on the spigot of favors and special treatment be enough to intimidate Fox News—or cause it to reconsider its fair and balanced coverage?

OBAMA'S FAVOR: HIS LARGESSE TOWARD GOLDMAN SACHS

But it's not only Obama's heavy-handed regulation that is to be feared. It's his demonstrable willingness to grant extreme benefits to corporations that help him politically.

Consider his administration's cozy relationship with Goldman Sachs.

Despite assuring us in a *60 Minutes* interview that "I did not run for office to be helping out a bunch of fat-cat bankers on Wall Street,"[227] Obama has showered incredible benefits on Goldman Sachs. He only talks like a populist.

Largely because of key decisions by his administration, Goldman reported record profits even as the rest of the nation was struggling with recession. As the *Wall Street Journal* reported, "Wall Street's meltdown fueled the most profitable quarter ever at Goldman Sachs Group Inc., which snatched business away from weakened rivals and churned out huge trading gains" during the second quarter of 2009. The *Journal* noted, "with competitors such as Lehman Brothers Holdings Inc. and Bear Stearns Cos. gone, and others like Citigroup Inc. flailing, Goldman appears to be pulling off one of the biggest market-share grabs in Wall Street history."[228]

Goldman's net income in the quarter was $3.44 billion, more than it earned in all of 2008. The *Journal* reported, "analysts had expected strong earnings, but were surprised by how much the firm exceeded expectations."[229]

It was a safe bet from the beginning that Goldman Sachs would make out well in the Obama White House: Goldman's partners and employees were the second-largest bundlers of Obama contributions in 2008, donating almost $1 million to his campaign. The *Washington Examiner* reported that Goldman's donations to Obama's campaign were "more than four times McCain's Goldman haul and more than any candidate has raised from any single company since the McCain-Feingold campaign finance regulations."[230]

The chart below, from OpenSecrets.org, shows that the people at Goldman Sachs were the second-largest cohort of donors to the Obama campaign. (These donations are from the employees and officers of the companies and institutions listed, not the organizations per se.)

TOP DONORS TO OBAMA CAMPAIGN

University of California	$1,591,395
Goldman Sachs	$994,795
Harvard University	$854,747
Microsoft Corp.	$833,617
Google Inc.	$803,436
Citigroup Inc.	$701,290
JPMorgan Chase & Co.	$695,132
Time Warner	$590,084
Sidley Austin LLP	$588,598

Source: OpenSecrets.org[231]

Of course, former president George Bush had as much to do with Goldman's record profits as Obama did: Bush's Treasury secretary, Henry Paulson, and his chief of staff, Joshua Bolten, were both Goldman men.

In September 2007, after the financial crisis doomed Lehman Brothers, federal regulators decided to stand aside and let the giant firm fail. The next company in peril was AIG. The *New York Times* reported that "although it was not widely known, Goldman, a Wall Street stalwart that had seemed immune to its rivals' woes, was A.I.G.'s largest trading partner, according to six people close to the insurer who requested anonymity because of confidentiality agreements. A collapse of the insurer threatened to leave a hole of as much as $20 billion in Goldman's side, several of these people said." [232]

As the *Times* noted, "days later, federal officials, who had let Lehman die and initially balked at tossing a lifeline to A.I.G., ended up bailing out the insurer for $85 billion. Their message was simple: Lehman was expendable. But if A.I.G. unspooled, so could some of the mightiest enterprises in the world." [233]

Obama extended Bush's policy of largesse to Goldman Sachs, carrying his favoritism toward his largest campaign donor to new heights.

His Treasury secretary, Timothy Geithner, appointed Mark Patterson, a former Goldman Sachs lobbyist, as his chief of staff. Melanie Sloan, executive director of the Citizens for Responsibility and Ethics in Washington, criticized the appointment, saying that Obama was backing away from his own ethics rules banning lobbyists from working on issues they lobbied about during the preceding two years. She said, "it makes it appear that they are saying one thing and doing another." [234]

The Obama administration also named a former Goldman staffer to an even more sensitive job: as the top cop policing Goldman and Wall Street. At twenty-nine, Adam Storch became the first chief operating officer in the Securities and Exchange Commission's enforcement division—after spending five years working in Goldman Sachs's business intelligence unit, which reviewed contracts and transactions for signs of fraud. [235] Without casting aspersions on Mr. Storch personally, his appointment to the top job in regulating his old (and future?) company raises serious issues of conflict of interest.

The president also tapped Goldman's ranks when he named the

company's vice chairman, Robert Hormats, to be undersecretary of state for economic, energy, and agricultural affairs.[236]

In addition, Goldman Sachs people have gotten other key Obama spots: Neel Kashkari is heading the TARP bailout; Gary Gensler is a top executive at the Commodity Futures Trading Commission; and Goldman's top lobbyist, Michael Paese, is the top aide to Congressman Barney Frank, the chairman of the House Financial Services Committee.[237]

But it was the administration's economic and financial policies that most benefited Goldman. When Treasury secretary Geithner announced that many of the major recipients of TARP money would have to raise new equity in order to pass the federally imposed stress test, he was forcing the banks to go back to the stock market for more funding. And, after the collapse of Lehman and Bear Stearns, the foremost remaining equity underwriter is Goldman Sachs. One by one, the major banks approached Goldman asking it to underwrite new equity issues on Wall Street. At a government-mandated 7 percent underwriting fee, Goldman did very well: In the second quarter of 2009 alone, its equity-underwriting department earned $736 million.[238]

Goldman also was able to issue $28 billion in debt backed by the Federal Deposit Insurance Corporation (FDIC) as part of Obama's efforts to stimulate lending to spur the economy. To be able to take advantage of this program, Goldman converted itself from an investment bank into a bank holding company so it could take advantage of the new program that lets commercial banks get FDIC backing for unsecured loans. The FDIC insurance gives Goldman access to cheap capital—and makes the taxpayers responsible if any of the loans go bad. Free profit. No risk.[239]

Obama has been so good to Goldman Sachs that its stock value increased from $53.31 a share when Obama was elected to close to $187.32 eight months later.[240]

As Goldman Sachs discovered at one end of the spectrum—and Fox News is finding out at the other—Obama does not rule without fear or favor.

CAP AND TRADE: THE MIDDLE-CLASS TAX INCREASE

Global warming and climate change may be a hoax backed by cooked data and ideological agendas. Or it could be the real threat many honest and objective scientists say it is. Whichever it is, one thing that's certain is that we don't need Obama's cap-and-trade legislation to fix it. And, if we do pass his program, it will mean higher electric bills for us all—and the virtual elimination of manufacturing in the United States, a disaster for our country.

Any responsible discussion of global warming should start with the fact that the United States is making great progress in cutting its carbon dioxide emissions—the supposed number-one cause of global warming.

Despite declining to ratify the Kyoto Protocol limiting carbon dioxide emissions, the United States has done relatively well in reducing them. President Obama has committed the United States to cutting its carbon emissions to 17 percent below its 2005 level. In 2005, the nation emitted 5,972 million metric tons (mmt) of carbon; Obama would have us slash our emissions to 4,957 mmts.[241]

And the surprising news is: We're already halfway there! In 2009, the United States emitted 5,476 mmts of carbon.[242] Just 519 mmts to go!

In a very short time, the normal workings of the free enterprise marketplace, the increase in gasoline prices, the recession, and an increased environmental consciousness among our citizens have brought us halfway toward achieving Obama's goal—without being bound by Kyoto, and without cap and trade. And we can get the rest of the way without the further taxes and regulations Obama wants to impose on us.

But no matter: The blunt fact is, Obama wants to tax and regulate us anyway—and climate change is just his latest excuse to do so.

Look at how well we're doing in cutting carbon emissions without government regulation or taxation:

U.S. CARBON DIOXIDE EMISSIONS: LEVELED OFF AND TRENDING DOWN!

Year	Millions of Metric Tons Emitted
1990	5,007
1995	5,296
2000	5,844
2005	5,972
2006	5,885
2007	5,967
2008	5,801
2009 (projected)	5,476 [243, 244]

If Obama is able to pass his proposed cap-and-trade legislation, the effects on us all will be horrific. During the 2008 campaign, Obama pledged not to raise taxes on the middle class. But he never mentioned utility bills. His cap-and-trade legislation will raise electric rates and gasoline prices, and it will fall disproportionately on the middle class and on the poor. There is no tax more regressive than an electric bill.

The federal EPA concedes, "a cap and trade policy increases the price of energy-intensive goods. The majority of this price increase is ultimately passed onto consumers. . . . Lower income households are disproportionately affected by [a] cap and trade policy because they spend a higher fraction of their incomes on energy-intensive goods." [245]

What is "cap and trade" anyway? It's just a fancy term for taxation.

Cap and trade works a bit like the papal indulgence system of the Middle Ages. The concept is that companies that sin by emitting carbon into the air must pay for the privilege. Under the cap-and-trade system, they would be allowed to buy the right to pollute from businesses that don't spew carbon into the atmosphere. So, ideally, if there are two utility companies— one that uses only nuclear power and the other that runs on coal—the nuclear company would be able to sell its right to pollute (which it doesn't need, because it emits no carbon) to the coal-based utility. The theory is that the coal-fired company will find it cheaper to pay for the right to emit carbon than to lower its own emissions. Cap and trade has worked very successfully in cutting back on acid rain emissions from Midwest utility companies that once seeded the clouds over their smokestacks with pollution, which then rained down on lakes in the Northeast.

But curbing acid rain was a lot easier than cutting carbon emissions. About two-thirds of America's electricity comes from coal-fired plants (the rest is about equally divided among nuclear, hydro, and natural gas). To curb these emissions—or to buy increasingly expensive permits to continue to pollute—will cost utilities a lot of money. And those costs will get passed on directly to the consumer. The federal Environmental Protection Agency (EPA)—pushing the bill—says it will force a 22 percent increase in electricity prices over the next twenty years, forcing the price of gasoline over $4 per gallon.[246] Many feel these estimates are ridiculously low.

Obama claims he will refund the money from higher utility and gas bills to the middle class and to the poor through tax credits. But these expenditures will only add to the deficit. When the time comes to vote for them, one can easily see them falling short.

And cap and trade will wipe out what is left of the American manufacturing industry. In 2008, when energy prices rose rapidly, American manufacturers caught a break. The high price of energy made it more expensive to ship products from China to the United States, and that difference in transportation costs began to outweigh the advantages of China's cheaper labor. But then, just as it looked like manufacturing was going to make a comeback in the United States, the Obama administration introduced its cap-and-trade bill.

If China, India, and other "developing" countries also imposed carbon taxes or made their polluters buy permits, there would be a level playing field. But, as it stands, China and India refuse to do so, pledging only to do their best to control carbon emissions. Since we'll have to pay the tax and they won't, the Heritage Foundation estimates cap and trade will cost the United States 400,000 manufacturing jobs a year.[247]

The cap-and-trade tax will hurt states in the central part of the country more than those on either coast. States from Minnesota to Pennsylvania, and down to Alabama, are dependent on coal-fired plants to generate their electricity.

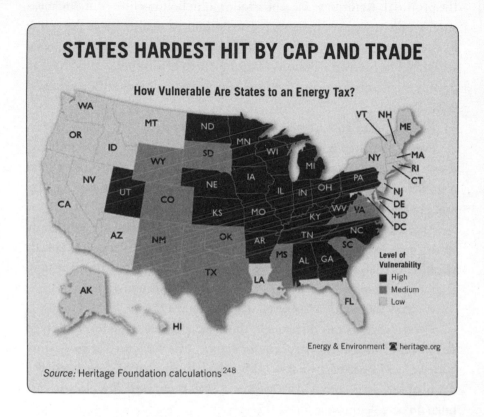

STATES HARDEST HIT BY CAP AND TRADE

How Vulnerable Are States to an Energy Tax?

Level of Vulnerability
- ■ High
- ■ Medium
- □ Low

Energy & Environment ☎ heritage.org

Source: Heritage Foundation calculations[248]

Why didn't the administration just propose a carbon tax and be done with it? Why insist on this extensive system of allowances and permits?

That's the key question. A carbon tax would simply add to the cost of doing business, like any other tax. But permits, issued by the government, give Washington the leverage that the Obama socialists need to take over American business. And Obama's people want to use cap and trade to further their takeover of the American economy.

To round up congressional support, Obama is promising to give away 85 percent of the permits in the first year of the bill's operation, selling 15 percent of them. The giveaway plan, of course, will only increase the Obama administration's political leverage. If you head a manufacturing business or a coal company or an electric utility, would you give money to Obama's challengers when he controls your access to a free permit?

Cap and trade is an excuse to take over the utilities and manufacturing industries in the United States. And that's not the only motive behind the proposal. As former UN ambassador John Bolton points out, the measure would trigger a "massive redistribution of wealth from the north to the south"—that is, from the developed world to the less-developed world.[249] The industrial nations of the northern hemisphere would have to pay for their emissions, and the funds would go to nations with less industrial capacity.

And here's the rub: *Cap and trade is not necessary.*

Even if you buy the evidence of global warming, rather than dismissing it as a fabricated nightmare of the left, the truth is that electric cars offer a simpler and better way to deal with both the problem of climate change and our dependence on foreign oil.

American cars account for nearly half the carbon dioxide emitted by vehicles worldwide every year (even though we have only 5 percent of the world's population and one-third of its cars).[250] Emissions from cars are responsible for one quarter of all U.S. carbon dioxide emissions.

We have the solution to end all that: electric cars.

Electric cars operate on batteries that need to be recharged every sixty to one hundred miles. (Inevitably, as they come into wider use, longer-lasting batteries will become available.) Once the battery charge runs down, the car operates on gasoline like any other; until then, however, electric cars burn no petroleum whatsoever.

If three-quarters of the U.S. car fleet were switched to electric power, it would save the United States 6.2 million barrels of oil per day, cutting our need for imported oil in half, according to the Pacific Northwest National Lab.[251]

And electric cars will do a lot to cut the global carbon emissions that the left points to as the cause of climate change. The Natural Resource Defense Council and the Electric Power Research Institute both found that carbon dioxide emissions could drop by 450 mmts annually if 60 percent of passenger cars were electric hybrids.[252] That's almost all the remaining 519 mmts we need to cut to meet Obama's goal.

Beyond cars, the most important measure would be to reduce emissions from trucks and buses, which account for about a quarter of the greenhouse gases emitted by all U.S. vehicles. Switching from diesel to natural gas reduces emissions by more than 80 percent.[253] Unlike cars, the nation's truck fleet is replaced every few years. Converting trucks to run on natural gas is a no-brainer. Obama should be directing his efforts toward converting trucks to natural gas, rather than to taxing our industrial base into oblivion.

We also need to switch our power plants from coal to natural gas. We have abundant supplies of gas in our country, far more than we can use, and gas contributes much less to global warming than coal does. But about two-thirds of our electric power comes from coal and only about one-tenth from natural gas. Since converting our cars to electric battery power would call for an increase in electricity generation, we need to get started converting our power plants.

More important, this combination of natural gas trucks and electric cars would largely free us of the need for imported oil from our enemies—and dramatically weaken the power of OPEC and the global sponsors of terror.

Oddly, environmentalists have been criticizing electric cars because they worry that the electricity that powers them must be generated by polluting, carbon-emitting, coal-fired plants. But most of the recharging will be done at night, during off-peak hours. In most parts of the country, clean sources—operating when there is little other demand for power—can provide most of the electricity needed.

The answer to such concerns is not to slow down the process of converting our cars to electricity (the first fully electric cars come on the market this year), but to hasten the conversion of our electricity-generating plants to natural gas. Though gas does give off some carbon emissions, they are much lower than those given off by gasoline or diesel—and we need not depend on foreign sources to buy it. And, eventually, hydrogen cars will emerge as the ultimate replacement for the gasoline engine: Hydrogen can be made from natural gas with no carbon emissions, because the hydrogen is released through the normal chemical process.

With these huge advances in car and truck carbon emissions on the table, what's the point of putting the country through the trauma of a cap-and-trade system or even a simple carbon tax?

We can achieve all the goals of the environmental community without regulating our industries—or taxing our citizens—to death.

But that's not the point. Barack Obama doesn't want regulation in order to stop global warming. He wants to use global warming as his excuse to enact further regulations. The cap-and-trade proposal is his way of extending government control to manufacturing and utilities, just as TARP expands it in the banking and financial sector. By regulating the banks in the name of financial solvency and risk management, and by shackling utilities and industries in the name of averting global climate change, he can achieve his socialist goals—all under the pretext of pursuing laudable objectives.

His real goal is to set up a government-run system of carbon credit allocation to strengthen government control of industry. Instead of a pragmatic effort to deal with our foreign oil dependency and environmental fears of carbon emissions, Obama is using these twin crises as an excuse to advance his program of government control when simpler solutions are readily available.

One real danger is that Democratic legislators will seek to adopt protectionist legislation to help domestic manufacturers cope with the extra costs of cap and trade. The idea would be to make up for the cost of carbon allowances by raising tariff barriers against countries like China and India that do not adopt cap-and-trade systems.

But this would be a disaster.

Foreign trade accounts for about a third of the U.S. economy, and generates 40 percent of our jobs.[254] To risk precipitating a trade war over cap and trade would be the height of stupidity. It was just this kind of protectionist legislation—the punitive Smoot-Hawley tariff of 1930—that helped fuel the Great Depression.

But Obama has often flirted with protectionism, as when he said in his campaign that he would renegotiate NAFTA. He never did, but if he gets his way with cap and trade, that kind of protectionism might be just around the corner.[255]

Cap and trade is still an Obama dream. It faces a long, tough fight in Washington before it graces our statute books. Most of the states that would be severely affected are represented by Democrats who aren't anxious to see their constituents socked with higher electric bills. This is the next great battle the Obama administration confronts. And we must wage it in 2010—and then use the issue to defeat the Democrats in the November election. Never has a president so openly—or so unnecessarily—pursued a policy that would hurt his own supporters!

All these expansions of government power would be scary enough. But an even more ominous warning comes from Alabama's governor, Bob Riley.

The governor notes that his state has "a distinct advantage over the states of the Northeast in three areas—lower taxes, lower energy costs and less unionization. As a result, there has been an influx of industries from the Northeast and Midwest to the South. The Northeast and Midwest are, of course, the president's political base. The South? Less so. I think his drive to stimulate unionization with card-check legislation, the higher energy costs we'll have with his cap-and-trade plan, and the taxes he will force many Southern states to raise with his unemployment benefit changes and health care reform, are all a way of neutralizing these advantages by raising taxes, energy costs and labor costs in the South."[256]

Could Obama's unionization, cap-and-trade, and tax policies be a way of impairing the economies of red states to allow blue states to keep their industrial base? Is he, perhaps, legislating only in the interest of half the country?

LOSING THE WAR ON TERROR

In our previous books, *Fleeced* and *Catastrophe*, we warned that Barack Obama would join those in the media who try to minimize the terrorist threat faced by this nation. Their collective view is, essentially, *What's the big deal?* They shrug their shoulders along with Michael Moore, who once said, "I don't know why we are making so much of an act of terror. It is three times more likely that you will be struck by lightning than die from an act of terror."[257]

This trivialization of terrorism, essentially treating it like any other crime, is just how the Clinton administration handled the 1993 attack on the World Trade Center. This policy—of failing to recognize that attack as an act of war, instead treating it like any other bombing or murder—led to the failure of both the Clinton and Bush administrations to take advance indications of future terrorist attacks seriously. And this attitude created institutional roadblocks that made 9/11 possible.

The Obama administration's lame response to the Fort Hood terrorist attack of November 5, 2009, smacked of the same refusal to take terrorism seriously, and its failure to head off the attack was characterized by the kinds of inhibition in taking preventative action that let 9/11 happen.

The fact is that the Obama administration has waged its own war of terror against the antiterrorism operatives, threatening prosecution for overly aggressive interrogation tactics. They are investigating the government's own investigators—not to make them more effective, but to protect the terror suspects themselves. In this world turned upside down, intelligence officials are reluctant to expose themselves to criticism by turning in suspects or reporting suspicious activity. But it is precisely this kind of inhibition that cleared a path for Major Nidal M. Hasan to murder thirteen soldiers at Fort Hood.

Obama's response to the massacre was to condemn it as an "act of violence" like that of a deranged schoolchild killing his classmates. Obama resisted using the word *terrorism* to describe the act, and the administration worked overtime to characterize the killings as a mass murder rather than a terrorist attack. They released information about how Major Hasan was distressed at his repeated deployments and was depressed over having to go back to Afghanistan. Only a few days after the killing did the evidence confirm, overwhelmingly, that this was indeed a terrorist attack—the first such on American soil since September 11, 2001.

This difference between a crime and an act of terrorism is profound, but it is also simple: A terrorist attack is an act of violence with a political motive. A terrorist need not be in contact with an organized group, or be supported by one financially or logistically, to be a terrorist. Bombing a storefront is a crime. Bombing an abortion clinic or a military recruiting station, on political grounds, is an act of terrorism. It has nothing to do with the number of people acting in concert, or with what communication they had with the outside world, or even with the statements they make upon commencing their mayhem.

Just as Timothy McVeigh was a terrorist when he bombed Oklahoma City's Murrah Federal Building, so is Major Hasan. It is irrelevant whether either man acted alone.

In fact, the Obama administration wants to avoid any mention of terrorism. In a March 2009 e-mail, the Defense Department's office of security review told Pentagon staff members that "this administration prefers to avoid using the term . . . 'Global War on Terror.' Please use 'Overseas Contingency Operation' " instead.[258]

And this is more than a question of semantics. By refusing to recognize the battle against terrorism as a war, or the terrorists as a foreign enemy, the Obama administration is sending every possible signal to the executive branch of government—including all our intelligence and counterterrorism agencies—that the fight is a lower priority, and that they are to bend over backward to avoid offending the sensibilities of the administration or the civil liberties of suspects (even if they aren't American citizens).

The inevitable result of treating terrorism as a back-burner issue is that investigators will be loath to pursue leads vigorously or to act decisively to head off possible terror threats. It's exactly that kind of failure of vigilance, in fact, that cleared a path for the Fort Hood massacre.

The military and intelligence agencies had ample warning of the possibility that Major Hasan was violent, and that he was a terrorist operative.

- Hasan had been "the focus of complaints by colleagues at Walter Reed Army Medical Center," the *Washington Post* reported, "and warned fellow Army physicians in 2007 that to prevent 'adverse events,' the military should allow Muslim soldiers to be released as conscientious objectors instead of fighting in wars against other Muslims."[259]

- He had also, according to the *Post*, "drawn the attention of terrorism investigators in San Diego and Washington, who tracked his e-mail correspondence from December 2008 to May 2009 with radical cleric Anwar al-Awlaki, a U.S. citizen and Islamic spiritual leader residing in Yemen who has exhorted followers to pursue violent jihad, or holy war."[260]

- Major Hasan had clearly come to the attention of the counterterrorism experts, but they kept the information to themselves. Hasan's superiors "were not told beforehand of the FBI-led review of the contacts with Awlaki. Likewise, concerns among military officials about his religious and political views were not in the files Defense officials provided to the FBI." [261] The *Wall Street Journal* reported, "the Pentagon said it was never notified by U.S. intelligence agencies that they had intercepted e-mails between the alleged Fort Hood shooter and an extremist imam until after last week's bloody assaults." [262]

- The *Washington Post* also reported that an FBI-led task force in San Diego "sent most of Hasan's suspect e-mails to counterparts in Washington early this year, which conducted an assessment but did not open a preliminary investigation or discuss the case with Hasan's superiors." Apparently, the Washington intelligence officials concluded that the e-mails were "innocent chatter and in keeping with Hasan's research interests." [263]

- After Washington decided Hasan was not a problem, the San Diego FBI office failed to forward to Washington two further e-mails lawmakers have identified as "troubling" since the agents "judged that they were in line with earlier correspondence." [264]

- ABC News reported, "U.S. intelligence agencies were aware months ago that Army Major Nidal Malik Hasan was attempting to make contact with an individual associated with al Qaeda." [265]

- After the attack, Al-Awlaki posted a blog—from his hideout in Yemen—titled "Nidal Hasan Did the Right Thing." He hailed Hasan as a "hero" and a "man of conscience." The Associated Press reported that Hasan attended a mosque in Falls Church, Virginia, when Al-Awlaki was imam there. [266]

- A fellow army doctor who studied with Hasan, Val Finell, told ABC News, "[Hasan] would frequently say he was a Muslim first and an American second. And that came out in just about everything he did at the University." Finell said he and other Army doctors complained to superiors about Hasan's statements. "And we questioned how somebody could take an oath of office . . . be an officer in the military and swear allegiance to the Constitution and to defend America against all enemies, foreign and domestic and have that type of conflict." [267]

So why was the FBI Washington office reluctant to attribute more than "innocent" motivation to Hasan's contact with Al-Awlaki? Why did it fall for the line that Hasan was just conducting research? And why didn't the FBI notify the Pentagon of its concerns or even report the fact of its investigation?

The answer, obviously, lies in the anxiety about political correctness, and the concern about ethnic and racial profiling, that has hampered the Obama administration's approach to global terrorism. In a time when antiterror investigators are being scrutinized by Attorney General Eric Holder's Justice Department, who could be expected to stick out his neck by making an accusation against an army major based on his e-mails or statements to his colleagues? Such incidents confirm that attitudes at the FBI and the CIA have changed radically to conform to the Obama administration's attitude; it should come as no surprise that their operatives are risk averse and fearful of making waves.

No longer will terrorism be treated as a war. It will henceforth be only a crime.

Nothing better epitomizes this change in federal attitudes than Holder's decision to try Khalid Sheikh Mohammed, the mastermind of the 9/11 attacks, in a federal criminal court in New York City. While it now appears that Mohammed will not be tried in New York, the fact that Holder initially decided to have him tried there indicates how lightly he takes the need for security in the city most victimized on 9/11. As former New York mayor Rudy Giuliani said, "What the Obama administration is telling us loud and clear is that the war on terror is over. . . . We are no longer going to treat these people as if this was an act of war. I do not understand why they cannot try Khalid Sheikh Mohammed in a military tribunal. That also would demonstrate that we are a nation of laws. That is the way we have tried enemy combatants in the past, whether it was the Second World War or the U.S. Civil War." [268]

Giuliani, a former federal prosecutor, said, "in this particular case, we are reaching out to give terrorists a legal benefit that is unnecessary." [269]

While the trial may not be in the Big Apple, it looks certain that it will be in a civilian civil court. That is clearly Obama's and Holder's preference. But how can federal prosecutors use much of the evidence they have against Mohammed? He was not read his rights; it's unlikely that his confessions were obtained pursuant to the constraints imposed by the Fifth Amendment. Even if the evidence is allowed in, how will the court treat the U.S. attorney general's boasts—at a congressional hearing—that Mohammed will be found guilty and that "failure is not an option," or the president's prediction that Mohammed would be given the death penalty?

So why are Holder and Obama proceeding with their plans to try Mohammed in a civilian court? Is it because a military tribunal would not get the coverage a federal district court will; neither would a panel of military judges allow the defense the leeway a federal judge would. Does Obama want to put the terror investigators on trial? Does he want a full airing of the details of the waterboarding and other means used in interrogating Mohammed, in order to elicit sympathy for Obama's efforts to handcuff our antiterror investigators?

Even as he puts our FBI and CIA on trial, Obama has asked that Congress not indulge in "political theater" by holding hearings on the Fort Hood massacre. But he wants to mount a piece of political theater in the Mohammed trial by putting the antiterror investigators in the hot seat. Unfortunately, we are only beginning to see the effects of Obama's standdown in the war on terror. On Christmas Day 2009, a twenty-three-year-old Nigerian Muslim, Umar Farouk Abdulmutallab, tried to explode a bomb on a flight bound for Detroit. As the plane approached the runway, alert passengers noticed smoke coming from his seat, pounced on him, and dismantled the device.

This last-minute intervention—and the failure of the bomb to go off in the first place—prevented the deaths of the three hundred passengers on board. Nevertheless, Homeland Security head Janet Napolitano hailed the incident as proof that the administration's efforts to prevent terrorism were succeeding.

Appearing on *Today*, she said, "the system has worked really very, very smoothly over the course of the past several days."[270] White House spokesman Robert Gibbs shared in the glee, claiming on CBS's *Face the Nation*, that "in many ways, this system has worked."[271]

After wiser people at the White House got hold of Napolitano and Gibbs, however, both backed off their statements of triumph. Obama, trying very much to look like the prosecutor attacking the security lapse—not the incumbent president whose government failed to anticipate them—sharply criticized the "systemic failure."[272]

The fact that Abdulmutallab—a man who was on a list of possible terrorists—was allowed to board a plane with a bomb, without being detected, illustrates not only a colossal flaw in the air safety system, but also the severely flawed antiterror policies in place today—and the skewed priorities of the Obama administration.

There was plenty of warning about Abdulmutallab's evil intentions. The *New York Times* reported that his "father, a prominent Nigerian banker and former government official, phoned the American Embassy in Abuja in October with a warning that his son had developed radical views, had disappeared and might have traveled to Yemen, American officials said, but the young man's visa to enter the United States, which was good until June 2010, was not revoked.

"Instead . . . embassy officials marked his file for a full investigation should he reapply for a visa. And when the information was passed on to Washington, his name was added to 550,000 others with possible terrorist connections—but not to the no-fly list. That meant no flags were raised when he used cash to buy a ticket to the United States and boarded a plane, checking no bags."[273]

In a world where you can be prosecuted for racial profiling, and where there is more concern about privacy and civil liberties than about stopping three hundred people from being blown up on an airplane, such things do slip through the cracks.

For example, why was Abdulmutallab's name not added to the no-fly list? The *Times* reports that the "government has spent the last several years cutting the size of the watch list, after repeated criticism that too many people were being questioned at border crossings or checkpoints."[274]

Today, the government's no-fly list contains only four thousand names; the selectee list, which triggers a more intrusive search at airport security, has only fourteen thousand. Obama has so terrorized our antiterror intelligence operatives that they have cut our scrutiny to the bone.

And why don't we have full-body screening available at airports? Because "privacy advocates," the *Times* reports, "have tried to stop or at least slow the introduction of advanced checkpoint screening devices that use so-called millimeter waves to create an image of a passenger's body, so officers can see under clothing to determine if a weapon or explosive has been hidden. Security officers, in a private area, review the images, which are not stored. Legislation is pending in the House that would prohibit the use of this equipment for routine passenger screening. To date, only 40 of these machines have been installed at 19 airports across the United States."[275]

Shockingly, ABC News reports, "one of the four leaders allegedly behind the plot to blow up a Northwest Airlines passenger jet over Detroit was released by the U.S. from Guantanamo prison in November 2007." Apparently, Guantanamo prisoner #372, Said Ali Shari, "was sent to Saudi Arabia on November 9, 2007, according to the Defense Department log of detainees who were released from American custody." He was released to Saudi Arabia, where "he entered into an 'art therapy rehabilitation program' and was set free according to U.S. and Saudi officials."[276]

(In our previous book, *Outrage*, we warned that released Guantanamo prisoners would go right back to their terrorist gangs after we let them go. Today our fears are stronger than ever.)

The most disturbing sign that Obama and Holder are compromising the war on terror is their appointment of Neal Katyal and Jennifer Daskal to major positions in the Justice Department. Katyal, according to the *New York Post*, was the "lawyer who defended Osama bin Laden's driver and bodyguard—and who sought constitutional rights for terrorists." He is to serve as the principal deputy solicitor general at Justice. Jennifer Daskal, who "just months ago was an anti-Guantanamo activist," is now in the Justice Department's National Security Division "working on detainee issues."[277]

As long as Obama sends the perverse signals he has been sending to our counterterrorism officials, incidents like the Detroit-bound flight or the massacre at Fort Hood will happen again and again, likely with increasing loss of life. But there is no evidence that Obama understands the connection between his posturing on privacy issues, interrogation techniques, and warrantless searches and the resurgence of domestic terrorism in the United States.

Until he does, we can only bring him back to reality by administering a shock in November 2010.

PART TWO

THE TARGETS

Partisanship used to be merely a crutch for those who were too simple to follow the records and positions of each individual candidate. Like any ideology, it was suspect because of its reliance on preconceived answers and formulaic responses to any issue.

But in light of the current Congress—when Democrats lined up like automatons to vote for the entire Obama program, dissenting only after first making sure their votes weren't needed—partisanship is the only accurate prism through which to watch events in Washington. There are now only Democrats and Republicans. No shades of meaning, at least on the Democratic side, make much sense. When the chips are down, they all vote as one.

So one must choose sides. And now is the time to put aside any latent streak of independence and back a solid Republican Party ticket. We used to be conservative Democrats. That's why we backed Bill Clinton. But, in today's atmosphere of extreme partisanship and no compromise, there is no such thing. The worst Republican is better than the best Democrat. After all, when Democrats vote the way their party leader tells them to more than 90 percent of the time, what is there to choose from?

So the way to save our country is to elect Republicans in 2010. (Not that they're always so good but because their Democratic opponents are always worse.) In this section, we'll focus on which Democrats should be our main targets.

THE SENATE

After the stunning and inspiring victory of Republican Scott Brown in Massachusetts, the Senate now has fifty-nine Democrats and forty-one Republicans. To get control, the GOP needs to win fifty-one seats, because as president of the Senate, Vice President Joe Biden is positioned to break any tie in the Democrats' favor.

That means we need to win ten new seats. And we can! There are fourteen we could win.

Here is how it breaks down:

Almost Certain Republican Pickups (2)

Delaware
North Dakota

Very Likely Republican Pickups (4)

Colorado
Nevada
Arkansas
Indiana

Toss-Ups (4)

Pennsylvania
Illinois
California
Wisconsin

Likely Democratic Wins, but Could Be GOP Pickups (4)

New York (Gillibrand)
Washington state
Oregon
Connecticut

It will be difficult, but it's far from impossible—in fact, it's downright likely!

Six Republican senators are retiring at the end of this term. To take control of the chamber, the GOP needs to win all six seats—and we can. Three of them are easy: Kentucky, Florida, and Kansas. Three are tougher, but still likely, Republican wins: Missouri, Ohio, and New Hampshire.

The open Republican seats are those currently held by: Kit Bond (Missouri), Sam Brownback (Kansas), Jim Bunning (Kentucky), Judd Gregg (New Hampshire), Mel Martinez (Florida), and George Voinovich (Ohio).

Here's how the Republican open seats stack up:

Missouri

The race to succeed Kit Bond is coming down to Congressman Roy Blunt, the Republican, against Missouri's Democratic secretary of state, Robin Carnahan. Blunt, the former House minority whip, is the father of Matt Blunt, Missouri's governor from 2005 to 2009. Robin is the daughter of former governor Mel Carnahan, who was killed in a plane crash. Robin's mother, Jean, took his place in the Senate but was defeated in 2002. Robin's brother Russ currently represents Missouri's Third District in the House of Representatives.

This race, pitting two dynasties against one another, will be a tough one. But we should win. A January 2010 Rasmussen Poll showed Blunt ahead 49–43 after having been three points behind a month before.[1] As the race heats up, Carnahan will likely be seen for what she is: a lightweight trying to cash in on sympathy for her father's death. Blunt's experience in the House should help him outshine her. *Missouri is a swing state but it leans Republican: Bush won it by seven points in 2004 and John McCain carried it by 4,000 votes in 2008. So the Republican, Blunt, should have an edge.*

Ohio

Senator George Voinovich's retirement is sparking a spirited race in this most swinging of all swing states. The Republican candidate will be Rob Portman, a former congressman who served as George W. Bush's budget director. The Democrats face a close primary between Lieutenant Governor Lee Fisher and Secretary of State Jennifer Brunner.

Rasmussen's January 2010 polls showed Republican Portman ahead of either Democrat, leading Fisher by 44–37, and Brunner by 43–40.[2] But this race has a long way to go. Again, because Ohio is such a swing state (Obama beat McCain there by 52–47, exactly his national margin), any national

Republican trend—to say nothing of today's tailwind—should bring Portman in.

New Hampshire

The toughest race among the open seats for the Republicans may be the fight for the one being vacated by Senator Judd Gregg. The Democratic candidate will be Congressman Paul Hodes; the Republican will probably be the state's former attorney general, Kelly Ayotte. Although attorney general is not an elected office in New Hampshire—Ayotte was appointed by the governor in 2004—she enjoyed an early lead of 49–40 over Hodes in a January 2010 Rasmussen poll.[3]

But Ayotte may face a primary challenge from conservatives Ovide Lamontagne and Bill Binnie, one an attorney and the other a businessman. Current polls show Hodes beating either of them, so with luck Ayotte will win the primary.

Hodes has problems of his own. His record of 95 percent support for Pelosi and Obama will not play well in New Hampshire; neither will his vote for the stimulus package, increased financial regulation, and the Obamacare health legislation.

With Massachusetts going Republican, it's hard to see how New Hampshire will go Democrat! But New Hampshire did vote for Obama by 55–45, about five points more than the national result. In a Republican landslide, Ayotte wins. In a close national race, it will be a toss-up.

Kentucky

When Hall of Fame pitcher Jim Bunning announced his retirement as senator from Kentucky, it was assumed that the Republican secretary of state, Trey Grayson, would be the nominee. But Congressman Ron Paul's son, Rand Paul, is challenging him in a primary. Endorsed by Sarah Palin, he is stirring up quite a fuss. The Democrats are having a primary of their own, between Attorney General Jack Conway and Lieutenant Governor Daniel Mongiardo. Both primaries could go either way.

But the seat should stay in Republican hands in any event. After all, McCain carried Kentucky by sixteen points, and the Obama administration is waging war against coal, a chief engine of the state's economy. The Rasmussen Poll, taken on February 2, 2010, shows either Republican beating either Democrat.[4]

Florida

In one of the year's early upsets, insurgent conservative candidate Mario Rubio, a former speaker of the Florida House, is leading Florida governor Charlie Crist in a February 2010 Rasmussen Poll, by 49–37.[5]

Even though Crist is the sitting Republican governor, it looks as though Rubio will be the Republican candidate, and he'll make a good one: articulate, forceful, and telegenic. He'd make a good senator, too. Either Rubio or Crist has a double-digit lead over the Democratic frontrunner, Congressman Kendrick Meek.

Kansas

A solidly Republican state. The only real contest is in the GOP primary between two good congressmen, Todd Tiahrt and Jerry Moran.

Of the six Republican open seats, then, the GOP can be reasonably sure of holding three: Kansas, Florida, and Kentucky. Missouri will be tougher, but will probably go Republican. Ohio will be tougher still, but in a national GOP landslide it will likely go Republican. New Hampshire could be a toss-up, but our best guess is that it, too, stays Republican. As of now, Republicans lead in all six states.

And here are the seats we could pick up:

Almost Certain Republican Pickups

Delaware
North Dakota

Delaware

Normally a solidly Democratic state, Delaware went for the Obama-Biden ticket by 62–37. But Republicans lucked out when GOP congressman and former governor Mike Castle decided to seek the seat. Since Delaware has only one congressman, Castle is elected at large; so he has served in state-wide elected office since 1980 (counting a stint as lieutenant governor). He has won eleven consecutive statewide races, and he's not likely to lose this one.

When Joe's son Beau Biden, the state's attorney general, decided not to run, the seat became a foregone conclusion for the Republicans. A January 2010 Rasmussen Poll had Castle thirty points ahead of the most likely Democratic candidate.[6]

North Dakota

A second virtually certain Republican pickup is in North Dakota, where Senator Byron Dorgan, under pressure for backing Obamacare, is not running again. The popular Republican governor, John Hoeven, was twenty points ahead of Dorgan when the latter decided to head for the hills; Hoeven should clean up against any other Democrat.

Very Likely Republican Pickups

Arkansas
Nevada
Colorado
Indiana

Arkansas

Democratic incumbent Blanche Lincoln seems headed for what Ronald Reagan called the "ash heap of history." She trails all four of her possible Republican challengers by margins of fifteen to nineteen points in a February 2010 Rasmussen poll.[7]

Nevada

The most lovely spectacle of 2010 should be the defeat of Senate majority leader Harry Reid, who richly deserves retirement. According to a Rasmussen poll in February 2010, he trails all three of his Republican rivals: Danny Tarkanian (47–39), Sue Lowden (45–39), and Sharon Angle (44–40).[8]

Colorado

Republican prospects are also bright in Colorado, where former lieutenant governor Jane Norton is running against appointed senator Michael Bennet, who has never been elected to office. Norton is very popular in Colorado and holds a commanding 51–37 lead over Bennet in a February 2010 Rasmussen poll.[9]

But Bennet has a primary on his hands against Colorado House speaker Andrew Romanoff. And a Norton-Romanoff race would be closer than a Norton-Bennet contest. The Republican tops Romanoff by only 45–38. Why would Norton run better against an incumbent than against a newcomer? For one simple reason: because Bennet is an incumbent who voted for Obamacare. Rasmussen notes "incumbency may be one of Bennet's biggest problems."[10]

Norton herself faces a primary against Republicans Ken Buck, a district attorney, and ex–state senator Tom Wiens. But the polls show neither one running as strong as Norton, so with luck Republican primary voters will nominate Jane.

Indiana

With the retirement of Indiana's incumbent senator, Evan Bayh, this seat in a red state is very likely to go Republican. Bayh only retired when it became clear to him that he would lose to former Senator Dan Coats (a past client of ours) who declared his candidacy just a few days before Bayh dropped out. Funny how these guys suddenly want to spend more time with their families when they read polls showing them losing! Bayh—once a moderate Democrat and now a liberal masquerading as a conservative—won't be missed. Bye bye Bayh!

Toss-Ups

Illinois
Pennsylvania
California
Wisconsin

Illinois

It might be too much to hope for that the Republican Party would win the former Senate seats of both the president and the vice president. But it's a real possibility.

After Roland Burris was appointed to fill Barack Obama's Senate seat by former governor Rod Blagojevich, in a transaction that stank to high heaven, a very strong Republican—Congressman Mark Kirk—emerged as the GOP candidate. Kirk has been a leader in the Congress in the fight against terrorism and has been pushing for strong sanctions against Iran.

The Democratic nominee is State Treasurer Alexi Giannoulias. How could the voters of Illinois be foolish enough to elect someone who comes from that snake pit of a state government in Springfield?

The Rasmussen Poll of February 3, 2010, shows Kirk ahead of Giannoulias by 46–40.[11] In a normal year, a Democratic victory in this race would be a given. But 2010 is not a normal year.

This contest will be one of the keys to taking control of the Senate in 2010. It will be hard-fought—and it's essential that Mark Kirk win!

Pennsylvania

Arlen Specter, a Republican who recently switched to the Democratic Party when he saw the Obama victory, should defeat his primary opponent, Joe Sestak. But Republican Pat Toomey led Specter by 49–40 in the Rasmussen Poll of January 2010.[12]

Wisconsin

At this writing, we don't know whether former Wisconsin governor Tommy Thompson, a Republican, will get into the race to challenge Democratic incumbent Russ Feingold. Here's hoping he does. The Rasmussen poll of January 28, 2010, shows him beating Feingold by 47–43. Wisconsin is a liberal state. But Feingold is so far to the left that it's hard to imagine any place outside Cuba where he'd be a safe bet for reelection.

California

Democratic incumbent Barbara Boxer is clinging to a very narrow lead over her three possible Republican opponents. She defeats former Hewlett-Packard CEO Carly Fiorina by just three points, state assemblyman Chuck Devore by six, and former congressman Tom Campbell by four in the January 2010 Rasmussen poll.[13] She's now ahead, but clearly could be defeated.

Likely Democratic Wins, but Could Be GOP Pickups

New York (Gillibrand)
Washington state
Oregon
Connecticut

New York

Kirsten Gillibrand, appointed to her seat by Governor David Paterson after Hillary Clinton resigned to become secretary of state, is very vulnerable. So far she's been able to scare off serious challengers, but she's not out of the woods. A number of credible candidates are in the offing, and even some who are now regarded as long shots could come in big—her liberal record is that terrible.

Connecticut

The Democratic hand in Connecticut was strengthened when Chris Dodd dropped out. The Democratic candidate will be Richard Blumenthal, the state's attorney general and the ultimate political insider, who is famous for his ability to get in front of a TV camera. But the Republicans have a primary between a good candidate in former congressman Rob Simmons and an entertaining one in Linda McMahon, the wife of the founder of World Wrestling Entertainment, Vince McMahon.

The national trend could hurt Blumenthal, but he leads Simmons by 19 points and McMahon by 20 in the latest Rasmussen poll.[14]

Washington State

Senator Patty Murray won her seat last time with only 55 percent of the vote—a slim margin for a three-term senator, when most romp to easy victories. But Murray's liberalism and uninspiring performance has kept her vote share down. She faces a tough challenge from an innovative young businessman, Paul Akers, who specializes in taking new technologies and making them work. With luck, he can work some magic here.

Oregon

Democrat Ron Wyden is seeking his third term in the Senate and, if he draws a good challenger, could be vulnerable.

Right now, Republicans hold a lead in enough states to hold all their open seats and take eight Democratic seats as well. We could gain the majority with a switch of only three points each in California and Indiana. Victory is in sight!

But the Democratic incumbents up for reelection this year don't just deserve to lose because they're Democrats, or because they backed Obama's miserable health-care legislation. Each deserves defeat on his or her own merits. Here's why:

Harry Reid (Nevada): The Prime Target

Democratic Party Loyalty in Voting: 95.6.2 percent[15]
Wealth Ranking (2008): 31/100[16]
Earmark Ranking: 32/100[17]
In fiscal 2009, Reid procured 146 earmarks totaling $211,798,429

The defeat of Senate majority leader Harry Reid in November should be the number-one priority for everyone who wants to stop the Obama agenda, the out-of-control spending in Washington, and the all-too-cozy relationship between lobbyists and elected officials.

Reid is an old-time dealmaker who's been accused of using his influence to line his own and his family's pockets. Like many of his colleagues, he has an ethical tin ear and he will never admit that he's wrong.

As majority leader of the Senate, Reid has been Obama's biggest cheerleader. Reid singlehandedly jammed Obama's costly liberal agenda through the Senate by introducing a bold new leadership tool—bribing members to get their votes. During the health-care debate, Reid brokered a deal to get the crucial sixtieth vote: He promised Senator Ben Nelson of Nebraska full federal funding for Medicaid expansion in his state—worth about $100 million—in exchange for his support. And that was just part of it. Nelson also made another deal with Reid to help insurance companies in Nebraska. According to published reports, Blue Cross/Blue Shield of Nebraska would save between $15 million and $20 million in new fees under the provision in the Senate bill that Nelson negotiated. And other Nebraska insurers will be excluded from taxes on supplemental Medigap insurance sold to the elderly. That's quite a deal! Reid is awfully generous in handing out millions of dollars in taxpayer money. Those of us from the other forty-nine states won't be so fortunate; we can be forgiven for criticizing Reid's magnanimous gift to Nelson. Not only won't we get the same subsidy, we'll be paying for the one Reid gave to Nebraska.

But Reid isn't worrying about people like us. He's spent his entire career worrying about the casino/gaming industry that dominates Nevada, and about the trial lawyers, banks, telecommunications companies, and lobbyists who pay for his campaigns. They're his constituents.

In running the Senate, money has been no object for Reid. It's the means to keeping his team in line and rewarding his friends. When Senator Mary Landrieu of Louisiana was wavering about voting for the health-care bill, for example, Reid handed her a $300 million gift for her state. She wasn't at all undecided after that. And Reid also tossed out another $100 million to his friend and fellow Obamacare advocate, Chris Dodd, for a $100 million new medical facility in Connecticut—a state that already has the prestigious Yale University and UConn medical centers to cover its 3 million people. What are the odds that the soon-to-be-former-senator Dodd finds his name on the new facility? But, hey, what are friends for?

Despite Reid's considerable power in Washington, his leadership in the Senate doesn't appear to matter too much to his constituents in Nevada. In fact, most people don't even like him. According to the *Wall Street Jour-*

nal, a recent poll commissioned by the *Las Vegas Review-Journal* found that 52 percent of Nevadans had an unfavorable opinion of Reid and only 40 percent indicated that they would vote for him. More ominous for Reid, he's running well behind three potential Republican opponents. But Reid won't go away quietly. He's announced that he'll raise $25 million for the race, if he needs to—and the special interests will be glad to help him out. They need him there. At the beginning of 2010, Reid had already raked in over $15 million. But money may not be enough. After spending $22,000 a day from October through December (for a total of almost $2 million), Reed hasn't made any significant inroads in the polls. The people of Nevada, it turns, out, just aren't wild about Harry.

Raising money won't be hard for Reid. He's always had the financial support of the casinos, personal injury lawyers, banks, telecommunications companies, lobbyists, and mines. They're his people and they'll come through for him. Just like he comes through for them.

Here's a list of his top campaign and PAC contributors:

TOP CONTRIBUTORS TO HARRY REID: 2010 ELECTION CYCLE

		TOTAL	INDIVIDUALS	PACS
1	MGM Mirage*	$180,400	$145,400	$35,000
2	Harrah's Entertainment*	$111,950	$86,950	$25,000
3	Weitz & Luxenberg**	$88,800	$88,800	$0
4	Law Offices of Peter G. Angelos**	$84,000	$84,000	$0
5	JPMorgan Chase & Co.	$82,100	$57,100	$25,000
6	Girardi & Keese**	$81,400	$81,400	$0
7	Simmons Cooper LLC**	$76,900	$76,900	$0
8	Station Casinos*	$76,200	$61,200	$15,000
9	Comcast Corp.***	$73,900	$38,900	$35,000
10	AT&T Inc ***	$73,050	$29,550	$43,500
11	Akin, Gump et al.**** (lobbyist for Harrah's)	$61,750	$39,750	$22,000

		TOTAL	INDIVIDUALS	PACS
12	Boyd Gaming*	$59,600	$49,600	$10,000
13	FMR Corp*****	$59,200	$33,200	$26,000
14	Blackstone Group	$50,800	$45,450	$5,350
15	National Cable & Telecommunications Assn.***	$50,000	$25,000	$25,000
15	United Health Group	$50,000	$0	$50,000
17	Sierra Nevada Corp.	$49,500	$32,500	$17,000
18	WPP Group****	$48,100	$45,100	$3,000
19	Apollo Advisors*****	$45,400	$45,400	$0
20	Walt Disney Co.	$45,400	$11,400	$34,000
21	DLA Piper*****	$45,000	$25,000	$20,000

Source: Center for Responsive Politics; OpenSecrets.org. As the Center's website specifies, "The organizations themselves did not donate, rather the money came from the organization's PAC, its individual members or employees or owners, and those individuals' immediate families." [18]
*Casino/gaming interests; **Personal injury lawyers;
***Telecommunications; ****Banks/financial, *****Lobbyists

Here are the top industries that have contributed to Reid's campaign and PAC:

TOP INDUSTRIES CONTRIBUTING TO HARRY REID (2010 ELECTION CYCLE)

	TOTAL	INDIVIDUALS	PACS
Lawyers/Law Firms	$1,851,425	$1,479,337	$372,088
Casinos/Gambling	$917,913	$766,414	$151,499
Lobbyists	$727,087	$703,622	$23,465
Securities and Investment	$669,910	$347,410	$322,500
Real Estate	$669,311	$443,811	$225,500
Health Professionals	$554,800	$226,200	$328,600
Insurance	$496,710	$148,710	$348,000

TV/Movies/Music	$429,200	$177,200	$252,000
Computers/Internet	$338,692	$109,575	$229,117
Commercial Banks	$338,096	$128,700	$209,396
Business Services	$297,359	$253,859	$43,500
Leadership PACs	$286,000	$0	$286,000
Public Sector Unions	$283,000	$1,000	$282,000
Misc. Finance	$277,865	$255,865	$22,000
Transportation Unions	$272,000	$0	$272,000
Retired	$240,195	$240,195	$0
Hospitals/Nursing Homes	$223,725	$65,725	$158,000
Pharmaceuticals/Health Products	$208,650	$15,150	$193,500
Finance/Credit Companies	$199,400	$67,100	$132,300
Air Transport	$197,850	$57,350	$140,500

Source: Center for Responsive Politics, OpenSecrets.org[19]

Champion of the Gambling Industry

It's interesting to note that Reid has received almost $1 million of the $4,447,000 that the casino/gaming industry has already shelled out in this election cycle. For good reason: Reid has been the industry's mouthpiece in fighting online gambling—a serious threat to Las Vegas. He's their boy. And, so far, he's kept the Internet folks at bay.

But it's not just the Las Vegas gambling interests that Reid has helped. He's been available to help other casinos, too. In fact, when the Jack Abramoff lobbying scandal broke, lobbying firm records revealed that Reid had intervened with the Department of Interior on behalf of several tribes who were Abramoff clients. Abramoff and his lobbying firm, Greenberg/Traurig, were at the core of a landmark lobbying investigation into the more than $80 million that Indian tribes paid to him and affiliated groups. Prosecutors were especially interested in the contributions of over $4 million that were made available to friendly congressmen. In 2006, Abramoff pled guilty to conspiracy, tax evasion, and corrupt practices arising from his lobbying and campaign activities.

According to John Solomon of the Associated Press, Reid sent a letter urging then Interior secretary Gale Norton to reject a casino project opposed by two Abramoff clients, the Louisiana Coushatta and Mississippi Choctaw tribes.[20] These tribes, of course, had nothing to do with Nevada. But Reid was only too happy to help them.

> **QUESTION:** Why would a Nevada senator go to bat for tribal gambling interests in Louisiana and Mississippi?

> **ANSWER:** Because he's just such a nice guy—he'd help out anyone.

Or was there more to it?

Well, Reid was probably happy when the very day after he sent his letter his PAC, the Searchlight Leadership Fund, received a $5,000 donation from the Coushatta tribe—at Abramoff's direction.[21] But, of course, that was just a coincidence. It had nothing to do with his concerns about the tribes. Reid was probably also happy about the additional contributions he received from Abramoff clients. Between 2001 and 2004, $68,000 in Abramoff-related donations went to Reid.[22]

But, again, we're sure that money was totally—totally—unrelated to his work for the tribes. Reid actively helped Abramoff's tribal clients on a number of occasions. According to Solomon, Reid sent four letters to officials in the Bush administration on their behalf and argued for their position once on the Senate floor, successfully opposing a fellow Democrat's bill. "Reid collected donations around the time of each action," Solomon reported.[23] Again, the timing? Just a coincidence. There were frequent phone contacts and meetings between Abramoff's firm and Reid's office. At one point, one of Reid's top aides quit the Senate office to go to work for Abramoff's firm as a lobbyist, where he quickly organized a fund-raiser for Reid. But that, too, was just a coincidence. Surely it had nothing to do with Reid's positions on gambling or his willingness to help the tribes.

As you can see, Reid is a master hypocrite. After the Abramoff scandal, Reid actually called for ethical reforms to control the influence of lobbyists, including:

> Closing the revolving door between the Congress and lobbying firms by doubling (from one year to two) the cooling-off period during which

lawmakers, senior Congressional staff, and Executive Branch officials are prohibited from lobbying their former offices.[24]

Did that, by any chance, include his own staff?

But Reid went even further: He criticized Republicans who accepted contributions from Abramoff, while at the same time he refused to refund the very same Abramoff-related contributions he himself had received. Because, you see, those were different. Reid claims that none of this was any problem—since he'd never met Abramoff himself. But how did Reid know to write the letters and speak up on the floor? How did he know to show up at the lobbyists' fund-raisers to benefit him?

Just another coincidence. It wasn't just the gambling interests that connected Reid and Abramoff's firm. The lobbying office's billing records documented twenty-one other contacts with Reid's office about another client—the Northern Mariana Islands, a U.S. territory. Dozens of phone calls and meetings with Reid's office about the extension of the minimum wage to the island were detailed:

> Reid, along with his Senate counsel, Jim Ryan, met with Abramoff deputy Ronald Platt on June 5, 2001, "to discuss timing on minimum wage legislation," according to an invoice that Greenberg Traurig—Abramoff's firm—sent to the Marianas. Three weeks before the meeting, Greenberg Traurig's political action committee donated $1,000 to Reid's Senate re-election committee. Three weeks after the meeting, Platt himself donated $1,000 to Reid.
>
> A Reid representative confirmed Platt had regular contacts with the Senator's office, calling them part of the "routine checking in" by lobbyists who work Capitol Hill. As for the timing of donations, Manley said, "There is no connection. This is just a typical part of lawful fund-raising."[25]

Unfortunately, he's right—it is very typical. That's what's wrong with Washington.

That's what's wrong with Harry Reid.

All in the Family: Reid's Three Sons and Son-in-Law All Represented Special Interests

Until several years ago, the Reid family were the folks to go to if you needed something in Nevada from the federal government. Reid's sons, who are lobbyists, could often be found in Harry Reid's Senate office, blurring the line between family and business.

But that all got a little uncomfortable after an investigation by the *Los Angeles Times* exposed the pervasive role of Reid's three sons and one son-in-law in representing special interests in Washington and Nevada. After the article, Reid finally—and belatedly—blocked the sons from working from his office or lobbying his staff. And while his sons went back to work on various projects in Nevada, Reid's son-in-law Steven Barringer stayed. He's still an active lobbyist at the D.C. firm of Holland & Hart, where he has been a rainmaker for the firm: The year before he joined, Holland & Hart made only $100,000 in lobbying fees.[26] Since he arrived in 2006, it has averaged about $2 million in lobbying fees.

It helps to be related to the majority leader of the Senate, doesn't it? By any measure, Reid and his family have set some kind of new record for inappropriate conduct. As the *Los Angeles Times* put it, when it came to lobbying by family members of a congressman or senator:

> Harry Reid is in a class by himself. One of his sons and his son-in-law lobby in Washington for companies, trade groups and municipalities seeking Reid's help in the Senate. A second son has lobbied in Nevada for some of those same interests, and a third has represented a couple of them as a litigator. In the last four years alone, their firms have collected more than $2 million in lobbying fees from special interests that were represented by the kids and helped by the senator in Washington. So pervasive are the ties among Reid, members of his family and Nevada's leading industries and institutions that it's difficult to find a significant field in which such a relationship does not exist.[27]

During that time, Reid was vice chairman of the Senate Ethics Committee. He apparently asked for an opinion on whether his sons could work as lobbyists—and was told that there was no problem. Talk about the goats guarding the garbage! Since then, Senate rules have prohibited lobbying of a member by a spouse or immediate family member. Of course, Reid himself saw nothing improper about Nevada clients paying his sons to lobby him!

Here are some of the significant findings from the *Los Angeles Times* story:

- Mining companies paid $200,000 in lobbying fees to the law firm where Barringer worked from 1999 to 2000.[28]

- When Barringer moved to another firm, Lionel Sawyer & Collins, in 2001, the mining interests followed him: The National Mining Association and other mining companies active in Nevada paid the new firm $780,000 and Barringer was their registered lobbyist on the mining accounts. "Doug Hock, a spokesman for Newmont Mining Corp., said the company used Barringer 'based on his expertise in mining and environmental law' and not because of his family ties."[29]

  Note: From 2001–2002, Lionel, Sawyer & Collins contributed $150,000 to Reid's PAC.[30]

- According to the *Los Angeles Times*, "In 2003, Reid's four sons—Rory, 40, Leif, 35, Josh, 31, and Key, 28—work[ed] for Nevada's largest law firm, Lionel Sawyer & Collins. Rory Reid was a partner in the firm and was a Nevada lobbyist before his election to the Clark County Board of Commissioners in November 2003. (Rory Reid is now a candidate for governor of Nevada. Leif Reid is a litigator who has represented mining and resort industry associations in Nevada.)"[31]

  Note: Rory Reid is still listed on the Lionel Sawyer & Collins website as a shareholder and attorney with a practice specializing in "gaming."[32]

- Key Reid was hired by the firm in 2002 to help open its Washington office.[33]

- According to the *Los Angeles Times*, "The mining firm Placer Dome Inc. paid the Lionel Sawyer law firm $5,000 a month in 2001 to be its 'eyes and ears' in Nevada and sought out Rory Reid's services."[34]

- The American Gaming Association followed Barringer from firm to firm and paid Lionel Sawyer over $180,000 from 2001 to 2003.[35]

- Barringer was hired by a helicopter-tour company fighting new federal flight restrictions near the Grand Canyon. Reid helped out on the matter.[36]

- "A chemical company seeking federal money to clean up radioactive waste and a hydrogen-fuel maker looking for a federal contract also got help from [Harry] Reid. Both hired son Rory to lobby on unrelated issues in Nevada."[37]

- The Howard Hughes Corp. paid $300,000 to Barringer's newly formed consulting firm "to push a provision allowing the company to acquire 998 acres of federal land ripe for development in the exploding Las Vegas metropolitan area."[38] Reid pushed the bill.

- "Other provisions of the same bill were intended to benefit a real estate development headed by a senior partner in Lionel Sawyer & Collins—the Nevada law firm that employed all four of Reid's sons—by moving the right-of-way for a federal power-transmission line off his property and on to what had been protected federal wilderness."[39]

- "Reid never told his senate colleagues or the public that the provisions he authored, some of which were technically and not apparently beneficial to anyone, were, in fact, introduced on behalf of clients who paid his sons and son-in-law over $2 million."[40]

- "The governments of three of Nevada's biggest cities—Las Vegas, North Las Vegas and Henderson—also gained from the legislation, which freed up tens of thousands of acres of federal land for development and annexation. All three were represented by Reid's family members who contacted his staff on their clients' behalf."[41]

- Steven Barringer is still very much involved as a lobbyist and partner at Holland & Hart. Since arriving at the firm, he has represented the following very familiar clients with businesses in Nevada:

STEVEN BARRINGER'S HOLLAND & HART CLIENTS

American Gaming Assn.*

Barrick Gold*

City of Henderson, Nevada*

Coeur d'Alene Mines Corp.*

Howard Hughes Corp.*

Newmont Mining*

Quinetiq Government Relations

Apogen Technologies

Note: Current clients are identified by an asterisk.
Source: Center for Responsive Politics, OpenSecrets.org.

It must be very helpful to have the ear of the majority leader—especially one who's shown just how willing he is to go out of his way to help his family.

Harry Reid has adamantly insisted that there was—and presumably still is—nothing wrong with his family members lobbying him and others on behalf of Nevada businesses. According to Reid, the fact that lobbyists have to file reports means that everything is transparent—that there's no issue.

What's *not* transparent is what motivates the introduction of certain amendments, like the ones Reid sponsored to secretly help out his sons and benefactors. What's not transparent are any conversations Reid had with his sons about helping their clients. What's not transparent is the kind of information a majority leader might give his lobbyist son-in-law.

What *is* transparent is that Reid needs to go.

Reid's Special Earmark: A Bridge to His Own Land

In 2005, Reid sponsored an earmark to the 2006 transportation bill that provided $18 million in federal funds to build a bridge over the Colorado River to connect Laughlin, Nevada, with Bullhead City, Arizona.[42]

Laughlin is a casino town but most of its workers live across the river in Bullhead. Also located in Bullhead—just a few miles from the bridge site—is a 160-acre parcel of land owned by Senator Harry Reid.[43]

So did Reid sponsor an amendment that would increase the value of his own land? Looks like the answer is yes.

In 2006, some local officials predicted that the construction of the new bridge would "undoubtedly hike land values in an already-booming commuter town, where speculators are snapping up undeveloped land for housing developments and other projects."[44] Of course, Rebecca Kirszner, Reid's communications director, insisted, "Sen. Reid's support for the bridge had absolutely nothing to do with property he owns." Of course. Construction on the bridge is expected to begin in 2010 and continue until 2013. Meanwhile, building continues in the town and a new "world-class" resort is planned.

Reid bought the property more than twenty years ago, paying $150,000 for one hundred acres; his friend Clair Haycock, the owner of Haycock Petroleum in Las Vegas, bought an additional sixty acres for $90,000. At one point in the 1990s, Reid and his partner sold the land for $1.3 million, but the buyer defaulted on the note and the land returned to the partners. Haycock sold his interest to Reid for $10,000 in 2002, even though the property was assessed at more than $2,000 an acre.[45]

So why didn't Haycock charge Reid $120,000 (sixty acres at $2,000 per acre)?

"The low price resulted from Haycock's need to sell and Reid's lack of interest in buying, the two men said."[46]

What's that supposed to mean? Presumably, if Hancock needed to sell, he needed the cash. But even if he did, why would he settle for less than 10 percent of his land's assessed value?

Years earlier, they'd been offered more than $1 million for the property. So the sale price makes no sense. Meanwhile, property prices began to jump after the bridge proposal. According to the *Los Angeles Times*, one California businessman bought property near the Reid property in 2006, "paying $240,000 for 37.52 acres, an average of $6,396 an acre."[47] Yet, strangely enough, Senator Reid has indicated a decrease, not an increase, in the value of the property. From 2001 to 2005, Reid disclosed that the property was worth $500,000 to $1,000,000. Then, in 2006, after the earmark for the bridge went into effect, he indicated that the entire 160-acre property was worth only $150,000. That same year, another nearby purchaser paid over $6,000 an acre. In 2007 and 2008, Reid valued the asset at $250,000 to 500,000.[48]

Is Reid's property the only one in town that's decreasing in value? Or has he failed to disclose the true value? And was the property a gift from his oil company pal?

Wishing You a Merry Christmas—with Campaign Funds

Although Reid is freehanded when he's doling out taxpayer funds, he can be quite the tightwad with his own money—even at Christmastime. When it came time to give out Christmas gifts to the service people who work at his luxurious condominium building in Washington, he apparently didn't want to dig into his own pockets. So he used a total of $3,300 of campaign contributions from his political action committee instead.

In 2002, Reid generously gave $600 in Christmas gifts to the help. In 2004, he gave $1,200. And in 2005 he gave $1,500. This money all came from campaign funds and it was all given "to an entity listed as the REC Employee Holiday Fund. His campaign listed the expenses as campaign 'salary' for two of the years and as a 'contribution' one year."[49] But for the tenacity of the astute John Solomon of the Associated Press, Reid would have gotten away with it. Once the gifts were disclosed, Reid's office suddenly claimed that listing the gifts as salary was a "clerical error" and that his lawyers approved the use of campaign money for the residential fund. "I am reimbursing the campaign from my own pocket to prevent this issue from being used in the current campaign season to deflect attention from Republican failures," he said.[50]

Hey, Harry, it wasn't Republicans who dug into campaign funds to pay your personal expenses. It was you. Reid actually tried to suggest that the money was related to his professional work because of the extra security he required.

Hey, Harry, do you really think cleaning floors and operating elevators qualifies as "security work"? Do you really think "distracting from Republican failures" is why the press raises these kinds of questions about the way you run your office?

Hey, Harry—you're a cheapskate and a fraud. Go back to Nevada.

Free Tickets to Professional Boxing Matches

Harry had yet another ethical problem: He accepted free tickets to three professional boxing matches from the Nevada State Athletic Commission while they were trying to persuade him not to pass legislation that would create a federal boxing commission.

Senate rules explicitly prohibit the acceptance of any gift that might appear to be an attempt to influence any official action by a senator. But that didn't bother Senator Reid. He took the free tickets anyway. He claimed it would help him do his job and that he wouldn't be influenced. Sure, Harry. We'll take your word for it.

Two other senators, who don't share Reid's ethical tin ears, didn't agree: Senator John McCain joined Reid at a championship match, but paid $1,400 for the tickets. At another match, Nevada's other senator attended, but recused himself from any votes on the boxing matter.

Only Reid took the valuable free tickets. And only Reid saw no problem with it.

The Land Grab: One More Ethical Issue

In 2004, Reid received a windfall profit of $1.1 million from the sale of Nevada property he hadn't personally owned for at least three years before the sale. Reid and his wife bought the property for $400,000 in 1998, but they sold it in 2001 for the same price. When Reid submitted his financial disclosure form to the Senate for that year, he failed to divulge the transfer of the property to a limited liability company he owned with a friend, Jay Brown, a former casino lawyer "whose name [has] surfaced in a major political bribery trial . . . and in organized crime investigations," according to USA Today.[51]

In 2004, after a change in zoning, Brown sold the land—and Reid made $1.1 million.

After John Solomon reported the 2001 transaction, Reid suddenly amended his 2001 disclosure form to reflect the sale.

Although Reid claimed he was a part owner of the limited liability corporation, public records don't list him as a shareholder.

Must have been another clerical error.

It's nice to triple your money on an investment.

So why didn't Reid disclose it?

Note: Brown is a longtime contributor to Reid, contributing $9,800 to his campaign and $20,000 to his PAC, the Reid Victory Fund, in 2009.[52] Brown was also a law partner with Reid's son-in-law, Steven Barringer: His firm was formerly known as Singer, Brown, & Barringer.

Reinventing Himself as a Civil Rights Leader

In January 2010, Reid was embarrassed by the disclosure of a private conversation in which he had referred to President Obama as "a light-skinned" black man whose absence of any "Negro dialect" enabled him to take a chance and run for president.

Some African Americans weren't too happy with his comments. Several weeks later, Reid seemed anxious to show just how supportive of African Americans he actually was. In an essay published on his website, Reid took credit for the integration of Las Vegas: "I worked hard during my time in local politics in Nevada to integrate the Las Vegas strip [sic] and the gaming industry."[53] But some civil rights leaders—who actually were involved in the process—don't remember seeing Reid. As Steve Friss points out in an article on aol.com:

> Joe Neal, a former Democratic state senator who was a key figure in the civil rights movement in Nevada, was baffled by the claim. For one thing, Reid was only 20 when a famous 1960 meeting between casino owners, progressive government officials and NAACP leaders resulted in an accord to integrate Las Vegas casinos for customers.
>
> The Nevada Legislature passed a civil rights act in 1965, but Reid did not become a member of that body until his 1966 election as an assemblyman. And a federal court decree in 1971 that set quotas for the hiring of minority casino workers was negotiated by the U.S. Department of Justice and handed down just months after he was sworn in as lieutenant governor.[54]

He's not the only one who didn't remember Reid as a civil rights leader. Reid himself made no mention of it in his memoir, *The Good Fight*.

Harry Reid, your Nevada home is yearning to call you back.

Blanche Lincoln: Arkansas, the 60th Vote for Obamacare!

Democratic Party Loyalty in Voting: 87.4 percent[55]
Wealth Ranking: 65/100[56]
Earmark Ranking: 26/100[57]
In fiscal 2009, Lincoln procured 115 earmarks for a total of
$222,902,125.

Notable Votes

- Blanche Lincoln opposed a bill to repeal automatic pay raises for members of Congress.

- She voted to allow terrorists involved in 9/11 to be tried in U.S. district courts, instead of in military tribunals.

- She voted against a bill to establish a national usury rate to prevent credit card companies from charging cardholders exorbitant interest rates.

- She voted with the banks against an amendment by Senator Dick Durbin (D-IL) to give troubled homeowners the ability to renegotiate their mortgage terms with the protection of the bankruptcy court.

- She voted for Obama's health-care reform package.

Arkansas senator Blanche Lincoln is one of the most vulnerable Democrats in the Senate. She should be defeated in the 2010 congressional election.

Don't be fooled by her claim to be a moderate who considers each issue on its merits. She's a puppet of the Senate leadership. When Harry Reid calls, she does what she's told. Like many of her colleagues, Lincoln has become a consummate Washington insider. She's spent her entire adult life and career in Washington—working first in Congress, then as a lobbyist, then as a congresswoman, and finally as a senator. She's never done anything else. And it shows. She's the darling of agribusiness, health-care professionals, TV and utility companies, banks and investment companies: They provide major bucks for her campaign and she doesn't disappoint them.

Industry Favorite

Of all of the members of Congress and all their likely challengers this year, Blanche Lincoln is the number-one recipient of campaign contributions from a wide variety of food and agribusiness companies. That's no small feat! She's also the number-two recipient from health-care professionals and TV and radio stations, and the number-three recipient from telephone utilities. The chart below reflects her prominent ranking as a recipient of campaign cash from each of these special interests.

BLANCHE LINCOLN'S RANKING AMONG SPECIAL INTEREST DONATION RECIPIENTS (BY INDUSTRY, FOR THE 2009–2010 ELECTION CYCLE)

Agricultural Services (#1)

Crop Production (#1)

Dairy (#1)

Food and Beverage (#1)

Food Process/Sales (#1)

Food Stores (#1)

Forest Products (#1)

Meat Processing and Products (#1)

Oil and Gas (#1)

Poultry and Eggs (#1)

Railroads (#1)

Restaurants and Drinking Establishments (#1)

Retail Sales (#1)

Sugar Cane and Sugar Beets (#1)

Commercial TV and Radio Stations (#2)

Health Professionals (#2)

Medical Supplies Manufacturing and Sales (#2)

Telephone Utilities (#3)

Source: Center for Responsive Politics[58]

After graduating from college in 1982, Blanche Lincoln moved to Washington when then Arkansas representative Bill Alexander hired her as a staff assistant. She returned the favor by running against him and defeating him in 1992 once he became enmeshed in the House banking scandal. She was easily reelected in 1994.

But she's worked for the special interests too. Between the end of her two-year stint as a congressional staffer and her first run for Congress, she spent years working as a lobbyist for the Dutko Group, one of the top ten lobbyist firms that caters to special interests in Washington. These folks represent the big boys in town—large corporations, foreign governments, and other interests. She made a few friends there who have doubtless been helpful along the way. Lincoln was elected to the Senate in 1998 after Senator Dale Bumpers (D-AR) retired; she was reelected handily in 2004. But now she's in serious trouble. Her ratings are terrible; she's running behind all her potential opponents.

Arkansans have good reason to question whether they want to send her back to Washington. Arkansas is one of the poorest states in the union, ranking 46th in per capita income—a step up in ranking (from 47th) for the first time in fifty years.[59] Despite that leap, it appears that Lincoln holds one standard for herself and another for her constituents. She's strongly in favor of the automatic annual cost-of-living pay raise given to members of Congress. But while she has no problem with spending taxpayer money, she's not nearly as generous to others as she is to herself—even when it comes to those who are especially needy. She's always there for big agribusiness, but when it comes to protecting consumers Blanche Lincoln is AWOL. We urgently need a national usury limit to stop credit card companies from charging unconscionable rates—some as high as 40 percent. There used to be state usury limits, but, as we noted in our book *Outrage*, these laws were invalidated when the Supreme Court ruled that the residence of the card issuer, not the consumer, determines which state law is binding. Because South Dakota has no limits, all the credit card companies happily moved there.

So the need for a national limit is obvious. But Lincoln supported the banks and voted against it. Now, thanks to Lincoln, they can—and do— charge whatever they want. That was no big concern of Blanche's; she's hardly likely to have a credit card debt problem of her own. Yet that vote may come back to haunt her: There's no doubt that many people in Arkansas, like people all across the country, struggle to overcome oppressive credit card debt—and might just disagree with her decision to side with the banks over her constituents. And Lincoln came through for the banks again when she voted against a Byron Dorgan amendment to permit some troubled homeowners to renegotiate their mortgages under the protection of the bankruptcy court—the so-called "cramdown provision." That legislation would have prevented 1.6 million foreclosures[60]—but Lincoln wasn't interested.

Maybe no one told her about the problems in her home state. In Arkansas, according to RealtyTrac, foreclosures reached 1,892 in October 2009—touching one of every six hundred and forty homes. Certain counties—Benton, Washington, Pulaski, Saline, and Sebastian—reported foreclosures on one of every one hundred seventy-five homes![61] Someone needs to clue Lincoln in on what's going on in her home state.

Lincoln may not believe we need a national usury rate, but she does think we should spend federal money on something else: teaching "financial literacy." She's supporting an amendment to provide millions of dollars for a *government* program to help teach *citizens* how to handle their own money. (This is not a joke!)

According to Politico.com, "The funding is part of a broader $375 million program aimed at promoting responsible lifestyles—a five-year plan to fund state efforts to educate adolescents on abstinence, contraception and other 'adult preparation subjects' such as healthy relationships, increased child-parent communication and 'financial literacy.'"[62]

Is she kidding? The federal government, which is $12 trillion in debt, is going to teach teenagers how to handle money? Maybe they'll bring the banks in to guest-lecture.

Lincoln defended the bill: "Financial literacy is one of the biggest problems we have in this country. Look at what happened in our stock markets, look at what happened in our economy with mortgages; people are indebting themselves into something more than what they can afford."[63] (If Lincoln had backed a federal usury law, perhaps it would have been more affordable.)

Blanche Lincoln has been in Washington for too long. It's time to send her back to Arkansas to see what the real world is all about. What it's *not* about is ignoring the needs of your constituents, or following the Democratic leadership like a robot when they demand it—but that's just what Lincoln does. Throughout the health-care debate, she's been in the glare of the media spotlight. Because the leadership needed every Democratic vote, her vote for the bill was decisive. In the past she's been a moderate. But when her vote is urgently needed—as it was in the critical vote to bring the health-care debate to the Senate floor—she votes solidly with the liberal Democrats. Her's was one of the key votes that paved the way for the health-care reform legislation to reach the floor of the Senate. The Democrats needed her and she came through with flying colors. As noted above, she has voted with her party leaders on 87.4 percent of the floor votes—a bit lower than most of the other Democratic sheep but still way too high to warrant reelection.

Still, from time to time—especially as the 2010 election draws near—Majority Leader Harry Reid, mindful of Lincoln's difficult position in Arkansas, has given her a pass when he knows he already has enough Republican votes to pass a controversial bill. That sometimes means Lincoln votes two different ways on the same piece of legislation: first against a bill, and then—when her vote is not actually needed—the opposite way.

Sound crazy? Well, that's exactly what happened during a December 5, 2009, vote to cut $42 million from home health-care benefits under Medicare. This was no matter of principle—it was pure, blind ambition. (With perhaps a dash of helping-out-her-contributors thrown in.) Once Lincoln changes her vote, it allows her to tell the folks back home that she's fighting for the elderly—and she takes that message and runs with it. Her website features boasts like "Lincoln: I Will Not Support Reform That Hurts America's Seniors."[64] That is, unless the leadership wants her to!

Of course, she never tells the folks at home about the vote she cast against them. Why confuse them? (For a video documenting Lincoln's unabashed flip-flop, go to http://trueslant.com/williamdupray/2009/12/05/blanche-lincoln-busted-on-a-cya-vote-on-medicare/. There you'll see her cast a vote supporting Harry Reid's move to cut health care for seniors . . . only to turn around and vote against the cuts—a position that would be more popular with her Arkansas constituents—after it became obvious that her vote wouldn't make a difference.) And that's not the only time Lincoln has flip-flopped. Although she righteously proclaimed that she would not support a final health-care bill with a public option when she voted to allow debate to begin, Lincoln obviously hadn't consulted her own website—which makes clear that she *did* in fact support a public option:

> [Health-care reform] . . . should include private plans as well as a quality, affordable public plan or non-profit plan that can accomplish the same goals as a public plan.[65]

According to the *New York Observer*, Lincoln also published an op-ed piece in an Arkansas newspaper in July 2009, using the same language in praise of a public option.

But then she did an abrupt about-face:

> For some in my caucus, when they talk about a public option, they're talking about another entitlement program, and we can't afford that right now as a nation. . . . I would not support a solely government-funded public option. We can't afford that.[66]

So which one is it? Is Lincoln for a public option? Or is she against it? Apparently, it depends on what the leadership tells her to do—or perhaps, what her health-care industry donors tell her.

Ultimately, of course, Lincoln followed her fellow Democrats and voted in support of the health-care reform bill. She may claim to be a moderate, but, in the end, she's whatever Harry Reid needs her to be. And one thing he doesn't need is a moderate. She can't be relied on to vote as a moderate, so don't send her back.

At this writing, with Election Day growing closer, Lincoln appears to be trying another metamorphosis: this time into a populist. After accepting more than $500,000 in campaign funds from the insurance industry in recent years, she's suddenly seen the light. Lincoln sponsored an amendment to prohibit any insurance company executive from receiving compensation higher than the salary of the president of the United States. Republicans opposed the bill, calling Lincoln a phony and calling on her to donate the $500,000 she accepted from the industry to charity.[67] She respectfully declined. The health-care industry has been very generous to Senator Lincoln, making her the single largest recipient of their contributions in the past five years:

DONATIONS BY TOP FIVE INDUSTRIES TO SENATOR BLANCHE LINCOLN'S CAMPAIGN COMMITTEE AND LEADERSHIP PAC, 2005–2010

Industry	Total	Individuals	PACs
Health Professionals	$483,250	$146,500	$336,750
Lawyers/Law Firms	$429,009	$317,041	$111,968
Securities and Investment	$328,850	$182,550	$146,300
Crop Production and Basic Processing	$285,325	$145,825	$139,500
Oil and Gas	$270,650	$125,050	$145,600

Source: Center for Responsive Politics[68]

Now Lincoln is chair of the Senate Agriculture Committee, which has been generous to her native state. Of course, given the campaign contributions Lincoln has accepted, that's no surprise—as this index of contributions reveals:

CONTRIBUTIONS TO BLANCHE LINCOLN'S 2010 ELECTION CAMPAIGN

By Both PACs and Individuals (as of December 2009)

Sector	Total	Individuals	PACs
Agribusiness	$666,546	$209,725	$456,821
Communications/Electronics	$346,020	$95,800	$250,220
Construction	$139,750	$57,400	$82,350
Defense	$29,250	$0	$29,250
Energy and Natural Resources	$375,581	$53,500	$322,081
Finance, Insurance and Real Estate	$982,290	$420,395	$561,895
Health	$878,068	$227,825	$650,243
Lawyers and Lobbyists	$667,633	$553,885	$113,748
Transportation	$205,693	$52,735	$152,958
Misc. Business	$629,562	$246,310	$383,252
Labor	$282,800	$2,000	$280,800
Ideological/Single-Issue	$440,220	$129,490	$310,730
Other	$298,105	$287,105	$11,000

Source: Center for Responsive Politics, OpenSecrets.org[69]

Apparently, there are some big expenditures Blanche Lincoln thinks we definitely *can* afford—notably subsidies for a handful of big farmers and agribusinesses back in Arkansas.

As *The Hill* noted, "back home in Phillips County, Ark., for example, where her family owns considerable acreage in rice and soybeans, big farmers have cashed U.S. government checks totaling more than $300 million over the past 10 years."[70]

Although Arkansas has fewer than three million people, it ranked seventh in farm subsidies from 1996 to 2006, receiving almost $8 billion. During that same period, California, with fifteen times the population, got slightly more than $6 billion.[71]

Lincoln has described herself as a "farmer's daughter."[72] She's certainly the big farmers' friend. But she's no buddy to small landowners without much money to donate. The big farmers will undoubtedly work hard to keep their favorite daughter and favorite benefactor as chair.

But the rest of Arkansas needs a voice, too.

Arkansans, it's time to call Blanche Lincoln home.

Barbara Boxer: The California Dreamer

Democratic Party Loyalty in Voting: 97.2 percent[73]
Wealth Ranking: 42/100[74]
Earmark Ranking: 34/100[75]
Thirty requests for $184,577,021

The California race against Barbara Boxer could give Republicans the key win they need to take control of the Senate.

At this writing, three Republicans are vying for the nomination to oppose Boxer: former Hewlett-Packard CEO Carly Fiorina, State Assemblyman Chuck Devore, and former congressman Tom Campbell. As the election gets closer, Boxer, a third-term senator, is losing support and is facing a serious decline in her popularity. She doesn't wear well. Even some hard-core Democrats must be uncomfortable about her failure to police ethics violations, her repeated use of campaign funds to pay her son, her numerous freebie trips for herself and her husband, her frequent gaffes, and her overall ineffectiveness.

To put it bluntly, Boxer is a loudmouthed, self-important, liberal ditz who should no longer be inflicted on the Congress or the American people. As the chair of the Senate Ethics Committee, she's ignored serious complaints and whitewashed everything that comes before her. If she has one good quality, it's that, as chair of the Senate Environment Committee, she's been completely ineffective.

Let's hope she stays that way—until she has to pack her things and head home.

Chair of the Do-Nothing Ethics Committee

In its mandatory year-end report, the Senate Select Committee on Ethics disclosed that it had received ninety-nine complaints of alleged violations of Senate rules in 2009; in addition, it carried over an additional twenty-six complaints from the previous year.[76] Yet, in response to these 125 separate allegations, Boxer's committee issued only *one* letter of admonition and not a single disciplinary sanction.

Wow. Those Washington types must be a pretty honest bunch. The ethics committee certainly does a good job of protecting senators; there's virtually no danger that any of them would incur a serious reprimand—whatever their conduct—as long as Boxer is in charge. The committee's proceedings are all conducted in secret, so the voters have no way of evaluating whether her dismissals have, in fact, been warranted. But, even so, it's inconceivable that only one complaint out of the one hundred twenty processed last year deserved a rebuke.

And it's interesting to note that the single disciplinary action taken by the committee was to send a "qualified disciplinary letter" to the infamous Senator Roland Burris of Illinois, who filled the Senate seat vacated by President Obama. Don't get us wrong: Burris deserved the admonition, and much more besides. But it's telling that the one figure Boxer's committee scolded was a senator who was never elected to office, and who cannot claim the bona fide insider status that would guarantee him the protection of the Senate club. Moreover, in Burris's case, the committee had virtually no choice. The evidence against him was incontrovertible: He was accused of lying in sworn testimony when he denied that he had neither discussed his interest in the Senate seat nor raised campaign contributions for indicted former Illinois governor Rod Blagojevich. There was no question that he did, in fact, raise money for the governor and seek the appointment—as he himself admitted when he amended his testimony to contradict his previous denials. By then, of course, the FBI had caught him on tape discussing all of this with the governor's brother. So there wasn't much to investigate. And yet, despite the clear evidence that Burris had lied and acted inappropriately, Boxer's committee did virtually nothing about it, applying only the lowest possible level of censure against him. Here's an excerpt from their tepid letter of admonition:

The Committee found that you should have known that you were providing incorrect, inconsistent, misleading, or incomplete information
to the public, the Senate, and those conducting legitimate inquiries into
your appointment to the Senate. The Committee also found that your November 13, 2008, call with [Gov. Rod] Blagojevich was inappropriate. . . .
When [he] called you, [he] was explicit about the purpose of his call:
to raise campaign funds for his brother. Yet, during this conversation
in which you appeared to agree to write a check and even potentially to
raise money for Governor Blagojevich, you repeatedly brought up your
desire to seek the Senate seat. You also implied that the people you might
raise the money from would be unhappy if you did not receive the appointment. The committee finds that this conversation was inappropriate
in its content and implications.[77]

Inappropriate? Isn't seeking a quid pro quo more than just inappropriate?
But, Barbara Boxer's committee concluded that Burris's conduct didn't rise
(or sink) to any more reprehensible level. Justice is supposed to be blind,
but Boxer and her colleagues are truly blind to justice: Even with clear evidence that Burris had lied in his testimony, they still gave him less than a
slap on the wrist—and that was more than they'd given anyone else.

Indeed, Boxer's ethics committee investigated only thirteen of the 125
complaints it has received—and dismissed eight. One letter was sent to
Burris; four investigations are apparently outstanding. The committee
dismissed complaints against senators Chris Dodd (D-CT) and Kent Conrad (D-ND) based on their VIP mortgages from Countrywide Financial.
No documents were released to support the finding of dismissal or to in-
spire confidence in the process or the results of the so-called investigation.
Under Boxer's leadership, the ethics committee has been completely use-
less. And this charade of ethical justice is likely to continue until there is an
independent agency to prosecute members of Congress. In 2007, Senator
Joe Lieberman (I-CT) introduced a bill to create an independent Office of
Public Integrity to police lobbying violations. The measure failed. Not sur-
prisingly, Boxer voted against it. The same kind of agency is needed to police Congress and its staff. (Nancy Pelosi has been equally AWOL on ethics
issues. When Congressman William Jefferson was caught with $100,000 in
cash in his freezer, Pelosi did nothing about it.)

All in the Family

But it may be that Barbara Boxer is just plain tone-deaf when it comes to ethical issues. Her own conduct speaks for itself: She actually paid her son $130,000 from her political action committee to run her PAC.[78] Apparently, it never occurred to her that such behavior might look a little like nepotism—or like she was using campaign funds to enrich her own family.

Boxer didn't stop this nefarious practice until 2007, when the Senate passed a rule prohibiting PACs and campaigns from paying spouses or immediate family members of the candidate. Boxer did not support the amendment and voted "Present." No more windfalls for the Boxers.

How the Boxers Travel the World—for Free

Boxer and her husband, Stewart, have taken luxurious, all-expenses-paid trips to Florence, Italy; San Juan, Puerto Rico; Grand Cayman; Dublin, Ireland; Barcelona, Spain; Banff, Canada; and Punta Mita, Mexico (four times), all as guests of the Aspen Institute. While not illegal, these trips are just another perk of the growing Imperial Congress, whose members believe they're entitled to royal treatment simply by virtue of being elected.

Why should Boxer—or any member of Congress—receive hundreds of thousands of dollars of free, tax-exempt trips to fabulous resorts? They shouldn't. Candidates should take a pledge to turn down these invitations. And senators who don't should be sent packing.

Boxer: Queen of the Faux Pas

Boxer has developed a well-deserved reputation as a flake, based on numerous inane comments she has made on the Senate floor and in committees. In one recent blunder, during a debate on an amendment sponsored by Senator Ben Nelson (D-NE) to prohibit federal funding of abortion, she left many scratching their heads in wonder:

> The men who have brought us this don't single out a procedure that's health care and say they have to get a special rider. There's nothing in this amendment that says if a man some day wants to buy Viagra, for exam-

ple, that his pharmaceutical coverage cannot cover it, that he has to buy a rider. I wouldn't support that. And they shouldn't support going after a woman using her own private funds for her reproductive health care. Is it fair to say to a man, You're going to have to buy a rider to buy Viagra, and this will be public information that could be accessed? No, I don't support that. I support a man's privacy, just as I support a woman's privacy.[79]

Equating access to abortion records with access to information about the purchase of Viagra? No wonder she isn't taken seriously.

And the polls make it clear that voters are catching on to her poor performance.

BARBARA SLIPPING . . . .

	BOXER	FIORINA
November 2009	46	37
January 2010	46	43

Source: Rasmussen Reports[80]

And there was more bad news for Boxer: More than a third of the voters have an unfavorable view of her. This is yet another place where California voters don't see eye to eye: The senator seems to have a very high opinion of herself. Though she's not especially well-known in Washington for either her intellect or her astute legislative skills, the ultra-liberal Boxer recently compared herself to the late Senator Ted Kennedy, an undisputed master of the Senate for over forty years. Deflecting criticisms about her lack of accomplishments as chair of the Senate Committee on Energy and Public Works, Boxer made the comment to reporters as she lamented the uphill battle she faced in trying to pass a bill on climate control:

Take Senator Kennedy, he tried to get health care reform done for his whole life. Was he a failure as a senator? He was a brilliant senator, one of the greatest of all time.[81]

Apparently, Boxer's failure to pass climate legislation—pending in the committee that she chairs—puts her in a league with the greats.

But many of her colleagues don't agree with her glowing personal assessment. Some are worried that "she's not up to the task" [82] of chairing the committee that has jurisdiction over all environmental bills. After all, that position puts Barbara Boxer in charge of Obama's benighted cap-and-trade bill.

Just another reason to hope she keeps up her ineffective streak.

One trait Boxer definitely didn't pick up from Ted Kennedy is the ability to cross the aisle, befriending Republicans and charming them into joining her causes. Quite the opposite: To put it bluntly, she's divisive, argumentative, and drives people crazy. According to Politico.com, "In private conversations, Senate staffers say that Boxer's abrasive personal style helped tank the climate bill that Sen. Joe Lieberman (I-Conn.) and former Sen. John Warner (R-Va.) sponsored last year." [83] She's never conciliatory—that's not her style—and apparently did little to convince her fellow senators to support the bill last year other than making righteous moral proclamations about the issue. That didn't fly; the bill went nowhere, and environmentalists weren't happy. "People don't look at her as the person who's going to make a deal and bring both sides to the table. Her way is the only way." [84]

And, by the way, her way includes reminding you constantly that she's a senator—not just a regular person. At all times, one must be sure to address her as *Senator* Boxer. She'll bite your head off if you don't.

One man who made that unfortunate mistake was Brigadier General Michael Walsh, of the U.S. Army Corps of Engineers. While testifying about efforts to restore the Louisiana coast after Katrina, Walsh called Boxer "ma'am," obviously following military protocol. This triggered the following exchange:

SEN. BOXER: You know, do me a favor, could you say "senator" instead of "ma'am"?

BRIG. GEN. WALSH: Yes, ma'am.

SEN. BOXER: It's just a thing—I worked so hard to get that title, so I'd appreciate it, yes, thank you.

BRIG. GEN. WALSH: Yes, senator. [85]

Walsh was simply showing the respect he would use when addressing anyone higher than himself in the chain of command.

But that was an insult to the senator from California.

Yet when it comes to insulting other people, Senator Boxer doesn't hold back. She shows no elegance, no professional demeanor, no politeness. One person who was on the receiving end of Boxer's biting sarcasm was Secretary of State Condoleezza Rice.

During a 2007 appearance before the Senate Foreign Relations Committee, Rice was attacked repeatedly by Boxer. First Boxer attacked the secretary's integrity, suggesting that her allegiance to President Bush and her support for the Iraq War had "overwhelmed [her] respect for the truth."[86]

But that wasn't enough. In a truly nutty exchange, Boxer went a step further, actually criticizing Rice for being childless: "Who pays the price" for the war, Boxer asked. "I'm not going to pay a personal price. My kids are too old, and my grandchild is too young. [And] *you're not going to pay a particular price, as I understand it, with an immediate family*" (emphasis added).[87]

The late Tony Snow, then serving as press secretary to President Bush, responded with incredulity to Boxer's comments: "I don't know if she was intentionally that tacky, but I do think it's outrageous. Here you['ve] got a professional woman, Secretary of State Condoleezza Rice, and Barbara Boxer is sort of throwing little jabs because Condi doesn't have children, as if that means that she doesn't understand the concerns of parents. Great leap backward for feminism."[88]

Well put, Tony.

Barbara Boxer's history of such spectacles has long since worn thin. And winning her seat in the Senate could well give the Republicans the margin they need to take back control of the Senate from Reid and Obama. It's the good fortune of the GOP—and the misfortune of the Democrats—that their majority hangs on such a flawed senator.

Kirsten Gillibrand: A Chameleon in Plaid[89]

Democratic Party Loyalty in Voting 97.2 percent[90]
Wealth Ranking: 55/100[91]
Earmark Ranking (In House): 127/435[92]
Twenty-five earmarks totaling $36,829,068 in fiscal year 2009

Kirsten Gillibrand, New York's junior senator, is living proof that the term "moderate Democrat" has been reduced to an anachronism. Gillibrand began her congressional career in 2007 as an independent-thinking centrist, but quickly morphed into a left-wing puppet of the Democratic leadership when she was appointed to the Senate in 2009 to fill Hillary Clinton's vacant seat.

Now Chuck Schumer does her thinking for her. And there's more: He raises her money, too. That's why she can't—and won't—say no to him. And that's why she, too, is no longer a moderate Democrat—rather, she's one of the most liberal members of the Senate. It's not just Schumer who calls the left-wing shots for Gillibrand. There's also Harry Reid, who "convinces" her to vote his way—without even making any of the huge payoffs he's given to other senators in return for their votes. No hundred-million-dollar medical schools for New York; no decrease in federal aid formulae. No, it looks like Gillibrand's liberal votes come pretty cheap. Why? Because she's desperate to keep her seat, desperate to avoid a primary, and desperate to keep any quality competition out of the race. Having been handed her Senate seat without an election, the last thing she wants is a challenge from a tough competitor. Her big strategy is to give the voters one choice: her. To do that, she needs the strong backing of the liberal Democratic establishment.

All of which explains her sudden conversion to hard-core liberalism.

Gillibrand Flip-Flops on Everything

Gillibrand's metamorphosis from the center to the left has been all too transparent. She hasn't even tried to cover up her ever-changing positions on gun control, immigration, and so on. No, she's proud of her growth and development. After all, she now represents all of New York State, not just a little congressional district along the Hudson. Doesn't that entitle her to do a complete turnaround on key issues? In her view, it makes complete sense.

But others suggest that her dramatic flip-flops point to a more fundamental lack of principle. The satirist H. L. Mencken once ridiculed FDR's character by saying: "If he became convinced tomorrow that coming out for cannibalism would get him the votes he so sorely needs, he would begin fattening a missionary in the White House backyard come Wednesday." [93]

He might have said the same thing of Gillibrand, if he had deigned to recognize her at all.

Gillibrand used to irritate liberals. On the day she was appointed to the Senate, New York mayor Michael Bloomberg attacked her opposition to gun control: "She has actively opposed the efforts of New York City, and cities around the state and nation, to enact common-sense measures that keep illegal guns out of the hands of criminals. . . . For instance, she has voted to keep critical data needed to track illegal gun traffickers from law enforcement, has voted to tie the hands of the ATF, and has also voted to protect dealers who sell guns illegally."[94]

But all that changed when Hillary's seat opened up, and she shamelessly promoted herself as a candidate to fill it. Within days Gillibrand's raw ambition had trumped her stated principles, and she began flipping and flopping wildly on all kinds of critical issues. As a new senator, Gillibrand was transformed from a rabid opponent of gun control—with a 100 percent rating from the National Rifle Association—to a cosponsor of gun control legislation. In 2007, she had sponsored a bill to delete background check information after twenty-four hours; now she suddenly voted to repeal her very own bill.

Now, she doesn't bother liberals at all. (Does she still keep two guns under her bed, as she claimed during the campaign? She hasn't said.)

But not everyone has fallen for her sudden conversion. Watching the former NRA darling announce that she would now sponsor a ban on assault weapons that she had earlier opposed, the *New York Post* noted:

> Gillibrand, formerly a single-term centrist congresswoman from a Republican-leaning Upstate district, is running as fast as possible from every position that used to separate her from the state's Democratic elite. . . . Those New Yorkers now getting their first good look at their new senator are entitled to wonder whether they can believe a word she says.[95]

Wayne Barrett of the *Village Voice* expressed even more cynicism on the subject:

> And speaking of targets, forget about guns. Gillibrand's 100 percent rating from the National Rifle Association occurred before she discovered that

there was gun violence in New York City, where she lived for a decade. The guns she kept under her bed upstate were for hunting.[96]

Gillibrand's sudden reformation had backfired: Even as she tried desperately to remake herself as a classic liberal in the Harry Reid mold, the press in New York—both liberal and conservative—saw her transformation for what it was, a blatant case of pandering to the voters. Judging by the polls in New York, the voters seem to feel the same way.

And gun control isn't the only issue where Gillibrand has seen the light—or, should we say, felt the heat. There was also her head-spinning turnaround on immigration. As a congresswoman, Gillibrand had unfalteringly opposed immigration reform. But when numerous Hispanic groups suddenly threatened to run a primary against her, Gillibrand suddenly saw the merit in their polar-opposite positions and swiftly did a complete and amazing reversal.

According to the *New York Times*, Gillibrand had

> opposed any sort of amnesty for illegal immigrants, supported deputizing local law enforcement officers to enforce federal immigration laws, spoke out against Gov. Eliot Spitzer's proposal to allow illegal immigrants to have driver's licenses and sought to make English the official language of the United States. . . . [S]he sided in favor of bills that required adult occupants of affordable housing to provide proof of residency and that penalized cities that protected undocumented immigrants, such as New York. . . . She also diverged from the overwhelming majority of Democratic representatives by voting in favor of bills that increased financing for law enforcement against illegal immigrants and that protected businesses requiring their employees to speak English on the job. . . . She is a co-sponsor of the SAVE Act, widely disparaged by immigrant advocates, which aims to crack down on illegal immigration with more border guards and surveillance technology, accelerated deportations and a mandatory program requiring employers to verify the immigration status of employees.[97]

In other words, she was the pro-immigration lobby's worst nightmare.

But all of that changed, too. Just days into her tenure, after meeting with Latino and Chinese political leaders, she suddenly dropped her opposition to paths to citizenship and her support for English as a second language.[98] Not only did she promise to work with Obama on immigration reform, she even pledged to take the lead in Congress on immigration reform and change her position on sanctuary cities and other issues that were important to pro-immigration groups.[99] Several months later, Gillibrand cosponsored a bill to permit illegal immigrants to apply for in-state college tuition credits.[100]

She's done a complete U-turn.

Gillibrand's opposition to gay marriage went by the wayside on the night before her appointment was announced. Reported sources suggest that Governor Paterson told her to call the head of the Empire State Pride organization and tell him that she now supported gay marriage, which she had earlier strongly opposed—making her position even more liberal than Clinton's and Schumer's![101] No problem. She did as she was told.

That's what moderate Democrats do.

Before her appointment to the Senate, one gay rights group gave her the lowest rating of anyone in the New York delegation. But now she's the biggest advocate for gay rights in the state of New York. Not only has she embraced gay marriage, she's introduced a bill to amend the federal budget to prohibit the use of federal funds to enforce the Don't Ask, Don't Tell policy. The New York Times described her latest move as "an apparent effort to court a voting bloc in her home state."[102]

It's clear that Gillibrand will do whatever it takes to appeal to all of those liberal folks who are now her constituents in the next election—which could include a primary challenge. That's surely what her conversion is about: It's not that she's had a change of heart, it's just that she's had a change in core voters. "There's nothing that defines her other than ambition, which explains the flip-flops, which explains the politics being used to clear her path," said Larry Sabato, director of the Center for Politics at the University of Virginia. "I don't associate her with anything, other than trying to hold her seat."[103]

And Gillibrand's first-year record of flip-flopping and groveling hasn't exactly won over the electorate. In January 2010, roughly a year after her appointment, a statewide poll by the Marist Institute for Public Opinion found that only 31 percent of Democrats and 24 percent of registered voters approved of the job she was doing.[104]

Apparently the voters just aren't as dumb as she thinks they are.

When former congressman Harold Ford announced that he was contemplating a primary challenge in early 2010, Gillibrand fiercely attacked him, claiming that his positions made him "out of touch" with New Yorkers. Out of touch? Hey, Senator, what's the problem? Ford can always follow your lead and just change his positions! After all, that's what moderate Democrats do.

Gillibrand's done a few other things to show just how liberal she is. She was one of only seven senators who voted against cutting federal funds to ACORN, the community activist group that's been embroiled in scandal since the 2008 election brought it to public attention. And she accepted a speaking invitation to appear on a panel in New York with Van Jones, the former Obama administration green jobs czar who resigned from his position after it was disclosed that he had signed a petition asking whether Bush administration officials had deliberately staged the 9/11 tragedy as a pretext to start the Iraq War. Jones also used a vulgar term to describe Republicans in a speech. You can't get much more liberal than Jones. Since he left the White House, Jones has kept a low profile—but his appearance with Gillibrand will be a high-profile return to the public stage.

Kirsten Gillibrand, Former Top Lawyer for Philip Morris

But Gillibrand's flip-flopping isn't the only troubling part of her public record. There's much more. For one thing, she's rewritten her own history. Gillibrand has deliberately buried the pivotal role she chose to play in defending Philip Morris, the world's largest cigarette company, against charges of criminal perjury and fraud arising out company executives' implausible testimony to Congress. This was made easier because of one simple fact: In those days, before her marriage, she was known as Tina and/or Kirsten Rutnick. "Tina Rutnick" doesn't exist anymore—she's gone the way of Gillibrand's moderate positions. But Kirsten Gillibrand marches on, gamely waving the liberal flag, refusing to discuss her work as a tobacco lawyer with the media, and hoping you don't notice the trail of unsavory associations behind her.

Rutnick had her work cut out for her representing Big Tobacco. The big boys at Philip Morris claimed to have absolutely no knowledge of either the addictive or cancer-causing qualities of tobacco; they even swore as much before a congressional committee. Only one problem: Their own internal documents contradicted their claims, showing that they marketed cigarettes despite the fact they were addictive and caused cancer. And Rutnick's efforts as an attorney helped them to keep incriminating documents from the prosecutors.

Those nine years of Gillibrand's career have been completely whitewashed from her biography, replaced by an exaggerated tale of public service. Amazingly, her pro-tobacco work never surfaced in her two congressional races; it wasn't until after she was appointed to the Senate that the information was disclosed. According to the *New York Times*, "More than half of her legal career was spent at the New York firm of Davis, Polk, which defended Philip Morris against criminal fraud and perjury charges stemming from testimony by its executives before Congress. Gillibrand was a key player on the high-powered team of Big Tobacco lawyers that spent years trying to prevent the release of documents that showed that the top company executives unquestionably knew when they pushed cigarette use that nicotine was addictive, its dosages could be manipulated, and it caused cancer. She and the team also focused on preventing anti-tobacco lawyers from getting company documents, including research on nicotine." [105]

During her campaigns, however, Gillibrand made no mention of what she was doing during those nine years. Not a word. Part of Rutnick's role was to prevent the release of damaging data from a secret research lab set up by Philip Morris in Cologne, Germany, to conduct studies on the role of tobacco in causing cancer. Because the lab was outside the United States, its studies were intended to be beyond the reach of Congress and the U.S. courts. Rutnick traveled to Germany several times, interviewed key researchers, and prepared witnesses for eventual testimony. Rutnick also worked on a committee dedicated to claiming attorney-client privilege to prevent the anti-tobacco lawyers from getting the incriminating documents.

In a separate landmark tobacco case, U.S. District Court judge Gladys Kessler commented on the lab and "cited Philip Morris's use of the German lab as a way for the company to suppress evidence and scolded the company for concealing information from consumers and government

regulators."[106] When the information about her role in protecting the tobacco companies became public, Gillibrand tried to spin her way out of it,
falsely claiming she was just a young associate who had to take whatever
cases came her way. But she left out one inconvenient fact: At the time, the
unusual policy at Davis, Polk was that associates could refuse to work on
any case that caused them moral or ethical concerns. Apparently Rutnick
had none.

Rutnick also worked on a high-level committee dedicated to claiming
attorney-client privilege to prevent the anti-tobacco lawyers from getting
incriminating documents. But their strategy failed:

> The State of Minnesota objected to the companies' claim of attorney-
> client privilege, invoking what is known as the crime-fraud exception: es-
> sentially, an assertion that the privilege did not apply because the lawyers
> were being used to help the companies commit fraud. A Minnesota judge
> agreed, saying that Philip Morris had engaged in an "egregious attempt to
> hide information" and, in a major blow to the industry, eventually forced
> the release of some 30 million pages of documents from industry files.
>
> Philip Morris and the other companies subsequently settled the Min-
> nesota case for $6 billion in 1998.[107]

Apparently, the folks at Philip Morris are still happy with Rutnick/
Gillibrand. She's one of the largest recipients of tobacco money, receiving
over $28,000 in her campaigns. Yet when these contributions from her
former client first became public, she seriously claimed to be ignorant of
them. "I didn't know one way or the other that the company had contributed," she said. "We have 10,000 contributors right now. I don't know all
of them."[108]

Believe that and she'll tell you another.

She thinks we'll buy that the woman who was named the most effective
fund-raiser in her congressional class in 2007 had no idea that a company
she once represented as a lawyer had become one of her five top contributors?

TOP CAMPAIGN CONTRIBUTORS
TO KIRSTEN GILLIBRAND
2007–2008 ELECTION CYCLE

	Total	Individuals	PACS
Boies, Schiller & Flexner	$120,524	$120,524	$0
Davis, Polk & Wardwell	$84,000	$84,000	$0
EMILY's List	$41,825	$39,650	$2,175
ActBlue	$24,930	$24,930	$0
Altria Group (formerly known as Philip Morris)	$20,500	$16,500	$4,000

Source: Center for Responsive Politics; OpenSecrets.org. As the Center's website specifies, "The organizations themselves did not donate, rather the money came from the organization's PAC, its individual members or employees or owners, and those individuals' immediate families."

One of Gillibrand's largest contributors in the 2007–2008 cycle was Steve Parrish, the senior vice president for corporate affairs at Altria, the new happy-talk name for Philip Morris. Parrish, one of her old colleagues in the tobacco wars, had recently begun promoting the regulation of tobacco, a cause Altria adopted. Gillibrand has actually pointed to her vote on that measure as a sign that she's not helping out her old client. But the fact is that Philip Morris/Altria supported the measure so that it could bolster its domination of the market.[109] So her vote was in support of the Philip Morris position.

It's also worth noting that Gillibrand received more than $240,000 from her old employers at Davis, Polk. When she left Davis, Polk and went to David Boies's firm in New York, Altria followed her as a client. And the folks at Boies were very generous to Gillibrand, too—indeed, they became the most generous of all her contributors. Since she first ran for Congress in 2005, employees of the firm have given her more than $400,000:

TOP CAMPAIGN CONTRIBUTORS TO
KIRSTEN GILLIBRAND, 2005–2010

	Total	Individual	PACs
Boies, Schiller & Flexner	$424,434	$424,434	$0
Davis, Polk & Wardwell	$247,042	$247,042	$0
EMILY's List	$140,214	$131,699	$8,515
Simpson, Thacher & Bartlett	$60,650	$60,650	$0
ActBlue	$57,746	$57,746	$0

Source: Center for Responsive Politics, OpenSecrets.org

There's one more connection to the tobacco company: Gillibrand's father, Douglas Rutnick, is a lobbyist for Altria; in 2008, he was paid $75,000 to work for them in New York.[110] Mr. Rutnick also worked for Philip Morris in 2004 and 2005, helping them fight legislation designed to limit damages in tobacco lawsuits and to defeat further restrictions on smoking in restaurants.[111] Seven of Mr. Rutnick's thirteen lobbying clients have contributed to his daughter's campaign.

She probably didn't know about that, either.

And the more you look into Gillibrand's record, the more troubling signs appear. In the days before Christmas 2008, when New York governor David Paterson was considering appointing Gillibrand to fill Hillary's seat, her former boss, David Boies, and his son Christopher each made a $25,000 contribution to Paterson.[112] Gillibrand may also not have cut all her ties with Boies: on her 2005 disclosure form, she indicated that she was on an unpaid leave of absence from the firm and could return if she chose. How closely she keeps in touch with Boies is anyone's guess.

And who runs the Boies firm? None other than David Boies, who famously represented Al Gore in the 2000 election controversy, and who has recently joined former solicitor general Ted Olson in a movement to challenge California's Proposition 8 and legalize gay marriages. Maybe Gillibrand is listening to her old boss.

Gillibrand's Ever-Changing Biography

It's interesting to compare the content of Gillibrand's various campaign biographies. Just as her positions change, so do the facts about her fifteen-year legal career.

As noted, Gillibrand's law practice was initially dominated by her work for Philip Morris at Davis, Polk. Then, after a short stint with Andrew Cuomo at HUD, she joined Boies, Schiller & Flexner. But Gillibrand never disclosed anything about her work for Philip Morris when she ran for Congress and gave few details about her short tenure at HUD. Here's how she described herself in her original campaign literature:

> Throughout her career, Gillibrand has demonstrated her commitment to public service. During the Clinton Administration, she served as Special Counsel to the Secretary of Housing and Urban Development (HUD), Andrew Cuomo. Gillibrand played a key role in furthering HUD's Labor Initiative and its New Markets Initiative, working on strengthening Davis-Bacon Act enforcement and drafting new markets legislation for public and private investment in building infrastructure in lower income areas.[113]

"Commitment to public service"? Is she kidding? Was defending tobacco companies her way of defending the public welfare? Apparently not, because she never mentioned it.

And she's still writing it out of the history books. Her official Senate website now says:

> During the Clinton Administration, Senator Gillibrand served as Special Counsel to the United States Secretary of Housing and Urban Development (HUD) Andrew Cuomo. *She then worked as an attorney in New York City before becoming a Member of Congress* [emphasis added].[114]

No mention of what she did *before* she served in the Clinton administration (that is, defend Big Tobacco). And no explanation that she served at HUD for just over one year of that eight-year administration. The rest of the time she was busy helping Philip Morris protect its hide.

And, after mentioning specifics about her work in earlier versions of her biography, Gillibrand later removed some of the earlier descriptions of her assignments at the housing agency. Once the subprime mortgage crisis erupted, she no longer included one entry, about her work on "new-market initiatives."

What were these "new-market initiatives"? Here's what former senator Jon Corzine had to say about them in testimony at a Senate hearing in 2001:

> With the help of Congress and the Clinton administration, HUD has sought to restore its credibility by remaining singularly focused on improving services for the poor, low-income and working-class families, the disabled and senior citizens. *It has transformed itself by launching new-market initiatives; integrating lower-income communities into the free market and creating renewal initiatives that spur private sector investment in both urban and rural communities. HUD has also helped America reach its highest homeownership rate ever—67.7 percent—and in the process helped African-American and Latino households attain record levels of homeownership* [emphasis added].[115]

HUD's "new-market initiatives" required Fannie Mae and Freddie Mac to significantly increase the number of loans purchased involving low-income borrowers: Borrowers who couldn't exactly *afford* the mortgages they were being offered. Borrowers who were given subprime mortgages. Borrowers who are now facing foreclosure in droves.

Gillibrand has erased her role at HUD from her biography—hardly a surprise, given that it was during her tenure that many of the policies that led to the current mortgage crisis were actually implemented.

As the *Wall Street Journal* noted:

> Along those lines, the Web site of the Department of Housing and Urban Development has an interesting item in its Archives section. Entitled "Highlights of HUD Accomplishments 1997–1999," the document chronicles the "accomplishments under the leadership of Secretary Andrew Cuomo, who took office in January 1997 . . ."
>
> Secretary Cuomo established new Affordable Housing Goals requiring Fannie Mae and Freddie Mac—two government-sponsored enterprises involved in housing finance—to buy $2.4 trillion in mortgages in the next

10 years. This will mean new affordable housing for about 28.1 million low- and moderate-income families. The historic action raised the required percentage of mortgage loans for low- and moderate-income families that the companies must buy from the current 42 percent of their total purchases to a new high of 50 percent—a 19 percent increase—in the year 2001.[116]

Gillibrand was a special assistant to Cuomo when these policies and regulations went into effect. Wayne Barrett of the *Village Voice* accuses Cuomo of making a series of decisions that "gave birth to the mortgage crisis" and resulted in three to four million people facing foreclosure.[117] And many commentators believe that the subprime mortgage crisis fueled the global financial crisis that began in late 2008.

But Gillibrand's responsibilities and experience at HUD during this critical time have disappeared from her résumé—just like her tobacco work.

Her latest description of her law career leaves out her New York City legal portfolio altogether. Now she was basically a pro bono lawyer offering "free representation":

As an attorney for 15 years, Kirsten worked on a wide range of legal and policy-related issues, often providing free legal representation to people who could not otherwise afford it.[118]

How nice.

The Gillibrand Family Finances: Betting on the Failure of Banks and Home Markets

Gillibrand's family finances are another issue. Since she was elected to Congress, her family's net worth has tripled—even as her salary decreased by 75 percent and her husband, Jonathan Gillibrand, made almost nothing each year. Although he is described as an adviser on venture capital, her husband is no tycoon. According to tax returns made public, his total business income for the years 2005, 2006, and 2007 was about $45,000—an average of about $15,000 per year.[119] Yet, during that same time period, their net worth increased from a low of $241,016 in 2006 to a low of $970,010 in 2008, with the high end increasing from $849,999 to $2,151,000.

Not bad. How'd you do during the same period?

NET WORTH OF THE GILLIBRAND FAMILY

	2006 (elected 11/06)	2008
low range	$241,016	$970,010
high range	$849,999	$2,151,000

(Data for 2009 will not be available until May 2010.)[120]
Source: Senate disclosure form at OpenSecrets.org

These assessments of net worth do not include personal residences or their contents. Even here there are small mysteries waiting to be unraveled: According to her 2007 tax returns, the Gillibrands took a $240 loss on "rental income." Yet no rental property has ever been disclosed as an asset.

Gillibrand Family Income

In February 2009, Gillibrand made copies of her 2005, 2006, and 2007 (2008 was not yet due) state and federal tax returns available for reporters to view, but not copy, for a three-hour period. Based on reports on the specifics of the tax documents and other publicly available data, the Gillibrand family income was as follows:

	2005	2006	2007	2008
TOTAL	$532,411**	$148,551	$198,163	$132,107+
HUSBAND*	20,390	11,402	13,755	unknown
CAPITAL GAIN/LOSS	–3,000	+48,535	+40,255	unknown
INTEREST	2,795	2,889	11,597	unknown
DIVIDENDS	2,460	2,328	1,331	unknown

Source: Center for Responsive Politics (OpenSecrets.org) and http://blog.timesunion.com/capitol/archives/11277/money-money-money
*Jonathan Gillibrand's business income
**Includes $509,269 earned by Kirsten Gillibrand at Boies, Schiller & Flexner

How did this family manage that amazing feat in the most troubled economy since the Great Depression? Our maddening disclosure laws make it hard to tell exactly where their good fortune came from. But one thing we do know: While she was in Congress and as the subprime mortgage crisis unfolded, Gillibrand's husband, Jonathan Gillibrand, invested in numerous banks and financial companies that were doomed to failure.

The Gillibrands Bet Against the Banks and Housing Markets

Jonathan Gillibrand's forte is evidently "puts"—options to buy or sell a stock in the future at a lower price.

As the Forbes website Investopedia.com explains:

> if a person purchases one March $10 put option on Ford Motor Co., it gives him the right to sell 100 shares of Ford at $10 before the expiration date in March. . . . If [a person] already holds 100 shares of Ford, his broker will simply sell these shares at the $10 price. . . . if, after the purchase the *put* shares fall to $5, he would still be able to sell 100 shares at $10 ($1,000) instead of the $500 ($5 x 100) for which he could currently sell the shares in the market. This transaction would represent an economic gain of $500.[121]

So, basically, by buying a put option, you are hoping that the price of a certain stock will drop below the price designated in the put. The more it drops, the more you make.

Based on financial disclosure statements, put options are a preferred form of investment in the Gillibrand family.

In 2007, as subprime lenders like Countrywide, IndyMac, Downey Financial, Bank United Financial, and Accredited Home Lenders began to tank, Mr. Gillibrand purchased puts and was basically rooting for the failure of mortgage banks, home builders, and others in the housing field. His strategy paid off. As the subprime mortgage crisis exploded, the stock in major mortgage banks and other housing businesses collapsed and Gillibrand cashed in, selling the puts in August, September, and October of 2007.[122] (Some of their puts did not pay off.)

That year, the Gillibrands reported over $40,000 in capital gains. Most of it was made by exploiting the desperate home loan situation.

How would those of her constituents who lost money in bank and home stocks feel about the senator's family's investments?

(*Note*: In Senator Gillibrand's first financial disclosure statement in 2005, she indicated that an ETrade account belonged to her. She did not describe it as a joint account. In 2006, she disclosed it in the same way and also listed a liability on the account based on the purchase of stock to cover a short sale. But suddenly in 2007, Gillibrand labeled the ETrade account and the list of puts as belonging to her husband.)

Jonathan Gillibrand's New Housing Career

After Gillibrand's election, her husband got a new job. According to her Senate disclosure in 2006, he went to work as a managing director for Redbrick Partners, a D.C. real estate investment firm run by two former HUD associates. According to CNN, the firm has a clear goal:

> "To Redbrick Partners, slow real estate markets mean a fast path to profits by acquiring cheap homes and turning them into rental properties." [123] Translation: The company buys thousands of homes in "distressed neighborhoods," where people are desperate to sell their homes. [124]

Some people might even call them slumlords. Because the generally accepted definition of "distressed neighborhoods" is

> the poorest urban areas generally identified as those with low income and high poverty rates along with a large percentage of female heads of household, high unemployment—specially among men, significant foreign born population, high percentage of high school drop-outs, and often a community of non-English speaking residents. [125] Some recent studies also include associate elevated incidences of homicides, foreclosures, and incidences of crime against property. [126]

Most "distressed properties" involve Section 8 housing rental subsidies. Did Redbrick's tenants get federal subsidies? But even with the federal government helping the tenants, trying to be an absentee landlord all over the country did not turn out to be a successful business model for Redbrick.

According to the *Wall Street Journal*, it is now trying to sell its rental properties. Initially, its first fund yielded a 20 percent return, "But the second and third funds have suffered heavy losses, according to letters recently sent to the investors. As of June 30, the value of a $100,000 limited-partnership investment in the second fund, including past distributions of cash to investors, had fallen to an estimated $56,099. For the third fund, the value fell to $45,633 as of June 30 from the original $100,000 of investment." [127]

Kirsten Gillibrand is a chameleon in plaid. She will say anything, vote for anything, change any position, reinvent herself, erase her past, and ignore her constituents to get what she wants: reelection to the Senate. She thinks the voters are idiots who will fall for her ridiculous stories, spins, and lies.

Voters throughout New York state, especially Independents, should be warned: Learn a lesson from Gillibrand and vote against her in November. She's a chameleon who has made it clear that she will do anything to get reelected. And what she wants may be even beyond the U.S. Senate; her friends say that she may want to be president someday.

Let's show her who's the real idiot.

An Embarrassing Specter Named Arlen

Democratic Party Loyalty in Voting: 95.7% [128]
Republican Party Loyalty in Voting: 76.8% [129] (2004)
70.5% [130] (2006)

Wealth Ranking: 38/100 [131]
Earmark Ranking: 22/100 [132]
318 requests for $241,393,246 in 2009

What can you say about Arlen Specter?

Start with this: He's a turncoat and a buffoon who has been in the U.S. Senate for far too long. He was first elected to the Senate from Pennsylvania in 1980 and reelected four more times as a Republican. But Specter has always been a wild card and never reliably Republican in his voting pattern: He consistently disagreed with the party about 25 percent of the time.

But while he was frequently at odds with numerous Republican positions, Specter never gave any indication at all that he might bolt from the party and ally himself with the Obama administration. That is, until 2009, when his poll numbers crashed and his chances of reelection looked impossible. Fearing that Republican voters would throw him out of the Senate in the 2010 election, Specter made a strategic decision to renounce the Republicans and switch to the Democratic Party.

His move gave the Democrats the critical sixtieth member they needed to block Republican filibusters until Scott Brown won a Senate seat in Massachusetts. At the time, giving the Democrats their sixtieth vote was a very big deal: It marked the first time that either party has had sixty votes in the Senate since 1978. It's no wonder that Vice-President Biden called him fourteen times during a two-week period to try to persuade him to dump the Republicans. And no wonder, too, that Obama dropped everything to call and welcome him to the party.

Specter's formal announcement of his resignation from the Republican Party gave new meaning to the word *obnoxious*. In a truly amazing performance, Specter rudely took a swipe at the Pennsylvania Republicans who had elected him over and over again:

> "I'm not prepared to have my twenty-nine-year record in the United States Senate decided by the Pennsylvania Republican primary electorate," he said, "not prepared to have that record decided by that jury." [133]

Talk about the lack of accountability in Washington.

Specter obviously has little regard for Republican voters—the same ones who sent him to the Senate repeatedly over the past thirty years.

Specter's contempt for his fellow citizens has not been limited to just Republicans. He has publicly made fun of Polish Americans. Aside from the obvious political incorrectness of a U.S. senator telling ethnic jokes, the sheer political stupidity of alienating a large block of the state's voters is mind-boggling. There are 824,000 Polish Americans in Pennsylvania, which is about 7 percent of the state's population.[134] Only three other states have larger Polish-American populations: Illinois, New York, and Michigan.

In December 2008, Senator Specter spoke in New York at a luncheon at the Rainbow Room hosted by a Pennsylvania organization. During his remarks, Specter suddenly looked around the room and asked if there were any Polish Americans in the group. After about ten hands went up (out of about one hundred), Specter proceeded to nevertheless reel off a series of offensive Polish jokes.

After a story about the jokes appeared in the *New York Post*, Specter apologized profusely. He then explained to one leader of a Pennsylvania Polish American organization that he'd first heard the jokes right before the event. So what? Was that any justification for his behavior—that the jokes were fresh in his mind? Doesn't Specter get it?

Apparently not. In fact, at times he seems almost out of control. In February, he insulted Republican congresswoman Michele Bachmann of Minnesota when they made a joint appearance on a Pittsburgh radio station. Frustrated that she was getting more airtime than he was, Specter tried to talk over her. When she continued talking, he started yelling at her to "stop interrupting me." Specter then told her: "Now, wait a minute, I'll stop and you can talk. . . . I'll treat you like a lady. *Now act like one*" [emphasis added]." [135] He repeated his patronizing comment a few minutes later. It was an appalling way to talk to any woman, but especially a fellow member of Congress. Bachmann told Sean Hannity that she felt she was being treated like a little girl, being told to sit down and shut up. Even *New York Times* commentator Gail Collins was horrified by Specter:

> Meanwhile, on a radio show in Pennsylvania, Senator Arlen Specter lost it completely and told Representative Michele Bachmann, the irrepressible heroine of the Tea Party movement, to "act like a lady."
>
> Specter, you will remember, switched parties last year. Democrats must be asking themselves why they wanted him. Oh, yes, the 60th vote . . .

Collins went on to call Specter "a self-important 79-year-old who makes wildly patronizing remarks about his female opponent during a radio debate." [136]

The Sixtieth Democrat

Specter proudly bragged about being that sixtieth Democrat, the one who can make things happen by stopping filibusters. He's gone as far to the left as he possibly can—a shift that probably has nothing to do with ideology and everything to do with the Democratic primary challenge he's facing from Congressman Joe Sestak.

Now that he's a Democrat, Specter is even trying to out-liberal Barack Obama. Although in his previous guise he voted with the Republicans three-quarters of the time, since becoming a Democrat he's voted with his new party on 95.7 percent of the votes he's cast after his conversion. The Democrats can surely count on him.

Immediately after President Obama announced his plan to boost the number of U.S. troops in Afghanistan, Specter came out against the surge and staked a position to the left of Obama:

> I oppose sending 30,000 additional American troops to Afghanistan because I am not persuaded that it is indispensable in our fight against Al Qaeda. If it was, I would support an increase because we have to do whatever it takes to defeat Al Qaeda since they're out to annihilate us. But if Al Qaeda can operate out of Yemen or Somalia, why fight in Afghanistan where no one has succeeded?
>
> I disagree with the President's two key assumptions: that we can transfer responsibility to Afghanistan after 18 months and that our NATO allies will make a significant contribution. It is unrealistic to expect the United States to be out in 18 months so there is really no exit strategy. This venture is not worth so many American lives or the billions it will add to our deficit.[137]

Specter also wants to be a liberal hero on health care. He has been loudly urging his Democratic colleagues to pass the health-care bill by using reconciliation, a move that requires only 51 votes—a strategy that would anger the voters, the Republicans, and even some Democrats.

But that's what Specter is all about.

Specter Was Forced to Return $850,000 in Campaign Contributions

When Specter announced he had become a Democrat, he magnanimously offered to return campaign contributions to anyone who felt betrayed by his change of party.

The switch, it turned out, cost him a lot: Nine hundred donors have taken him up on his offer, and he has had to return $850,000 in campaign contributions—to donors who never expected their candidate to turn tail and head for the Democratic fold.

Shilling for the Trial Lawyers

Specter is one of the Senate's biggest supporters of the trial lawyers' lobby. He's introduced a bill to allow additional tax deductions for lawyers in contingency cases, a benefit that's said to be worth more than $1.6 billion.[138] He's opposed caps on medical malpractice fees.

He even wants to let trial lawyers sue people when they have no evidence of any grounds for such a suit. Recently, the U.S. Supreme Court ruled that plaintiffs who file a lawsuit must allege sufficient facts to state a credible claim.

Sounds reasonable? Specter didn't think so. He sponsored the Notice Pleading Restoration Act of 2009 to overturn the Court's decision. He wants trial lawyers to be able to sue even when they have no grounds, and then to be able to use the discovery process to find a reason to sue. (Once a lawyer starts discovery, he can pull in virtually anyone to give a sworn deposition.) *Sue now, explain later* seems to be Specter's motto.

But another unintended consequence of the bill, according to the *Wall Street Journal*, is that it "would make it easier for terrorists to sue military and federal law-enforcement officials."[139] In the original Supreme Court decision, *Ashcroft v. Iqbal,* a Pakistani national who was arrested after 9/11 and designated as a person of "high interest" to the government was detained and deported. Iqpal, the plaintiff, later sued more than three dozen government officials and corrections officers, including the attorney general of the United States and the head of the FBI, claiming he'd been discriminated against and physically abused because of his race and religion. Iqpal made no specific allegations against the government officials and the case was dismissed on that basis.

William McGurn, writing in the *Wall Street Journal*, pointed out the possible problems with the bill:

> We know that al Qaeda operatives are trained to claim abuse when they
> are captured. If Mr. Specter's legislation succeeds, what is to prevent them

from alleging all sorts of violations so they can go on discovery expeditions against, say, Gen. David Petraeus or Defense Secretary Robert Gates? And how would that affect the ability of these men to prosecute the war?

Justice Kennedy made this point when he wrote about the "heavy costs" imposed on government officials trying to do their jobs. These costs, he noted, "are only magnified when Government officials are charged with responding to, as Judge [Jose] Cabranes aptly put it, 'a national and international security emergency unprecedented in the history of the American Republic.' "[140]

If Specter's bill passes, plaintiffs could try to use discovery and our legal system to go searching for information of interest to our enemies. That's a big problem.

But Specter is only trying to please the trial lawyers. Why? Because they're his biggest contributors:

INDUSTRIES CONTRIBUTING TO THE ARLEN SPECTER CAMPAIGN COMMITTEE

	Total	Individuals	PACS
Lawyers/Law Firms	$1,567,888	$1,357,238	$210,650
Securities and Investment	566,750	540,250	26,500
Lobbyists	442,669	413,429	29,240
Health Professionals	440,183	289,183	151,000
Real Estate	433,450	430,050	3,400
Pharmaceuticals/Health Products	416,449	217,550	198,899
Retired	380,058	380,058	0
TV/Movies/Music	340,830	244,980	95,850
Hospitals/Nursing Homes	289,726	188,576	101,150
Computers/Internet	217,843	112,250	105,593
Misc. Business	210,733	207,733	3,000
Misc. Finance	208,301	203,301	5,000

Education	201,090	200,590	500
Electric Utilities	194,649	108,350	86,299
Insurance	178,773	116,273	62,500
Misc. Manufacturing and Distributing	159,700	110,300	49,400
Leadership PACs	146,500	0	146,500
Business Services	145,300	137,800	7,500
Pro-Israel	134,800	84,300	50,500
Construction Services	116,700	96,700	20,000
Oil and Gas	114,150	70,650	43,500
Commercial Banks	112,750	63,800	48,950
Food Processing and Sales	107,673	68,100	39,573
Chemical and Related Manufacturing	105,383	56,483	48,900
Retail Sales	95,650	66,150	29,500
Steel Production	90,950	60,650	30,300
Building Trade Unions	83,500	0	83,500
General Contractors	82,684	68,184	14,500
Health Services/HMOs	79,200	49,900	29,300
Accountants	70,350	53,850	16,500
Air Transport	68,349	48,850	19,499
Railroads	66,700	53,700	13,000
Food and Beverage	63,700	52,100	11,600
Republican/Conservative	59,483	64,483	−5,000
Printing and Publishing	53,500	40,000	13,500
Building Materials and Equipment	53,500	50,500	3,000
Lodging/Tourism	45,101	40,101	5,000
Civil Servants/Public Officials	44,970	44,970	0
Nonprofit Institutions	42,500	41,500	1,000
Misc. Health	40,250	40,250	0
Transportation Unions	39,750	750	39,000
Mining	38,200	18,700	19,500
Public Sector Unions	33,350	0	33,350

Telecom Services and Equipment	33,200	18,700	14,500
Automotive	33,200	29,200	4,000
Recreation/Live Entertainment	32,100	23,600	8,500
Trucking	31,700	19,200	12,500
Misc. Defense	31,700	15,700	16,000
Sea Transport	31,100	14,100	17,000
Human Rights	29,250	20,850	8,400

Source: Center for Responsive Politics, OpenSecrets.org[141]

More than almost any other senator, Arlen Specter is a total opportunist. It's time to send him home. He's done enough damage in Washington.

HOUSE OF REPRESENTATIVES

The election of 2008 left the House solidly in Democratic control, with 258 Democrats squared off against only 177 Republicans. The recent switch of Alabama congressman Parker Griffith from Democrat to Republican reduced the Democratic margin to 257–178, meaning that the GOP has to pick up thirty-nine seats in order to take control.

Some say that closing such a wide gap is impossible.

They are dead wrong.

The Republican Party will take back scores of seats in the House, and will take control if we all do our work. We've come from this far behind before—as recently as 1994, when the Republican Party gained fifty-four House seats. And we can do it again!

In any election, the easiest seats to win are open seats where the incumbent is leaving for greener pastures. As Obama's health-care package increasingly alienates voters, and unemployment persists at high levels, a lot of incumbent Democratic congressmen are reading the handwriting on the wall and are getting out while the getting is good—sparing themselves the agony of a losing campaign by quitting in droves. Already fourteen Democrats have announced their retirement, many in swing districts. Seventeen Republicans have also said they are not going to run again, many to seek Senate seats or governorships, but most come from safe Republican districts.

The chart below shows the Democrats and Republicans who are not seeking reelection in 2010, along with the vote share John McCain received in their districts in 2008.

Of the seventeen Republicans who are leaving, eleven are from safe districts; four others are from districts Republicans should win. Only two come from swing districts. Our best guess is that we'll hold sixteen open seats and lose only one.

RETIRING REPUBLICANS (17)

Safe Republican Districts (11)	McCain vote
Mary Fallin (Oklahoma, 5th District)	59%
Nathan Deal (Georgia, 9th District)	75
John Boozman (Arkansas, 3rd District)	64
J. Gresham Barrett (South Carolina, 3rd District)	64
Roy Blunt (Missouri, 7th District)	63
Todd Tiahrt (Kansas, 4th District)	58
Zach Wamp (Tennessee, 3rd District)	62
Jerry Moran (Kansas, 1st District)	69
Henry Brown (South Carolina, 1st District)	56
John Shadegg (Arizona, 3rd District)	56
Adam Putnam (Florida, 12th District)	50
Districts Leaning Republican (4)	
George Radanovich (California, 19th District)	52%
Peter Hoekstra (Michigan, 2nd District)	51
Adam Putnam (Florida, 12th District)	50
Jim Gerlach (Pennsylvania, 6th District)	41
Swing Districts (2)	
Michael Castle (Delaware at large)	38%
Mark Kirk (Illinois, 10th District)	38

BEST GUESS: REPUBLICANS LOSE ONE

But there are also fourteen Democratic congressmen retiring, and more will probably have packed it in by the time you read this. Only three of the fourteen are in districts that are safe for their party. Our best guess is that the GOP will pick up eleven open Democratic seats. With one loss of an open Republican seat, that comes to a net gain of ten seats among the retiring Congressmen.

DEMOCRATIC RETIREES (14)

Safe Democratic Districts (3)

Artur Davis (Alabama, 7th District)	26%
Kendrick Meek (Florida, 17th District)	13
Robert Wexler (Florida, 19th District)	34

Districts Leaning Democratic (2)

Joe Sestak (Pennsylvania, 7th District)	43%
Neil Abercrombie (Hawaii, 1st District)	30

Swing Districts (4)

Brian Baird (Washington, 3rd District)	45%
Dennis Moore (Kansas, 3rd District)	48
Paul Hodes (New Hampshire, 2nd District)	43
John Murtha (Pennsylvania, 12th District)	49

Districts Leaning Republican (1)

John Tanner (Tennessee, 8th District)	56%

Strong Republican Districts (4)

Charlie Melancon (Louisiana, 3rd District)	61%
Bart Gordon (Tennessee, 6th District)	62
Marion Berry (Arkansas, 1st District)	59
Vic Snyder (Arkansas, 2nd District)	54

BEST GUESS: DEMOCRATS LOSE ELEVEN
NET GOP GAIN FROM RETIREMENTS: TEN SEATS

But this is all a work in progress. Three of the Democratic retirements and Griffith's party change came in the last two weeks of 2009. And more are likely!

Assuming there are no other switches or retirements, the Republican Party would need to gain twenty-nine more seats to take control.

And yes we can!

But conservatives can't just leave campaigning to the candidates in each district. If you happen to live in one of the districts where a vulnerable Democratic incumbent congressman can be toppled, that's an important opportunity: You can make a real national difference right in your own hometown. But even if you don't, it's important that you get involved. Remember, to return control to the Republican party, thirty-nine seats have to change hands. That's only 9 percent of the seats in the House of Representatives—and, therefore, only 9 percent of the population.

So the remaining 91 percent of us need to get involved in the campaigns for these swing seats—even if we don't live in one of the targeted districts. We may have friends who live there. We can send money to the Republican candidate. Some of us might even pack our bags and move there for the final few weeks before Election Day to pitch in and help out. It's our country, too!

But we need to choose the right targets.

We should focus our efforts on the seats now held by Democrats whose districts voted for John McCain in 2008. Some of these members disguise their liberalism by voting against a few big pieces of legislation—like health care—but still give Pelosi the majority she needs to govern. Others have been in office so long that the voters have almost forgotten they're there. Some even ran unopposed for reelection in 2008.

Those days are over. Come 2010, we're going to take back most of these blue seats in red states!

There are also the newly elected Democratic congressmen (some from districts where McCain won) who took their seats by relatively narrow margins in 2008. Now is the time to dislodge them, before they sink deep roots in their districts. And, finally, there are some Democrats who won by the skin of their teeth in 2008, and should be very vulnerable in 2010.

Of course, these categories overlap; some seats that appear to be vulnerable really aren't. But here's a list of fifty-four truly vulnerable Democratic incumbents in 2010. Undoubtedly, a few of these folks will win reelection.

But with fifty-four in play, we can afford a few reversals. What's *more* likely is that several incumbents who now appear invulnerable will actually lose. After all, tsunamis are not neat things: It's impossible to predict exactly how high the water will rise.

Much depends on how Obama does in 2010. More depends on how hard we work.

But one thing is sure: Control of the House in 2010 is within reach!

Here are the fifty-four vulnerable seats (and remember, we need only twenty-nine after we consider the likely Republican net gain of ten seats where incumbents are retiring):

DEAD MEN WALKING: THE MOST VULNERABLE HOUSE DEMOCRATS (16)

State (District)	Dem Congressman	'08 vote	Freshman	McC vote
Alabama (2)	Bobby Bright	50%	Y	63%
Col (4)	Betsy Markey	56	Y	50
Florida (8)	Alan Grayson	52	Y	47
Idaho (1)	Walt Minnick	51	Y	62
Indiana (9)	Baron Hill	58		50
Maryland (1)	Frank Kratovil	49	Y	59
Mich (7)	Mark Schauer	49	Y	47
Miss (1)	Travis Childers	54	Y	62
Nevada (3)	Dina Titus	47	Y	43
NH (1)	Carol Shea-Porter	52		47
NM (2)	Harry Teague	56	Y	50
Ohio (1)	Steven Driehaus	52	Y	44
Ohio (15)	Mary Jo Kilroy	46	Y	45
Pennsylvania (3)	Kathy Dahlkemper	51	Y	49
Virginia (2)	Glenn Nye	52	Y	49
Virginia (5)	Tom Perriello	50	Y	51

Even without a landslide, these folks would find it hard to get back to Washington. As it is, they'd better switch parties if they want to stay there.

Bobby Bright

Alabama 2nd District (Montgomery)

2008 vote share	50%
McCain vote	63%
Freshman	
Party support score	71%[142]

Bobby Bright is a prime example of the kind of chicanery that keeps the likes of Nancy Pelosi in power. He's a freshman who comes from a district represented by a Republican since 1965. Though the district gave McCain 63 percent of its vote, it elected Bright in a squeaker last year.

Bright votes with the Democratic Party 71 percent of the time. But on the big votes—the stimulus package, health care, raising the debt limit, and federal funding for abortion—he votes with the Republicans. Pelosi is perfectly happy to have him vote against her—as long as he keeps his seat as a Democrat, thus helping keep her in power. She's got plenty of party faithful to pass her socialist legislation. She doesn't need Bright's votes. She just needs him to stay in office, and stay in the party.

And that's why we have to defeat Bobby Bright. Though he had a good record as mayor of Montgomery, Alabama, his major contribution to politics today is keeping the likes of Pelosi and Charlie Rangel in power—while doing his party leaders' bidding more than two-thirds of the time.

He's a liberal posing as a moderate to fool the voters into keeping him in office.

Don't let him get away with it.

Betsy Markey

Colorado 4th District (entire eastern part of the state, including Fort Collins, Greeley, Lamar, and Sterling)

2008 vote share	56%
McCain vote	50%

Freshman

Party support score   94%[143]

Before Betsy Markey defeated Republican congresswoman Marilyn Mus-grave in 2008, she "spent much of the general election promising to work with Republicans as well as Democrats," according to *The Almanac of American Politics*.[144] But that little promise fell apart as soon as she got to Washington. Since she's been there, she's voted with Pelosi, Obama, and her party 94 percent of the time.

Can she fool her district again in 2010?

Markey's voting record in Washington will clearly count against her. She voted for the stimulus package, for allowing federal takeover of the financial industry, and in favor of federal funding for abortion. The fact that Pelosi let her vote against Obama's health-care bill—after the Democrats had enough votes to pass it anyway—is a mere shadow of the moderation she pledged so prominently in the 2008 campaign.

Alan Grayson

Florida 8th District (Orlando area)

2008 vote share	52%
McCain vote	47%
Freshman	
Party support score	98%

Alan Grayson is a trial lawyer from Orlando who ranks sixth among the 435 members of the House of Representatives in wealth. His net worth is between $31 million and $78 million.[145]

Elected in 2008 with only 52 percent of the vote, Grayson comes from a district that should go Republican in a GOP year.

Grayson sees no problem in voting to cut Medicare benefits or to spend the United States into a huge deficit. He votes with his party leaders 98 percent of the time and loyally supported Obamacare, the stimulus package, increased government regulation of the financial industry, and raising the debt limit. He supports federal funding of abortions.

He made his name fighting against contractor fraud in Iraq. As we noted in *Outrage*, this was an important issue, and he deserves credit for his whistle-blowing efforts.

Too bad he's done nothing good since!

This swing district doesn't need an extreme-left congressman like Alan Grayson. He'll undoubtedly use his massive personal wealth to try to buy reelection in 2010, talking about values and moderation and fiscal responsibility.

Don't listen. Grayson is a liberal automaton who deserves to lose his seat.

Walt Minnick

Idaho 1st District (Boise and western half of Idaho)

2008 vote share	51%
McCain vote	62%
Freshman	
Party support score	68%[146]

Minnick is another Democrat who got elected in a Republican district (McCain got 62 percent of the vote here) and then went to Washington to support Pelosi and her gang. Minnick tells his district that he deserves reelection because he voted against Obamacare and the stimulus package—yet he supports the Democratic position 68 percent of the time.

Walt Minnick is no independent.

Among other things, Minnick voted for one of the most dangerous bills this year: HR 4173, the measure to increase regulation of the financial industry and of American business in general. That's part of the Obama-Geithner plan to give themselves the power to take over any business they want, replace the board, fire the management, and shortchange the stockholders just because they think it's in financial difficulty and fear it's too big to fail. For that vote alone, he deserves to be dispatched back to Idaho.

He's only a freshman. It shouldn't be hard.

Baron Hill

Indiana 9th District (from the Kentucky border up to Bloomington)

2008 vote share	58%
McCain vote	50%
Seeking third term	
Party support score	86%[147]

Baron Hill, a basketball star in school, served as congressman from 1998 to 2004 before losing his seat. He regained it in 2006 and was promoted to the national party leadership as a chief deputy whip.

Pelosi's faith in Hill has been well rewarded: He votes with her 86 percent of the time, and backed Obamacare, the stimulus package, and the increase in the debt ceiling. In a district McCain narrowly carried, these votes won't go down very well.

We should be able to beat Hill: If we run a good campaign, the district should recognize his true colors as a loyal supporter of the left-wing agenda.

Frank Kratovil Jr.

Maryland 1st District (Eastern Shore)

2008 vote share	49%
McCain vote	59%
Freshman	
Party support score	83%[148]

Kratovil, a forty-one-year-old freshman, won this heavily Republican seat only because the nine-term GOP incumbent, Wayne Gilchrest, lost a primary to state senator Andy Harris, which split the vote and let Kratovil get elected.

By all rights, however, this should be a Republican seat! After all, John McCain got almost 60 percent of the vote here.

Kratovil votes with his party 83 percent of the time, voting in favor of both the Obama stimulus package and the financial regulation bill. He also voted for federal funding of abortion. He did vote against Obamacare, but that was obviously because he had reelection on his mind.

An opportunist, Kratovil may pose as a moderate, but he backs Pelosi on more than four out of five votes. He deserves to lose and probably will.

Mark Schauer

Michigan 7th District (Branch, Calhoun, Eaton, Hillsdale, Jackson, Lenawee, and Washtenaw counties)

2008 vote share	49%
McCain vote	46%
Freshman	
Party support score	94%[149]

In 2008, Schauer defeated Republican congressman Tim Walberg, himself a freshman, in a narrow race. He is only the second Democrat to represent the district since World War I. (That's no typo: the First World War!)

Schauer votes the straight liberal agenda, supporting Pelosi 94 percent of the time, even though his district is essentially moderate. He supported Obamacare, the stimulus package, the stepped-up regulation of business, the elevation of the debt limit, and federal funding of abortion.

McCain got 46 percent of the vote here in 2008, one point below his national showing. So if there's any national Republican trend this fall, Schauer will be a one-term wonder.

Travis Childers

Mississippi 1st District (northeastern Mississippi, including Columbus and Tupelo)

2008 vote share	54%
McCain vote	62%
Freshman	
Party support score	81%[150]

Why on earth did the voters of Mississippi elect a liberal like Travis Childers, who votes with Nancy Pelosi 81 percent of the time? Childers comes from a district that voted 62 percent for McCain—but he voted for the stimulus package and for vastly increased federal regulation of the financial industry.

For Republicans to have a chance to take Congress in 2010, Travis Childers has to go!

We won't be losing much. Many congressmen come to the House with distinguished resumes; Travis Childers, on the other hand, was a chancery clerk for Prentiss County, Mississippi, for sixteen years. That's it—his complete public résumé.

It'll be tough, but we'll have to find a way to manage to run the country without his special skills and experience.

Dina Titus

Nevada 3rd District (Las Vegas area)

2008 vote share	47%
McCain vote	43%
Freshman	
Party support score	97%[151]

Nicknamed "Dina Taxes" by one political opponent, Dina Titus defeated incumbent Republican congressman Jon Porter by a margin of 47–42 in 2008. She had just lost the race for governor of Nevada in 2006 when she sought the consolation prize of congresswoman.

In Washington, Titus has voted with the Democratic Party leadership 97 percent of the time—backing Obamacare, the stimulus package, and increased government control over the financial industry. She's done a lot to earn her nickname!

Obama swamped McCain in Titus's district by 55–43, so we have a steep hill to climb in knocking her out. But there's no such thing as a real incumbent in Nevada, where migration is so heavy that a new state is born every election year. Besides, Harry Reid should lose his bid for another term—and he could drag Titus down with him.

Just in case, though, let's help make sure she leaves!

Carol Shea-Porter

New Hampshire 1st District (Portsmouth, Manchester, Lakes Region)

2008 vote share	52%
McCain vote	47%
Seeking third term	
Party support score	98%[152]

As liberal as they come, social worker Carol Shea-Porter voted with Pelosi 98 percent of the time. She backed Obamacare, the stimulus package, raising the debt limit, permitting federal takeover of financial businesses, and federal funding for abortions.

Shea-Porter was elected in 2006 as part of a backlash against the Iraq War, and she continues to vote as far left as she can. But she has one big problem: Her district is distinctly middle-of-the-road. Elected with 51 percent of the vote in 2006, she managed just 52 percent in 2008 even amid a Democratic landslide.

The backlash against the ultra-liberal policies she has championed in fiscally conservative New Hampshire should sweep Shea-Porter away in 2010. Look at what happened next door in Massachusetts!

Harry Teague

New Mexico 2nd District (southern New Mexico, including Las Cruces, Roswell, Socorro, Los Lunas, and Hobbs)

2008 vote share	56%
McCain vote	50%
Freshman	
Party support score	89%[153]

The ninth richest member of the House—an oilman with a net worth between $36 million and $40 million—Harry Teague not only spent big to get elected, he also spent our money lavishly. As soon as he got to Congress, he voted for the stimulus package. Overall, he's rewarded Obama and Pelosi for their support by backing their agenda 89 percent of the time. And he comes from a district McCain narrowly carried in 2008—and that Bush won in 2006 by seventeen points!

Teague was elected in a slugfest between millionaires seeking to fill an open seat vacated by a Republican congressman. Before that, however, the district had been controlled by the GOP since 1980: The people of the area are solidly Republican, and it's time to return their district to GOP control.

Steven Driehaus

Ohio 1st District (Cincinnati and west to the Indiana border)

2008 vote share	52%
McCain vote	44%
Freshman	
Party support score	94%[154]

Elected with only 52 percent of the vote in 2008 after beating seven-term Republican Steve Chabot, Driehaus has voted the straight party line ever since. He supported Pelosi 94 percent of the time, backing Obamacare, the stimulus package, and the bill allowing takeover of any financial institution Obama wants. Then, in an act of ultimate hypocrisy, he voted against raising the debt limit. All right, Steven, you voted for the stimulus package. Just how are we going to pay for it if you won't even let the feds borrow the money?

Driehaus calls himself "a raging moderate," claiming that he "tend[s] to be open-minded on a whole host of issues."[155] Some freethinker: He just happens to conclude that Obama and Pelosi are right 94 percent of the time!

Fortunately, we can beat Driehaus. He won narrowly in 2008 largely on the strength of a large African American turnout (28 percent of the vote) that had been drawn to the polls by Obama. With the president not on the ballot, and high unemployment cooling the ardor of his erstwhile supporters, Driehaus should be very beatable.

Mary Jo Kilroy

Ohio 15th District (Columbus and west to the Indiana border)

2008 vote share	46%
McCain vote	45%
Freshman	
Party support score	98%[156]

Kilroy, who votes a solid liberal line in Congress, won an open seat in 2008. She supported Pelosi and Obama 98 percent of the time. She voted for Obamacare, the stimulus, raising the debt limit, federal funding of abortion, and the legislation to permit takeover of financial institutions. She is way too liberal for her district—and, since she was elected with only 46 percent of the vote last time, she may be in her last term.

Actually, Kilroy nearly didn't make it to Congress at all: She was losing on Election Day, but with the usual Democratic shenanigans, she won in subsequent recounts. It was a close race, and the only reason she was elected was that two independents (one antiabortion and the other libertarian) siphoned votes away from the Republican candidate.

Kilroy also sided with Hamas and against Israel on January 21, 2010, when she signed a letter with fifty-three other Democratic congressional members protesting the Israeli blockade of Gaza. She forgot to mention that it was the daily shower of rockets aimed at civilians in Israel from Gaza that provoked the blockade.[157]

This is a must-win seat in 2010.

Kathy Dahlkemper

Pennsylvania 3rd District (Erie)

2008 vote share	51%
McCain vote	49%
Freshman	
Party support score	94%[158]

Dahlkemper defeated incumbent Republican congressman Phil English in a close race in 2008. She comes from the ultimate swing district, one where the 2008 presidential vote was evenly divided between Obama and McCain. When she ran for office, she argued that she was "not a professional politician but a concerned citizen." [159]

But Dahlkemper sure votes like a pro, toeing the Democratic line from morning to night. She voted the way they told her to 94 percent of the time. She voted for Obamacare, the stimulus package, increased government regulation of the financial industry, and raising the debt ceiling. When they say "jump," Kathy asks, "How high?"

We need to get someone in Congress from Erie, Pennsylvania, who's looking out for us—and send Dahlkemper back to her favorite role—as a "concerned citizen."

Glenn Nye

Virginia 2nd District (Hampton Roads and the Eastern Shore)

2008 vote share	52%
McCain vote	49%
Freshman	
Party support score	84%[160]

Nye comes from a foreign service background. Only forty years old, he has served in Eastern Europe, Iraq, Afghanistan, Singapore, and Gaza. He comes from a district where McCain and Obama won basically equal vote shares, and defeated Republican incumbent Thelma Drake by a very narrow margin. He may have served too long in Gaza. He displayed his true sympathies on January 21, 2010, when he joined fifty-three other Democratic congressmen in signing an anti-Israel letter blaming the blockade for inflicting harm on the poor people of Gaza.[161] The same poor people who regularly fire rockets into Israel.

In Washington, Nye backs the Democratic line 84 percent of the time and voted for the stimulus package. He voted no on Obamacare, but he probably had no choice, given his district.

He vigorously opposes drilling in Alaska or offshore, and used the issue to help win his seat in 2008. Presumably, he's happier having us depend on the likes of Venezuela and Saudi Arabia for our oil.

Nye's campaign contributors included Nancy Pelosi, Steny Hoyer, and

Charlie Rangel. That says it all: We need a new congressman from the 2nd District of Virginia.

Tom Perriello

Virginia 5th District (south central Virginia, down to the North Carolina line; includes Charlottesville, Bedford, Timberlake, Martinsville, and Danville)

2008 vote share	50%
McCain vote	51%
Freshman	
Party support score	89%[162]

Elected by a margin of only 727 votes in 2008, Perriello ran as a religious conservative. According to *The Almanac of American Politics*, he claimed that "his nonprofit work was a way of answering God's calling."[163] He defeated six-term incumbent conservative Republican congressman Virgil Goode, after it turned out that Goode's press secretary had appeared in a low-budget gay-themed film.

Once in Washington, however, Perriello turned sharply left, backing Pelosi's agenda 89 percent of the time. He voted for Obamacare and for the stimulus package. One wonders how he justifies slicing $500 billion in Medicare benefits.

Perriello's district leans conservative; McCain carried it with 51 percent of the vote. Many wonder whether Perriello would have won if it hadn't been for the gay film scandal. Can he get his district to overlook his support for socialized medicine and cuts in Medicare? We hope not.

Then there are the seats now held by Democrats that we might well win in a Republican sweep. Normally, most of these would be off-limits. But with Obama's popularity in free fall, we've got a good shot at winning most of them.

SEATS WE SHOULD WIN: VULNERABLE DEMOCRATS (38)

State (District)	Dem Congressman	'08 vote	Freshman	McC vote
Arizona (5)	Harry Mitchell	53%		51%
Arizona (8)	Gabrielle Giffords	55		52
Arizona (1)	Ann Kirkpatrick	56	Y	54
Arkansas (4)	Mike Ross	86		58
California (11)	Jerry McNerney	55		44
Colorado (3)	John Salazar	62		50
Connecticut (4)	Jim Himes	51	Y	40
Florida (2)	Allen Boyd	62		54
Florida (24)	Suzanne Kosmas	57	Y	51
Georgia (8)	Jim Marshall	57		56
Illinois (14)	Bill Foster	58	Y	44
Michigan (9)	Garry Peters	52	Y	43
Missouri (4)	Ike Skelton	66		60
New Jersey (3)	John Adler	52	Y	47
New York (1)	Tim Bishop	58		48
New York (13)	Mike McMahon	61	Y	51
New York (19)	John Hall	59		48
New York (23)	Bill Owens	49	Y	47
New York (24)	Mike Arcuri	52		48
New York (25)	Dan Maffei	55	Y	43
New York (29)	Eric Massa	51	Y	51
North Carolina (8)	Larry Kissell	55		47
North Dakota (at large)	Earl Pomeroy	62		53
Ohio (16)	John Boccieri	55	Y	50
Ohio (18)	Zack Space	60		53
Pennsylvania (4)	Jason Altmire	56		55

Pennsylvania (8)	Patrick Murphy	57%	45%
Pennsylvania (10)	Christopher Carney	56	54
Pennsylvania (11)	Paul Kanjorski	52	42
South Carolina (5)	John Spratt	62	53
Tennessee (4)	Lincoln Davis	59	64
Texas (17)	Chet Edwards	53	67
Utah (2)	Jim Matheson	63	58
Virginia (9)	Rick Boucher	unopposed	59
West Virginia (1)	Alan Mollohan	unopposed	57
West Virginia (3)	Nick Rahall	67	56
Wisconsin (8)	Steve Kagen	54	45

Harry Mitchell

Arizona 5th District (northeastern suburbs of Phoenix)
2008 vote share	53%
McCain vote	51%
Seeking third term	
Party support score	81%[164]

Elected in 2006, Mitchell voted for Obamacare and the stimulus package. He backs his party line 81 percent of the time. A former chair of the Arizona Democratic Party, he's a classic party hack who put together the political machine that picked up seats in the 2006 and 2008 elections.

And he defeated a very, very good man: Republican Congressman J. D. Hayworth, a stalwart opponent of amnesty for illegal immigrants.

Mitchell's district is a quintessential toss-up: Even though he ran as an incumbent Democrat in the Democratic landslide of 2008, he managed to get only 53 percent of the vote—and McCain took the district in the same election.

Mitchell should be ripe for the picking!

Gabrielle Giffords

Arizona 5th District (southern Arizona including Tucson)
        2008 vote share   55%
        McCain vote   52%
        Seeking third term
        Party support score   90%[165]

Elected in 2006, Giffords votes the way her party leaders tell her 90 percent of the time. She has gone right down the party line, backing Obamacare, the stimulus package, socialization of the financial sector, and federal funding for abortion. We might as well elect a robot for all the independent thought she shows.

Giffords, of course, is a career politician, elected to the Arizona House at age thirty. She became a state senator at thirty-two, and went to Congress at thirty-six.

She took an open seat in the House of Representatives in 2006, campaigning against a strongly anti–illegal immigration Republican. She won reelection by the seemingly comfortable margin of 55 percent of the vote in 2008. But how comfortable can a pro-Obamacare liberal be in a district that went for McCain?

This is just the sort of district we've got to recapture to win back the House!

Ann Kirkpatrick

Arizona 1st District (about three quarters of Arizona, the entire
    northeastern part of the state; includes Apache, Coconino, Gila,
    Graham, Greenlee, Pinal, Navajo, and Yavapai counties)
        2008 vote share   56%
        McCain vote   54%
        Freshman
        Party support score   86%[166]

Arizona's 1st District is solidly Republican. The only reason Kirkpatrick was elected is that the incumbent Republican congressman, Rick Benzi, didn't run for reelection after being indicted in an alleged extortion scheme.[167] The Republican nominee won the designation after a bitter primary and the state party decided not to fund the race. Kirkpatrick outspent her GOP adversary by three to one.

According to *The Almanac of American Politics*, what made the difference for Kirkpatrick was that her "more moderate views resonated with voters." [168] But if that's the case, they were fooled. Once Kirkpatrick got to Washington, she backed the Democratic agenda 86 percent of the time. Pelosi relied on her to vote for both the stimulus package and the Obama health-care bill.

But Ann Kirkpatrick's district is Republican: It backed McCain with 54 percent of the vote. And if a good candidate steps forward, the district should turn Kirkpatrick out in 2010.

Mike Ross

Arkansas 4th District (southern half of the state)

2008 vote share	86%
McCain vote	58%
Seeking sixth term	
Party support score	95%

Mike Ross votes with Pelosi on 95 percent of all votes.[169] He voted for the stimulus bill and backed raising the debt limit. He was a total hypocrite on the health-care bill: In committee, where his vote would have helped to kill the bill, he made a big stink about how he wasn't going to back Obamacare— but then he folded like a cheap suit and voted to report it to the floor anyway. When it reached the floor, and his vote no longer made any difference, he voted against it. This kind of thing is typical of his trickery.

Ross was implicated in a 2007 real estate deal in which he sold his property to an Arkansas-based pharmacy, USA Drug, for between $1 million and $1.67 million. According to the watchdog group OpenSecrets (OpenSecrets.org), that's "much more than a county assessment said the property was worth." [170]

As OpenSecrets notes, this sale means that Ross has "money in his pocket from a company that not only employs his wife—she's still a pharmacist at Holly's Health Mart, which USA Drug bought from the couple—but that has also been outspoken against a government option" for health care.[171] Right position—wrong reason.

Ross's two Democratic colleagues in the four-person Arkansas congressional delegation have both retired and won't run again in 2010. Ross should listen to their wisdom and pack it in. Otherwise, let's beat him!

Jerry McNerney

California 11th District (Stockton and Pleasanton)

2008 vote share	55%
McCain vote	44%
Seeking third term	
Party support score	95%[172]

McNerney was elected in 2006 as a result of a surge of support from Democratic bloggers. Endorsed early on by Howard Dean, he was the ultraliberal candidate. A Pelosi clone, he has not been seriously challenged since his election and should be in for the fight of his life in 2010. We think he'll lose.

Part of the reason for his defeat will be his support of Obamacare, the stimulus package, and draconian financial regulation. His 95 percent score of supporting Pelosi and Obama shows what a liberal he has been in Congress.

John Salazar

Colorado 3rd District (Pueblo area)

2008 vote share	62%
McCain vote	50%
Seeking fourth term	
Party support score	97.4%[173]

Interior Secretary Ken Salazar's big brother, John, was elected in 2004 after the incumbent Republican congressman retired. He "crafted a moderate image." [174] Then, like most of these self-styled moderate Democrats, he went to Washington and toed the party line 97.4 percent of the time, backing Obamacare, the stimulus package, raising the debt limit, and financial regulation. Some centrist!

But McCain beat Obama here, and the district is getting to know Salazar's liberal ways. The fact that his brother is in Obama's cabinet won't help much. This year he can be beaten!

Jim Himes

Connecticut 4th District (Fairfield County)

2008 vote share	51%
McCain vote	40%[175]
Freshman	

Himes defeated longtime incumbent Republican congressman Chris Shays in this liberal Connecticut district. Shays, who was quite independent of the Republican line, finally succumbed to the Obama sweep, which carried his district by 60–40. But the 4th District is a rich one, and Obama's war on prosperity may not play well here.

Himes's vote in favor of Obamacare will prove especially unpopular as will his support for tax increases. He won by only two points last time. Let's oust him in 2010.

Allen Boyd

Florida 2nd District (Panhandle, including Tallahassee and Panama City)

2008 vote share	62%
McCain vote	54%
Seeking eighth term	
Party support score	95%[176]

Easily reelected despite coming from a Republican district, Allen Boyd has a formula: Vote against tax cuts, support massive spending and borrowing, but get a piece of the action for the folks at home, to keep them in line. Boyd sponsored or cosponsored forty-eight earmarks in 2009 alone, for a total of $75,956,157. He ranked thirty-eighth out of 435 congressmen in earmarks. Among his pet projects are $1.2 million for citrus canker research, $2.5 million for climate forecasting, and $267,000 for a fringe organization called the Green Institute in Florida.[177]

But should we be happy when Boyd recycles our own money back to us and uses it to get reelected? Or should we remember that he voted against Bush's tax cuts in 2001 and backed the stimulus package in 2009? (Actually, it's even worse than that: At first he voted against the stimulus, but then, after he got some goodies inserted in the bill, he switched his vote to come around.)

Many experts say that a guy like Boyd can't be beaten, and that voters will reelect him out of habit. But with McCain winning 54 percent of the vote in his district, it's time Republicans realized what a fraudulent deal he's giving us.

Suzanne Kosmas

> Florida 24th District (Florida's Atlantic coast, from South Daytona to Cape Canaveral and inland to Winter Park)

2008 vote share	57%
McCain vote	51%
Freshman	
Party support score	92%[178]

Kosmas is another Democrat elected in 2008 on the heels of a scandal involving the Republican incumbent. This time it was former congressman Tom Feeney, who was reprimanded by the House Ethics Committee for having accepted a free trip to St. Andrews, Scotland, paid for by former lobbyist Jack Abramoff. Feeney repaid the Treasury the cost of the $5,000 trip, but the damage was done. (We reported and criticized the trip in *Outrage*.)

As a result, Kosmas was able to win in this Republican district that McCain carried. Her 57 percent vote share shows that she'll be a strong incumbent. But her voting record may be her undoing. She backs Pelosi and Obama 92 percent of the time, and voted for both the stimulus package and the government takeover-and-regulation bill affecting the financial industry. When it became evident that her vote wasn't needed, she voted against Obamacare, but that shouldn't be enough to save her.

Jim Marshall

Georgia 8th District (Macon area)

2008 vote share	57%
McCain vote	56%
Elected in 2002	
Party support score	89%[179]

Seeking his fifth term, Marshall should be a shoo-in. He won with 57 percent of the vote in 2008 and probably expects to return in 2010.

But Marshall has one small problem: He's way too liberal for his district.

Even though 56 percent of his constituents voted for McCain, Marshall loyally supports the Pelosi leadership 89 percent of the time.

We need to ensure that his voters remember that figure: 89 percent!

Marshall voted for the stimulus package. He supported giving Obama and Geithner the power to take over financial institutions at will. He voted to raise the debt ceiling so he could continue his big-spending ways. His sole concession to reason was voting against Obamacare, but that was probably a vote he had to cast to get reelected. (Nancy will understand.) Marshall opposes tort reform and wants to continue the Death Tax.

Though he's a social conservative, Marshall votes with the big spenders 89 percent of the time. Let's elect a real conservative—a Republican—from this district.

Bill Foster

Illinois 14th District (Batavia, Dixon, and Geneseo)

2008 vote share	58%
McCain vote	44%
Freshman	
Party support score	91.5%[180]

Foster holds the seat recently vacated by Republican former House speaker Dennis Hastert. He won it 53–47 in a special election in March 2008 after winning the Democratic primary by four hundred votes. He wasn't strongly opposed in the November 2008 election and held on to his seat. Obama beat McCain here, perhaps out of home state loyalty, but it's really a swing district. Bush trounced Kerry in Foster's district 55–45.

Voters will be disappointed that Foster backs Pelosi 91 percent of the time and voted for Obamacare, the stimulus package, and for more financial regulation. He'll have a tough fight this year and should be vulnerable.

Gary Peters

Michigan 9th District (Oakland County)

2008 vote share	52%
McCain vote	43%
Freshman	
Party support score	95%

Gary Peters, a freshman from Michigan's 9th District, got elected in 2008 with only 52 percent of the vote. His Democratic district went heftily for Obama, but Peters pulled only a thin margin, so he has a stiff challenge ahead. He has backed the party line 95 percent of the time,[181] and voted for Obama's health-care bill, the stimulus package, and the socialist bill to allow the government to take over financial firms at will.

Ike Skelton

Missouri 4th District (Blue Springs, Jefferson, Lebanon, and Sedalia)

2008 Vote share	66%
McCain vote	60%
Seeking eighteenth term	
Party support score	95%[182]

Ike Skelton represents rural Missouri, a very conservative district that voted overwhelmingly for McCain. First elected in 1976 as a conservative Democrat (back when there was such a thing), he has been moving to the left ever since. Now he backs Pelosi and Obama 95 percent of the time. He's a reliable rubber stamp who backed raising the debt limit, and backed the pork-laden stimulus package. He voted against Obamacare only after it was clear that his vote wasn't needed.

Skelton is head of the House Armed Services Committee and brings lots of goodies to his district. But he's become a liberal during his years in Washington, and it's time to bring him home.

John Adler

New Jersey 3rd District (Burlington, Ocean Counties, and Cherry Hill)

2008 vote share	52%
McCain vote	47%
Freshman	
Party support score	91%[183]

Narrowly elected in 2008 to an open seat in a swing district, John Adler immediately joined the House Financial Services Committee, where he became a loyal acolyte of its chairman, Barney Frank. Adler helped craft the bill that gave Obama and Geithner the power to take over any financial institution they consider too big to fail and potentially insolvent. As a member of the committee, Adler has been part and parcel of the greatest power grab in the modern history of American government.

Adler voted for the stimulus program but voted against Obamacare on the floor of the House. But the damage he has done in committee to the American economy is cause enough to throw him out of Congress in 2010.

Tim Bishop

New York 1st District (eastern Suffolk County)

2008 vote share	58%
McCain vote	48%
Seeking fifth term	
Party support score	96.8%[184]

The congressman from the Hamptons, Bishop holds a seat that is exactly at the center of the nation's politics. Obama carried it by four points (while winning the nation by five) and Bush beat Kerry here by less than one point (while he won by three points nationally). But Bishop votes like an ultra-liberal, backing Pelosi an astounding 97 percent of the time. He voted down the line for Obamacare, the stimulus package, raising the debt ceiling, and giving the government power to seize private businesses. He has escaped serious challenges in recent contests, but he'll get one this time—and we hope he'll lose.

Mike McMahon

New York 13th District (Staten Island and a bit of Brooklyn)

2008 vote share	61%
McCain vote	51%
Freshman	
Party support score	92.6[185]

McMahon stumbled into this seat in the 2008 election when Republican incumbent Vito Fossella was busted for drunk driving in Virginia. The arrest led to all sorts of lurid stories about extramarital affairs, and three weeks later Fossella pulled out of the race. Then, to make matters worse for the GOP, the Republican candidate slated to succeed Fossella died of a heart attack four months before the election. The candidate who ended up running was unpopular among his fellow Republicans, and *The Almanac of American Politics* reports that he was rejected by his own party "because of questionable business dealings." [186]

The district thought it was electing a moderate in McMahon—only to be disappointed when he supported the stimulus package, raising the debt limit, and financial regulation, backing the party 92 percent of the time.

In 2010, the district will recover its senses and vote Republican again.

John Hall

New York 19th District (northern Westchester and Peekskill counties, including Peekskill, Mount Kisco, Beacon, Port Jervis, and Arlington)

2008 vote share	59%
McCain vote	48%
Seeking third term	
Party support score	98%[187]

Hall, a former rock star who founded the group Orleans, hopes he'll be "Still the One" in 2010. But New York's 19th district may have other thoughts. His 98 percent support for Pelosi makes him little better than a robot. He voted for Obamacare, the stimulus bill, raising the debt limit, and allowing government takeover of any financial institution that struck its fancy.

But Hall's district isn't that liberal. McCain lost here only narrowly (with 48 percent of the vote) and Congresswoman Susan Kelly, a Republican whom Hall defeated in 2006, represented the district quite well.

In 2008, the Republican candidate who was supposed to oppose Hall dropped out after putting $1.5 million of his own money into the race. The GOP quickly recruited a challenger to take up the slack, but he never seriously endangered Hall, who won with 59 percent of the vote.

But Hall's not that strong. There's a good chance he won't still be the one in 2010.

Bill Owens

New York 23rd District (Plattsburgh, near the Canadian border)

2009 vote share	49%
McCain vote	47%
Freshman	
Party support score	93.9[188]

Owens won a special election on November 3, 2009, winning a House seat the Republicans had controlled since 1872. He was elected only because the

Republican candidate, Assemblywoman Dede Scozzafava, was so liberal that the district's GOP voters rejected her. Three weeks before the election, she dropped out and endorsed the Democrat. Meanwhile, conservatives waged a strong campaign for Doug Hoffman, who ran as the nominee of the Conservative Party. Despite all these handicaps, Owens won only 49–45. Democrats hailed it as a great victory, but it was really a fluke.

We can reverse it this November.

Even though he has served less than one year in the House, Owens has established himself as a left-wing liberal with his votes for Obamacare and for giving the secretary of the Treasury the power to seize and dismember any business he considers too big to fail.

Mike Arcuri

New York 24th District (Utica and south central New York state)

2008 vote share	52%
McCain vote	48%
Seeking third term	
Party support score	91%[189]

Mike Arcuri was elected in 2006 on a totally fraudulent premise: He told the district he would follow in the footsteps of twelve-term Republican congressman Sherwood Boehlert, calling himself a "Boehlert Democrat." Then, when he entered Congress, he turned right around and voted as a liberal, following Nancy Pelosi's dictates 91 percent of the time.

Arcuri voted for Obamacare, the stimulus package, and the government takeover of financial institutions, and backed raising the debt limit. Some conservative!

The Democratic Congressional Campaign Committee even had the audacity to run an ad accusing Republican state senator Ray Meier, Arcuri's opponent, of "spending like a drunken sailor" in the legislature. This from a man who voted to triple the federal deficit as soon as he went to Washington!

In Congress, Arcuri joined Barney Frank's House Financial Services Committee, where he backed legislation allowing Obama and Geithner to take over virtually any private company they wanted.

But his district may be getting wise to his ways. Elected in 2006 with 54 percent of the vote, he saw his margin drop to 52 percent in 2008 despite the Democratic landslide.

Let's finish the job in 2010 and vote him out of office.

Dan Maffei

New York 25th District (Syracuse)

2008 vote share	55%
McCain vote	43%
Freshman	
Party support score	97%

Dan Maffei, a freshman from New York's 25th District, won with only 55 percent of the vote. His 97 percent party support score included votes for Obamacare, the stimulus, and financial regulation.[190] He comes from a Democratic district, but they can't be happy with his votes: He's vulnerable.

Eric Massa

New York 29th District (Pittsford, Corning, Elmira, and Olean)

2008 vote share	51%
McCain vote	51%
Freshman	
Party support score	95%[191]

What do you call someone who defeats his opponent by criticizing him for taking money from special interest Washington PACs—and then, the minute he's elected, takes their money himself? As they would say on *Jeopardy*, what is a hypocrite?

That's what Eric Massa did. He ran against Republican congressman Randy Kuhl in 2006 and lost narrowly. In their rematch, he used the PAC issue to unseat Kuhl, carrying 51 percent of the vote.

Once elected, Massa flip-flopped and took the same kind of PAC money he had scolded his opponent for accepting.

Worse yet was Massa's hypocrisy in selling himself to his district as a moderate—only to vote with his liberal-minded party leadership 95 percent of the time once he reached Washington, including voting for the stimulus package. Massa doubtless hopes his vote against Obama's health-care bill will convince his voters he's a conservative. But we need to make them understand that he does Pelosi's bidding *nineteen out of twenty times.*

Massa was also one of fifty-four Democratic congressmen who signed a letter on January 21, 2010, attacking Israel for its blockade of Gaza. Citing the economic hardship it causes, he conveniently ignored the shower of rockets Hamas fires from Gaza at civilians in Israel.[192]

Larry Kissell

North Carolina 8th District (Concord, Albemarle, Monroe, and
Laurenberg)

2008 vote share	55%
McCain vote	47%
Seeking third term	
Party support score	96%[193]

After being narrowly defeated in his first race for the seat in 2006, Larry Kissell won in 2008, defeating five-term Republican incumbent Robin Hayes. Hayes had stumbled when he declared that "liberals hate real Americans that work and achieve and believe in God,"[194] a comment for which he had to apologize. Kissell campaigned heavily against the Central American Free Trade Agreement, which cost his district textile jobs. But after he was elected he did nothing to repeal the deal or to help Obama fulfill his campaign pledge—which he broke—to renegotiate NAFTA.

In 2010, it'll be fun watching Kissell explain to his district why he does his part to keep the Democrats in power—even though they back the cap-and-trade tax, which will destroy what is left of the textile mills in his district. Although he voted against the stimulus package and Obamacare, he backs his party line 96 percent of the time. He backed the financial industry takeover bill, and generally does what Pelosi tells him to do.

Kissell will doubtless try to cite his votes to show how independent he is, but voters in his district should recognize that he was only free to vote that way because Pelosi already had enough votes to pass the bills without him. He'll probably criticize the cap-and-trade bill, but his North Carolina constituents are smart enough to realize that, as long as Democrats like him hold on to their seats, Nancy Pelosi will remain in charge—and she'll try her best to ram cap and trade through Congress.

Earl Pomeroy

North Dakota (at large)

2008 vote share	62%
McCain vote	53%
Seeking tenth term	
Party support score	97.3%[195]

Elected a decade ago as a populist, Earl Pomeroy voted for Obamacare—a decision that may well cost him his seat in this heavily Republican state. North Dakota Democratic senator Byron Dorgan has already thought better of running for reelection and dropped out, and the state's very popular governor, Republican John Hoeven, is a shoo-in to become its new senator.

But health care is just one of a seemingly endless series of liberal votes Pomeroy has cast, including his votes for the stimulus, financial regulation, and raising the debt ceiling. His 97 percent party support voting record isn't what North Dakota had in mind.

Pomeroy is under great pressure to join Dorgan in retirement, and may well be defeated if he runs.

John Boccieri

Ohio 16th District (Stark, Wayne, and parts of Ashland and Medina counties)

2008 vote share	55%
McCain vote	50%
Freshman	
Party support score	94%[196]

Boccieri came to Congress in 2008, winning a seat that was being vacated by Ralph Regula, an eighteen-term Republican incumbent. The Democratic Congressional Campaign Committee effectively bought the seat for Boccieri, dumping $300,000 into the race in the final days before the election. By then the Republicans were out of money, and Boccieri coasted to an unexpectedly wide 55–45 margin of victory. But McCain still narrowly carried the district; Boccieri's 94 percent party voting score isn't likely to be sitting well with his constituents.

Boccieri voted for the stimulus package and the federal takeover of financial firms. He sanctimoniously voted against raising the debt limit after his stimulus spending required its elevation. He did vote against Obamacare—but, as with most of the dissenting votes, he did so only after the leadership was able to let him off the hook because they had the votes to pass it without him.

Zack Space

Ohio 18th District (Dover, Zanesville, and Chillicothe)

2008 vote share	60%
McCain vote	53%
Seeking third term	
Party support score	93.9[197]

Zack Space, from Ohio's 18th District, has represented a community that went for Bush by fourteen points and for McCain by seven. Yet, it reelected him with 60 percent of the vote in 2008. He originally won in 2006, taking the seat of Republican congressman Bob Ney, who pled guilty to corruption charges stemming from the Abramoff scandal and was forced to give up his seat.

Space votes with Pelosi 94 percent of the time. He backed Obamacare and the stimulus package. With luck, this will be the year when his district gets to realize whom they've sent to Washington to represent them.

Jason Altmire

Pennsylvania 4th District (western Pennsylvania, northwest of
Pittsburgh along the Ohio border, including part of Allegheny
County and Beaver and Lawrence counties)

2008 vote share	56%
McCain vote	55%
Seeking third term	
Party support score	88%[198]

Altmire is the typical so-called moderate Democrat who hides his true liberalism from his district. Pro-life on abortion, he votes against federal funding and uses his social conservatism to convince the district that he's a Republican in Dems' clothing.

But he's not. He voted for the Obama stimulus package, for raising the debt limit so the deficit could grow, and in favor of the extreme left-wing financial takeover bill written by Barney Frank. He voted against Obamacare, one of the thirty-eight Democrats from swing districts whom Pelosi let go so they could come back in 2011 and assure her continued control.

The fact is, Altmire votes with his party 88 percent of the time. He even got Al Franken and Howard Dean to come into his district to help him raise funds—and then had the gall to use that money to try to convince us he's a moderate!

Fifty-five percent of Altmire's district voted for John McCain. This is the kind of district we have to win to take control of the House in 2010.

Patrick Murphy

Pennsylvania 8th District (Bucks County)

2008 vote share	57%
McCain vote	45%
Seeking third term	
Party support score	96.9%[199]

Patrick Murphy, elected in 2006, is an Iraq War veteran who ran against the Iraq War. As such, he was able to appeal to the district's hawks and doves at the same time and upend a newly elected Republican freshman congressman.

But was his conservative district ready for a liberal with a 96.9 percent party support score who voted for Obamacare and the deficit-creating stimulus package? We doubt it. This should be his last term in Congress. The war in Iraq is winding down, and he is now left to face his conservative district as a liberal incumbent.

Christopher Carney

> Pennsylvania 10th District (northeastern corner of Pennsylvania
> along the New York and New Jersey borders, including Sunbury,
> Williamsport, Carbondale, and Shamokin)

2008 vote share	56%
McCain vote	54%
Seeking third term	
Party support score	91%[200]

Elected in 2006 after his opponent, a Republican congressman, was implicated in a messy and noisy sex scandal, Carney backs his party hierarchy 91 percent of the time. Thanks to the unfortunate lapses of his 2006 opponent, we're saddled with a congressman who voted for Obama's health bill, the stimulus package, and the socialist regulation of the financial industry. All this from a district that backed John McCain with 54 percent of the vote. In 2008, the Republican Party was hamstrung by a divisive primary fight that allowed Carney to win a second term. Let's be sure it's his last!

Paul Kanjorski

> Pennsylvania 11th District (Scranton/Wilkes-Barre area)

2008 vote share	52%
McCain vote	42%
Seeking fourteenth term	
Party support score	97%[201]

When an incumbent Democrat gets only 52 percent of the vote amid the Obama landslide of 2008—after twenty-six years in office—something's wrong. His district is Democratic, after all, and Obama won there by fifteen points.

So what's up? His district wised up to him.

Kanjorski is the number-two Democrat on the Financial Services Committee in the House, right under Barney Frank. He was a key author of the TARP $700 billion bank bailout and of the new legislation that would give Obama and Geithner the power to nationalize banks virtually at will.

Kanjorski voted for Obamacare, for the stimulus bill, and for raising the debt limit. His unexpectedly close margin of victory in 2008 shows that he might be vulnerable in 2010.

Thus far, his survival can be attributed largely to his talent for getting earmarks for his district. The *New York Times* called him "a master of earmarking."[202] He delivered $21 million of pork to his district in 2009.[203] At some point, the voters of Wilkes-Barre and Scranton should realize that it's *their own money* he's recycling to them and stop voting for him.

Kanjorski is an example of a Democrat who picks your pocket with taxes and spending—and then sends back a pittance to the district in earmarks to try to ensure his reelection. It's time to put an end to his game.

John Spratt

South Carolina 5th District (rural South Carolina between Columbia and Charlotte, North Carolina)

2008 vote share	62%
McCain vote	53%
Seeking fifteenth term	
Party support score	97.9%[204]

More than any other House Democrat, it was John Spratt Jr. who led this nation into a tripling of its budget deficit. Called Pelosi's "maestro of the budget" by *The Almanac of American Politics*,[205] he was responsible for engineering the 2009 budget, which turned out to be $1.4 trillion in the red. He votes with Pelosi, his master, almost all the time, and hopes his district—which went for McCain 53–46—won't notice. He also hopes they won't notice that he voted for Obamacare, raising the debt limit, and stepped-up regulation and government takeover of the financial industry. But this might be the year when this conservative South Carolina district wakes up and realizes who represents them in Congress.

Lincoln Davis

> Tennessee 4th District (roughly one quarter of Tennessee, from the
> northern to the southern border of the state; includes Colum-
> bia, Jamestown, McMinnville, and Rockwood)

2008 vote share	59%
McCain vote	64%
Seeking fifth term	
Party support score	94%[206]

If the Civil War were still raging, a congressman named Lincoln Davis would have it made—straddling the gap between the two presidents. But Davis will have trouble getting reelected in his heavily Republican district, which voted for McCain by almost two to one. His record of voting with Pelosi and Obama 94 percent of the time won't help, either. He voted for the stimulus package and for raising the debt limit. He voted against Obamacare, but only after Pelosi had enough support to pass it without him. And Davis has funneled $18.4 million in earmarks to his Tennessee district.

If the Republican Party cannot count on a district that backed McCain with 64 percent of the vote to send a Republican congressman back to Washington, we *deserve* Nancy Pelosi as speaker!

Chet Edwards

> Texas 17th District (Waco and Bosque, Brazos, Grimes, Hill, Hood,
> Johnson, Madison, McLennan, and Somervell counties)

2008 vote share	53%
McCain vote	67%

Seeking eleventh term
Party support score   97%[207]

What's wrong with this picture? Chet Edwards is from Texas. His district voted for McCain over Obama two to one. But Edwards votes with the liberal leadership of his party 97 percent of the time; he voted for the stimulus package, for raising the debt limit, and for the Death Tax; he even voted against banning partial-birth abortions. If any seat should be held by a Republican, it's this one.

Chet Edwards is a reliable performer for the Democratic leadership. As *The Almanac of American Politics* points out, in 2008 "Pelosi enthusiastically encouraged Obama to place Edwards on his short list of potential vice presidents." [208] (Maybe the Democratic Party had some leftover "Edwards for Vice President" bumper stickers from 2004.)

Edwards casts the occasional vote against liberal legislation as a sop to conservatives—opposing Obama's health-care bill, for instance, after he was sure it had enough votes to pass anyway. But that's not good enough: We need a reliable conservative in this district.

Edwards shows his real colors—and stays in power—by feeding us back our own tax money in the form of earmarks. In 2009, he ranked sixth in earmarks in the entire House.[209] He sponsored sixty-seven earmarks in 2009, for a total of $152 million—including $1,762,000 for a honey bee lab in Weslaco, Texas. No wonder he voted to triple the deficit with the stimulus package: He was in on the feeding frenzy.

Aren't we sick and tired of congressmen who vote to pick our pockets through debt and taxes, and then give us back a pittance in earmarks and ask for our votes?

The district is getting wise to Edwards. In 2006, he was reelected with 58 percent of the vote. But in 2008, against an opponent with little money, he got only 53 percent. Next year, let's get rid of him and put in a real Republican instead.

Jim Matheson

Utah 2nd District (the eastern and southern borders of Utah, including South Salt Lake, Price, and St. George)

2008 vote share	63%
McCain vote	58%
Seeking his sixth term	
Party support score	91%[210]

Despite frequent challenges, Matheson keeps fooling his district, painting himself as a conservative while he backs his party line 91 percent of the time. But this time he may have gone a little too far, especially in a district that McCain carried by seventeen points. He supported Obama's stimulus plan, backed his proposal for massive takeovers of private financial institutions, supported raising the debt limit, and voted against Obamacare only after Pelosi had enough support to pass it without him.

The entire process of watching Obama ram through his program has made voters understand the chicanery involved in getting them to vote for people like Matheson, who then enable Pelosi, Rangel, and the other radicals to control the House. This year, a major challenge could oust him.

Rick Boucher

Virginia 9th District (southwest Virginia)

2008 vote share	unopposed
McCain vote	59%
Seeking fifteenth term	
Party support score	97.3%[211]

Virginia's Rick Boucher was unopposed in 2008. Yet McCain carried Boucher's district with 59 percent of the vote. His district is heavily dependent on coal and doesn't seem to realize that Obama and Pelosi have declared war on their principal product. Cap and trade will put them out of business. But don't count on Boucher to defy his party. He does what they tell him 97 percent of the time and backed both the stimulus package and raising the debt limit.

Alan Mollohan

West Virginia 1st District (Wheeling, Morgantown)
2008 vote share	unopposed
McCain	57%
Seeking fifteenth term	
Party support score	97.8%[212]

West Virginia's Mollohan has been under FBI investigation for personally profiting from financial deals with the heads of nonprofit companies for whom he wangled earmarks. (In *Outrage* we discuss his shenanigans in detail.) Mollohan helped nonprofit organizations in his district get federal earmarks. Then he went into real estate deals with the heads of the non-profits. But the Obama/Holder Justice Department dropped the investigation just in time for the election of 2010.

Whether or not he is financially dishonest, Mollohan does not represent the wishes of a district that voted for McCain by fourteen points. He voted for Obamacare, the stimulus package, raising the debt limit, and socialistic financial regulation. He backed Obama and Pelosi an astonishing 98 percent of the time. He was unopposed the last time he ran. But this time he can, and should, be defeated.

As with other Democratic congressmen from this coal-producing region, he will have a hard time explaining to the voters of his district how he can back a party leadership dedicated to the extinction of its principal product in the name of climate change.

Nick Rahall

West Virginia 3rd District (Huntington)
2008 vote share	67%
McCain vote	56%
Seeking eighteenth term	
Party support score	96.9%[213]

Nick Rahall's district went 56 percent for McCain, but reelected him at the same time by a two-to-one margin. Rahall is no moderate: He votes with Pelosi 97 percent of the time and reliably supports her on health care, stimulus, raising the debt limit, and financial regulation.[214] His big thing has been supporting the coal industry. But his constituents must realize that his very first vote at the start of each session of Congress—for Pelosi as speaker, Henry Waxman as Energy Committee chairman, and Charlie Rangel as Ways and Means chairman—vitiates all of his efforts over the subsequent two years for coal. This team is united in its determination to eradicate coal as an energy source in the name of global climate change. Unless Rahall becomes a Republican, he cannot be a supporter of coal.

Rahall also sided with Hamas against Israel on January 21, 2010, when he signed a letter with fifty-three other Democratic congressmen opposing the blockade of Gaza. Nick forgot to mention that the Israelis only imposed the blockade after Hamas used Gaza to shower rockets on its cities and civilians.[215]

Steve Kagen

Wisconsin 8th District (Green Bay)

2008 vote share	54%
McCain vote	45%
Seeking third term	
Party support score	98.2%[216]

Finally, there's Wisconsin's Steve Kagen, who might be defeated. His district went for Obama, but McCain got 45 percent of the vote and Kagen got only 54 percent. Elected in 2006, he hasn't done a good job of consolidating his hold on his seat, and his district won't like the fact that he backed Obama on health care, the stimulus, raising the debt limit, and on financial regulation. His party support score is 98 percent.

So that's the list of the forty-four most vulnerable Democrats. We need to beat twenty-nine of them to throw out Madam Pelosi. But there are many other Democrats who deserve defeat and might be vulnerable in what we hope will be the coming Republican sweep of 2010! (This list, and others throughout this book, has been assembled after consulting with

Cookpoliticalreport.com, and after studying *The Almanac of American Politics*, both invaluable tools for handicapping races.)

Dennis Cardoza, California
Jim Costa, California
Loretta Sanchez, California
Ed Perlmutter, California
Christopher Murphy, Connecticut
Ron Klein, Florida
John Barrow, Georgia
Melissa Bean, Illinois
Debbie Halvorson, Illinois
Joe Donnelly, Indiana
Brad Ellsworth, Indiana
Bruce Braley, Iowa
Leonard Boswell, Iowa
John Yarmuth, Kentucky
Ben Chandler, Kentucky
Martin Heinrich, New Mexico
Scott Murphy, New York
Tim Walz, Minnesota
Heath Schuler, North Carolina
Kurt Schrader, Oregon
Tim Holden, Pennsylvania
Stephanie Herseth Sandlin, South Dakota
Ciro Rodriguez, Texas
Gerald Connolly, Virginia
Ron Kind, Wisconsin

With more than sixty Democratic seats potentially in play in the House and more than a dozen in the Senate, the chances are very good that Republicans can take control. But only if we wage a smart campaign.

PART THREE

THE STRATEGY

Defeating Obama's efforts to destroy all that is best in our country won't be easy. But there is no more urgent or important task.

Very simply: If we want our way of life to continue, and our free enterprise–based economy to survive, we must win the congressional elections of 2010.

Gaining the ten Senate and thirty-nine House seats we need to take power will be a real challenge. The best model for this political earthquake is the 1994 elections, when the Republicans captured control of both houses (marking the first time in forty years that they'd controlled the House of Representatives).

Can we achieve another 1994? The off-year election results in Virginia and New Jersey—and the amazing GOP victory in Massachusetts—all suggest that we can.

In 1993—the year before the GOP landslide—Republicans also won upset victories for governor in New Jersey and Virginia. And their margins of victory were very similar to those of 2009.

If we believe that "as go Virginia and New Jersey, so goes the nation" we could, indeed, take over both houses. Let's take a closer look at these two bellwether races.

Virginia, which doesn't allow its governors to seek a second term, elected a Democratic governor in 1993 and in 2009. In 1993, Republican George Allen defeated Democrat Mary Sue Terry by 58–41%. In 2009, Republican Bob McDonnell beat Democrat Creigh Deeds by 58–40%.

New Jersey, too, elected a Democratic governor, Jim Florio, in 1993, and another, Jon Corzine, in 2009. Florio and Corzine each sought reelection, and each lost his bid. In 1993, Republican Christie Todd Whitman beat Florio by 49–48%. And, in 2009, Republican Chris Christie defeated Corzine by 49–45%. The similarity of these scenarios suggests that, just as the early races of 1993 presaged the sweeping Republican victories of 1994, the early wins of 2009 could point the way to 2010.

And what more evidence of our chances for victory could skeptics want than the incredible election of Republican Scott Brown to the Senate seat held by Ted Kennedy in (the People's Republic of) Massachusetts since 1962!

The handwriting is on the wall.

But victory will not come automatically, just as it did not in Virginia, New Jersey, or Massachusetts. It will take hard work and the right strategy.

Here's how we can do it.

DEBUNK THE MYTH OF THE MODERATE DEMOCRAT

The single most important message of the 2010 campaign should be this: *It doesn't matter who the Democratic candidate is.* Once they reach Congress, they all morph into rubber stamps, endorsing whatever Obama, Pelosi, and Reid want.

There's no such thing as a moderate or conservative or "blue dog" Democrat. They are all just Democrats. They may vote against the leadership when they're allowed, like a dog occasionally let off his leash in the park. But when the leaders need an important vote, it's always there. The leash comes back on.

Every year, voters get more and more sophisticated as the 24/7 cable news cycle brings them new information and insights. Five years ago, no one outside of a few congressional parliamentarians knew what "reconciliation" meant. Now, any taxi driver might ask if you think Reid will use the strategy to pass Obama's program with only fifty-one votes instead of the sixty required to shut off debate.

And those super-educated voters are catching on to the paradox of modern American politics: It's the swing districts and swing voters who determine who gets elected and which party controls Congress. And swing voters are, by definition, moderates—in the middle of the political spectrum. They aren't real liberals or dedicated conservatives. Sometimes they agree with one party, sometimes with the other. That's democracy at work.

But here's the problem: In recent years, the votes of these moderate voters have too often gone to elect congressmen and senators who pose as moderates to win those swing votes—but then roll over as soon as they get elected and allow their extreme liberal leaders to run Congress. These votes pave the way for extreme liberals like New York's Charlie Rangel to take over the House Ways and Means Committee and jam through huge tax increases.

It's their votes that let radicals like Nancy Pelosi and Harry Reid steer our nation toward socialism.

Generally, the political parties are smart enough to run moderates for office in swing districts. A candidate like this may be a Democrat in name, but many of them campaign against government spending; some oppose gun control; some are even pro-life. They run for office saying all the right things. Sometimes, they even go to Congress and vote against Obama's programs. But none of this matters. The only vote that counts is the first vote: the vote that elects Pelosi speaker or Reid majority leader. After that, these "moderates" are free, within reason, to do what they need to keep their jobs.

In fact, even their votes against Obama's programs are usually phony. In the Senate, Reid needs every last Democrat to get what he wants: He needs sixty votes to pass a bill, and until Republican Scott Brown won there were only sixty Democrats for him to work with. In the House, on the other hand, all Nancy Pelosi needs is 218 votes to pass legislation—and she has 257 Democrats to choose from. So when it comes to passing the unpopular programs the Obama administration is pushing, she can afford to let thirty-nine Democrats off the hook.

For example, when health care came up for initial passage in the House, it passed by only 220–215. Thirty-eight Democrats voted against it. Some called this a close vote, but it would have passed however many votes the Democrats needed. If they had to make every single Democrat support the bill, they would have gotten the votes, just as Reid does in the Senate. But as long as they needed only 218 for passage, the House leaders were content to give some of their moderate and marginal members a break and let them vote against the bill.

The ultimate goal, sadly enough, is to fool the voters. After the dust has settled, these moderates come home and tell their constituents *I'm a moderate. I voted against the Obama health plan, but it passed over my objections*—hoping that will be enough to get them reelected.

But it's our job to make sure voters see through that kind of bait-and-switch. These days, a Democrat is a Democrat is a Democrat.

It wasn't always this way: In the 1990s there was an actual split between the liberal and moderate wings of the Democratic Party. When welfare reform passed in 1996, for example, ninety-nine House Democrats voted for it and ninety-nine voted against it.

With the coming of Obama, though, all that has changed.

Why? In part, because these days the party itself controls most of the campaign funding its candidates receive. They get the bulk of their money from PACs, party committees, rich donors, or independent expenditures on their behalf that are controlled by the party leaders. Only a small part of their money comes from their own initiative. If they stray from the party line—without permission from the leadership—they can, and will, be cut off. Connecticut senator Joe Lieberman found out how painful that can be. He was denied his party's renomination in 2006, and won only by running as an Independent!

So as we head into the 2010 election season, it's your job—it's all our jobs—to explain these facts to every potential voter. Show them why the Democrats in your state always do what the party asks them to do. Trace where their money comes from. Show that the party that funds their campaigns controls them. Only by making that clear will your fellow voters understand that a few stray votes of dissent do not a moderate make.

Here's a sample TV ad that makes the point (if you're involved in a campaign yourself, you have our blanket permission—and encouragement— to use any sample ad in this book, without any obligation to us; what's important is just that we get the message out there!):

JONES'S FUNDING

Visual	Text
Print on screen:	
Democratic National Committee: $700,000	The Democratic National Committee gave Congressman Joe Jones $700,000
Democratic House Campaign Committee: $300,000	And the Democratic House Campaign Committee gave him $300,000
Democratic Leadership PACs: $150,000	And PACs controlled by party leaders gave him $150,000.
Photo of Rep. Joe Jones	Is Joe Jones independent? Whose bread he eats, his praises he sings.

Educate your fellow voters. Show them that your opponent votes the party line, whatever he says to the contrary. Cite his party support score in your ads. (Look it up online, or in part 2 of this book.)

When the Democrats won sixty votes in the Senate (by stealing the Al Franken election), they may have helped us to discredit the myth of the moderate Democrat. When they had the majority—but not sixty votes— Reid had to negotiate with Republicans to pass a bill. But last year he didn't have to. He could tell Republicans to get lost and concentrate on cutting deals with his so-called moderate Democrats to hang on to his sixty votes.

By lining up his soldiers and marching them in lockstep to vote for the most radical of Obama's programs, Reid showed the nation how fraudulent the very idea of a moderate Democrat truly is. When push comes to shove, they all vote the way they're told. If Reid needs sixty votes, he gets sixty votes—no exceptions allowed.

Are some senators dooming themselves to defeat by their votes? You bet they are! Arkansas's Blanche Lincoln, for instance, will probably be defeated because of her vote for health care. She knows it. But with Obama in power, she can look forward to her reward: a cabinet post, an ambassadorship, and support for another run at public office. A cushy future awaits her—as long as she disregards what the people of Arkansas want and votes the way Obama and Reid tell her to vote.

Forty-eight Democratic congressional representatives come from districts that John McCain carried in 2008. It's a disgrace to the intelligence of the voters of their districts that these Democrats can fool them into voting for them year after year.

Five of these Democrats, who represent Republican districts, were reelected unopposed in 2008 (Marion Berry of Arkansas, Charlie Melancon of Louisiana, John Tanner of Tennessee, Rick Boucher of Virginia, and Alan Mollohan of West Virginia). How outrageous! All they do is go back to Washington and keep the Democrats in power.

Perhaps these so-called conservative Democrats know that the jig is up! Of the five conservative Democratic congressmen listed above, three have dropped out and are not seeking another term.

Why does the state of Mississippi, one of the most conservative states in America, have two Democratic congressmen out of four to represent it in Washington? They are Travis Childers and Gene Taylor. They have their districts convinced that they're really conservative Democrats. But their votes keep Pelosi and Rangel in charge of the House of Representatives. It doesn't matter how they vote after they have backed Pelosi and Rangel. *That's* the vote that determines what will pass. These two, and all others like them, have to go!

Utah is the most Republican state in America, but it sends Jim Matheson, a Democrat, as one of its three representatives to the Congress. Why do the voters of Utah vote to keep the radical liberal socialists in charge in Washington by reelecting Matheson? With luck, they'll see the error of their ways in 2010.

This television commercial (or any adaptation of it you care to make for literature or radio or the Internet) really brings the point home well.

Do you remember "The Anvil Chorus" (from the opera *Il Trovatore*), with its pounding, repetitive beat? Well, that would make a great soundtrack for this video or radio ad. Instead of blacksmiths pounding their hammers, have a guy with a rubber stamp keeping time to the music, stamping bill after bill after bill with a big YES—or, if it's radio, use the sound of a rubber stamp throughout the ad. Here's the text:

PARTY HACK

Visual	Text
Man in a suit stamping bills. "Anvil Chorus" plays in background.	Congressman Joe Jones voted the way his party leaders told him to 94 percent of the time. When they said to vote for more spending, he did. Cut Medicare? Okay with him. Raise the deficit? Yes again. Jones runs as a moderate. He says he's his own man. But when the party leaders, like President Obama, Nancy Pelosi, and Harry Reid, tell him to jump, he's got only one question: How high?

Every American voter needs to understand that there's no such thing as a blue dog. They don't exist in real life, and they don't exist in Congress, either. Those mutts called blue dogs are just a bunch of yellow dogs pretending to be blue!

NATIONALIZE THE CAMPAIGN AND MAKE OBAMA THE ISSUE

By Election Day, one fact will be undeniable in every single state or district where Republicans have a chance to defeat incumbent Democratic senators and congressmen: The incumbent Democrat—no matter how unpopular—will have a higher approval rating than Obama!

So don't run against the popular local incumbent—run against Obama! Show how your opponent never strays far from the Obama party line. Make his knee-jerk support for the president's legislative program the issue in the campaign. By pointing out his sycophantic support for whatever Obama wants, you can pave the way to his defeat.

So far, Obama's crash—from 70 percent approval, at the start of his term, to less than 50 percent in every poll today—has been historic. No previous president ever fell so far so fast. So the Democratic strategy will be obvious: *Hide Obama.* Congressional representatives and senators will campaign on their own, rarely mentioning the president, and try to cast themselves as moderates and independents.

But we can't let them set the terms of the debate. Our job is to remind everyone that this race is about Barack Obama.

We have to stop the Democrats from obscuring that fact. We have to make the election a referendum on the Obama presidency. A job you can help perform, whether you're a local candidate, a party organizer, a canvasser, or simply a concerned citizen. Go after Obama's policies and programs. Attack his record of high and continuing unemployment. Warn of the dangers of his health-care program. Speak out about the huge federal budget deficit and its catastrophic implications for our country. Criticize his cap-and-trade proposals and point out how they will raise utility bills. Describe the inflation his policies are going to trigger. Hammer away at the global loss of confidence in the dollar and our abandonment of economic control to European banks. Point to the higher taxes that will certainly follow a Democratic victory. Make clear your opposition to a government takeover of the economy, of further bailouts of banks, and of its continued ownership of General Motors. Talk about how we're letting our guard against terrorism down. These are the issues!

But don't just *talk about* issues, like a professor in an economic class. You need to bring these issues home to the average voter—by drawing the link between the financial situation of individual households and that of the federal government. People are wrestling, in their own lives—and at their own kitchen tables—with just the sort of dilemmas into which Obama has plunged us. Just as many American families worry about how to pay the mortgage, electric bill, and credit card debt, the American people have to start worrying about how we're going to pay for this gargantuan deficit with which Obama has saddled us.

Here's an example of a television ad that the Republican campaigns ought to be running in markets all over the country this year. It can also work as a radio ad or a piece of direct-mail literature.

THE GROWING NATIONAL DEBT

Visual

A middle-aged man is pounding away on his calculator. He looks more and more frustrated.

Text

Bills got you down? Can't pay your debts?

Now the man morphs into Uncle Sam, still working on the calculator.

The government's in the same boat. Obama has increased our debt by more than $3 trillion.

Uncle Sam is now sweating and mopping his brow . . .	Up 33 percent in one year. With debt like that, who can afford health care, jobs, education, anything?

Cut to Barack Obama signing a bill.	But Obama has a solution. He keeps borrowing to pay off his borrowing.
Cut back to middle-aged man.	And we end up paying the bill!
NAME OF REPUBLICAN CANDIDATE	Vote No on Obama Vote for _____.

Why did the Republicans win in 1994?

Because they all ran against Bill and Hillary Clinton.

The tax increases the Clinton administration got passed, and the health-care bill they tried and failed to pass, were the key issues that propelled the Republican Party to its most sweeping congressional victory in more than fifty years.

There's always a temptation to fragment congressional and senatorial campaigns and to treat each as a discrete and separate contest—to deal with each Democratic and Republican candidate on his or her own. No candidate or state party wants to see itself as merely a cog in a fifty-state national election.

But that is what they will be in 2010—only one part of a larger mosaic. The radicalism of the Obama agenda, how it affects every facet of our lives and changes our country so completely, guarantees that it will be *the* issue in 2010. Individual candidates won't matter nearly as much as the outcome of the giant national referendum on Obama's policies.

In the usual off-year election, the fate of the candidates moves up or down based on the ebb and flow of their debate and dialogue. The national party trend manifests itself only at the very end of the election year, a sudden wave that can move the candidates of the favored party up five to ten points right before Election Day. This is largely because the impact of party trend voting is generally limited to downscale voters who pay too little attention to politics to know much about the candidates. Only when the noise of the approaching election reaches cacophonic proportions are they left with no choice but to pay attention. (These voters are like those who ignore football until right before the Super Bowl, or Christmas shoppers who don't enter a store until December 23.)

Forced to focus with Election Day right around the corner, they usually fall in line behind their political party. Until then, they may have told pollsters that they're undecided, or may have said they would vote for the incumbent—the only name they knew. But now they focus on partisan choices—and return to the banner of their traditional party affiliation. (Because there are more downscale Democrats than Republicans, this process is often referred to as "Democrats coming home" in the final days of the campaign.)

But 2010 won't work that way. The issues are too important and receive far too much attention for voters not to follow them. Who can ignore the massive unemployment and the misery of the recession? The radicalism of Obama's health-care proposals? The prospect of huge tax increases? A deficit and debt that is consuming our economy? Now, in 2010, everybody is paying attention to the race from the very beginning. This intense focus on the issues surrounding Obama will drown out normal party trends on one hand, and the merits or demerits of each individual candidate on the other. It doesn't matter so much who's running. This election will be a referendum on Obama—from beginning to end.

In some off-year elections, local issues dominate the debate. In 2010, however, they have been drowned out by the defining national issues of our time. With unemployment up around 10 percent, the deficit tripled, the national debt up 33 percent, and seven million jobs lost, the only issues that count are the national ones.

Tip O'Neill, the former Democratic House speaker, famously said, "all politics is local."[1]

Not this year! In 2010, the tables are turned: All politics is national.

In some states—in the past—voters tended to vote one way for president and another way for Senate or Congress. Their local congressman or senator courts them by sending mailings, issuing press releases, and bringing home pork barrel projects. He or she shows up at picnics and town fairs and cultivates the voters. Confronting them on the local level is fighting their fight on their turf. As Winston Churchill once said about trying to mount a land war against Japan in Asia, fighting local candidates on local issues is like "going into the water to fight the shark."

Don't do it! The way to win is to make the fight about national issues.

When you're stirring up debate about the 2010 election, don't waste your time on local dustups. Talk about the national policies—the ones that make red-state voters see red.

And don't confuse partisanship with opposition to Obama! The national polling shows far more antipathy to the president than support for the Republican Party. Even in blue states, Obama's policies are becoming so unpopular that you can gain all the traction you need just by opposing them. With his approval scores dropping every month, you can use Obama to defeat your local Democratic federal elected officials.

But remember: This isn't about attacking Democrats. It's about attacking *Obama*. Leave plenty of room for those who are still Democrats to vote against Obama because of their disenchantment with high unemployment and continuing hard economic times.

Go into depth on these national issues. Use the arguments and facts in this book. (That's why we wrote it!) Lucidly and clearly explain to your fellow voters the dangers we face—and why Obama's programs aren't working.

DON'T BE LIMITED BY IDEOLOGY

Another trap to avoid when campaigning against Obama is framing everything in terms of ideology. Just as Obama's failures transcend ideology, so too should our attacks. Don't rely on left-versus-right issues like health care or government spending. Attack him for his basic failures of leadership, for breaking his promises, for being ineffectual or weak, and for failing to listen to the people. Your attacks don't have to be ideological. They just have to resonate with the voters.

After all, the voters don't have to agree with us on every issue to cast the right vote in 2010. Plenty of voters who backed Obama in 2008 have since become disillusioned; if they're thinking of voting Republican in 2010, we'll welcome their support, not ask them to repudiate the ideology that led them to support Obama in the first place. It doesn't matter why they vote against Obama. It only matters that they do.

When voters become disappointed with a president for whom they voted, their angst over his performance hardens and eventually leads them to draw negative conclusions about his character, ability, energy, commitment to the job, or sincerity. We need these voters. They may once have embraced Obama, but now they're disillusioned. We can't let our ideology drive them back into Obama's arms. Let them vote for us without making them recant their entire ideology.

There are plenty of reasons to recognize that Obama is a bad president—and that his congressmen and senators need to be replaced—that have nothing to do with ideology.

Obama doesn't keep his campaign promises. Conservatives don't always go out of their way to point this out—after all, they're happy that Obama has decided to stay in Afghanistan. But that doesn't matter. The fact is, this president was elected on a platform of peace and jobs—and he's given us anything but.

That kind of reversal gets liberals and even moderates who supported Obama very angry. They feel conned and fooled. They feel buyer's remorse. Regardless of what *you* thought of all his crazy promises, the real point is that Obama flips and flops.

Here's a basic axiom for when a politician changes his mind and alters his position: The only people who believe he's really changed are those who used to agree with him and now are angry that he's flipped. The folks who used to disagree with him don't really buy that he's come around to their point of view. He loses them both.

So Obama won't gain any new friends by fighting in Afghanistan. The hawks still consider him too weak and unwilling to stand up for American interests. And the doves are upset that he went back on his word.

It's impossible to know whether the Afghan war can be won, but one thing's for sure: It won't be if we pursue Obama's policies. When you attack Obama over Afghanistan, the real thing to attack is the *way* he's conducting the war. Even raising the issue will catch the attention of the antiwar base that elected him in the first place.

The litany of broken Obama promises is amazing:

He promised to get us out of Iraq. But we're still there.

He promised cap and trade. But he hasn't produced.

He said he'd end Don't Ask, Don't Tell and allow gays in the military. But he hasn't.

He promised not to raise taxes on the middle class. But he has.

He said he'd bring down the deficit. But he's tripled it.

He promised to close Guantanamo. But it's still open for business.

He said he'd fix Social Security. But he hasn't touched it.

He promised to preserve Medicare. But he cut it by $500 billion.

He said he'd reform immigration law. But it's the same as when he took office.

He promised to renegotiate NAFTA. But he flipped as soon as he took office.

He told Big Labor he'd make it possible to organize new unions without a secret ballot. But that bill died.

You may disagree with many of these promises. You're probably glad they failed. But don't let that stop you from using them to defeat Obama.

Here's a radio ad that makes this point:

OBAMA'S PROMISES

(A female voice reads Obama's promises. A male voice reads his reactions.)

Woman: When Barack Obama was running for president, he said he'd pull out of Iraq.

Man: But we're still there.

Woman: Candidate Obama promised to cut the deficit.

Man: Instead, he tripled it.

Woman: He said he'd create jobs.

Man: He's actually lost three million.

Woman: He promised to hold down federal spending.

Man: He raised it from three trillion to four trillion.

Woman: Obama told us he wouldn't raise taxes on the middle class.

Man: But he did.

Woman: Said he'd fix Social Security.

Man: Nope.

Woman: Who can trust Obama?

Man: Well, Congressman Jim Jones still believes him.

Woman: Well, I don't!

You can also hit Obama on his weakness. Everyone agrees that Obama has shown himself to be incredibly ineffective in the face of foreign enemies. You don't need to be a conservative to appreciate that in the face of America's most serious and threatening adversaries, he has consistently backed down.

Voters usually see foreign policy as a test of a president's character. Because he has such leeway to do what he wants in international affairs, they see it as the surest indication of his firmness and decisiveness.

Obama is flunking on both counts.

By the time you read this book, we hope that Obama will finally have taken action against Iran, arresting its progress toward the development of nuclear weapons. If not, we hope and pray that Israel finds a way to avert a second Holocaust by acting on her own. But the record of Obama's submissiveness in the face of Iran and North Korea, and his refusal to stand up to Russia's Putin or Venezuela's Chavez, is obvious to all.

Most voters, at least initially, were hopeful when the president reached out to the "Arab street" to make it clear that America was not opposed to Islam or to Muslims in general. But we see that his initiatives have not been reciprocated. The terrorists are as busy as ever, as the widows and orphans of the slain soldiers at Fort Hood will attest. So go after Obama for his failures in foreign policy.

On the domestic front, even if you buy wholeheartedly into Obama's ideology and his political agenda, you have to admit he's not been very effective in achieving it. At this writing, we don't know the fate of all his legislative initiatives, but so far the record is pretty sparse. Even the president's most ardent admirers must be disappointed.

Liberals don't like that he promised a public option in his health-care plan, only to cave.

They're mad that he settled for a face-saving solution at the Copenhagen climate talks, rather than getting a real global commitment for action.

And they're severely disappointed that he hasn't pushed through cap and trade.

Liberals want gays accepted in the military and can't understand why they're not.

Hispanics, who voted for Obama by two to one, are alienated because he hasn't pushed for immigration reform, giving the cause only lip service.

And the entire Michael Moore crowd is beside itself that Guantanamo is still open and wiretapping in terror investigations hasn't been stopped. And they're going crazy because they think Obama is too cozy with Wall Street.

Keep hammering away at these issues to erode voter turnout from Obama's base.

DO NOT MOVE TO THE CENTER

This may sound like odd advice coming from the exponent of triangulation, the strategy that moved Bill Clinton to the center and led to his reelection in 1996.

But it's good advice all the same.

American politics moves in cycles. There are times when voters *want* to hear debate and disagreement. As they face new problems, they urge left and right alike to explain and elaborate their proposed solutions, critiquing one another's ideas. This is different from the process in Japan, for instance, where the political process is *never* used to hash out real debates; everything is decided by consensus behind closed doors.

But, in the United States, there always comes a moment when voters have heard enough and are ready to make a decision. When that time comes, they want their elected officials to put aside party and ideology and enact the national consensus. (That doesn't happen in Italy or France, where the debates never end. Italy still has a fascist party; France still has Bonapartists and Monarchists.)

And both phases—debate and consensus—come from the dialectic first explained by the German philosopher Friedrich Hegel. He observed that in any debate there is always a thesis—a governing wisdom—and an antithesis to combat it. After the conflict has raged, he writes, a new consensus, a synthesis, appears and history moves on.

It's very important to recognize when the public wants debate and when it demands consensus. Getting it right is the most important element in judging the mood of the electorate.

After the 2000 election, the debate over the validity of the election count lasted for months after the matter was settled by the Supreme Court. But then 9/11 brought us back together again. It was a time for synthesis. In 2004, John Kerry lost because he misjudged where voters were on this triangular progression. He ran as the antithesis when voters wanted synthesis. He ran as the candidate of the left at a time when voters wanted consensus. But then Iraq pulled us apart again and it was John McCain's turn to misjudge the public mood. In 2008, he ran as the candidate of synthesis, of consensus, while Obama demanded change, and McCain lost.

Today, Obama's radical program has kindled the debate anew. The public wants to hear what Republicans think of Obama's proposals. Frustrated with the economy and high unemployment, they want the left and the right to thrash it out and explain how they think we can get out of this mess.

Now is no time for the middle of the road. It's a time for contrast and debate.

It will probably take the election of 2010 for this cycle to enter its next phase. Once those votes have been counted, the electorate will have rendered its verdict. Then it will want Washington to implement its consensus. Synthesis will be in order.

But not now!

OFFER A POSITIVE ALTERNATIVE

When the Republican Party controlled at least one House of Congress from 1994 to 2006, they screwed up. Their earmarks were just as outrageous as the Democrats' had been. Their spending was just as profligate. Their conflicts of interest were just as profound; their ties to lobbyists just as cozy and corrupt. In *Outrage*, *Fleeced*, and *Catastrophe*, we documented these abuses and railed against them.

If the GOP just offers more of the same, it will not win and will not deserve to win.

The party has to make clear that it points in a decidedly new direction in 2010 and that its leaders have learned their lessons from the defeats of 2006 and 2008.

Just as House speaker Newt Gingrich electrified the nation by publishing a Contract with America before the 1994 election, so the Republican Party must make specific commitments to the voters as the elections of 2010 approach.

Here's what they must pledge to get our support:

1. An end to earmarking
2. A ban on families of members of Congress serving as lobbyists
3. No free travel, whether sponsored by foundations or lobbyists. Only government trips on official business—*real* official business—should be allowed.
4. No tax increases
5. Support for the line-item veto
6. Full disclosure of the precise amounts of members' net worth, debts, investments, and holdings
7. No use of taxpayer-funded staff or offices for political campaigning
8. The establishment of a special prosecutor for congressional ethics violations and an end to the self-serving ethics committees made up of members of the club
9. A ban on spouses of members of Congress serving on boards or accepting employment by any company or organization that receives federal funds.
10. Full publication, online, of all committee votes
11. A ban on members of Congress, or congressional staffers, lobbying Congress for five years after the end of their tenure or employment or being employed by a company that performs lobbying services.

12. And if a senator or congressman is absent more than 10 percent of the time for reasons other than illness—dock his pay (especially if he's in Iowa running for president.)

An agenda like this can and will show voters that the Republican Party can be trusted to change Washington.

DON'T TRIP OVER YOUR OWN PROPOSALS: STAY ON OFFENSE

One danger Republicans face as the 2010 election heats up is being forced onto the defensive, into proposing detailed answers to every issue. The Democrats running in 2010 are already on the ropes, trying to defend Obama. Don't give them ammunition by making specific proposals for them to attack. Stay on the offense. Keep the upper hand.

Like a good defense attorney, or a negative debater, we have to stay focused on the job—which is to stop the incumbent and his party from successfully defending Obama. The president's record is what's under attack, and we need to keep it that way.

Unemployment, the deficit, skyrocketing spending, and Obama's socialist designs on our health-care system, banks, and auto industry will give us the ammo we need in 2010.

Here's a piece of advice for all aspiring politicians: If you're running as a Republican in 2010, don't complicate things by making detailed affirmative proposals on issues. The time for that will come when you're in Congress!

And, for the many, many Americans we hope will get involved in actively supporting these Republican candidates, the advice is much the same: You won't convince your friends and neighbors by spending all your time talking up the new proposals your candidate's going to bring to Washington next year. The way to win is to focus on what's wrong right now: the Obama Democrats who are ruining our country.

Raise a stink about Obama's big-spending ways. Everyone knows that Obama has been spending money like a madman ever since he reached the White House. If you're asked where spending should be cut, just read off the list of all the wasteful projects in the stimulus package. You don't need to make sure the numbers add up to a balanced federal budget. Just enumerate the waste and you'll have made your point.

The economic program most identified with President Obama is the stimulus package he jammed through Congress in the opening week of his presidency. This massive dose of government spending, plus the supplemental appropriations package he passed in 2009 and the second stimulus or "jobs" package he's planning as this is written, are among his greatest vulnerabilities. The list of ways he's spent taxpayer money is incredible. And because your Democratic congressman or senator most likely voted for the stimulus package, you can lay the blame equally on him or her and Obama!

And when you list the ridiculous projects this job-killing deficit has funded, voters will turn against the Democrats even more dramatically.

When Obama decided to spend his way to recovery, he didn't much care where the money would go. He just wanted it spent. The sooner the better. So whoever was "shovel ready" got the funding. The result is the weirdest collection of federal projects you can imagine. Humor is always a great weapon in politics, and the list of stimulus spending projects we enumerated earlier practically begs for satire:

OBAMA'S STIMULUS SPENDING LIST [2]

1. $300,000 for a GPS-equipped helicopter to hunt for radioactive rabbit droppings at the Hanford nuclear reservation in Washington state.

2. $30 million for a spring training baseball complex for the Arizona Diamondbacks and Colorado Rockies.

3. $11 million for Microsoft to build a bridge connecting its two headquarters campuses in Redmond, Washington, which are separated by a highway.

4. $430,000 to repair a bridge in Iowa County, Wisconsin, that carries ten or fewer cars per day.

5. $800,000 for a backup runway for the John Murtha Airport in Johnstown, Pennsylvania, serving about twenty passengers per day.

6. $219,000 for Syracuse University to study the sex lives of freshman women.

7. $2.3 million for the U.S. Forest Service to rear large numbers of arthropods, including the Asian long-horned beetle, the nun moth, and the woolly adelgid.

8. $3.4 million for a thirteen-foot tunnel for turtles and other wildlife attempting to cross U.S. 27 in Lake Jackson, Florida.

9. $1.15 million to install a guardrail for a persistently dry lake bed in Guymon, Oklahoma.

10. $9.38 million to renovate a century-old train depot in Lancaster County, Pennsylvania, that has not been used for three decades.

11. $2.5 million in stimulus checks sent to the deceased.

12. $6 million for a snowmaking facility in Duluth, Minnesota.

13. $173,834 to weatherize eight pickup trucks in Madison County, Illinois.

14. $20,000 for a fish sperm freezer at the Gavins Point National Fish Hatchery in South Dakota.

15. $380,000 to spay and neuter pets in Wichita, Kansas.

16. $1.5 million for a fence to block would-be jumpers from leaping off the All-American Bridge in Akron, Ohio.

17. $1 million to study the health effects of environmentally friendly public housing on three hundred people in Chicago.

18. $356,000 for Indiana University to study childhood comprehension of foreign accents compared with native speech.

19. $983,952 for street beautification in Ann Arbor, Michigan, including decorative lighting, trees, benches, and bike paths.

20. $148,438 for Washington State University to analyze the use of marijuana in conjunction with medications like morphine.

21. $462,000 to purchase twenty-two concrete toilets for use in the Mark Twain National Forest in Missouri.

22. $3.1 million to transform a canal barge into a floating museum that will travel the Erie Canal in New York State.

23. $1.3 million on government arts jobs in Maine, including $30,000 for basket makers, $20,000 for storytelling, and $12,500 for a music festival.

24. $71,000 for a hybrid car to be used by student drivers in Colchester, Vermont, as well as a plug-in hybrid for town workers decked out with a sign touting the vehicle's energy efficiency.

25. $1 million for Portland, Oregon, to replace one hundred aging bike lockers and build a garage that would house 250 bicycles.

26. $300 apiece for thousands of signs at road construction sites across the country announcing that the projects are funded by stimulus money.

The goal of an incumbent is to make the challenger the issue. Don't make that easy for the incumbent you're trying to beat by making a controversial proposal that can have you on the defensive.

The FairTax, for example, might be a very good idea. But if you push the idea too loudly or too often, it could become perceived as your campaign's only issue. Then, as soon as your opponent claims you "want to eliminate the mortgage interest deduction on your taxes," your campaign will get tied up in knots trying to explain how the FairTax works—and you could leave voters more confused than engaged.

This isn't the time for creative thinking. This is the time to stay focused on the problems that face America today—and the biggest problem of all is the Obama administration.

THE UNEMPLOYMENT ISSUE

Just as health care was the leading issue of 2009 and the early months of 2010, unemployment will be the key focus as the congressional elections come into play.

It won't be enough to cite how many jobs Obama has lost or how high the unemployment rate has risen. Republican campaigns will have to dig deeper, to explain *why* these trends are occurring.

Stubbornly high percentages of voters still blame the Bush administration for those problems. As recently as late December 2009, the Rasmussen Poll reported that 51 percent blamed the "recession that started under President Bush" and only 41 percent said that the "policies Obama has adopted since taking office" are primarily at fault for the economic misery.[3] To them, high unemployment and low growth just reinforces their preconception of how bad a president Bush was; they do little to dampen support for Obama.

But campaigns that explain how Obama has caused the current misery will be welcomed by angry voters. Americans love speeches, campaign literature, and even ads that *explain* situations, rather than simply repeat partisan arguments. We love to be educated and informed—especially when we're all wondering how things got so bad and how long they'll stay that way. We need to give the voters the real answers they want! Empty rhetoric isn't enough.

While voters do not necessarily yet blame continuing high unemployment on Obama, they do blame excessive Washington spending and high deficits on him. What we need to do is to *explain* how the spending and the deficit is causing our persistent unemployment.

Deficit spending has a horrible reputation with American voters. For six decades, ever since the 1950s, they've been warned over and over that deficits are the root of all evil. Americans have never taken to Keynesian economics. They never bought into the idea that deficits were good for the economy. Even when first Kennedy and then Nixon tried to sell the idea, they recoiled.

And their rejection of the idea of deficit spending continues to this day. A February 2010 Rasmussen poll found that "only 11% of American adults . . . think the nation needs to increase its deficit spending at this time . . . 70% disagree and say it would be better to cut the deficit. In fact, 59% think Keynes had it backwards and that increasing the deficit at this time would hurt the economy rather than help." [4]

There's a simple reason for this view: Deficit spending just runs too counter to the voters' own daily experience to be a credible solution to our national economic woes. When every household must balance its budget—and the consequences of high personal debt have been brought home to almost every American family—it's impossible to convince Americans that racking up huge debts is an acceptable way to run the American economy. We've all seen too many credit card bills carrying 18 percent interest rates or higher to be comfortable with the idea of living off debt.

If we want to win in 2010, we need to emphasize the deficit and explain how it creates unemployment. Then we can lay the blame for the resulting unemployment squarely on Barack Obama's shoulders.

Obama has tried to equate government spending with job creation. The idea that the two are linked was the basis of his first stimulus package, and of the second "jobs" stimulus package.

We need to discredit this idea. We must explain that government spending, when it is financed by borrowing, does *the opposite* of creating jobs—it destroys jobs. With all the native distrust of deficits, this shouldn't be a hard sell—but it takes some explaining.

It isn't enough just to complain about the debt and the deficit. We have to explain, clearly and simply, why they cause more unemployment than they solve.

Obama believes that the key to curing the recession and unemployment is more and more stimulus spending, running up larger deficits, and piling up more debt. We need to explain that the more government borrows, the more it crowds out small businesses that need to borrow money to expand. There's only so much capital to go around, and by hogging it Washington stops the private sector from creating the jobs we need.

Here's how you might explain it in a piece of campaign literature. (Again, feel free to adapt these for use in supporting your own candidates, whether in paid ads or online. And don't underestimate the effectiveness of a homegrown handout: It may seem low-tech in the Internet age, but a simple flyer is still an efficient and effective way of getting the word out.)

HOW TO WRITE CAMPAIGN BROCHURES

In writing campaign literature, it's important to bear a few simple facts in mind:

1. Draw the reader in by making the cover nonpolitical. And try to make it funny.

2. Use headlines to grab attention.

3. Keep the text to a minimum.

4. Caption each photo you use.

5. Use multicolored graphics.

6. Always include contact information, so the reader can find out more.

Here's some sample text you could use in a flyer or adapt for an online ad:

DEFICIT AND UNEMPLOYMENT

Page 1:

Caption: *What If the Medicine Is Making Him Sicker?*

Page 2: (Photo of a big sack of money weighing down poor Uncle Sam.)

Headline: That's what Obama's big spending is doing to us.

Text: Under Obama, the federal deficit has tripled, rising from less than $500 billion in 2008 to $1.4 trillion in 2009! The higher the deficit goes, the more the U.S. government has to borrow. And the more the government borrows, the less money there is for small businesses to borrow to create jobs.

Congressman Jim Jones has voted yes to all this spending. He has helped Obama amass the deficit that is sinking our economy.

Photo:

Caption: Unemployment is sky-high because the deficit is killing small businesses that try to create jobs.

Page 3: John Doe (our candidate) will cut the deficit . . .

  . . . But Congressman Jim Jones just votes to make it higher.

Text: Jim Jones voted:

- To raise government spending by $1 trillion
- To raise the federal debt ceiling
- To increase federal borrowing

  But John Doe will fight to hold the line on spending, oppose higher taxes, and demand cuts to balance the budget.

Photo: (Photos of Jones and Doe)

Caption: Congressman Jim Jones voted to triple the deficit . . .

  . . . But John Doe will vote to cut it and create jobs.

DOE FOR CONGRESS; CUT THE DEFICIT; CREATE JOBS

Page 4: (Photo of Doe and family, captioned with their names.)

(Brief bio of Doe, repeating his commitment to cutting the deficit and creating jobs.)

(Coupon including website, e-mail address, physical address, and a box to check to volunteer or contribute.)

Here's a way the unemployment and deficit might be treated in a TV commercial:

THE DEFICIT MONSTER

Visual	Text

A hog keeps getting fatter and fatter	Under Bush, the budget deficit was $500 billion. Under Obama, it's grown to $1.4 trillion.

The hog is now crushing a car.

The government has to borrow so much each day that there's no money for car loans . . .

Now he's crushing a house.

or for home mortgages . . .

And now he's crushing a store.

or for small businesses . . .

Now he's crushing a family.

or for ordinary consumers to live their lives.

The hog looks up and smiles.

Barack Obama and Senator Jones will never cut the deficit. They created it.

The hog frowns and gets thinner.

But John Doe sure will.

Another tool you can use in spreading the word is the chart on page 89 showing how U.S. debt has skyrocketed since 2008. That chart is a great way of showing voters at a glance how government borrowing is crowding out consumer, mortgage, and business credit.

Making the jobs issue a deficit-spending issue helps to pin the blame squarely on Obama, where it belongs. And when he proposes more government spending to "create jobs," your criticism—that the spending won't create jobs, it will grow the deficit and *cost* jobs—will click with anyone who's listening.

Voters agree by 59–24% that more government spending will hurt the economy. And Rasmussen reports that "by a three-to-one margin, [voters] believe tax cuts would create more jobs than additional [government] spending."[5]

So here is the formula that works:

More spending = bigger deficit = more unemployment

Because everyone agrees that Obama is for more spending, you just have to elaborate the formula to its conclusion to assign the blame for unemployment where it belongs: on Barack Obama's shoulders.

But Obama isn't listening. No matter how high the deficit goes, Obama just proposes more and more spending. He's a bit like the medieval doctors who felt the key to curing illness was to rid the patient of evil humors by bleeding him. The more blood they drained from the poor victim's veins, the weaker he got and the closer he came to death—but the doctors concluded that his deterioration only proved they hadn't drawn enough blood, so they kept going until the poor soul died.

THE HEALTH-CARE ISSUE

It was the fierce debate over health care that cost Obama the bulk of his support. Once voters looked at the package of proposals, they ran screaming! By the time you read this, we'll know whether we've finally defeated this legislative monstrosity. But what is clear is that voters oppose it by at least a margin of 58 percent.[6] And what is also clear is that if Obama wins the elections of 2010, socialized medicine will be back on the agenda . . . with a vengeance.

But the depth of the public's distrust of the health-care bill runs deeper than even these numbers suggest. According to the Rasmussen Poll, only 13 percent of Americans believe that Obama's health-care legislation will reduce the cost of medical care. Sixty-three percent say it will increase costs. And voters believe by 54–24% that the bill will make the quality of medical care worse.

A plan to cut the quality of health care that costs more! Great plan![7]

If the candidate you're trying to beat is one who voted for the legislation, you should hang the features of the bill around his neck one at a time. It's not enough merely to say "He voted for Obamacare" and leave it at that! Soon the charge will become accepted wisdom and voters will move past it. But if we parade each of the provisions before the voters, and make the plan's supporters eat them for breakfast, lunch, and dinner, the issue can remain fresh and dominate the election. Remember: The more detailed the attack, the more effective it will be.

Here are the key items you should feature in your attack on Obamacare:

WHAT'S WRONG WITH OBAMACARE?

- It slices $500 billion from Medicare, sharply cutting funding for elderly care.

- It repeals the Medicare Advantage program, which subsidized premiums that gave the elderly coverage beyond what Medicare provides. Now they would have to buy more limited Medigap coverage at higher cost with no subsidies available.

- It sets up a Medical Review Board to rule on what kind of care is allowed and what is not permitted under Medicare—specifying who can get procedures like hip replacements, bypass surgery, and high-cost cancer chemotherapy. The board's decisions would be based on age, condition, and other personal factors; doctors who refuse to follow their rules would be fined or face cuts in their reimbursement.

- Uninsured Americans would be required to get insurance, costing an average of $6,000 for an individual and more than $10,000 for a family. Those who fail to do so would have to pay fines of $1,000 to the government. Subsidies will be available, but only after the uninsured pay a specified percentage of their income ranging from 2 percent (or $600 for those making a household income of $30,000) to 10 percent ($8,000 for those making $80,000). For families making $45,000 a year, the subsidies would kick in only after they have spent 6 percent of their income ($2,700) on insurance.

- We would all face higher insurance premiums as our money goes to subsidize those who must now be covered by our insurers. Since these companies would no longer be able to raise their rates or deny coverage for preexisting conditions, we would face increases of up to $2,000 per family to pay for them.

- Medical devices such as pacemakers, heart valves, prosthetic limbs, and automated wheelchairs would all be subject to taxation.

- One-third of our health insurance policies would be taxed at a rate of 40 percent.

- Our state taxes would go up dramatically as the states expand their Medicaid coverage to conform with the bill. Every state will be obliged to offer free medical care to anyone making up to $33,000 for a family of four—and we'll have no choice in the matter.

Here's a sample TV ad attacking a candidate who voted for the new health-care plan:

HEALTH CARE

Visual	Text
Old man speaking	Senator Lincoln, why did you cut my Medicare?
Old woman speaking	You even taxed my pacemaker!
Young family speaking	And you're making us pay a $1,000 fine for not having insurance . . . or we go to jail!
Family in their forties speak	And now our insurance company has hiked our premiums way up!
Blanche Lincoln's photo	[Voiceover] Blanche Lincoln for Senate?
Everyone in ad shouting together	*Are you kidding?*

If Obama does not pass his health-care bill this year, the issue will still loom large in 2010. He won't and can't back away from it. He's invested too much, too publicly, and over too long a period to stop now.

But if his bill does pass in some form, it will be even more of an issue—because the cuts in Medicare in Obama's bill take effect immediately, but the benefits don't start until 2013. The administration thought this was a clever move, designed to present the program as not adding to the deficit. But now that strategy will backfire in a major way: As the 2010 election approaches, we'll have a full list of proposed cuts in Medicare to run against.

The best way to drive home the point about health care for the elderly is to be *very, very specific*. Here's the kind of ad that will work:

CUTS IN DOCTOR REIMBURSEMENT

Visual	Text
Doctor closes the door to his office.	He remembers every driveway, every patient, every heartbeat.
He walks to his car, gets in, and drives away. On his door is a sign: PRACTICE CLOSED	But now he's retiring. Obama's program fines him if he spends too much treating his patients. Washington wants him to cut corners. But he's always put his patients first. They're family. And he's too old to change his ways. So it's time to retire. Since Obamacare passed, thousands of doctors have quit. And fewer doctors means less medical care.
NAME OF REPUBLICAN CANDIDATE	Vote No on Obama Vote for _____.

When it comes to health care, the more moving the ad is, the more effective it will be.

THE TAX ISSUE

Every once in a while, a politician says something everyone knows isn't true. But when he's the president, and he bases his entire administration on the lie, he becomes very, very vulnerable.

Barack Obama's pledge not to raise taxes on anyone making less than $250,000 a year was one of the two signature promises of his campaign. The other was that he would cut taxes for 95 percent of all Americans. Those were his most widely publicized pledges.

Today, the American public no longer believes them.

Rasmussen reports that 48 percent of voters "nationwide now expect their own taxes to go up during the Obama years." Only 9 percent expect them to drop.[8]

Yet this pledge remains the rhetorical underpinning of the Obama presidency. Democrats in the 2010 congressional races will repeat it like a mantra. But even they won't believe it.

All the Republican candidates need to do is point out that Obama has tripled the deficit, *and* raised the national debt by 25 percent, *and* now wants to pay for health care for the uninsured, *and* impose a cap-and-trade carbon tax on utilities and manufacturers. After hearing that, only a totally deluded partisan would agree that Obama has no tax increases up his sleeve.

And yet the Democrats will hang in there, promising they won't raise your taxes.

This disjuncture between what everyone believes—knows—to be true, and what the Democrats say, is so wide that it can power the Republican campaigns of 2010.

The more any Democratic candidate pledges not to raise taxes (on anyone making $250,000 or less), the more he'll damage his credibility. Voters don't like being deceived. No one wants to be taken for a fool.

And while the Democratic candidates of 2010 will doubtless pay lip service to cutting the deficit and reducing spending, their voting records supporting the massive stimulus package and other Obama spending vehicles belie their protests.

In the world of winner-takes-all politics, there's much to be said for making your opponent repeat a promise everyone knows is a lie. By challenging the Democrats over taxes, the deficit, and spending, we'll be forcing them to make—and repeat—promises the voters know to be untrue.

Obama is going to have to raise taxes on the middle class. He'll raise income taxes. Through cap and trade, he'll raise utility bills and the cost of manufactured goods. He'll make the uninsured pay $15,000 per family for health insurance. He's going to tax one-third of the health insurance policies at a rate of 40 percent. He will force states to raise taxes by billions by expanding Medicaid. He has said he'll put all income under the Social Security tax, not just the first $100,000, as at present. He campaigned promising to raise the capital gains tax and to tax dividends as ordinary income. There will probably be an extra surtax on those with incomes of

$500,000 or more (for individuals) or $1 million (for couples); at first few will pay this surtax, but wait until Obama's inflation takes hold and more and more will have to write out bigger checks.

Just wait and see: All these taxes will be coming thick and fast.

The more Republicans predict new taxes—and the more Democrats deny it—the more their credibility will sink and ours will rise.

And voters agree, overwhelmingly, that tax increases will hurt the economy. Rasmussen tells us that 59 percent of voters believe tax hikes will hurt the economy, while just 19 percent believe they can help. (Eleven percent say they have no impact.)[9]

But how should Republican candidates handle the tax issue? By arming themselves with one basic fact: tax cuts—not increases—generate additional revenue.

By squelching economic activity and reducing consumer buying power, higher taxes hurt the economy, dry up commerce, and reduce tax revenues. Tax cuts do just the opposite: By adding to buying power, incentivizing ambition and productivity, and catalyzing investment, they add revenue.

This isn't just theory. It's what has happened every time.

When George W. Bush cut taxes for the wealthiest Americans, he cut their tax rates—but the amount they paid rose sharply. Yes, that's right: Lower rates generated higher revenues. In 2001, before Bush's tax cuts took effect, the richest 1 percent of the country paid $301 billion a year in taxes. By 2006, they were paying $408 billion a year.[10] And the share of total tax payments by the richest tenth of the country rose from 65 percent before Bush's tax cuts to 71 percent in 2006.[11]

So remember that mantra: *Lower tax rates produce higher revenues.* It's one of the most powerful messages we have.

Nor must we shy away when the Democrats say they want to increase taxes only on the rich. Asked by Rasmussen whether they'd be more likely to support a candidate who says he'll increase taxes on the rich or one who says he won't increase taxes at all, voters backed the no-tax candidate by 48–38%. (During the election of 2008, the voters held the opposite view according to Rasmussen's polls.)[12]

And Obama's pledge not to raise taxes on the middle class extended only to federal taxes. A key component of his health-care program is a vast expansion of the Medicaid program, part of which is funded through state taxes. Indeed, some estimate that as many as three-quarters of those who will be newly covered by insurance under the plan will get their benefits from the Medicaid program.

While the new federal law would require every state to cover anyone making 150 percent of the federal poverty level (a measure that would put anyone making less than about $30,000 under Medicaid), current Medicaid levels vary widely. Some states—Texas, for example—cover only those making less than 27 percent of the poverty level, or about $5,000 a year. This low level of Medicaid coverage is a key reason why taxes are lower in Texas and, indeed, why the state can survive without having a state income tax.

Texas now spends only $8 billion in state revenues on its Medicaid program while the state of New York spends $12 billion. Under the new Obama law, Texas will have to upgrade to the New York level, costing the state almost $3 billion extra in the first year alone. By itself, this whopping increase will drive up taxes by 10 percent in Texas, reducing its low-tax edge and, perhaps, requiring a new state income tax.

The chart below shows how much each state is going to have to come up with in additional state tax revenues under the Obama bill:

STATE SPENDING INCREASES IN MEDICAID REQUIRED BY OBAMA'S HEALTH BILL[13]

Alabama	$394 million
Alaska	39
Arizona	217
Arkansas	402
California	1,428
Colorado	163
Delaware	35
Florida	909
Georgia	495
Hawaii	41
Idaho	97

Iowa	77
Indiana	586
Kansas	186
Kentucky	199
Louisiana	432
Maryland	194
Michigan	570
Mississippi	136
Missouri	836
Montana	29
Nebraska	00
Nevada	54
New Hampshire	59
New Mexico	102
North Carolina	599
North Dakota	14
Ohio	399
Oklahoma	190
Oregon	231
Pennsylvania	1,490
South Carolina	122
South Dakota	33
Texas	2,749
Utah	58
Virginia	601
Washington state	311
Wyoming	25
West Virginia	132

Did you notice that Nebraska won't have to come up with any new money? That's because the $80 million they would have normally had to raise will be picked up by the U.S. government—a privilege extended only to Nebraska, under a deal Senate majority leader Harry Reid cut with Senator Ben Nelson (D-NE) to get his vote.

(Some states, like New York and Massachusetts, won't have to pay any more in Medicaid because they already cover 150 percent of the poverty level.)

THE AFGHANISTAN ISSUE

You may support sending troops to Afghanistan. But that shouldn't stop you from pointing out that the way Obama is running the war, it can't be won. You don't have to be an advocate of withdrawal to point out that, by fixating on a timetable for pulling out our troops, Obama is encouraging the Taliban to hang on until we go home. He is, in effect, telling the local warlords not to side with us because soon we'll have pulled out and left them to face the Taliban alone.

Afghanistan might be more important as an issue than all the usual causes Republicans hold dear. That's because issues like health-care reform, climate change, the deficit, unemployment, and the debt are basically Republican issues. Liberals and Democrats can take a pounding on them and fight back all day. Each side is rooted in ideology: They have theirs; we have ours.

But as an issue Afghanistan has a bipartisan appeal. Democrats and Republicans are equally suspicious of foreign entanglements. Of course, the two sides tend to express their concerns differently. Republicans are likely to talk about the corruption of other nations and how they're not worthy of our aid or sacrifice. They're more apt to cite our own financial limitations and ask if it is worth adding to the deficit to preserve the regime in Kabul.

Democrats usually talk about giving priority to our domestic problems. With poor people at home and problems in our cities, they will say, why should we go abroad in search of danger? And both parties will ask the question that haunts us all: Is the human cost in dead and wounded soldiers worth it?

But most Republican candidates, focused on the war on terror, will support Obama's decision to send additional troops to Afghanistan. The problem a Republican candidate has in 2010 is how to get political mileage out of Obama's embroilment in Afghanistan without clearly opposing our involvement.

The way to do it is to focus on Obama's personal conduct regarding the war. Make it not a test of policy but of personality. When Bill Clinton wouldn't intervene in Bosnia as the news of civilian deaths and widespread rape mounted, he began to be seen as too weak to be a good president. When Bush refused to alter his tactics in Iraq, despite their lack of success, he began to be seen as too rigid and single-minded to be effective. And this is nothing new: When Lyndon Johnson wouldn't reexamine our strategy in Vietnam, the American people soon perceived him as overbearing, arrogant, and closed to new ideas.

Obama's off-again, on-again approach to Iraq and Afghanistan suggests that he's weak and malleable. He seems determined to have things both ways: to please the generals by sending troops, and to placate the liberals by promising to pull them out again. When Obama set a withdrawal date even as he signed the orders for troop deployment, it was the classic sign of a flip-flopper who never met a bet he didn't hedge.

And as Obama wrestles with how to fight a war while counting down the days until he abandons it, we can point out that he is merely encouraging the Taliban to dig in, fight harder, and outwait the United States. We've already seen Obama hedging on his date for withdrawal: One minute it was firm, set in stone, and the next day his aides were scrambling to explain it was just a guideline for commanders "on the ground." These rhetorical contortions are the kind of thing that happens when you're trying to have your cake and eat it too—and they make Obama look weak and indecisive.

Remember, too, that Obama was elected as a peace candidate. His entire campaign—right up to the time of his convention—was focused on getting out of Iraq. Now, while he abandons most of his policies and breaks his promises, he comes across as insincere, getting elected over the Iraq War and then refusing to end it any sooner than Bush had already said he would.

Obama's endless rumination on the Afghan issue and his inability to act quickly and decisively, give the impression of a president handicapped by his own intellect—of a latter-day Jimmy Carter who's unable to see the big ideas behind the details. He appears waffling, unsure, pushed and pulled one way and then the other by his advisers.

All these personal negatives stem from Obama's decision-making performance over the wars in Afghanistan and Iraq. Republicans basically agree with what he is doing in both these nations. In Afghanistan, we applaud his commitment of extra forces; in Iraq we're glad he hasn't tried to accelerate Bush's timetable for pulling out. So it's important that we address both wars not as policies, but as indicators of the character, style, strength, decisiveness, and forcefulness of Barack Obama as president. Leave the policy alone and focus on the persona. And use the issue to win.

HOW TO ANSWER A NEGATIVE CAMPAIGN

Every challenger who takes on an incumbent expects to run an aggressive campaign attacking his opponent. His attacks usually find their mark; at some point you come within striking distance of your adversary. But then *his* negative ads start—and then, even if you've never served in public office before, your every action as a private citizen or businessman will come under scrutiny.

It's the only way the Democrats can win. They know that their own record is so shabby that there's no way to defend it and get reelected. The incumbent Democrats of 2010 can only win by negative campaigns.

Voters don't really dislike negative campaigning. Sure, they *say* they do in focus groups, but that's mostly because such ads are often perceived as tawdry. But most of the electorate regards negative advertising as a way to find out the truth. As voters, we're sophisticated enough to know that some of the candidates we vote for will end up being corrupt. And we know we're not likely to find out about it until they're walked out of their offices in handcuffs. Naturally, we want to find out if our candidates are corrupt *before* we vote for them, and negative ads are one way to learn the truth. We don't trust the media to dig up the information, but we do watch what the candidates say about one another in the hopes of finding out the real story.

That's why it's very important for candidates to answer every negative attack ad their opponents run against them. If a candidate doesn't answer an attention-getting ad, the public has to assume it's true. Voters look to the candidates themselves for answers—to "say it ain't so, Joe," and give them the truth.

Bill Clinton's political career thrived because he lived by one rule: "Don't go to sleep with an unanswered negative out there. Always, always, always answer!" Clinton's ability to parry negatives—right down to surviving a presidential impeachment—was largely due to his speed in answering attacks and his inventiveness in discrediting his attackers. It's like the old political saying: Deny the allegation—and then shoot the alligator!

The key to answering an attack quickly and effectively is to anticipate the attack *before it's made*. If the first time a candidate hears about an attack is when his opponent has a negative ad on the air, chances are he's already too late to make an effective comeback. It takes time to dig up the kinds of old records that can disprove an attack. When your opponent's negative researchers have been doing their homework for months digging up dirt— and you have twenty-four hours to cook up an answer before the charge becomes conventional wisdom—you're sunk.

So all candidates must do their own negative research—not just on their opponents, but on themselves! The only way to anticipate the most dangerous attacks is to go through your *own* record, just like your opponent will, and come up with answers for everything he might use to hit you. Public officials must go through their own voting records and ask themselves: Have I ever supported tax increases? Have I missed many meetings or votes? Have I supported controversial bills my opponent could use to attack me? How would my expense account look to a critic? Every questionable vote should be examined in the worst possible light—because that's how it will look in an opposition ad or speech. Perhaps you voted against raising $1 billion in new taxes, but did support $50 million. Your opponent will never mention the $1 billion, but you can be sure you'll see an ad that says you voted for higher taxes!

As a private citizen, are there any court judgments against you? Have you ever been sued? Have you ever lost or settled a suit? Be assured, all that will come out. Any DWIs? (Remember that George W. Bush almost lost in 2000 when his DWI came out at the last minute.) Any childhood arrests?

Candidates running for public office are generally expected to release their income tax returns. (They should only do so if their opponents release theirs. Once the other side has done so, there's really no choice—

unless the candidate wants to spend the whole campaign explaining his refusal.) And every candidate will be subjected to a checklist: Did he pay at least 20 percent of his adjusted gross income in taxes? Did she take any legal deductions that absolved her of any tax liability? Has he incurred any IRS penalties for late payment?

Businessmen have their own set of inquiries to face: Have they had any OSHA complaints? FDA? Department of Health citations? Serious workers' comp cases? Accusations of unfair labor practices? Sex discrimination or harassment complaints? However ugly the truth may be, any candidate must assume the other side will find it out—and must get some answers ready before the shells begin to fall.

For example, one recent Senate candidate ran a business that renovated distressed properties. He would turn around the building, renovate it, and put it back on the tax rolls. But by the time he got the property, there would be millions in unpaid taxes due. He would apply to the city and get the taxes removed since they accrued before he bought the property. Since the property was abandoned and paying no taxes, the city was happy to get anything at all.

But just as he took the lead in this Senate race, his Democratic opponent ran a negative ad saying that he hadn't paid millions in property taxes.

The businessman was in the right, but he didn't answer the attacks, because he worried about "going on the defensive." He figured that "people wouldn't fall for the negative ad." He felt that his side of the story was too complicated to explain in a thirty-second ad. But he was wrong. Here's what he should have said:

"Have you seen the attack by Senator X on John Doe for not paying property taxes? It's a lie. Doe takes over buildings that have been abandoned and already owe millions in taxes. He gets the city to forgive the taxes the previous owner didn't pay, renovates the building, and creates new affordable housing. So when Senator X says Doe didn't pay his property taxes, he's not telling the truth. You can't trust Senator X."

Had the challenger answered with that ad, he would have won. As it was, he snatched defeat from the jaws of victory and lost.

Usually, the best way to answer an attack is by going deeper into the issue and explaining it. In a recent campaign, an incumbent attacked his

Republican challenger, saying he had opposed requiring mammograms on health insurance policies. So the challenger answered:

"Our state has a long list of things every insurance policy must cover. But that adds to the cost, and a lot of people don't need all that coverage. So John Doe says it doesn't make sense, for example, to make men pay premiums for mammograms, so he voted to make coverage available but not mandatory. Now Governor X says Doe opposes mammograms. No way. You just can't trust Governor X."

When you explain the context of an issue, this kind of negative attack often doesn't hold up. Without the explanation, though, a negative can be a knockout punch.

The nice thing about rebuttal advertising is that it lets you undermine your opponent's credibility. By explaining his fabrication and reciting what the facts really are, you catch him in the act of dissembling. That ends up being far more effective than turning around and attacking your opponent for something he did years ago: Here you've caught him red-handed, trying to pull the wool over the voters' eyes. After one such exchange, your opponent's credibility will be damaged. After a few, it will be destroyed.

When Bill Clinton ran for his final term as governor of Arkansas in 1990, his Republican opponent, Sheffield Nelson, ran a very effective negative ad on the final weekend of the campaign. He took a tape of Bill's own voice saying the words "raise and spend" and put it in a negative ad. "What did Bill Clinton do to us in 1983?" the ad asked. " 'Raise and spend.' And in 1987? 'Raise and spend.' And if we give him another term what will he do? 'Raise and spend.' "

The results were a disaster: Clinton's vote share tanked and Nelson took the lead.

Late on Saturday night, Bill Clinton taped this reply:

"Have you seen Sheffield Nelson's negative ad using my own voice saying 'raise and spend' to convince you I was pushing higher taxes? Well, here's what I actually said in my speech to the legislature. 'Unlike our friends in Washington, we can't write a check on an account that is overdrawn. Either we raise and spend or we don't spend.' All I was doing was fighting for a balanced budget. But Nelson went to work and cut out the words 'raise and spend' from my speech to give you the wrong impression. You can't trust Sheffield Nelson."

Clinton regained the lead and won. Had he lost, he would never have been president!

See what Clinton did? He didn't deny that he'd raised taxes twice before. (He had.) He didn't say he wasn't going to raise them if he got reelected. (He did.) What he did was dismantle Nelson's gimmick, discrediting the attack—and the attacker!

Political consultants—especially Republicans—tend to be skeptical of rebuttal ads. They see them as going into defensive mode and surrendering control of the dialogue. But they're dead wrong. Rebuttal advertising is the best way to destroy your opponent—and a failure to answer a serious charge is the best way to lose.

Democratic candidates often try to overwhelm their Republican opponents with negative ads. They'll run five different ads with three separate attacks in each. The key is to answer—not every attack, but the one you can! If a candidate is pro-life and an ad attacks him for being against a woman's right to choose, there's not much you can say in answer. But if the Democrats throw fifteen different charges at a candidate, there's bound to be at least one with a good answer. That's the one to target. A Republican who discredits one attack will make voters doubt any accusation the Democrats throw at him—and make his opponent look like a dirty fighter.

Everyone likes a fighter. Nobody likes a dirty one.

Sometimes, of course, there is no answer. In one of his early runs for public office, it came out that Ed Rendell, now Pennsylvania's governor, had thousands of dollars in unpaid parking tickets. His wife had driven the government car and parked it for hours in front of her beauty parlor. Rendell lost that race but then came back to win years later.[14] The candidate who steps out of a race in the light of an unanswerable attack can save millions—and save his party from a big defeat.

But how is a candidate supposed to stave off all these attacks and still remain on the offensive? How can we keep reminding voters about Obama's disastrous policies if the Democrats mount a nonstop barrage of attacks, fair or unfair?

The key is to sandwich the reply in between the attack.

When Clinton ran for governor in 1986, he was facing Governor Frank

White, who had defeated him for reelection in 1980 (and whom he had defeated in his 1982 comeback). White ran a negative ad attacking Hillary Clinton for allegedly taking legal fees from the Rose Law Firm for a specific piece of state business while Bill was governor. The fees were for representing Arkansas in a utility rate case—and Bill had hit White for taking money from utility companies in his campaign.

So Clinton answered: "Frank White would let the utility companies raise their rates at will. That's why they are financing his campaign. Now White attacks Hillary Clinton for representing Arkansas in a lawsuit against the utilities. Says she took fees from tax money. But she didn't. She represented the state for free. Hey, Frank: If you want to attack Bill, attack Bill. But not his wife. After all, you're running for governor . . . not for first lady."

It worked: Clinton festooned the state with "Frank White for First Lady" bumper stickers, and White's campaign was cooked.

(FYI: It later came out that while Hillary did not collect any fees for this lawsuit, she increased her share of other Rose Law Firm revenues to make up for it!)

The key is to stay on the attack even when you're playing defense. It's hard to do—but in this critical year, when the Democrats are going to throw out everything they can in their desperation to keep their hold on Congress, you can bet it'll be necessary.

PART FOUR

THE ELECTRONIC PRECINCT

HOW YOU CAN HELP BEAT OBAMA AND THE DEMOCRATS

Politics is no longer a spectator sport. Those in the grandstands must leave their seats and come down on the playing field to help their side score. That is the key lesson of the Obama campaign. He didn't just have supporters. He had campaign workers—millions of them.

Every caller who dialed Obama's headquarters in 2008 was greeted with a question: "What can you do for us?"

The Internet has made each of us the center of our own political campaign. We *are* the campaign. The days when the candidate and a small group of professionals ran things—and the rest of us chipped in money, showed up at rallies, and voted—are over. Now each of us must conduct our own campaign within our own circle of acquaintances, until the circle spreads to include thousands of voters. Some of us will use the Internet to do so. Others need not feel disqualified by their technophobia. Just do it by old-fashioned word of mouth and snail mail!

In a way, political campaigns are coming full circle, to the way they were in the nineteenth century. Back then campaigns were waged on the stump throughout the country. Candidates themselves rarely spoke in public; they were often no more than franchises used by the political parties to win the election. Abraham Lincoln, for example, did very little actual campaigning when he ran for president. (His debates with Douglas actually occurred during his Senate race two years before—and were very unusual for his day.) Lincoln's few speeches and letters were designed to provide ammunition for his local party workers to use in their districts to sell his candidacy and their party. It was on these local workers that the real burden of waging the campaign fell.

But television interrupted this process and permitted a candidate and a small staff of media professionals to reach the entire electorate. No need to bother with grassroots organizations or campaigning out on the stump. Campaigns stayed indoors, at headquarters, grinding out commercials, speeches, and talking points.

Too many of us still labor under the illusion that politics is a top-down game, driven by the manager and candidate whose initiatives filter down to the lowly campaign workers—the foot soldiers on the ground. We wait for our phones to ring or e-mails to arrive telling us what to do to help win the election.

But in today's politics, those initiatives have to come from us, not from on high.

This development mirrors what's happening in society. Political advertising, like all advertising, is losing its effectiveness—for two key reasons.

First and most obviously, the Internet is replacing television. We're no longer watching the same shows at the same time of day as our neighbors. The mass audiences traditional advertising depends on just aren't there anymore. With hundreds of cable or satellite channels, we're all watching different shows. Many of us are tuned in to movies. And roughly a third of us are online during prime time; we're not even watching television.

Some of us are even talking to each other at night!

Prime-time television audiences are far smaller than they once were. In the 1980s, a prime-time show would reach 20 to 30 percent of all U.S. households. Now it's lucky if it reaches one in ten. And many of those folks are watching recorded shows—and fast-forwarding through the commercials.

When they were first confronted with this cosmic shift, most political candidates and media advisers reacted by advertising *more*, not less, in the hope that they could still reach enough voters to make a difference. They bought more time and ran ads for longer periods, hoping that eventually they would reach everybody.

It is now clear, however, that the Internet is becoming the most powerful forum for political campaigning. And we all have equal access to the Web.

This means one thing: *You are the campaign!* You can be your own campaign media guru, strategist, and manager. You don't need money. You don't need fame. You just need to be able to produce cogent and effective campaign messages to send to your friends and associates by e-mail and to the world at large on YouTube, Twitter, Facebook, and whatever else is invented between now and when you read these words.

But there's a second, more important reason that the conventional top-down media-driven political campaign isn't working anymore: because we don't believe what we hear from strangers.

Our politicians suffer from a huge credibility gap. Advertisers face an even wider gap. So it's no surprise that we attach virtually no credibility to paid political ads. After watching our politicians disappoint us for decades on end, we're all reluctant to believe the promises they make in their campaigns. (And after listening to Obama's pledge to be a candidate who was above party and would bring Washington together, we're just that much more cynical about believing anything a politician says.)

Here's an interesting corollary: The more we disbelieve those we *don't* know, the more we *do* believe and rely upon those we *do* know. The old regimen of media propaganda is swiftly being supplanted by old-fashioned word of mouth—recommendations from friends, trusted colleagues, and established, credible commentators—as our main source of information. We no longer want intermediaries to dictate what we should know or should like.

And not just in politics. We trust dining guides like Zagat, or online reviews from everyday consumers, more than we do paid ads or even reviews. We're more likely to visit a vacation spot because a friend had a good time there than because we've seen a well-produced television ad. Despite the massive spending the carmakers do every year on TV and in magazine ads, a recommendation from a friend carries far more weight with us than a glossy photo. The same goes for computers, appliances, electronic equipment—nearly everything we buy . . .

. . . and for political candidates.

In this new era, we—the party's and candidate's supporters—must do the heavy lifting. We, not the candidate or his staff, must get the message out. The campaigns themselves—with their budgets and exposure—become ammunition factories producing shells for us to fire. Why? Because *we* have a credibility *they* do not. If we tell our friends that we've met a new Republican candidate in the area and he's brilliant, persuasive, and compelling, that makes a big difference. Likewise, if we tell our friends about a bad experience we've had with the staff of our incumbent Democratic senator, then that can have a strong influence.

We each have our areas of expertise. A doctor or nurse's opinion of Obama's health-care bill will carry great weight with his or her peers, relatives, patients, and friends. A small business owner will be very credible discussing the problems he's facing in the marketplace and how Obama's policies are stopping him from expanding his business or creating new jobs. The opinions of soldiers and their families carry great weight when they report on how Obama's Afghanistan policy is hampering the war effort and emboldening the opposition. A construction worker's opinion of the housing market will get our attention. Everyone listens intently when a banker or investor describes the chaos Obama has caused in the markets.

We are all experts. We are all media creators now. We are all the campaign.

In the mid-1990s, Matt Drudge of drudgereport.com predicted that each of us would become publishers. He sure got that right. Our audience is a large circle of people and we're at its center. We have in our circle school and college buddies, office colleagues, family members (even if we have to climb pretty far out on the family tree), members of civic and fraternal groups, clients, social friends, and other associates. We have in our circle the parents of our children's friends and people we know from their schools. There are people we forward jokes to, share articles about our favorite sports teams with, or send out Christmas cards or letters to every year.

If you want to make a difference in 2010, now's the time to start reaching out to all those people to spread the word. They are your constituents— your electronic precinct.

The Internet allows you to reach those in your circle with little effort and no cost. You do it all the time. In 2010 you should make it part of your campaign.

In the old political-machine days, campaign workers were each assigned an election district or precinct to canvass. Their political task was defined geographically, and our politically minded ancestors walked from one house to the next spreading the message—identifying favorable voters, working on the undecided, answering arguments or questions, resolving doubts, and, finally, making sure their party's supporters actually voted.

Now our precinct is an electronic network that can spread across the nation. It includes everyone we know and those strangers whom we can reach. They don't live in one neighborhood, but they are our beat nonetheless.

They are the votes we need to deliver on Election Day.

So follow the example of the precinct workers of old Tammany Hall: Make a list of your constituents and go talk to each of them—by e-mail, by Twitter, by YouTube, by Facebook, even by phone.

Sound them out about their political preferences. Learn what issues matter to them. Make notes on their criticisms of Obama—and their positive ideas, too. Figure out what gets them motivated.

Then craft a strategy for each voter on your list. As any good precinct captain would, you will find some voters you need to ignore. There is no reason to get in their faces, since they'll probably vote for the Democrats. You certainly don't want to make them mad; that will only encourage them to get out and vote, if only to spite you!

Formulate a plan to win over those who are persuadable. Work on which issues to push, which themes to strike, and how to approach each voter.

Remember to think of yourself as a publisher. The job of the campaign staff, and the candidate, is to produce ammunition in the form of issue positions, statements, and campaign material. Yours is to fire it off, distributing it to the right people. You've probably been trying your friends' patience by forwarding jokes or baby pictures via e-mail. Now you can use the same tool to send something they may actually be interested in: videos of a promising candidate or stories about his or her campaign speeches. Surf the Web for articles and other materials that are helpful to your campaign. Reach out to other sources of information that might generate good material for your campaign. (Make sure to get our columns from dick morris.com). Search far and wide for ammunition—material to send to your list, aiming each blast at the right targets.

One good place to start is the list of columnists on drudgereport.com. Spend a couple of hours reading each of them. See who's generating material you find interesting and relevant. Follow their columns each week, always reading with one goal in mind: To generate interesting copy to send to those on your list, your virtual precinct.

When the candidates in your race debate each other, stay glued to the TV—and then write a review of the debate to send to your list. If you don't have confidence in your own writing, read your columnists the next morning and circulate the columns with which you agree.

When your candidate throws a punch at the other side, go to his website, download the ad, and send it around to your list. Give the attack the amplification it needs to be successful. Conversely, when the other side hits your candidate, go to your guy's website and download rebuttal material to send out to your list, exposing the truth about the false charges being leveled at your candidate.

Whenever any piece of anti-Obama news breaks, circulate it to your list. When the new unemployment figures show thousands of jobs lost, or the new budget deficit figures are released, circulate them to your list. Be an opportunist: Seize anything that comes your way that might be persuasive and interesting.

Watch shows on Fox News—O'Reilly, Hannity, Beck, Greta—and forward what you learn to your list, whether it's a video clip or an article from one of their websites.

Follow your candidate's schedule. When he comes to your city or town, e-mail your precinct to come out to greet him. Make *his* rallies *your* rallies. His appearances will give you a marvelous chance to meet the people on your list, share enthusiasm for the campaign, and enjoy some of the hoopla together. And it'll give you a great chance to expand your precinct, tap into new circles, and widen your reach.

Be the epicenter of communication for your virtual precinct. Spread the word!

The key to an Internet campaign is to remember that receiving information over the Web is completely voluntary. Many people delete most of the e-mails they receive—especially the unsolicited ones, whether or not they have an official "spam folder." And most people frequent only a handful of Internet sites. Every site, every e-mail correspondent, every blogger is his or her own brand. Does this brand deliver serious, interesting material or frivolous, unreliable, and petty stuff? Every morning we scan through our e-mails and delete the ones that come from people whose causes we don't care about. We don't open their jokes. We don't download their photos. It's not worth the time and they're usually not funny. But we almost always open those from people and groups we value. Make sure you're on the plus side of the ledger of your virtual precinct. Don't pound away, sending material every day regardless of whether it's worthy of circulation. Wait for really good stuff before you send it around. Keep your brand pure.

In this respect, the principles of an Internet campaign are the exact opposite of a traditional media campaign. The keys in advertising are condensation and repetition: Shrink your message down to a seven-second sound bite or slogan and then repeat it until it sinks in.

On the Web, though, condensation is deadly! No one goes online for seven seconds. It's an active way to be in touch with the world, not a passive time-killer: We surf the Web to find interesting stuff. A short blurb or bite doesn't occupy anyone's attention for more than a moment before it gets lost in the plethora of other material.

Similarly, no one wants repetition on the Web. We just delete anything we've seen before. Advertising is largely based on involuntary learning: We hear the same message, slogan, phrase, gimmick, or song so frequently that it gets tattooed on our brains whether we want it there or not. But learning through the Internet is voluntary. It's a cerebral process, not a matter of rote memorization. We have to *want* to learn and retain what we are reading. Repetition turns us off, and then we click off and move on.

So the lesson is this: The stuff you send out has to be good, funny, interesting, graphically intriguing, original, and worth opening.

Let your creativity have free rein. Create your own videos and post them on YouTube. Do your own graphic designs. Make your own cartoons. Come up with your own one-liners, headlines, and campaign slogans. You are your own media guru. Go for it!

The advent of YouTube has changed the political game entirely. No longer is the television advertisement the sole preserve of sophisticated media experts hired for big fees by the main campaigns. Now everyone can become a media creator, post free ads on the Web, and reach out to your own electronic precinct and others to generate traffic.

The wonder of YouTube is that good ads spread virally. They don't need the constant stoking of paid outreach, or big-dollar media buys, to be seen and heard. They just have to be good! Like Super Bowl ads, they can captivate viewers so completely that they lose focus on the lopsided game on the field.

And whether or not you're tech-savvy enough to create videos for

YouTube, you can surely do your own blogging. Follow the campaign in your own blog online. Record your reactions to what's happening—even minor stuff. This kind of daily coverage builds your brand, bolsters your credibility, and helps you persuade voters to back your candidate.

Be yourself on the blog. Be funny or irreverent. Don't dress it up and try to be someone you're not. And don't hold back—let your creativity fly!

The history of modern political campaigning has increasingly demonstrated the superiority of this kind of homegrown, bottom-up campaigning.

The Internet first emerged as a political force during the late 1990s, in response to Republican efforts to impeach President Clinton. Liberals were exasperated at being on the defensive over the president's affair. They set up Moveon.org, encouraged by leaders of the left like George Soros. Moveon .org built an online list of millions and made the leftist voting base easily accessible through the Internet. It raised funds to fight against impeachment, and when the smoke cleared had developed the best online political list in the country.

In our 1998 book *Vote.com* we offered an early—and eerily prescient— look at the potential of the Web to transform American politics. (It also has a bunch of predictions that haven't yet come true, but will.) The Internet came of age politically a few years later during the Howard Dean campaign of 2004. Guided by political consultant Joe Trippi, the campaign vaulted an unknown former governor of Vermont into the lead for the Democratic presidential nomination. Since Vermont has fewer voters than the average New York City high school, Trippi's was quite an achievement.

The Dean campaign did it by harnessing political forces that were then still on the fringes of our politics—the gay and peace movements. Dean had signed the nation's first gay marriage law (back then they were still known as "civil unions") and had won the undying affections of homosexual men and women throughout the land. And he was the first political candidate to dissent from the post-9/11 consensus in favor of the war in Iraq and the Bush-directed war on terror. He echoed, on the political playing field, the critique of Michael Moore in *Fahrenheit 911* and became the hero of the increasingly mobilized extreme left.

It was Trippi's genius to drive these movements online, moving the campaign's focus away from a traditional media campaign. Backed by millions of new donors and activists who joined online, Dean vaulted to the lead in the polls. (Read Trippi's book *The Revolution Will Not Be Televised* to hear how they did it.)

It took the combined efforts of the Clintons and the Kennedys—who were alarmed at the prospect of an overtly leftist Democratic candidate—to torpedo Dean's surging candidacy and nominate instead the more reliable and less incendiary John Kerry.

The right had its shot at grassroots mobilization in the aftermath of the Kerry convention of 2004, which unwisely featured the candidate-as-war-hero extolling his service on swift boats during the Vietnam War. War hero was an unlikely role for a world-famous former antiwar activist, but the Democratic Party spent its convention trying to sell the odd notion.

That only lasted until John O'Neill, a swift boat vet himself, saw the Kerry charade and decided to do something about it. He understood that even though he held no office, had no pulpit, and was unknown nationally, his status as a Vietnam veteran willing to speak out gave him an inherent power to affect public opinion. So, backed by relatively nominal financing, he filmed a political ad casting doubt on Kerry's self-aggrandizing accounts of his war service. Even though the ad only ran in a few small media markets, it had an immediate national impact because it spread rapidly and virally online to tens of millions of people. (For a fuller account of O'Neill's historic campaign, read his book *Unfit for Command: Swift Boat Veterans Speak Out Against John Kerry.*)

But Moveon.org, the Dean campaign, and the swift boat attack all used the Internet to raise funds to air their attacks over the traditional media. The counterattack against Dan Rather's biased account of President Bush's National Guard service was the first all-online campaign to win national support.

Rather tried to prove that Bush had sought special treatment in the Guard, citing letters to and from its commander. Computer users everywhere noticed that the letter, which purported to be contemporaneous with Bush's service, featured a superscript *th* symbol after a number (as in 5th). Yet back when Bush served in the Guard, only typewriters, not computers, would have been available and a *th* superscript of that kind was impossible to create on a typewriter. The documents were obviously recently concocted forgeries. Even as the media tried to ignore the controversy, the scandal sped over the Internet to millions of homes; CBS stood by Rather's account and tried to stonewall the growing outcry. Eventually it had to admit the forgery, and Rather resigned shortly thereafter. The Internet had brought down one of the most powerful men in the nation—a network news anchor.

Then came Barack Obama. By now Joe Trippi was backing John Edwards, but the Obama people took a page out of Trippi's playbook and set out to build the biggest and best Internet base in political history. They used the massive crowds at Obama's book signings in 2007 to amass a huge e-mail list. And when the Illinois senator became a presidential candidate the list just kept on growing.

Federal election law doesn't require campaigns to report the identities of donors who give less than $100. But Obama's people took great care to copy down the e-mail addresses of everyone who bought a T-shirt or bumper sticker or a book nonetheless. Those addresses, they realized, would be more important than money to the campaign.

And this list defeated Hillary Clinton.

Mrs. Clinton assumed that the 2008 race for the nomination would be like any other. The process would unfold until it climaxed in a dramatic primary, the winner would move on to the nomination, and the loser would gracefully drop out. This is the way it had always been. Reagan knocked out Bush in the 1980 New Hampshire primary. Dukakis decked Jesse Jackson in Wisconsin, New York, and Pennsylvania in 1988 to win the nomination. Clinton put Tsongas away on Super Tuesday.

But a close analysis of these races shows that the victories—and the knockouts—came not because the loser lacked *political* viability, but because he couldn't raise any more money. His finances drove him out of the race.

In 2008, Hillary failed to realize that an Internet-funded candidate could not be knocked out for lack of funds. If he ran out of money, he'd just double-click and his base would send in a deluge of small donations to keep him going.

Hillary expected that, even if she lost some early primaries, a big win on Super Tuesday would allow her to capture the nomination.

And win she did. Hillary carried California, New York, and New Jersey, the biggest prizes available on that pivotal night. But then a funny thing happened: Obama wasn't knocked out. To be sure, he suffered a bad few days as the media anointed Hillary the winner—and on the day after the primaries both candidates were broke. But Obama didn't go down. Instead, he double-clicked on his list and his appeal went out to his entire donor base. And, just as rapidly, they sent in their money—*Instantly.* Unlike the defeated candidates of past years, Obama was still in business.

For Hillary, that meant a return to her Rolodex to call people who hadn't already given to her campaign. But she had already maxed out (gotten the legal limit of donations) from all her supporters. Having tapped out her friends and then her acquaintances, she was now reduced to calling people who disliked her only a little!

She got the extra money, but it took time: Time to gather the potential donors; time to make the calls; time to hold the fund-raisers; time to get the checks; time to deposit them and wait for them to clear; time. And while Hillary had the media adulation and a lead in delegates, the one thing she didn't have on her side was time. The primary and caucus calendars kept ticking, and in the two weeks after Super Tuesday a dozen states selected their delegates. They weren't really big states, but there were a bunch of medium-size ones—Maryland, Virginia, Louisiana, and Washington state among them.

And the Democratic Party in all these states used proportional representation—not the winner-take-all rule used in the Republican Party—to allocate delegates.

By then, Obama was the only candidate with the funds to compete. Unlike Hillary, he had foreseen that he would neither win nor lose on Super Tuesday. Rather than risking everything on one throw of the dice, he had invested in organizing in these February states (and in a bunch of Super Tuesday caucus states that Hillary ignored as she went for the big wins in California and New Jersey). In fact, in most cases he had the only organization on the ground. So when the delegates voted, whether in primaries or in caucuses, he won a disproportionate share, building up a big lead by the middle of the month.

By the time Hillary recovered her financial base it was too late. Obama's lead was insurmountable. The Internet had nominated Barack Obama.

The most recent chapter in the grassroots' growing domination of our political scene is being written right now with the Tea Party movement.

With no clear national leaders, the Republicans in Congress have been largely impotent as Obama has swept through Washington with his radical agenda. Unable even to filibuster in the Senate, the GOP's efforts to mount an opposition in Congress has thus far been pathetically ineffective.

So it's up to the grassroots—which means us. As Obama's health-care bill loomed on the horizon in the spring of 2009, local activists organized Tea Parties throughout the nation, protesting the big-spending, high-taxing ways of Democratic Washington. Galvanized, summoned, and organized via the Internet—and without visible national leadership—ordinary people began to attend rallies that grew larger and larger as the season progressed.

As Democratic congressmen held town meetings in the summer of 2009—usually tame affairs where they recited their achievements—Tea Party members thronged to attend them, besieging their representatives with questions, speeches, and tirades about the evils of the pending health-care bill. So intense were these gatherings that the congressmen stopped holding meetings and retreated to Washington, D.C., returning home without publicity or fanfare lest their constituents bother them again.

This same conservative cyber-roots activism must resurface as we work to take back our country. Don't wait for instructions. Don't look for leaders. Take politics into your own hands and mobilize your precincts! As they sing in "La Marseillaise": *"Aux armes, citoyens!"*

But canvassing your own electronic precinct is only part of your assignment. You must also get your friends to join you as precinct captains, bringing their own list of friends, family, colleagues, and associates. One pebble cast into the water will generate its share of ripples. But only when many are thrown at once can we build a wave. Take to heart Robert F. Kennedy's famous metaphor:

Each time a man stands up for an ideal, or acts to improve the lot of others, or strikes out against injustice, he sends forth a tiny ripple of hope, and crossing each other from a million different centers of energy and daring those ripples build a current which can sweep down the mightiest walls of oppression and resistance.[1]

So be a recruiter for your electronic campaign. Tell your friends what you're doing. Most people just don't realize how politics has changed. They assume that once they've sent in a check or two to their favorite candidates, their work is done until Election Day. You need to let them know: Politics is now a participatory sport! And you have to explain how to do it. Show them your own list and your own e-mails. Help them think about how to develop their own electronic precincts. For, as Bobby Kennedy said, only when the ripples overlap and run into one another will a true wave build that can help us to take back our country. None of us can do it on our own.

Underlying all our efforts is one fundamental conviction: Conservatism is too important a cause to leave to the establishment of the Republican Party. Even if we assume their good faith, they don't yet know how to translate their convictions into action.

The GOP has been slipping since Gingrich quarterbacked them to victory in 1994.

The Republicans lost in 1996 because Clinton moved to the center just in time.

Unable to capitalize on even the Lewinsky scandal, they lost the election of 1998.

Though Bush won in 2000, he lost the popular vote by nearly half a million.

The Republicans gained ground in 2002 in an election animated by the shadow of 9/11. And Karl Rove's genius for knitting together the GOP coalition of economic free marketers, national security voters, and social conservatives helped the party retain power in 2004.

Since then, however, the party's record has been ghastly. It lost control of Congress in 2006 and was swept from the White House in 2008. Its losses were so huge, and its performance so pathetic, that it only recently acquired the power to block Obama's radical agenda.

We can't wait for headquarters to call. If we want to take back our country we need to run our own campaigns in our own electronic precincts.

But that doesn't mean we can't call headquarters ourselves! Some modern campaigns become so introverted, so out of touch with reality, that one wonders if they'd even notice if their outgoing phone service was turned off.

You'll know more than most campaign staffers about what the voters are thinking, feeling, and saying from your contact with your own electronic precinct. You'll know when your candidate has made a faux pas long before the professionals spot it. It'll be apparent to you from the instant feedback you get from your own list if he has zigged when he should have zagged.

That's when your responsibility to your candidate and his campaign kicks in. Go to the headquarters and make yourself heard. Show them the e-mails you've received from your list and explain how the campaign got it wrong.

Be their early warning system, and you can save them from key mistakes.

It's tough to transform oneself from political couch potato to activist. But you don't have to leave home to do it. Politics has changed and we need to absorb the lessons of the success the left has had in changing with it.

Many people like to villainize leftist activists like George Soros or groups like ACORN, blaming them for the resurgence of the left in 2006 and 2008. But we shouldn't be condemning them; we should be stealing their playbook—not the dirty tricks or the alleged fraud or the monkeying with voter lists, of course. We can win fairly. But we do need to learn to play the grassroots/cyber-roots game as effectively as they have.

The Tea Parties are a great start. But if we're to win the elections of 2010, we need to have hundreds of thousands of electronic precincts throughout the country, all of them worked by dedicated activists who are willing to put in the time and creativity necessary to make their work count.

Our country is too important to do anything less. Victory in 2010 depends on you!

Join us in a peaceful, permanent voters' coup!

ACKNOWLEDGMENTS

We'd like to say a special thanks to Morgan Buehler for her excellent research on this, our third book together.

Barry Elias, an economist, offered us important substantive insights that helped us wade through the various policies that emerged after the global meltdown. Chuck Brooks helped enormously with his unending supply of timely information. And Norah Maxwell helped us decipher government formulae and became our resident statistician.

We're grateful to retired U.S. ambassador V. Manuel Rocha, whose wisdom and knowledge were unerring.

Dr. Don Gordon, a close personal friend and our physician, helped us to understand how difficult the choices are for doctors in America today.

We want to thank Scott Rasmussen, whose excellent polling provided so much important information for our books, as well as the Center for Responsive Politics and its website, opensecrets.org, which faithfully unmasks what Congress wants to conceal. We also want to thank *The Almanac of American Politics* and its editor Michael Barone—once you start to drill down to state-by-state Congressional district politics, they are the best source out there.

And thanks also to cookpoliticalreport.com for its great coverage of the 2010 races. Thanks to Jim Dugan for his help with editing.

Our thanks to former HarperCollins publisher Judith Regan for her insights and encouragement. Thanks also to Jonathan Burnham, Kathy Schneider, Angie Lee, Cindy Achar, Susan Kosko, Josh Marwell, Doug Jones, Brian Grogan, Tina Andreadis and Kate Blum for their work in publishing the book as quickly as possible. Thanks to John Sprengelmeyer for his drawings, which show just how good political ads can look.

And our personal thanks to our special cousins Irma and Tom Gallagher and our sister Maureen Maxwell. Together, they make everything work and keep each of us on target and on schedule.

NOTES

INTRODUCTION

1 "The agreements . . .": Edmund Andrews, "Leaders of the G-20 Vow to Reshape Global Economy," *New York Times*, September 25, 2009.
2 Obama predicted: Ibid.
3 "Sometimes party loyalty": William Safire, Spring Commencement Address, James Madison University, Harrisonburg, Virginia, May 5, 2001, available at www.jmu.edu/jmuweb/general/news2/general_2001522102018.shtml.
4 "For I will give you shepherds after my own heart, who will lead you with knowledge and understanding." Jeremiah 3:15
5 "We few, we happy few": William Shakespeare, *Henry V*, Act IV, scene iii.

PART ONE

1 "The U.S. has . . . the economy": "America Must Reassert 'Stability and Leadership,' " *Der Spiegel*, December 12, 2009, www.spiegel.de/international/business/0,1518,666757,00.html.
2 Printing Press: The Increase in Money Supply: "St Louis Adjusted Monetary Base," StLouisFed.org, http://research.stlouisfed.org/fred2/data/BASENS.txt.
3 "My concern is that": Marc Davis, "Greenspan: Higher Taxes are Certain," MoneyNews .com, October 5, 2009, http://moneynews.newsmax.com/streettalk/greenspan_taxes_certain/2009/10/05/268667.html?s=al&promo_code=8B2C-1.
4 "The wisdom of the": James Harrington, *The Founders' Constitution*, 1656, http://press-pubs.uchicago.edu/founders/documents/v1ch11s2.html.
5 "Of all tyrannies": "C. S. Lewis Quotes," http://quotes.liberty-tree.ca/quotes_by/c.+s.+lewis.
6 "Give me your": Emma Lazarus, "The New Colossus," www.libertystatepark.com/emma.htm.

7 Europe vs. America: Socialism vs. Capitalism: Bruce Stokes, "Happiness Is Increasing in Many Countries—But Why?" *National Journal*, July 24, 2007, http://pewglobal.org/commentary/display.php?AnalysisID=1020.

8 "The sad fact for Europeans": Ibid.

9 "In contrast, America maintained": Ibid.

10 "Europeans may be poorer": Ibid.

11 "the average U.S. worker": Arthur C. Brooks, "Happy for the Work," *Wall Street Journal*, June 20, 2007, http://online.wsj.com/article/SB118230180318341380-search.html.

12 "two in three Americans": Stokes, "Happiness Is Increasing in Many Countries—But Why?"

13 Happiness: The United States and Europe Compared: Ibid.

14 Suicide Rates in the United States and Europe: "Suicide Rates of the World, and Why People Kill Themselves," May 11, 2007, WordPress.com, http://nitawriter.wordpress.com/2007/05/11/suicide-rates-of-the-world/.

15 Alcohol Consumption in the United States and Europe: Robert Malone and Tom Van Riper, "The World's Hardest-Drinking Countries," Forbes.com, November 28, 2007, www.forbes.com/2007/11/27/drinking-europe-alcohol-biz-commerce-cx_tvr_1128drinking.html.

16 "American's work 50%": Adam Okulicz-Kozaryn, "Why Europeans Work to Live and Americans Live to Work," HappinessEconomics.net, April 12, 2009, www.happinesseconomics.net/ocs/index.php/heirs/relationalgoods/paper/viewFile/21/78.

17 Asked to rate: Ibid.

18 The *Wall Street Journal*: Brooks, "Happy for the Work."

19 "For most Americans": Ibid.

20 a Rasmussen Poll: "America's Best Days," RasmussenReports.com, November 5, 2009, www.happinesseconomics.net/ocs/index.php/heirs/relationalgoods/paper/viewFile/21/78.

21 Obama's Change: More Unemployment: "Employment Status of the Civilian Noninstitutional Population by Sex and Age, Seasonally Adjusted," Bureau of Labor Statistics, ftp://ftp.bls.gov/pub/suppl/empsit.cpseea3.txt.

22 Only 59.2 percent of Americans: Rich Miller, "Unemployment Confronts Obama Rhetoric With Chronic Joblessness," Bloomberg.com, September 28, 2009, www.bloomberg.com/apps/news?pid=20601109&sid=aDx_Srx0Sv8Q.

23 (As recently as): "Table 575. Civilian Labor Force and Participation Rates With Projections: 1980 to 2016," U.S. Bureau of Labor Statistics, www.census.gov/compendia/statab/2010/tables/10s0575.pdf.

24 In November 2009: "Table A-12. Alternative Measures of Labor Underutilization," U.S. Bureau of Labor Statistics, December 4, 2009, www.bls.gov/news.release/empsit.t12.htm.

25 "the long-term jobless rate": Mary Pilon, "Life on Severance: Comfort, Then Crisis," *Wall Street Journal*, November 10, 2009, http://online.wsj.com/article/SB125780714976639687.html.

26 And more than half: Miller, "Unemployment Confronts Obama Rhetoric with Chronic Joblessness."

27 European and American Unemployment: "Clouds Mar Europe's Sunnier Outlook," *Financial Times*, December 15, 2009, p. 7.

28 "It's a change . . . and robotics": Peter S. Goodman, "The Recession's Over, but Not the Layoffs," *New York Times*, November 7, 2009, www.nytimes.com/2009/11/08/weekinreview/08goodman.html.

29 Why Aren't the Jobs Coming: Tom Raum, "Higher Jobless Rates Could be Here to Stay," *USAToday*, October 19, 2009, www.usatoday.com/money/economy/2009-10-19-high-unemployment-remains_N.htm.

30 Almost two thirds: "Just 12% Would Prefer a Car from a Bailed-Out Automaker," RasmussenReports.com, March 10, 2009, www.rasmussenreports.com/public_content/business/auto_industry/march_2009/just_12_would_prefer_a_car_from_a_bailed_out_automaker.

31 Since 2008, all categories: Serena Ng and Liz Rappaport, "Lending Squeeze Drags On," *Wall Street Journal*, December 8, 2009, http://online.wsj.com/article/SB126021724472580609.html.

32 Manufacturing jobs have been: Marlene A. Lee and Mark Mather, "Population Bulletin," PBR.org, June, 2008, www.prb.org/pdf08/63.2uslabor.pdf.

33 Decline in Manufacturing Jobs: "Employees on Nonfarm Payrolls by Major Industry Sector, 1959 to Date," Bureau of Labor Statistics, ftp://ftp.bls.gov/pub/suppl/empsit.ceseeb1.txt.

34 And, during the recession: "The Employment Situation—November 2009," Bureau of Labor Statistics, December 4, 2009, www.bls.gov/news.release/empsit.nr0.htm.

35 "In the middle": Goodman, "The Recession's Over, but Not the Layoffs."

36 "our view of the business": Ibid.

37 "such industries as science": "Is the U.S. Job Market Broken?" Reuters.com, October 5, 2009, http://blogs.reuters.com/columns/2009/10/05/is-the-us-job-market-broken/.

38 "firms are continuing": Jon Hilsenrath and Luca di Leo, "Productivity Soared in Third Quarter," *Wall Street Journal*, November 6, 2009, http://online.wsj.com/article/SB125742744080829139.html.

39 The Labor Department noted: Ibid.

40 "may be mismatched": "Is the U.S. Job Market Broken?"

41 "is in the process": Louis Woodhill, "More Stimulus Equals More Unemployment," November 11, 2009, www.realclearmarkets.com/articles/2009/11/11/more_stimulus_equals_more_unemployment_97503.html.

42 "the 500 largest": Ibid.

43 And, at the same time: Ibid.

44 "this means that selling": Ibid.

45 Instead, the *New York Times*: Michael Cooper and Ron Nixon, "Reports Show Conflicting Numbers of Jobs Attributed to Stimulus Money," *New York Times*, November 5, 2009, www.nytimes.com/2009/11/05/us/05stimulus.html.

46 Economist Barry Elias: E-mail from Barry Elias dated December 30, 2009.

47 For example, the purchase of a $1,047: Cooper and Nixon, "Reports Show Conflicting Numbers of Jobs Attributed to stimulus Money."

48 The higher birthrates . . . may be deliberate: Joshua Zumbrun, "Best-Case Scenario: Unemployment Rises," Forbes.com, November 12, 2009, www.forbes.com/2009/11/12/ unemployment-recession-economy-business-washington-jobs.html?feed=rss_business _beltway.

49 In October 2009: Woodhill, "More Stimulus Equals More Unemployment."

50 those workers who *do*: Ianthe Jeanne Dugan, "Returning Workers Face Steep Pay Cuts," *Wall Street Journal*, November 12, 2009, http://online.wsj.com/article/ SB125798515916944341.html.

51 Kenneth S. Rogoff: Goodman, "The Recession's Over but Not the Layoffs."

52 "is really just . . . 6 percent": Ibid.

53 "so-called natural . . . natural rate": Miller, "Unemployment Confronts Obama Rhetoric With Chronic Joblessness."

54 U.S. pension funds: Joshua Brockman, "Stocks Weigh Down U.S. Pension Funds," NPR .org, February 18, 2009, www.npr.org/templates/story/story.php?storyId=100818937.

55 According to the Federal Reserve: "St. Louis Adjusted Monetary Base," http://research .stlouisfed.org/fred2/data/BASENS.txt.

56 "most Americans saved": Sara Murray, "Most 2008 Stimulus Checks Were Saved, Not Spent," *Wall Street Journal*, December 17, 2009, http://blogs.wsj.com/economics/2009/ 12/16/most-2008-stimulus-checks-were-saved-not-spent/.

57 The Rising Price of Gold: "5 Year Gold Price History in US Dollars Per Ounce," Gold Price.org, November 13, 2009, http://goldprice.org/gold-price-history.html#5_year _gold_price.

58 Ratio of the Dow to the Price of Gold: Adrian Ash, "Dow Gold Ratio: Where Next?" April 17, 2008, http://goldnews.bullionvault.com/dow_gold_ratio_price_ounce_inflation_ 041720082.

59 "uncertainty over the outlook": Krishna Guha, "Inflation Outlook Uncertainty, 'High,' " FT.com, November 9, 2009, www.ft.com/cms/s/0/6cbdd4fe-cccd-11de-8e30-00144feabdc 0.html.

60 "inflation will emerge": Vincent Del Giudice and Thomas R. Keene, "Harvard's Feldstein Sees U.S. Inflation Danger After 2010," Bloomberg.com, April 23, 2009, www.bloomberg .com/apps/news?pid=20601087&sid=aGAGdAyBd6dY.

61 "concerns about inflation": Matt Phillips, "Warren Buffett Says His Concern about Inflation 'On the Rise,' " *Wall Street Journal*, July 24, 2009, http://blogs.wsj.com/marketbeat/ 2009/07/24/warren-buffett-says-his-concern-about-inflation-on-the-rise/.

62 "what we are doing": "Buffett's inflation prediction could boost Gold Investment," May 7, 2009, http://goldnews.bullionvault.com/Goldbug/gold_investment/buffetts_inflation_ prediction_could_boost_gold_investment_19158916.

63 "100 percent sure": Chen Shiyin and Bernard Lo, "U.S. Inflation to Approach Zimbabwe Level, Faber Says," Bloomberg.com, May 27, 2009, www.bloomberg.com/apps/news?pid= 20601110&sid=avgZDYM6mTFA.

64 "once business activity": Puru Saxena, "Inflation is Our Future," FinancialSense.com, September 24, 2009, www.financialsense.com/editorials/saxena/2009/0924.html.

65 The federal government: E-mail from Barry Elias, December 15, 2009.

66 According to Elias: Ibid.

67 "it would be . . . of the above": Matthew Jaffe, "Are We Witnessing the Demise of the Dollar?" ABCNews.com, October 6, 2009, http://abcnews.go.com/Business/dollar-versus-global-currency-world-leaders-deny-dollar-demise/story?id=8763491.

68 "provide domestic producers": E-mail from Barry Elias, economist, November 15, 2009.

69 "come to fear that": Paul A. Samuelson, "Heed the Hopeful Science," New York Times, October 23, 2009, www.nytimes.com/2009/10/24/opinion/24iht-edsamuelson.html.

70 "if we don't get our": Jaffe, "Are We Witnessing the Demise of the Dollar?"

71 The United Nations, too: Edmund Conway, "UN Wants New Global Currency to Replace Dollar," Telegraph, September 7, 2009, www.telegraph.co.uk/finance/currency/ 6152204/ UN-wants-new-global-currency-to-replace-dollar.html.

72 "to increase global": Ambrose Evans-Pritchard, "The G20 Moves a Step Closer to a Global Currency," Telegraph, April 3, 2009, www.telegraph.co.uk/finance/comment/ambrose evans_pritchard/5096524/The-G20-moves-the-world-a-step-closer-to-a-global-currency.html.

73 "a single clause . . . financial order": Ibid.

74 "putting a de . . . sovereign body": Ibid.

75 "Mr. Soros suggested": Alessandro Torello, "Soros Proposes Way to Fund CO_2 Cuts," Wall Street Journal, December 11, 2009, http://online.wsj.com/article/SB126044605972885237 .html.

76 "are planning to move": Jaffe, "Are We Witnessing the Demise of the Dollar?"

77 Its loan volume has quadrupled: Phil Hirschkorn, "Is the FHA at Risk?" CBSNews.com, November 29, 2009, www.cbsnews.com/stories/2009/11/29/eveningnews/main5826890 .shtml.

78 The FHA is using: "On U.S. Housing and Debased Lending Standards," November 20, 2009, http://seekingalpha.com/article/174510-on-u-s-housing-and-debased-lending -standards.

79 "just one out of twenty-two": Tim Cavanaugh, "Government Is Encouraging Lax Lending Standards," Reason, October 27, 2009, http://reason.com/blog/2009/10/27/government -is-encouraging-lax.

80 "FHA insurance Armageddon": Ibid.

81 The Federal Reserve Bank: "US Financial Data," StLouisFed.org, December 11, 2009, http://research.stlouisfed.org/publications/usfd/20091211/usfd.pdf.

82 At an Oval Office: The Associated Press, "Obama Urges Banks to Increase Lending to Businesses," nola.com, December 14, 2009, www.nola.com/business/index.ssf/2009/12/ obama_urges_banks_to_ease_lend.html.

83 "the Obama administration": Jim Puzzanghera, "Obama Administration Pushes to Make Mortgage Modifications Permanent," Los Angeles Times, December 1, 2009, www.latimes .com/business/la-fi-obama-mortgages1-2009dec01,0,1687963.story.

84 "the administration is hoping": Ibid.

85 "the removal of the": Sammy Benoit, "Democratic Senator Feinstein to Obama—No More Gitmo to Yemen Transfers," December 30, 2009, http://yidwithlid.blogspot.com/2009/12/sen-feinstein-to-obama-no-more-gitmo-to.html?utm_source=feedburner&utm_medium=email&utm_campaign=Feed%3A+YidWithLid+%28YID+With+LID%29.

86 "I'm worried": David Streitfeld, "New Slip in Housing Prices Undercuts Fragile Optimism," New York Times, December 29, 2009, www.nytimes.com/2009/12/30/business/economy/30econ.html?_r=1&ref=business.

87 "Those who cannot": http://en.wikiquote.org/wiki/George_Santayana.

88 The richest one percent: Gerald Prante, "Summary of Latest Federal Individual Income Tax Data," TaxFoundation.org, July 30, 2009, www.taxfoundation.org/news/show/250.html.

89 Right now, the top: Brian M. Riedl and Curtis S. Dubay, "Income Tax Surtax Should Not Fund Government Health Care Expansion," Heritage.org, July 15, 2009 www.heritage.org/Research/Taxes/upload/wm2544_table1.gif.

90 How Obama and Pelosi Will Increase the Top Tax Rate: Ibid.

91 "higher than the top": Ibid.

92 Top Tax Rate by Nation: Ibid.

93 "showed that . . . better life": "Night of the Living Death Tax," Wall Street Journal, March 31, 2009, http://online.wsj.com/article/SB123846422014872229.html.

94 What We Face: Obama's New Taxes: Martin Vaughn, "Medicare Tax on High Earners and Other Levies Stir Debate," Wall Street Journal, November 20, 2009, http://online.wsj.com/article_email/SB125868229026056763-lMyQjAxMDI5NTI4MDYyODAyWj.html.

95 Fifty billion dollars: "The Cost of Dying," CBSNews.com, November 22, 2009, www.cbsnews.com/stories/2009/11/19/60minutes/main5711689.shtml?tag=contentMain;contentBody.

96 And those who do: Esha Clearfield and Jeanne Batalova, "Foreign-Born Health-Care Worker in the United States," Migration Information Source, February 2007, http://www.migrationinformation.org/USFocus/display.cfm?ID=583; and Boulet, Cooper, Seeling, Norcini, and McKinley, "US Citizens Who Obtain Their Medical Degrees Abroad: An Overview, 1992–2006," Medscape Today, March 9, 2009, http://www.medscape.com/viewarticle/587050.

97 "already a catastrophic": Pat Wechsler, "Doctor Shortage to Spur Delays, Crowded ERs in Health Overhaul," Bloomberg.com, November 13, 2009, www.bloomberg.com/apps/news?pid=20601103&sid=aOd7mHLJIhJc.

98 "underserved areas in the": Ibid.

99 "now we're talking": Ibid.

100 "the average waiting time": Ibid.

101 "as many as half": Ibid.

102 "The primary lesson": Ibid.

103 "we're not going to": Janet Adamy, "Bill Complicates Drive to Add Primary-Care Doctors," Wall Street Journal, November 27, 2009, http://online.wsj.com/article/SB125928189292865761.html.

104 "if you expand coverage": Katharine Mangan, "Health-Reform Momentum Highlights Need for More Primary-Care Doctors," *Chronicle*, November 9, 2009, http://chronicle .com/article/Health-Reform-Momentum/49102/.

105 "Primary care . . . of reversal": H. Kenneth Walker, "Primary care is dying in the United States: Mutatis Mutandis," January 2006.

106 Since 1997, Dr. Walker: Ibid:

107 "one must complete": E-mail from Dr. Donald Gordon, November 30, 2009.

108 The number of U.S.: Janice Lloyd, "Doctor Shortage Looms as Primary Care Loses Its Pull," *USA Today*, August 18, 2009, www.usatoday.com/news/health/2009-08-17-doctor -gp-shortage_N.htm.

109 "considering it takes": Ibid.

110 Doctors' Starting Salaries, 2007: Ibid.

111 Medical school tuition and expenses: Ibid.

112 The president's program: Adamy, "Bill Complicates Drive to Add Primary-Care Doctors."

113 "increases funding for": Ibid.

114 "It is utterly . . . afford to": Mangan, "Health-Reform Momentum Highlights Need for More Primary-Care Doctors."

115 *Investor's Business Daily*: Terry Jones, "45% of Doctors Would Consider Quitting if Congress Passes Health Care Overhaul," Investors.com, September 15, 2009, www.investors .com/NewsAndAnalysis/Article.aspx?id=506199.

116 "Americans who lack": Lloyd, "Doctor Shortage Looms as Primary Care Loses It's Pull."

117 "finding a doctor": Ibid.

118 "if a patient goes": Ibid.

119 "At the time we need": Ibid.

120 In March 2009: Ibid.

121 "once the home of": Nadeem Esmail, "Canadian Medicare Deserves Its Criticism," Frasier Institute.org, October 9, 2009, www.fraserinstitute.org/newsandevents/commentaries/ 6839.aspx.

122 In 1993, it took: Ibid.

123 The Rasmussen poll reports: "78% Believe Health Care Plan Will Cost More Than Projected," RasmussenReports.com, December 30, 2009, www.rasmussenreports.com/ public_content/politics/current_events/healthcare/december_2009/78_believe_ health_care_plan_will_cost_more_than_projected.

124 Congressional leaders projected: Michael F. Cannon, "ObamaCare's Cost Could Top $6 Trillion," Cato-At-Library.com, November 27, 2009, www.cato-at-liberty.org/2009/ 11/27/obamacares-cost-could-top-6-trillion/.

125 "another gimmick": Ibid.

126 "on- and off-budget": Ibid.

127 "if the [Obama]": Dana Bush and Kristi Keck, "Special Deals, Carve-Outs Keep Health Care Afloat," CNN.com, December 22, 2009, http://edition.cnn.com/2009/POLITICS/ 12/22/health.care.favors/index.html.

128 What They got: The Senate Deals Behind Health-Care "Reform" Package: "The Price of 'History,' " *Wall Street Journal*, December 23, 2009, http://online.wsj.com/article/SB1000 142405274870430450457461047307722355 0.html?mod=WSJ_newsreel_opinion.

129 Federal Deficit as Percentage: "US Federal Deficit As Percent Of GDP Fiscal Years 1900 to 2010," www.usgovernmentspending.com/federal_deficit_chart.html.

130 "With our mounting": Lawrence Kadish, "Taking the National Debt Seriously," *Wall Street Journal*, October 12, 2009, http://online.wsj.com/article/SB2000142405274870442 93045.74467071019099570.html.

131 "the United States government": Edmund L. Andrews, "Wave of Debt Payments Facing U.S. Government," *New York Times*, November 22, 2009, www.nytimes.com/2009/11/23/ business/23rates.html?_r=1&scp=1&sq=Federal%20government%20faces%20balloon %20in%20debt%20payments&st=cse.

132 "the government faces": Ibid.

133 "the government is on": Ibid.

134 While our budget deficit: Adam Cohen, "Offers Reprieve on Deficits, But Gives Ultimatum to Greece ," *Wall Street Journal*, November 12, 2009, http://online.wsj.com/article/ SB125794136510943495.html.

135 Of the $10.7 trillion: Michael Hodges, "Federal Government Debt Report," October 2009, http://mwhodges.home.att.net/debt.htm.

136 "What a good country": Andrews, "Wave of Debt Payments Facing U.S. Government."

137 "the credit market": George Melloan, "Government Deficits and Private Growth," *Wall Street Journal*, November 23, 2009, http://online.wsj.com/article/SB100014240527487039 32904574511243712388988.html.

138 Change in Debt Since 2008: Ng and Rappaport, "Lending Squeeze Drags On."

139 Obama recently announced: Peter Barnes, Major Garrett, and the Associated Press, "Obama Pitches Jobs Program, Points Finger at GOP for Economic Mess," FOXNews.com, December 8, 2009, www.foxnews.com/politics/2009/12/08/obama-takes-joblessness/.

140 "the Federal Reserve . . . manage risk": Ibid.

141 "By official definition": Ibid.

142 "under the new management": Ibid.

143 As economist Barry Elias: E-mail from Barry Elias, economist, December 15, 2009.

144 "feeding the government": Melloan, "Government Deficits and Private Growth."

145 "first post-American president": Author interview with John Bolton, Fox News Green Room, November 16, 2009.

146 It has a male: "Life Expectancy in Russia WisdomCard," http://organizedwisdom.com/ Life_Expectancy_in_Russia.

147 At number 145: "The 2006 Transparency International Corruption Perceptions Index," Transparency.org, www.infoplease.com/ipa/A0781359.html.

148 Saudi Arabia ranks: Ibid.

149 Indonesia is ranked: Ibid.

150 GDPs of G-20 Nations: "Report for Selected Countries and Subjects," IMF.org, http:// imf.org/external/pubs/ft/weo/2009/02/weodata/weorept.aspx?pr.x=79&pr.y=12

&sy=2007&ey=2014&scsm=1&ssd=1&sort=country&ds=.&br=1&c=512%2C941%2C914.

151 The current executive: Charles Bremner, "Nicolas Sarkozy Dismay as Dominique Strauss-Kahn in Sex Scandal," *Times*, October 20, 2008, www.timesonline.co.uk/tol/news/world/europe/article4972855.ece.

152 Among his female: Ibid.

153 "Mr Strauss-Kahn": Ibid.

154 "help the G-7 talk": Lesley Wroughton and Frances Kerry, "Snap Analysis: New World Economic Order Takes Shape at G-20," Reuters.com, www.reuters.com/article/ousiv-Molt/idUSTRE58O1FB20090925.

155 "Europeans [are] . . . it's finished": Steve Hargreaves, "G-20 Shaping a New World Order," CNN.com, November 14, 2008, http://money.cnn.com/2008/11/14/news/economy/g20_powerplay/index.htm.

156 "greater oversight of hedge": Ibid.

157 These bureaucrats: "Snap Analysis: New World Economic Order Takes Shape at G-20," www.reuters.com/article/ousivMolt/idUSTRE58O1FB20090925.

158 "as a board of directors": Bob Davis and Stephen Fidler, "Nations Ready Big Changes to Global Economic Policy," *Wall Street Journal*, September 22, 2009, http://online.wsj.com/article/SB125348959155226421.html.

159 "have to define . . . to the U.S.": Ibid.

160 "leaders from the G-20": Ibid.

161 "The U.S. is pressing . . . back in line": Ibid.

162 "none of the countries": Ibid.

163 "new limits on corporate": Ibid.

164 "coordinated capitalism": Barry Eichengreen, *The European Economy Since 1945*, Princeton, 2007, p. 7.

165 "The same institutions": Ibid.

166 "Bank-based financial": Ibid.

167 "The generous employment": Ibid.

168 "State holding companies": Ibid.

169 "discourage risk-taking": Davis and Fidler, "Nations Ready Big Changes to Global Economic Policy."

170 The stress test results: Binyamin Applebaum, "10 Banks Allowed to Repay $68B in Bailout Money," *Washington Post*, June 10, 2009, www.washingtonpost.com/wp-dyn/content/article/2009/06/09/AR2009060900891.html.

171 Big Banks Ordered: Jim Puzzanghera and E. Scott Reckard, "Bank 'Stress Test' Results Hint at Economic Recovery," *Los Angeles Times*, May 8, 2009, http://articles.latimes.com/2009/may/08/business/fi-stress-tests8.

172 "pay cuts for the top": Judson Berger, "Pay Czar's Move to Cut Salaries Raises Questions About Limits of Authority," FoxNews.com, October 22, 2009, www.foxnews.com/politics/2009/10/22/pay-czars-cut-salaries-raises-questions-limits-authority/.

173 "the move raises": Ibid.

174 "He has a lot of": Ibid.

175 "the Washington pay czar": Ibid.

176 Bainbridge points out: Ibid.

177 "Since these companies": Ibid.

178 "In early October": Ibid.

179 "The fear by executives": Ibid.

180 "the Federal Reserve": Ibid.

181 "give federal officials . . . an assessment": Jim Puzzanghera, "Geithner Makes a Pitch for Regulation of Financial Industry," *Los Angeles Times*, October 30, 2009, www.latimes .com/business/la-fi-geithner-regs30-2009oct30,0,3248143.story.

182 "place no limit": Ibid.

183 Provisions of the Financial Institutions Regulation Act: Damian Paletta, "Financial Bill Hits Big Banks Hardest," *Wall Street Journal*, December 8, 2009, http://online.wsj.com/article/SB126023676584581197.html.

184 Now, like a monument: Sharon Terlep, "GM Reports $1.5 Billion Loss, Plans Repayment," *Wall Street Journal*, November 17, 2009, http://online.wsj.com/article/SB10001424052748704431804574539284255805824.html.

185 The workforce will be: Micheline Maynard, "A Primer on the New General Motors," *New York Times*, July 10, 2009, www.nytimes.com/2009/07/11/business/11primer.html.

186 "Fritz Henderson, chief": Steven J. Dubord, "GM's Bailout Money May Go Overseas," TheNewAmerican.com, November 16, 2009, www.thenewamerican.com/index.php/economy/sectors-mainmenu-46/2333-gms-bailout-money-may-go-overseas.

187 Seven of ten: Satya J. Gabriel, "Restructuring State-Owned Enterprises in China," MtHolyoke.edu, May 1998, www.mtholyoke.edu/courses/sgabriel/soe.htm.

188 "are very unlikely": Committee for a Responsible Federal Budget, "Troubled Asset Relief Program: Year-End Review December 9, 2009," December 9, 2009, www.scribd.com/doc/23899423/Troubled-Asset-Relief-Program-Year-End-Review-1.

189 "an individual mandate": Randy Barnett, Nathaniel Stewart, and Todd F. Gaziano, "Why the Personal Mandate to Buy Health Insurance is Unprecedented and Unconstitutional," Heritage.org, December 9, 2009, www.heritage.org/research/legalissues/lm0049.cfm.

190 "nowhere in the Constitution": Ibid.

191 "class of activity": Ibid.

192 "proponents of the individual": Ibid.

193 "never in this nation's": Ibid.

194 Single-person households: "2009 Federal Poverty Level," Foundation for Health Coverage Education, January 23, 2009, www.azdhs.gov/phs/hiv/pdf/adap/FHCE_FedPoverty Level.pdf.

195 "short-term private benefit": Andrew Napolitano, ". . . They Violate Good Sense and the Constitution," *Wall Street Journal*, February 6, 2009, http://online.wsj.com/article/SB123388405082355077.html.

196 "by saving some businesses": Ibid.

197 "the power to spend": Ibid.

198 "doctrine against unconstitutional": Ibid.

199 "condition corporate welfare": Ibid.

200 "The salary caps also": Ibid.

201 The Constitution clearly: "Bill of Attainder," www.techlawjournal.com/glossary/legal/attainder.htm.

202 "possession of secured": Ken Klukowski, "Senior Democrat Says Obama's Czars Unconstitutional," TownHall.com, June 15, 2009, http://townhall.com/columnists/Ken Klukowski/2009/06/15/senior_democrat_says_obamas_czars_unconstitutional.

203 "possession of secured . . . and Fiat": John Carter, "Seizing Property: The Federal Takeover of the Auto Industry," BobBeauprez.com, June 24, 2009, www.bobbeauprez.com/seizing-property-the-federal-takeover-of-the-auto-industry.

204 "Truman Administration['s] contention": Ibid.

205 "Court flatly rejected": Ibid.

206 "Indiana suit . . . contends": Fred Lucas, "Indiana Challenges Constitutionality of TARP Money for Auto Bailout," CNSNews.com, June 4, 2009, www.cnsnews.com/public/content/article.aspx?RsrcID=49096.

207 "speculators range from retired": Dr. Mark W. Hendrickson, "Team Obama's Auto Coup," MensNewsDaily.com, June 15, 2009, http://mensnewsdaily.com/2009/06/15/team-obamas-auto-coup/.

208 "Congress only approved": Lucas, "Indiana Challenges Constitutionality of TARP Money for Auto Bailout."

209 "On its face": Ibid.

210 "Plaintiffs' arguments have even": Ibid.

211 "Passage of that": Ibid.

212 The result is that: Christopher Neefus, "UAW Bondholders to Receive More Equity in GM than Others," CNSNews.com, June 2, 2009, www.cnsnews.com/news/article/48942.

213 How did the White House: Ibid.

214 "from the beginning": Ibid.

215 "an arm of the": "Anita Dunn: Fox News an Outlet for GOP Propaganda," Huffington Post.com, October 11, 2009, www.huffingtonpost.com/2009/10/11/anita-dunn-fox-news-an-ou_n_316691.html.

216 "push back . . . the president": Ibid.

217 But a study: "White House Escalates War of Words with Fox News," FOXNews.com, October 12, 2009, www.foxnews.com/politics/2009/10/12/white-house-escalates-war-words-fox-news/

218 there was a difference: Ibid.

219 Pew reports: Ibid.

220 Media Coverage: Ibid.

221 "Is this why": Ibid.

222 "informed by the": Ibid.

223 "the way we would": Brian Stelter, "Fox's Volley with Obama Intensifying," New York Times, October 11, 2009, www.nytimes.com/2009/10/12/business/media/12fox.html.

224 The list included: "Nixon's Enemy List," Wikipedia.org, http://en.wikipedia.org/wiki/Nixon's_Enemies_List#Master_list_of_political_opponents.

225 "American society must": Leonard Downie Jr. and Michael Schudson, "Finding a New Model for News Reporting," *Washington Post*, October 19, 2009, www.washingtonpost.com/wp-dyn/content/article/2009/10/18/AR2009101801461.html.

226 "whether government . . . copyright laws": Brent Kendall and Thomas Catan, "FTC to Examine Possible Support of News Organizations," *Wall Street Journal*, December 2, 2009, http://online.wsj.com/article/SB10001424052748704107104574569661532881656.html.

227 "I did not run": Timothy P. Carney, "Obama Brings Purrs from Wall Street's Fat Cats," WashingtonExaminer.com, December 16, 2009, www.washingtonexaminer.com/politics/Obama-brings-purrs-from-Wall-Street_s-fat-cats-8658762-79346897.html.

228 "Wall Street's . . . Wall Street history": Suzanne Craig and Aaron Luchetti, "Goldman Gains on Rivals' Pain," *Wall Street Journal*, July 15, 2009, http://online.wsj.com/article/SB124755439431437571.html.

229 Goldman's net income: Ibid.

230 "more than four": Carney, "Obama Brings Purrs from Wall Street's Fat Cats."

231 Top Donors to Obama Campaign: "Barack Obama (D) Top Contributors," OpenSecrets.org, www.opensecrets.org/pres08/contrib.php?cycle=2008&cid=N00009638.

232 "although it was not": Gretchen Morgenson, "Behind Insurer's Crisis, Blind Eye to a Web of Risk," *New York Times*, September 27, 2008, www.nytimes.com/2008/09/28/business/28melt.html?_r=1&hp=&oref=slogin&pagewanted=all.

233 "days later, federal officials": Ibid.

234 "it makes it appear": Fredreka Schouten, "Geithner Names Ex-Lobbyist as Treasury Chief of Staff," *USA Today*, January 27, 2009, www.usatoday.com/news/washington/2009-01-27-lobbyist_N.htm.

235 At twenty-nine: "SEC Unit Hires Ex-Goldman Sachs Worker as Chief Operating Officer," *Los Angeles Times*, October 16, 2009, http://articles.latimes.com/2009/oct/16/business/fi-sec-coo16.

236 The president also tapped: Janine Zacharia, "Obama Names Goldman Sach's Hormats to State Department Post," Bloomberg.com, July 17, 2009, www.bloomberg.com/apps/news?pid=20601103&sid=aIGwcAuMUcFI.

237 In addition, Goldman Sachs: "Why Obama is Owned by Goldman Sachs," October 23, 2009, http://gdayworld.thepodcastnetwork.com/2009/10/23/why-obama-is-owned-by-goldman-sachs/.

238 In the second quarter: Matt Taibbi, "The Real Price of Goldman's Giganto-Profits," TrueSlant.com, July 16, 2009, http://trueslant.com/matttaibbi/2009/07/16/on-goldmans-giganto-profits/.

239 Goldman also was able: Ibid.

240 Obama has been: "Why Obama is Owned by Goldman Sachs."

241 In 2005, the nation: "U.S. Carbon Dioxide Emissions from Energy Sources 2008 Flash Estimate," EIA.gov, May 2009, www.eia.doe.gov/oiaf/1605/flash/flash.html.

242 In 2009, the United States: Mark Long, "EIA: 2009 US Co2 Emissions from Fossil Fuels Seen Down 5.6%," *Wall Street Journal*, November 10, 2009, http://online.wsj.com/article/BT-CO-20091110-713634.html.

243 U.S. Carbon Dioxide Emissions: "U.S. Carbon Dioxide Emissions from Energy Sources 2008 Flash Estimate."

244 2009 (projected) 5,476: Long, "EIA: 2009 US Co2 Emissions from Fossil Fuels Seen Down 5.6%."

245 "a cap and trade": Matt Cover, "EPA: Cap-and-Trade Bill Could Hurt U.S. Manufacturing, Send Factory Jobs Overseas," CNSNews.com, May 25, 2009, www.cnsnews.com/news/article/48552.

246 The federal Environmental Protection: Ibid.

247 Since we'll have: Daniella Markheim, "Energy Cap and Trade Threatens American Prosperity," Heritage.org, June 16, 2009, www.heritage.org/Research/EnergyandEnvironment/wm2488.cfm.

248 States Hardest Hit by Cap and Trade: "Waxman-Markey Cap and Trade's Biggest Losers: Manufacturing," June 25, 2009, http://blog.heritage.org/2009/06/25/waxman-markey-cap-and-trade's-biggest-losers-manufacturing/.

249 "massive redistribution": Author interview with John Bolton, November 10, 2009.

250 American cars account: Julian Borger, "Half of Global Car Exhaust Produced by US Vehicles," *Guardian*, June 29, 2006, www.guardian.co.uk/environment/2006/jun/29/travelandtransport.usnews.

251 If three quarters: Josie Garthwaite, "Surprise: Electric Cars Not Actually Zero-Emission," November 12, 2009, http://earth2tech.com/2009/11/12/surprise-electric-cars-not-actually-zero-emission/.

252 The Natural Resource: Eric Loveday, "ETA Warns That Switching to EVs Will Increase Emissions in Coal Dependent World," AllCarsElectric.com, November 24, 2009, www.allcarselectric.com/blog/1038867_eta-warns-that-switching-to-evs-will-increase-emissions-in-coal-dependent-world.

253 natural gas reduces: "Rolling Smokestacks: Cleaning Up America's Trucks and Buses," UCSUSA.org, March 7, 2003, www.ucsusa.org/clean_vehicles/vehicle_impacts/diesel/rolling-smokestacks-cleaning.html.

254 Foreign trade accounts: Markheim, "Energy Cap and Trade Threatens American Prosperity."

255 But Obama has often: Ibid.

256 "a distinct advantage": Speech by Governor Bob Riley in Costa Rica at Alabama International Business Conference, January 16, 2010.

257 "I don't know why": Dave Kopel, *Fahrenhype 9/11*, Michael and Me, LP, 2004.

258 "this administration prefers": Al Kamen and Scott Wilson, " 'Global War On Terror' Is Given New Name," *Washington Post*, March 25, 2009, www.washingtonpost.com/wp-dyn/content/article/2009/03/24/AR2009032402818.html.

259 "the focus of complaints": Spencer S. Hsu and Carrie Johnson, "Agencies Reporting to White House of Ft. Hood," *Washington Post*, December 1, 2009, washingtonpost.com/wp-dyn/content/article/2009/11/30/AR2009113003883.html.

260 "drawn the attention": Ibid.

261 "were not told": Ibid.

262 "the Pentagon said": Yochi J. Dreazen and Evan Perez, "Army Wasn't Told of Hasan's Email," *Wall Street Journal*, November 12, 2009, http://online.wsj.com/article/SB125788890000142139.html.

263 "sent most of Hasan's . . . research interests": Hsu and Johnson, "Agencies Reporting to White House on Ft. Hood."

264 After Washington decided: Ibid.

265 "U.S. intelligence agencies": Matthew Cole, Richard Esposito, and Brian Ross, "Officials: U.S. Army Told of Hasan's Contacts with Al Qaeda," ABCNews.com, November 9, 2009, http://abcnews.go.com/Blotter/fort-hood-shooter-contact-al-qaeda-terrorists-officials/story?id=9030873.

266 After the attack: Ibid.

267 "[Hasan] would frequently . . . type of conflict": Ibid.

268 "What the Obama": "Khalid Sheikh Mohammed Civilian Trial Blasted by Giuliani," BigNewsNetwork.com, December 10, 2009, http://feeds.bignewsnetwork.com/?sid=565796.

269 "in this particular": Ibid.

270 "the system has": Peter Baker and Scott Shane, "Obama Seeks to Reassure U.S. After Bombing Attempt," *New York Times*, December 28, 2009, www.nytimes.com/2009/12/29/us/29terror.html?pagewanted=1.

271 "in many ways": Ibid.

272 "systemic failure": Peter Baker, "Obama Faults 'Systemic Failure'; in U.S. Security," *New York Times*, December 29, 2009, http://thecaucus.blogs.nytimes.com/2009/12/29/obama-faults-systemic-failure-in-us-security/.

273 "Instead . . . embassy officials": Ibid.

274 "government has spent": Ibid.

275 "privacy advocates . . . across the United States": Ibid.

276 "one of the four . . . Saudi officials": Rehag El-Buri, Joseph Rhee, and Brian Ross, "Al Qaeda Leader Behind Northwest Flight 253 Terror Plot Was Released by U.S.," ABCNews.com, December 28, 2009, http://abcnews.go.com/Blotter/northwest-flight-253-al-qaeda-leaders-terror-plot/story?id=9434065&page=1.

277 Lawyer who defended: "Come Clean Mr. Holder," *New York Post*, January 27, 2010, http://www.nypost.com/p/news/opinion/editorials/come_clean_mr_holder_qakritP0Paijq DmUny929I.

PART TWO

1 The latest Rasmussen: "Election 2010: Missouri Senate," RasmussenReports.com, February 11, 2010, http://www.rasmussenreports.com/public_content/politics/elections2/election_2010/election_2010_senate_elections/missouri/election_2010_missouri_senate.

2 Rasmussen's January 2010: "Election 2010: Ohio Senate," RasmussenReports.com, February 8, 2010, http://www.rasmussenreports.com/public_content/politics/elections 2/election_2010/election_2010_senate_elections/ohio/election_2010_ohio_senate.

3 she enjoyed an early: "Election 2010: New Hampshire Senate," RasmussenReports.com, February, 11, 2010, http://www.rasmussenreports.com/public_content/politics/elec tions2/election_2010/election_2010_senate_elections/new_hampshire/election_2010_ new_hampshire_senate.

4 The Rasmussen Poll: "Election 2010: Kentucky Senate," RasmussenReports.com, February 4, 2010, http://www.rasmussenreports.com/public_content/politics/elections2/ election_2010/election_2010_senate_elections/kentucky/election_2010_kentucky _senate.

5 In one of the: "Election 2010: Florida Republican Primary for Senate," RasmussenReports .com, February 1, 2010, http://www.rasmussenreports.com/public_content/politics/ elections2/election_2010/election_2010_senate_elections/florida/election_2010 _florida_republican_primary_for_senate.

6 A January 2010: "Election 2010: Delaware Senate," RasmussenReports.com, January 26, 2010, http://www.rasmussenreports.com/public_content/politics/elections2/election _2010/election_2010_senate_elections/delaware/election_2010_delaware_senate.

7 She trails all four: "Election 2010: Arkansas Senate," RasmussenReports.com, February 2, 2010, http://www.rasmussenreports.com/public_content/politics/elections2/ election_2010/election_2010_senate_elections/arkansas/election_2010_arkansas_senate.

8 According to a Rasmussen: "Election 2010: Nevada Senate," RasmussenReports.com, February 5, 2010, http://www.rasmussenreports.com/public_content/politics/elections2/ election_2010/election_2010_senate_elections/nevada/election_2010_nevada_senate.

9 Norton is very: "Election 2010: Colorado Senate," RasmussenReports.com, February 5, 2010, http://www.rasmussenreports.com/public_content/politics/elections2/election _2010/election_2010_senate_elections/colorado/election_2010_colorado_senate.

10 "incumbency may be": Ibid.

11 The Rasmussen Poll: Ibid.

12 But Republican Pat: "Election 2010: Pennsylvania Senate," RasmussenReports.com, February 8, 2010, http://www.rasmussenreports.com/public_content/politics/elections2/ election_2010/election_2010_senate_elections/pennsylvania/2010_senate_election/ election_2010_pennsylvania_senate.

13 She defeats former: "Election 2010: California Senate," RasmussenReports.com, February 15, 2010, http://www.rasmussenreports.com/public_content/politics/elections2/ election_2010/election_2010_senate_elections/california/election_2010_california _senate.

14 The national trend: "Election 2010: Connecticut Senate," RasmussenReports.com, February 3, 2010, http://www.rasmussenreports.com/public_content/politics/elections2/ election_2010/election_2010_senate_elections/connecticut/election_2010_connecti cut_senate.

15 Democratic party loyalty: "Members of Congress / Harry Reid," *Washington Post,* http://projects.washingtonpost.com/congress/members/r000146/.

16 Wealth ranking: "Personal Finances Harry Reid (D-Nev), 2008," OpenSecrets.org, http://www.opensecrets.org/pfds/CIDsummary.php?CID=N00009922&year=2008.

17 Earmark ranking: "Other Data Senator Harry Reid 2005–2010," OpenSecrets.org, http://www.opensecrets.org/politicians/otherdata.php?cycle=2010&cid=N00009922&type=I.

18 Top Contributors to Harry Reid: "Top 20 Contributors to Campaign Cmte," Open Secrets.org, http://www.opensecrets.org/politicians/contrib.php?cycle=2010&cid=N00 009922&type=I&mem=.

19 Top Industries Contributing: "Top Industries Senator Harry Reid 2005–2010," Open Secrets.org, http://www.opensecrets.org/politicians/industries.php?cycle=2010&cid=N 00009922&type=I&mem=.

20 According to John Solomon: Jerry Doyle, "Harry Reid Ethics Complaint," FreeRepublic.com, April 17, 2006, http://www.freerepublic.com/focus/news/1618473/posts.

21 Well, Reid was probably: Ibid.

22 Between 2001 and 2004: Ibid.

23 "Reid collected donations": "Harry Reid," SourceWatch.org, http://www.sourcewatch.org/index.php?title=Harry_Reid.

24 Closing the revolving: "Democrats Pledge to Provide Honest Leadership, Open Government," Democrats.Senate.gov, January 18, 2006, http://democrats.senate.gov/newsroom/record.cfm?id=250503.

25 Reid, along with his: Associated Press, "Top Democrat Reid Aided Abramoff Clients," MSNBC.com, February 9, 2006, http://www.msnbc.msn.com/id/11261035/.

26 The year before he: "Lobbying Holland & Hart," OpenSecrets.org, http://www.opensecrets.org/lobby/firmsum.php?lname=Holland+%26+Hart&year=2009.

27 Harry Reid is in a class: Richard T. Cooper and Chuck Neubauer, "The Senator's Sons," *Los Angeles Times,* June 23, 2003, http://newsmine.org/content.php?ol=cabal-elite/w-administration/big-money/lobbyists-senators-sons.txt.

28 Mining companies paid: Ibid.

29 When Barringer moved to another: Ibid.

30 From 2001–2002: "Harry Reid [D-NV] The Most Corrupt Senator in DC," PipeLineNews.org, October 17, 2006, http://www.pipelinenews.org/index.cfm?page=reidfixer.htm.

31 "In 2003, Reid's four": Cooper and Neubauer, "The Senator's Sons."

32 Rory Reid is still: "About the Firm," LionelSawyer.com, http://www.lionelsawyer.com/index.cfm?page_id=2.

33 Key Reid was hired: Cooper and Neubauer, "The Senator's Sons."

34 "The mining firm Placer": Ibid.

35 The American Gaming Association: Ibid.

36 Barringer was hired: Ibid.

37 "A chemical company seeking": Ibid.

38 The Howard Hughes Corp.: Ibid.

39 "Other provisions of the same": Ibid.

40 "Reid never told his senate": Ibid.

41 "The governments of three": Ibid.

42 In 2005, Reid sponsored: Tom Hamburger and Chuck Neubauer, "Will the Pork Stop Here?" *Los Angeles Times,* November 13, 2006, http://www.latimes.com/news/politics/la-na-earmarks13nov13,0,6626376,full.story?coll=la-home-headlines.

43 Laughlin is a casino town: Ibid.

44 "undoubtedly hike land": Ibid.

45 "Sen. Reid's support": Ibid.

46 "The low price resulted": Ibid.

47 "paying $240,000 for 37.52": Ibid.

48 From 2001–2005: Reid financial disclosures for 2001, 2001, 2003, 2004, 2005, 2006, 2007, 2008;

49 In 2002, Reid generously: Associated Press, "Reid Used Campaign Money for Christmas Bonuses at Personal Condo," *USA Today,* October 17, 2006, http://www.usatoday.com/news/washington/2006-10-17-reid-christmas-bonuses_x.htm?csp=34.

50 Once the gifts were: Ibid.

51 "whose name [has]": Kathleen Hennessey and John Solomon, "Democrat Leader Reaped $1.1 Million from Sale of Land he didn't Own," *USA Today,* October 11, 2006, http://www.usatoday.com/news/washington/2006-10-11-reid_x.htm.

52 (Brown is a longtime): "Jay Brown's Federal Campaign Contribution Search," NewsMeat.com, http://www.newsmeat.com/fec/bystate_detail.php?zip=89101&last=BROWN&first=JAY

53 "I worked hard": "Black History Month Column Questions," AOLNews.com, February 2, 2010, http://www.aolnews.com/nation/article/sen-harry-reids-black-history-month-column-raises-questions/19341444?icid=main|main|dl1|link1|http%3A%2F%2Fwww.aolnews.com%2Fnation%2Farticle%2Fsen-harry-reids-black-history-month-column-raises-questions%2F19341444.

54 "Joe Neal, a former": Ibid.

55 Democratic Party Loyalty: "Other Data Senator Blanche Lincoln 2005–2010," Open Secrets.org, http://www.opensecrets.org/politicians/otherdata.php?cycle=2010&cid=N00008092&type=I.

56 Wealth Ranking: "Top Industries Senator Blanche Lincoln 2005–2010," OpenSecrets.org, http://www.opensecrets.org/politicians/industries.php?cycle=2010&cid=N00008092&%20type=C.

57 Earmark Ranking: Rob Moritz, "Beebe: Per Capita Income Up to 46th, Revenues Still Falling," ArkansasNews.com, November 2, 2009, http://arkansasnews.com/2009/11/02/beebe-per-capita-income-up-to-46th-revenues%20-still-falling/.

58 Blanche Lincoln's Ranking: "Bank's Beat Homeowners: Foreclosure Bill Killed in Senate," HuffingtonPost.com, April 30, 2009, http://www.huffingtonpost.com/2009/04/30/banks-beat-howeowners-for_n_193902.html.

59 Arkansas is one of: Manu Raju, "Health Bill Sparks Nanny State Debate," Politico.com, December 14, 2009, http://www.politico.com/news/stories/1209/30543.html.

60 That legislation would have: Ibid.

61 Certain counties: Blanche Lincoln, "Lincoln: I Will Not Support Legislation that Hurt's America's Seniors," Lincoln.senate.gov, December 7, 2009, http://lincoln.senate.gov/newsroom/2009-12-7-2.cfm.

62 "The funding is part": Ezra Klein, "Blanche Lincoln was for the public option before she was against it," *Washington Post*, November 23, 2009, http://voices.washingtonpost.com/ezra-klein/2009/11/blanche_lincoln_was_for_the_pu.html.

63 "Financial literacy is one": Joe Conason, "Masking Inaction with Drivel," *New York Observer*, November 23, 2009, http://www.observer.com/2009/politics/masking-inaction-drivel.

64 "Lincoln: I Will Not": Blanche Lincoln, "Lincoln: I Will Not Support Legislation that Hurt's America's Seniors," Lincoln.senate.gov, December 7, 2009, http://lincoln.senate.gov/newsroom/2009-12-7-2.cfm.

65 [health-care reform]: "Blanche Lincoln," OpenSecrets.org, http://www.opensecrets.org/politicians/summary.php?type=C&cid=N00008092&newMem=%20N&cycle=2010.

66 For some in my: "Top Industries 2007–2008," OpenSecrets.org, http://www.opensecrets.org/politicians/industries.php?cycle=2008&type=C&cid=N0000809%202&newMem=N&recs=20.

67 Lincoln sponsored an amendment: Tony Romm, "NRSC Hits Lincoln for Insurance Industry Contributions," *The Hill*, December 5, 2009, http://thehill.com/blogs/blog-briefing-room/news/70759-nrsc-hits-lincoln-for-insurance-industry-contributions.

68 Donations by Top: Farm Subsidy Database, http://farm.ewg.org/farm/progdetail.php?fips=00000&progcode=total&page=states.

69 Contributions to Blanche: Chris Edwards, "Congressional Conflict of Interest," www.CATO-at-Library.org, September 10, 2009, www.cato-at-liberty.org/2009/09/10/congressional-conflict-of-interest/.

70 "back home in": Conason, "Masking Inaction with Drivel."

71 Although Arkansas has: "Arkansas," Farm.EWG.org, http://farm.ewg.org/region.php?fips=05000.

72 "farmer's daughter": Blanche Lincoln, "Lincoln Next Chairman for Senate Committee on Agriculture, Nutrition, and Forestry," Lincoln.senate.gov, September 9, 2009, http://lincoln.senate.gov/newsroom/2009-09-09-1.cfm.

73 Democratic party loyalty: "Members of Congress/Barbara Boxer," *Washington Post*, http://projects.washingtonpost.com/congress/members/b000711/.

74 Wealth Ranking: 42/100: "Personal Finances Barbara Boxer (D-Calif), 2008," OpenSecrets.org, http://www.opensecrets.org/pfds/CIDsummary.php?CID=N00006692&year=2008.

75 Earmark Ranking: 34/100: "Other Data Senator Byron L Dorgan 2005–2010," Open Secrets.org, http://www.opensecrets.org/politicians/otherdata.php?cycle=2010&cid=N00004615&type=I.

76 In it's mandatory year-end: "Annual Report of the Select Committee on Ethics 111th Congress, First Session," Ethics.senate.gov, http://ethics.senate.gov/downloads/pdffiles/2009_Annual_Report.pdf.

77 The committee found that: Ibid.

78 She actually paid: Chuck Neubauer, Richard Simon, and Rone Tempest, "Political Payrolls Include Families," *Los Angeles Times*, April 14, 2005, http://articles.latimes.com/2005/apr/14/nation/na-campaign14?pg=2.

79 "The men who have brought": Nick Wing, "Boxer: Nelson Amendment Wouldn't Require Men to Purchase Riders for Viagra," HuffingtonPost.com, December 8, 2009, http://www.huffingtonpost.com/2009/12/08/boxer-nelson-amendment-wo_n_383908.html.

80 Barbara Slipping: "Election 2010: California Senate," RasmussenReports.com, January 15, 2010, http://www.rasmussenreports.com/public_content/politics/elections2/election_2010/election_2010_senate_elections/california/election_2010_california_senate.

81 Take Sen. Kennedy: "Internal Affairs: Barbara Boxer is No Ted Kennedy," *Mercury News*, October 25, 2009, http://www.mercurynews.com/breaking-news/ci_13630074?nclick_check=1.

82 "she's not up to the": Lisa Lerer and Manu Raju, "Democrats Raise Concerns About Barbara Boxer," Politico.com, July 23, 2009, http://www.politico.com/news/stories/0709/25309.html.

83 "In private conversations": Ibid

84 "People don't look": Ibid.

85 Sen. Boxer: You: "Boxer, the U.S. Senator, Chides Brigadier General for Calling her 'Ma'am,' " FoxNews.com, June 18, 2009, http://www.foxnews.com/politics/2009/06/18/boxer-senator-chides-brigadier-general-calling-maam/.

86 "overwhelmed [her] respect": "Rice Spars with Democrats in Hearing," CNN.com, January 19, 2005, http://www.cnn.com/2005/ALLPOLITICS/01/18/rice.confirmation/index.html.

87 "Who pays the price": Melissa Drosjack and Greg Simmons, "White House Spokesman Blasts Sen. Boxer's Exchange with Secretary Rice," FoxNews.com, January 13, 2007, http://www.foxnews.com/story/0,2933,243359,00.html.

88 "I don't know": Ibid.

89 Kirsten Gillibrand: a phrase used by Herbert Hoover to describe President Franklin Delano Roosevelt.

90 Democratic Party Loyalty: "Members of Congress/Kirsten Gillibrand," *Washington Post*, http://projects.washingtonpost.com/congress/members/g000555/.

91 Wealth Ranking: "Personal Finances Kirsten Gillibrand (D-NY), 2008," OpenSecrets.org, http://www.opensecrets.org/pfds/CIDsummary.php?CID=N00027658&year=2008.

92 Earmark Ranking: "Other Data Senator Kirsten Gillibrand 2005–2010," OpenSecrets.org, http://www.opensecrets.org/politicians/otherdata.php?cycle=2010&cid=N00027658&type=I.

93 "If he became": William E. Leuchtenburg, "The FRD Years," *Washington Post*, http://www.washingtonpost.com/wp-srv/style/longterm/books/chap1/fdryears.htm.

94 "She has actively opposed": Keith B. Richburg, "Rep. Gillibrand Chosen for Clinton Senate Seat," *Washington Post*, January 24, 2009, http://www.washingtonpost.com/wp-dyn/content/article/2009/01/23/AR2009012300297.html.

95 "Gillibrand, formerly a": "Flip-Flopping with Kirsten," *New York Post*, February 10, 2009, http://www.nypost.com/p/news/opinion/editorials/item_sbOWG6tiAea2bbUeHvJz1J;j sessionid=2CC72469155E32654D9008E899E2F0D9.

96 "And speaking of targets": Wayne Barrett, "Barrett: How Will the Ballot Police Protect Kirsten Gillibrand from the Harold Ford Invasion?" VillageVoice.com, January 13, 2010, http://blogs.villagevoice.com/runninscared/archives/2010/01/barrett_harold.php.

97 opposed any sort of: Kirk Semple, "Gillibrand's Immigration Views Draw Fire," *New York Times*, January 27, 2009, http://www.nytimes.com/2009/01/28/us/politics/28immigration. html.

98 Just days into: "In Chinatown, Sen Gillibrand Softens Immigration Stance," *Sing Tao Daily*, February 3, 2009, http://news.newamericamedia.org/news/view_article .html?article_id=a71a87d3b6a75d64b48dc7ab120262a6.

99 Not only did she: Michael Powell, "Gillibrand Hints at a Change of Mind on Immigration," *New York Times*, February 1, 2009, http://www.nytimes.com/2009/02/02/ny region/02kirsten.html?_r=1.

100 Several months later: "Sen. Gillibrand Changes Tune on Illegal Immigration," Rochester Homepage.net, April 3, 2009, http://rochesterhomepage.net/content/fulltext/?cid=81711.

101 Gillibrand's opposition: Elizabeth Benjamin, "Gillibrand's Gay Marriage Evolution," NYDailyNews.com, January 23, 2009, http://www.nydailynews.com/blogs/dailypolitics/ 2009/01/gillibrands-gay-marriage-evolu.html.

102 "an apparent effort": Jeremy Peters, "Gillibrand Seeks to Stop Funding for 'Don't Ask, Don't Tell,'" *New York Times*, February 5, 2010, http://thecaucus.blogs.nytimes .com/2010/02/05/gillibrand-jumps-on-dont-ask-dont-tell-retreat/.

103 "There's nothing that defines": "Gillibrand Remains a Political Question Mark," Times Union.com, February 6, 2010, http://www.timesunion.com/AspStories/story.asp?storyI D=897747&TextPage=2#ixzz0eskTwQTR.

104 In January 2010: Mary Azzoli, Barbara Carvalho, and Lee Miringoff, "Democrats Duke it Out in New York State: Gillibrand vs. Ford," MaristPoll.edu, January 15, 2010, http://maristpoll.marist.edu/wp-content/misc/nyspolls/NY100113/Complete%20 January%2015,%202010%20NYS%20Poll%20Release%20and%20Tables.pdf.

105 "More than half": Raymond Hernandez and David Kocieniewski, "As new Lawyer, Senator Was Active in Tobacco's Defense," *New York Times*, March 26, 2009, http://www.nytimes .com/2009/03/27/nyregion/27gillibrand.html?pagewanted=all.

106 "cited Philip Morris's": Ibid.

107 "The state of Minnesota": Ibid.

108 "I didn't know": James M. Odato, "Gillibrand's Tobacco Past Includes Philip Morris," TimesUnion.com, October 16, 2008, http://www.timesunion.com/AspStories/story.asp ?storyID=729940&TextPage=1#ixzz0ennDeh4x.

109 But the fact is: John Stossel, "Crony Capitalism V," FoxBusiness.com, January 14, 2010, http://stossel.blogs.foxbusiness.com/2010/01/14/crony-capitalism-v/.

110 Gillibrand's father, Douglas: Odato, "Gillibrand's Tobacco Past Includes Philip Morris."

111 Mr. Rutnik also: Benjamin Lesser and Greg B. Smith, "Senator-Designate Kirsten Gillibrand has Tapped Dad's Lobbyist Connetions," NYDailyNews.com, January 25, 2009, http://www.nydailynews.com/news/2009/01/24/2009–01–24_senatordesignate _kirsten_gillibrand_has_.html#ixzz0enuu8xyc.

112 In the days before: Wayne Barrett, "Wayne Barrett: Is Gillibrand too Republican to Replace Clinton," VillageVoice.com, January 22, 2009, http://blogs.villagevoice.com/ runninscared/archives/2009/01/the_pudgy_papa.php.

113 Throughout her career: "The New York State Pipe Trades Would Like To Congratulate Kirsten Gillibrand in Winning the New York State Congress Seat!" NYSPipeTrade.org, February 9, 2007, http://www.nyspipetrades.org/viewarticle.asp?a=363.

114 During the Clinton: Kirsten Gillibrand, "Senator Kirsten Gillibrand A Voice for the People of New York," Gillibrand.Senate.gov, http://gillibrand.senate.gov/about/biog raphy/.

115 "With the help": "Opening Statement of Senator Jon Corzine (D-NJ)," April 25, 2001, Banking.Senate.gov, http://banking.senate.gov/01_04hrg/042501/corzine.htm.

116 "Along those lines": Russell Roberts, "How Government Stoked the Mania," *Wall Street Journal*, October 3, 2008, http://online.wsj.com/article/SB122298982558700341 .html.

117 "gave birth to the": Wayne Barrett, "Andrew Cuomo and Fannie and Freddie," Village Voice.com, August 5, 2008, http://www.villagevoice.com/2008–08–05/news/how -andrew-cuomo-gave-birth-to-the-crisis-at-fannie-mae-and-freddie-mac/2.

118 "As an attorney": "About Kirsten," KirstenGillibrand.com, http://www.kirstengillibrand .com/about?id=0001.

119 According to tax returns: "Money, money, money," Jennifer A. Dlouhy, TimesUnion.com, http://blog.timesunion.com/capitol/archives/11277/money-money-money.

120 Net Worth of the Gillibrand: "Personal Finances Kirsten E. Gillibrand (D-NY), 2006," OpenSecrets.org, http://www.opensecrets.org/pfds/CIDsummary.php?CID= N00027658&year=2006, and "Other Data, Senator Kirsten Gillibrand 2005–2010," OpenSecrets.org, http://www.opensecrets.org/politicians/otherdata.php?cycle=2008& cid=N00027658&type=I.

121 "... if a person": "How is a put option exercised?" Investopedia.com, http://www .investopedia.com/ask/answers/06/putoptionexcercise.asp.

122 In 2007, as sub prime: "Financial Disclosure Statement," OpenSecrets.org, http://pfds .opensecrets.org/N00027658_2007.pdf.

123 "To Redbrick Partners": Les Christie, "Florida Foreclosure Future Shock", CNNmoney .com, July 9, 2007, http://money.cnn.com/2007/07/05/real_estate/futureshock_Florida _housing_will_fall/index.htm.

124 "distressed neighborhoods": Mark Mather and William O'Hare, "The Growing Number of Kids in Severely Distressed Neighborhoods: Evidence from the 2000 Census," PBR.org, October 2003, http://www.prb.org/pdf/KidsDistressedNeighborhoods.pdf.

125 "the poorest urban areas": Ibid.

126 Some recent studies: James Jennings, "Community-based Nonprofits and Neighbor-hood Distress in Boston, Massachusetts," Tufts.edu, February 2009, http://www.tufts.edu/~jjenni02/pdf/community-basedNonprofits2009.pdf.

127 Initially, it's first fund: James R. Hagerty, "Beware the Foreclosure Allure," *Wall Street Journal*, September 24, 2008, http://74.125.113.132/search?q=cache:UWawYmcuOjMJ:online.wsj.com/article/SB122222286574070071.html+REDBRICK+PARTNERS+FUND&cd=1&hl=en&ct=clnk&gl=us.

128 Democratic Party Loyalty: "Members of Congress/Arlen Specter," *Washinton Post*, http://projects.washingtonpost.com/congress/members/s000709/.

129 76.8% (2004): "109th Congress/Senate/Members Voting with their Parties," *Washington Post*, http://projects.washingtonpost.com/congress/109/senate/party-voters/.

130 70.5% (2006): "110th Congress/Senate/Members Voting with their Parties," *Washington Post*, http://projects.washingtonpost.com/congress/110/senate/party-voters/.

131 38/100: "Personal Finances 2008," OpenSecrets.org, http://www.opensecrets.org/politicians/otherdata.php?cycle=2010&cid=N00001604&type=http://www.opensecrets.org/pfds/CIDsummary.php?CID=N00001604&year=2008.

132 22/100: Ibid.

133 "I'm not prepared to have": Carl Hulse, "Specter Switches Parties," *New York Times*, April 28, 2009, http://thecaucus.blogs.nytimes.com/2009/04/28/specter-will-run-as-a-democrat-in-2010/.

134 There are 824,000: "Census 2000 Demographic Profile Highlights," Census.gov, http://factfinder.census.gov/servlet/SAFFIteratedFacts?_event=Search&geo_id=01000US&_geoContext=01000US&_street=&_county=&_cityTown=&_state=04000US42&_zip=&_lang=en&_sse=on&ActiveGeoDiv=geoSelect&_useEV=&pctxt=fph&pgsl=010&_submenuId=factsheet_2&ds_name=DEC_2000_SAFF&_ci_nbr=551&qr_name=DEC_2000_SAFF_A1010&reg=DEC_2000_SAFF_A1010%3A551&_keyword=&_industry=.

135 "stop interrupting me": Andrew Malcolm, "Specter May be Haunted by Exchange with Bachmann," *Los Angeles Times*, January 24, 2010, http://articles.latimes.com/2010/jan/24/nation/la-na-ticket24–2010jan24.

136 "Meanwhile, on a radio": Gail Collins, "The Lady and the Arlen," *New York Times*, January 22, 2010, http://www.nytimes.com/2010/01/23/opinion/23collins.html.

137 "I oppose sending": Arlen Specter, "Why I Oppose the Afghan Surge," Specter.senate.gov, December 9, 2009, http://specter.senate.gov/public/index.cfm?FuseAction=NewsRoom.Articles&ContentRecord_id=74014b58-ae36-4ec0-8013-4ae2fb279e33.

138 He's introduced a bill: David Freddoso and Kevin Mooney, "Trial Lawyers Seek Return on Contributions to Senate Democrats," *Washington Examiner*, August 14, 2009, http://www.washingtonexaminer.com/opinion/blogs/beltway-confidential/Trial-lawyers-seek-return-on-contributions-to-Senate-Democrats-53177542.html.

139 "would make it easier": "Terror by Trial Lawyer," *Wall Street Journal*, November 30, 2009, http://online.wsj.com/article/SB10001424052748703939404574568130713843644.html.

140 "We know that al Qaeda": Ibid.

141 Industries Contributing to the: "Industries Contributing to Campaign Cmte," Open Secrets.org,http://www.opensecrets.org/politicians/industries.php?cid=N00001604&cycle =2010&type=I&newMem=N&recs=0.

142 Bobby Bright: "Members of Congress/Bobby Bright," *Washington Post,* http://projects .washingtonpost.com/congress/members/b001264/.

143 Betsy Markey: "Members of Congress/Betsy Markey," *Washington Post,* http://projects .washingtonpost.com/congress/members/m001172/.

144 "spent much of the": Michael Barone and Richard E. Cohen, *The Almanac of American Politics,* National Journal Group, 2010, p. 289.

145 Alan Grayson: "Personal Finances Alan Grayson (D-Fla), 2008," OpenSecrets.org, http:// www.opensecrets.org/pfds/CIDsummary.php?CID=N00028418&year=2008.

146 Walt Minnick: "Members of Congress/Walt Minnick," *Washington Post,* http://projects .washingtonpost.com/congress/members/m001175/.

147 Baron Hill: "Members of Congress/Baron Hill," *Washington Post,* http://projects .washingtonpost.com/congress/members/h001030/.

148 Frank Kratovil Jr.: "Members of Congress/Frank Kratovil," *Washington Post,* http:// projects.washingtonpost.com/congress/members/k$00371/.

149 Mark Schauer: "Members of Congress/Mark Schauer," *Washington Post,* http://projects .washingtonpost.com/congress/members/s001178/.

150 Travis Childers: "Members of Congress/Travis Childers," *Washington Post,* http:// projects.washingtonpost.com/congress/members/c001074/.

151 Dina Titus: "Members of Congress/Dina Titus," *Washington Post,* http://projects .washingtonpost.com/congress/members/t000468/.

152 Carol Shea-Porter: "Members of Congress/Carol Shae-Porter," *Washington Post,* http:// projects.washingtonpost.com/congress/members/s001170/.

153 Harry Teague: "Members of Congress/Harry Teague," *Washington Post,* http://projects .washingtonpost.com/congress/members/t000466/.

154 Steven Driehaus: "Members of Congress/Steven Driehaus," *Washington Post,* http://proj-ects.washingtonpost.com/congress/members/d000609/.

155 Driehaus calls himself: Michael Barone and Richard E. Cohen, *The Almanac of American Politics,* National Journal Group, 2010, p. 1168.

156 Mary Jo Kilroy: "Members of Congress/Mary Jo Kilroy," *Washington Post,* http:// projects.washingtonpost.com/congress/members/k$00372/.

157 Kilroy also sided: "Washington—Muslim Congressman Leads 54 Congressional Mem-bers to Sign Letter to Pressure Israel," *Minnesota Independent,* January 30, 2010, http:// www.vosizneias.com/48158/2010/01/30/washington-muslim-congressman-leads-54 -congressional-members-to-sign-letter-to-pressure-israel/feed/atom/.

158 Kathy Dahlkemper: "Members of Congress/Kathy Dahlkemper," *Washington Post,* http:// projects.washingtonpost.com/congress/members/d000608/.

159 "not a professional": Kathy Dahlkemper, "Biography," Dalhkemper.house.gov, August 17, 2009, http://www.dahlkemper.house.gov/index.php?option=com_content&view=artic le&id=71&Itemid=21.

160 Glenn Nye: "Members of Congress/Glenn Nye," *Washington Post,* http://projects
.washingtonpost.com/congress/members/n000183/.

161 He displayed his true: "Washington—Muslim Congressman Leads 54 Congressional
Members to Sign Letter to Pressure Israel."

162 Tom Perriello: "Members of Congress/Tom Perriello," *Washington Post,* http://projects
.washingtonpost.com/congress/members/p000600/.

163 "his nonprofit work": Michael Barone and Richard E. Cohen, *The Almanac of American
Politics,* National Journal Group, 2010.

164 Harry Mitchell: "Members of Congress/Harry Mitchell," *Washington Post,* http://
projects.washingtonpost.com/congress/members/m001167/.

165 Gabrielle Giffords: "Members of Congress/Gabrielle Giffords," *Washington Post,* http://
projects.washingtonpost.com/congress/members/g000554/.

166 Ann Kirkpatrick: "Members of Congress/Ann Kirkpatrick," *Washington Post,* http://
projects.washingtonpost.com/congress/members/k$00368/.

167 The only reason: Michael Barone and Richard E. Cohen, *The Almanac of American Politics,* National Journal Group, 2010, p. 287.

168 "Kirkpatrick's more moderate": Michael Barone and Richard E. Cohen, *The Almanac of
American Politics,* National Journal Group, 2010, p92.

169 Mike Ross: "Members of Congress/Mike Ross," *Washington Post,* http://projects
.washingtonpost.com/congress/members/r000573/.

170 "much more than a": Lindsay Renick Mayer, "Blue Dog Democrat Mike Ross Benefits
from Real Estate Deal with Drug Company," OpenSecrets.org, September 22, 2009,
http://www.opensecrets.org/news/2009/09/real-estate-transaction-with-p.html.

171 "money in his pocket": Ibid.

172 Jerry McNerney: "Members of Congress/Jerry McNerney," *Washington Post,* http://
projects.washingtonpost.com/congress/members/m001167/.

173 John Salazar: "Members of Congress/John Salazar," *Washington Post,* http://projects
.washingtonpost.com/congress/members/s001158/.

174 He "crafted a moderate": Michael Barone and Richard E. Cohen, *The Almanac of American Politics,* National Journal Group, 2010, p. 287.

175 Jim Himes: "Members of Congress/James Himes," *Washington Post,* http://projects
.washingtonpost.com/congress/members/h001047/.

176 Allen Boyd: "Members of Congress/Alan Boyd," *Washington Post,* http://projects
.washingtonpost.com/congress/members/b000716/.

177 Boyd sponsored: "Other Data Congressman Allen Boyd 2009–2010," OpenSecrets.org, http://
www.opensecrets.org/politicians/otherdata.php?cycle=2010&cid=N00002743&type=I.

178 Sazanne Kosmas: "Members of Congress/Suzanne Kosmas," *Washington Post,* http://
projects.washingtonpost.com/congress/members/k$00370/.

179 Jim Marshall: "Members of Congress/Jim Marshall," *Washington Post,* http://projects
.washingtonpost.com/congress/members/m001146/.

180 Bill Foster: "Members of Congress/Bill Foster," *Washington Post,* http://projects
.washingtonpost.com/congress/members/f000454/.

181 Gary Peters: "Members of Congress/Gary Peters," *Washington Post,* http://projects .washingtonpost.com/congress/members/p000595/.

182 Ike Skelton: "Members of Congress/Ike Skelton," *Washington Post,* http://projects .washingtonpost.com/congress/members/s000465/.

183 John Adler: "Members of Congress/John Adler," *Washington Post,* http://projects .washingtonpost.com/congress/members/a000364/.

184 Tim Bishop: "Members of Congress/Tim Bishop," *Washington Post,* http://projects .washingtonpost.com/congress/members/b001242/.

185 Mike McMahon: "Members of Congress/Michael McMahon," *Washington Post,* http:// projects.washingtonpost.com/congress/members/m001174/.

186 "because of questionable": *The Almanac of American Politics,* p. 1065.

187 John Hall: "Members of Congress/John Hall," *Washington Post,* http://projects .washingtonpost.com/congress/members/h001039/.

188 Bill Owens: "Members of Congress/William Owens," *Washington Post,* http://projects .washingtonpost.com/congress/members/o000169/.

189 Mike Arcuri: "Members of Congress/Mike Arcuri," *Washington Post,* http://projects .washingtonpost.com/congress/members/a000363/.

190 Dan Maffei: "Members of Congress/Dan Maffei," *Washington Post,* http://projects .washingtonpost.com/congress/members/m001171/.

191 Eric Massa: "Members of Congress/Eric Massa," *Washington Post,* http://projects .washingtonpost.com/congress/members/m001173/.

192 Massa was also: "Washington—Muslim Congressman Leads 54 Congressional Members to Sign Letter to Pressure Israel."

193 Larry Kissell: "Members of Congress/Larry Kissell," *Washington Post,* http://projects .washingtonpost.com/congress/members/k$00369/.

194 "liberals hate real Americans": Michael Barone and Richard E. Cohen, *The Almanac of American Politics,* National Journal Group, 2010, p. 1130.

195 Earl Pomeroy: "Members of Congress/Earl Pomeroy," *Washington Post,* http://projects .washingtonpost.com/congress/members/p000422/.

196 John Boccieri, "Members of Congress/John Boccieri," *Washington Post,* http://projects .washingtonpost.com/congress/members/b001263/.

197 Zach Space: "Members of Congress/Zachary Space," *Washington Post,* http:// projects.washingtonpost.com/congress/members/s001173/.220 Space votes with: Ibid.

198 Jason Altmire: "Members of Congress/Jason Altmire," *Washington Post,* http://projects .washingtonpost.com/congress/members/a000362/.

199 Patrick Murphy: "Members of Congress/Patrick Murphy," *Washington Post,* http:// projects.washingtonpost.com/congress/members/m001168/.

200 Christopher Carney: "Members of Congress/Christopher Carney," *Washington Post,* http://projects.washingtonpost.com/congress/members/C001065/.

201 Paul Kanjorski: "Members of Congress/Paul Kanjorski," *Washington Post,* http:// projects.washingtonpost.com/congress/members/k$00008/.

202 "a master of earmarking: Michael Barone and Richard E. Cohen, *The Almanac of American Politics*, National Journal Group, 2010, p. 1289.

203 He delivered $21 million: "Paul E. Kanjorski: Earmarks (Fiscal Year 2009,)" http://www.opensecrets.org/politicians/earmarks.php?cid=N00001509.

204 John Spratt: "Members of Congress/Paul Kanjorski," *Washington Post,* http://projects.washingtonpost.com/congress/members/s000749/.

205 "maestro of the budget": Michael Barone and Richard E. Cohen, *The Almanac of American Politics*, National Journal Group, 2010, p. 1350.

206 Lincoln Davis: "Members of Congress/Lincoln Davis," *Washington Post,* http://projects.washingtonpost.com/congress/members/d000599/.

207 Chet Edwards: "Members of Congress/Chet Edwards," *Washington Post,* http://projects.washingtonpost.com/congress/members/e000063/.

208 "Pelosi enthusiastically encouraged": Michael Barone and Richard E. Cohen, *The Almanac of American Politics*, National Journal Group, 2010, p. 1454.

209 In 2009, he ranked: "Other Data Congressman Chet Edwards 2009–2010," OpenSecrets.org, http://www.opensecrets.org/politicians/otherdata.php?cycle=2010&cid=N00005794&type=I.

210 Jim Matheson: "Members of Congress/Jim Matheson," *Washington Post,* http://projects.washingtonpost.com/congress/members/m001142/.

211 Rick Boucher: "Members of Congress/Rick Boucher," *Washington Post,* http://projects.washingtonpost.com/congress/members/b000657/.

212 Alan Mollohan: "Members of Congress/Alan Mollohan," *Washington Post,* http://projects.washingtonpost.com/congress/members/m000844/.

213 Nick Rahall: "Members of Congress/Nick Rahall II," *Washington Post,* http://projects.washingtonpost.com/congress/members/r000011/.

214 He votes with: Ibid.

215 Rahall also sided: "Washington—Muslim Congressman Leads 54 Congressional Members to Sign Letter to Pressure Israel."

216 Steve Kagen: "Members of Congress/Steve Kagen," *Washington Post,* http://projects.washingtonpost.com/congress/members/k$00365/.

PART THREE

1 "All politics is local": Martin Tolchin, "Thomas P. O'Neill Jr., a Democratic Power in the House for Decades, Dies at 81," *New York Times,* January 7, 1994, http://www.nytimes.com/learning/general/onthisday/bday/1209.html.

2 Obama's Stimulus Spending List: Susan Ferrechio, "After a Flurry of Stimulus Spending, Questionable Projects Pile Up," *Washington Examiner,* November 3, 2009, http://www.washingtonexaminer.com/politics/After-a-flurry-of-stimulus-spending_-questionable-projects-pile-up-8474249-68709732.html.

3 As recently as late: "51% Say Bad Economy Bush's Fault, 41% Blame Obama," Rasmussen Reports.com, December 22, 2009, http://www.rasmussenreports.com/public_content/

politics/obama_administration/december_2009/51_say_bad_economy_bush_s
_fault_41_blame_obama.

4 A February 2010: "Americans Reject Keynesian Economics," RasmussenReports.com,
February 5, 2010, http://www.rasmussenreports.com/public_content/business/general
_business/february_2010/americans_reject_keynesian_economics.

5 "by a three-to-one": "48% Expect Tax Hike, Fundamental Challenge for Obama Administration," RasmussenReports.com, November 25, 2009, http://www.rasmussenreports
.com/public_content/politics/obama_administration/november_2009/48_expect_tax
_hike_fundamental_challenge_for_obama_administration.

6 But what is clear: "Health Care Reform," RasmussenReports.com, February 11, 2010,
http://www.rasmussenreports.com/public_content/politics/current_events/health
care/september_2009/health_care_reform.

7 According to the Rasmussen: "Health Care Reform," RasmussenReports.com, January
4, 2010, http://www.rasmussenreports.com/public_content/politics/current_events/
healthcare/september_2009/health_care_reform.

8 Rasmussen reports that: "48% Expect Tax Hike, Fundamental Challenge for Obama
Administration."

9 Rasmussen tells us: Ibid.

10 In 2001, before Bush's: Gerald Prante, "Summary of Latest Federal Individual Income
Tax Data," TaxFoundation.org, July 30, 2009, http://www.taxfoundation.org/news/
show/250.html.

11 And the share of: Ibid.

12 Asked by Rasmussen: Ibid.

13 State Spending Increases: author's calculations from data on http://www.kaiser
permanente.org and interviews with the staff of the Senate Finance Committee, December 14, 2009.

14 In one of his: Sherley Uhl, "Casey: Rendell 'fixed' tickets," *Pittsburgh Press*, March 28,
1986, http://news.google.com/newspapers?nid=1144&dat=19860328&id=AQUIAAAAI
BAJ&sjid=OmIEAAAAIBAJ&pg=5940,8547012.

PART FOUR

1 "Each time a man": Robert F. Kennedy, "Day of Affirmation Address (as Delivered),"
www.JFKLibrary.org, June 6, 1966, www.jfklibrary.org/Historical+Resources/Archives/
Reference+Desk/Speeches/RFK/Day+of+Affirmation+Address+News+Release+P
age+2.htm.

INDEX

Page numbers in *italics* refer to tables

ABC, 120, 136, 140
Abdulmutallab, Umar Farouk, 138–39
abortion, 69, 178–79, 209, 210, 215, 217, *222*, 237, 241
Abramoff, Jack, 156, 157, 158, 226, 236
absenteeism, 267
Abu Dhabi, 58
Accredited Home Lenders, 195
ACORN, 16, 186, 308
Adjusted Monetary Base (AMB), 13, 38
    see also money supply
Adler, John, *220*, 229
Afghanistan, 218
Afghanistan War, 200, 261–62, 284–86, 298
agribusiness, 168
agricultural subsidies, 174–75
Akers, Paul, 152
alcohol consumption, 26
Alexander, Bill, 169
All-American Bridge, *269*
Allen, George, 249
Almanac of American Politics, 210, 219, 223, 230, 239, 241, 245
Al Qaeda, 136, 200, 201
Alternative Minimum Tax, 67
Altmire, Jason, *220*, 237
Altria, *see* Philip Morris
American Academy of Family Physicians (AAFP), 73, 77
American College of Physicians, 71
American colonies, 92

American Express, 104
American Gaming Association, 161
American International Group (AIG), 106, 124
anesthesiologists, 74
Angle, Sharon, 148
Ann Arbor, Mich., 269
"Anvil Chorus, The," 254, *255*
Arcuri, Mike, *220*, 232–33
Argentina, 2, 16, 93–94, *93*, 95, *95*, 99
Arizona Diamondbacks, *268*
Arkansas, 169
    in 2010 election, 144, 148
ARM mortgages, 38
asbestos, *81*
Ashcroft v. Iqbal, 201
Asian financial crisis (1999), 97
Aspen Institute, 178
Associated Press, 37, 38, 41, 107, 136, 164
Association of American Medical Colleges (AAMC), 72, 76
ATF, 183
Australia, *95*
Austria, 96
automobile industry, 17, 37–38, 47, 49, 267
Awlaki, Anwar al-, 135, 136, 137
Ayotte, Kelly, 146

baby boomers, 77, 88
Bachmann, Michele, 199
Bainbridge, Stephen, 106, 107
Ballard, James, 53

bank loans, 37, 39
Bank of America, *104*, 106
Bank of New York Mellon, 104
bankruptcy, 170
banks, 298
  bad debts cleared by, 39, 46
  Obama's desire for control of, 103–9,
    267
  rescue of, 15, 39, 49, 60, 256
Bank United Financial, 195
Barr, Michael, 61
Barrett, Wayne, 183–84, 193
Barringer, Steven, 159, 160, 161–62, *162*,
  166
Bayh, Evan, 149
BB&T, 104
Bear Stearns Cos., 123, 125
Belgium, 64, 96
Bennet, Michael, 149
Benzi, Rick, 222–23
Berkshire Hathaway, 53
Bernanke, Ben, 56
Berry, Marion, 253
Biden, Beau, 148
Biden, Joe, 148, 198
Binnie, Bill, 146
birthrates, 44
Bishop, Tim, *220*, 229–30
Bixby, Robert, 87
Blagojevich, Rod, 150, 176, 177
blogs, 302
Bloomberg, Michael, 183
Bloomberg News, 53, 71
Blumenthal, Richard, 151
Blunt, Matt, 145
Blunt, Roy, 145
Boccieri, John, *220*, 235–36
Boehlert, Sherwood, 232
Boies, David, 190
Boies, Schiller & Flexner, 191
Bolshevik Revolution, 28
Bolton, John, 92, 124, 130
Bond, Kit, 145
bonds, *see* Treasury securities
Boom, Doom, and Gloom Report, 53
boom, economic, of early 2000s, 48
Boucher, Rick, *221*, 242, 253
Boxer, Barbara, 151, 175–82
  on abortion, 178–79

campaign funds received by, 175
environmental work of, 179–80
ethics and, 175, 176–77, 178
PAC of, 178
slipping popularity of, *179*
slips of the tongue of, 178–81
Boxer, Stewart, 178
Boyd, Allen, *220*, 225–26
Brazil, 16, *93*, 94, *95*
Bretton Woods Conference, 12, 55
Bright, Bobby, *208*, 209
Brown, Jay, 165
Brown, Scott, 143, 198, 250, 251
Brownback, Sam, 145
Brunner, Jennifer, 145
Buck, Ken, 149
budget, U.S., of 2011, 67
Buffett, Warren, 53
Bullhead City, Ariz., 162–63
Bumpers, Dale, 169
Bunning, Jim, 145, 146
bureaucracy, 19–20, 24
Burris, Roland, 150, 176, 177
Bush, George H. W., 304
Bush, George W., 32, 102, 145, 181, 228,
    270, 304
  bank regulation increased by, 103
  DWI of, 287
  Goldman Sachs and, 124
  increased spending by, 91–92
  Iraq War strategy of, 285, 302
  National Guard service of, 303–4
  stimulus checks sent out by, 49–50
  tax cuts by, 39, 54–55, 65, 67, *67, 68*, 102,
    226, 281
Bush (G. W.) administration, terrorism
    and, 133
bypass surgery, *277*
Byrd, Robert, 115

Cabranes, Jose, 202
California, 190
  in 2010 election, 144, 149, 151
California, University of, *123*
campaign brochures, *272*
campaign laws, 266
Campbell, Tom, 151, 175
Canada, 78, *93*, *95*
cancer, 14, *277*

Cannon, Michael F., 78, 79
cap-and-trade legislation, 40, 41, 47,
    126–33, 180, 234, 235, 242, 256, 262,
    264, 280
capital gains tax, 68, 47, 54, 67, 68
Capital One Financial, 104
carbon credits, 10, 19
carbon dioxide emissions, 126–28, 127, 130
carbon tax, 10, 14, 41, 131
car loans, 49
Carnahan, Jean, 145
Carnahan, Mel, 145
Carnahan, Robin, 145
Carney, Christopher, 221, 238
Carter, Jimmy, 32, 285–86
Carter, John, 116
Case, Karl E., 62
Castle, Mike, 148
Catastrophe (Morris and McGann), 9, 49,
    133, 266
Cato Institute, 78
CBS, 120, 138, 304
Central American Free Trade Agreement,
    234
CEOs, salaries of, 19
Chabot, Steve, 216
Chavez, Hugo, 15, 94, 263
chemotherapy, 277
Childers, Travis, 208, 213–14, 254
China, 14, 15, 16, 98, 100
    cap-and-trade and, 128, 132
    dollar under siege by, 58
    economic growth in, 111
    GDP of, 95
    GM in, 111
    low labor costs in, 41
    political prisoners in, 94
    U.S. debt purchased by, 12, 47, 55, 87
    U.S. imports from, 55, 99, 128
Choctaw tribe, 157
Christie, Chris, 249
Chrysler, 19, 106, 116, 118
Chrysler Financial, 106
Churchill, Winston, 57, 260
CIA, 138
Citigroup, Inc., 104, 106, 123, 123
Citizens for Responsibility and Ethics in
    Washington, 124
civil liberties, 19

Clark County Board of Commissioners,
    160
climate change, 19, 29, 58, 126, 130, 132,
    179–80, 243
Clinton, Bill, 42–43, 54, 59, 258, 264, 285,
    303
    as conservative Democratic, 143
    negative campaigns answered by, 287,
        289–91
    scandal and impeachment of, 302, 307
Clinton, Hillary, 151, 182, 183, 185, 258,
    291, 303, 304–5
Clinton administration, 133
Club for Growth, 43
CNBC, 53, 120
CNN, 97, 120, 196
coal, 127–29, 131, 147, 244
Coats, Dan, 149
Collins, Gail, 198
Colorado, in 2010 election, 144, 149
Colorado Rockies, 268
Committee for a Responsible Federal
    Budget, 111
Commodities Futures Trading
    Commission, 125
communism, 33, 84
Conference on Trade and Development,
    U.S., 56
Congress, U.S., 47
    Obama's lackeys in, 3, 143
    see also elections, U.S., of 2010
Congressional Budget Office, 79
Connecticut:
    Obama's health-care reform and, 80,
        80, 153
    in 2010 election, 144, 151
Connecticut, University of, 80, 153
Conrad, Kent, 177
Constitution, U.S., 112–18
construction industry, 37, 38
consumer confidence, 32, 46
consumer spending, 37, 38
Contract with America, 266
Conway, Jack, 146
Cookpoliticalreport.com, 245
coordinated capitalism, 100–101
Copenhagen Climate Talks, 264
copper, 51
Corzine, Jon, 30, 192, 249

cost-push inflation, 50
Couch, Kenneth, 45
Countrywide Financial, 59, 177, 195
Coushatta tribe, 157
cramdown provision, 170
credit card debt, 49
credit cards, 43, 256
  usurious rates charged by, 167, 169–70,
    171
Crist, Charlie, 147
Cuomo, Andrew, 191, 192–93

Dahlkemper, Kathy, *208*, 217–18
Daschle, Tom, 72
Daskal, Jennifer, 140
Davis, Lincoln, *221*, 240
Davis, Polk, 187, 188, 189, 191
Dean, Howard, 237, 302
death panels, 70
death tax, 2, 65–67, *68*, 227, 241
debt, of businesses, 50
Decision Economics, 36–37
Deeds, Creigh, 249
Defense Department, U.S., 134–36
defense spending, 86, *86*
deficit:
  health-care reform and, 78
  as increased by stimulus, 12, 55, 272
  inflation and, 38, 50
  interest rates forced up by, 9
  Obama's enlargement of, 5, 12, 15,
    46, 54, 84–90, 256, 262, 267, 271,
    272, *273*, *274*, 275–76, *275*,
    280
  as percentage of GDP, *84–85*
  taxes and, 5, 15, 39, *67*
deflation, 53
Delaware, in 2010 election, 144, 147–48
demand-pull inflation, 48
Democratic Party, U.S., 16–17
  in control of legislative branch, 2
  moderation absent from, 3–4, 143,
    250–55
  stimulus passed by, 4
  in 2010 elections, 204–8
Denmark, 64, 96
"depressflation," 48, 54
dermatologists, 74
Der Spiegel, 11

Devore, Chuck, 175
diesel, 130
distressed neighborhoods, 196
doctors:
  foreigners as, 10, 71, 77–78
  pay of, 10, 73–74, *73*, 75, 78, 79, *279*
  potential fining of, 76
  scarcity of, 10, 13–14, 70, 71–74, 77,
    81
  student loans of, 10, 74–76
Dodd, Chris, 80, 151, 153, 177
dollar, 47
  confidence in, 9, 12
  threat to, 5, 12, 47–48, 53, 55–57
Don't Ask, Don't Tell policy, 185, 262
Dorgan, Byron, 148, 170, 235
Douglas, Stephen, 295
Dow Jones Industrial Average, 52, *52*
Downey Financial, 195
Downie, Leonard, Jr., 121
downsizing, 42–43
Driehaus, Steven, *208*, 216
Drudge, Matt, 298
drudgereport.com, 298, 299
Dubord, Steven J., 111
Dukakis, Michael, 304
Duluth, Minn., 269
Dunn, Anita, 119, 120
Durbin, Dick, 167
Dutko Group, 169

earmarks, 4, 152, 162–64, 167, 175, 181,
    197, 266
Edwards, Chet, *221*, 240–41
Edwards, John, 304
Eichengreen, Barry, 100–101, *101*
elderly, health reform as threat to, 10,
    171–72, 279
election, U.S., of 2010:
  Afghanistan War as issue in, 284–86,
    298
  deficit as issue in, 271, 272, *273*, *274*,
    275–76, *275*, 280
  health care as issue in, 256, 259, 260,
    264, 276–77, *277*, 278–79, *278*, *279*,
    280–82, *282*, 283–84, *283*, 297–98
  importance of, 1, 2, 3, 4, 5, 6, 11, 16, 33,
    46, 55, 58, 68–69, 83, 112, 132–33,
    249

money for, 252
negative campaigning in, 286–91
Obama as issue in, 255–56, 258–59,
    260–64, 267–68, *268, 269, 270,*
    276–86
possible advertisements for, 252–53,
    252, 254–55, *255,* 256, *257, 258, 262,*
    263
Republican possibilities in, 143–52,
    204–8
spending as issue in, 156, 259, 260
strategy for, 249–91
taxes as issue in, 279–82, 283–84, *283,*
    284
unemployment as issue in, 256, 259, 265,
    270–76
elections, U.S.:
    of 1980, 304
    of 1988, 304
    of 1994, 249, 258, 307
    of 1996, 307
    of 2000, 190, 307
    of 2008, 119, 228, *228,* 281, 304–5
    of 2012, 11, 16
electric cars, 130
Electric Power Research, 130
El-Erian, Mohamed, 46
Elias, Barry, 44, 53–54, 90
emergency rooms, 72
Empire State Pride, 185
Enclosure Acts, British, 43
Environmental Protection Agency (EPA),
    47, 127, 128
Epperly, Ted, 77
Erie Canal, *269*
ethnic profiling, 137
euro, 56, 58, 87
Europe, 23–27, 28–29
    post-World War II economy of, 100–101
    unemployment in, 23, 24, 36, *36*
European Bank for Reconstruction and
    Development, 96
European Economy Since 1945, The
    (Eichengreen), 100–101
European Union, 23, 29, 95, *95*
    lack of democracy in, 99–100
executive compensation, 107, 115
executive pay, 3
experts, 22–23

Faber, Marc, 53
Facebook, 296, 299
Face the Nation, 138
Fannie Mae, 59, 61–62, 105, 192–93
farms, 66
Fayetteville National Cemetery, 44
FBI, 135, 136, 137, 138, 176, 243
FDA, 288
Federal Deposit Insurance Corporation
    (FDIC), 125
Federal Housing Authority (FHA), 59–60
Federal Reserve, U.S., 12, 16, 49, 50, 54, 56,
    90–91
    early 2000s low interest rates of, 48, 59,
    83
    money pumped into economy by, 11,
    48–49
    TARP overseen by, 104
Federal Reserve Bank of St. Louis, 53
Federal Trade Commission (FTC), 121,
    122
FedEx, 22
Feeney, Tom, 226
Feinberg, Kenneth, 105, 106, 107, 115,
    116
Feingold, Russ, 123, 150
Feldstein, Martin, 53
Fiat, 116
FICA, 39, 63, *67*
Fifth Amendment, 138
Fifth Third, *104*
finance industry, 42
financial firms, 15
financial instruments, regulation of, 3
    see also specific instruments
"financial literacy," 170–71
financial regulations, 3
    Democratic support for, 22, 146, 209,
        210, 214, 215, 216, 217, 218, 224, 225,
        227, 228, 229, 230, 231, 232, 233, 235,
        236, 238, 239, 240, 242, 243, 244
    international, 97
    subprime loans pushed by, 61
    see also banks
Financial Times, 53
Finell, Val, 136
Fiorina, Carly, 151, 175, *179*
Fisher, Lee, 145
Fleeced (Morris and McGann), 9, 133, 266

Florida:
    Obama's health-care reform and, *80*
    in 2010 election, 144, 147
Forbes.com, 44–45
Ford, Harold, 186
Ford Motor Co., 195
foreign policy, of Obama, 1, 14–15
Forest Service, U.S., *269*
Fort Hood terrorist attack, 134, 135–36,
    138, 140
Fossella, Vito, 230
Foster, Bill, *220*, 227–28
Fox News, 106–7, 114, 119, 122
    Obama's criticism and blackballing of,
        10, 16, 119–22, 125
France, 2, 23, 24, 27, 28, 93, 95, 97, 101–2,
    265
    deficits of, 87
    dollar under siege by, 58
    GDP of, *95*
    taxes in, 64
Frank, Barney, 125, 229, 232, 237, 239
    financial bill drafted by, 108–10, 111–12
Franken, Al, 237, 253
Fraser Institute, 78
Freddie Mac, 59, 61–62, 192–93
free markets, 29, 249
Friss, Steve, 166
full body screening, 139–40

G-7, 93
G-8, 97–98
G-20 Nations, 57, 96–97, 98, 102, 107
    U.S. sovereignty threatened by, 2–3, 10,
        16, 93–97, *93*, 98–99
Gallup poll, 4
gambling, 156–58
Gates, Bill, 31
Gates, Robert, 202
gays, gay marriage, 185, 190, 264
Gaza, 217, 218, 234
Geithner, Timothy, 15, 124, 125, 211, 227,
    229, 232, 239
    financial bill drafted by, 108–10, 111–12
    TARP overseen by, 104, 105, 107
General Motors, 15, 19, 38, 106, 109,
    110–11, 112, 116, 118, 256
General Social Survey, 27
Gensler, Gary, 125

Germany, 23, 24, 27, 93, 95, *95*, 100
    deficits of, 87
    exports of, 99
    taxes in, 64
Giannoulas, Alexi, 150
Gibbs, Robert, 138
Giffords, Gabrielle, *220*, 222
Gilchrest, Wayne, 212
Gillibrand, Jonathan, 193, 195, 196–97
Gillibrand, Kirsten, 144, 151, 181–97
    campaign biographies of, 191–93
    campaign contributors of, 188–89, *189*
    financial dealings of, 193–97, *194*
    flip-flopping of, 182–86
    Philip Morris work of, 186–90, 191, 193
Gingrich, Newt, 54, 103–4, 266
Giuliani, Rudy, 137
global economic meltdown, 55, 59, 61, 83,
    195
global warming, *see* climate change
GMAC, *104*, 106
gold, 51–52, *51*, *52*, 58
Goldman, Peter S., 41
Goldman Sachs, 32, *104*, 114, 119, 122–25,
    123
Good Fight, The (Reid), 166
Google Inc., *123*
Gordon, Donald, 72
Gore, Al, 190
Goroll, Allan, 72
Grayson, Alan, *208*, 210–11
Grayson, Trey, 146
Great Britain, 2, 93, 95
    capital flight to, 28
    debt of, 57
    deficits of, 87
    GDP of, *95*
    taxes in, 64
    unemployment in, 36
Great Depression, 36, 37, 91, 132
*Great Money Binge, The: Spending Our
    Way to Socialism* (Melloan), 88
Greece, 56, 96
Greenberg/Traurig, 156, 158
Green Institute, 226
Greenspan, Alan, 13
Gregg, Judd, 79, 145, 146
Griffith, Parker, 204, 207
Gross, William H., 88

gross domestic private investment, 43
Gross Domestic Product (GDP), 36, *95*
Grover, Atul, 72
Guantanamo prison, 140, 262
Gulf Arab states, 58
Gulf Co-operation Council, 58
Guymon, Okla., 269

H1N1 virus, 31–32
Hall, John, *220*, 231
Hamas, 217, 234
Hannity, Sean, 198
Harrington, Jane, 20
Harris, Andy, 212
Harvard University, 27, *123*
Hasan, Nidal M., 134, 135–36
Hastert, Dennis, 227
Haycock, Clair, 163
Haycock Petroleum, 163
Hayworth, J. D., 221
Health and Human Services, U.S., 14
health-care industry, Blanche Lincoln's
    support for, 168, 173
health-care reform, 69–81, 111
    cost of, *79*, 81, 276
    Democratic support for, 146, 149, 152,
        153, 167, 171–73, 200, 209, 210, 212,
        214, 215, 217, 218, 219, *222*, 223, 224,
        226, 227, 228, 229, 232, 233, 234, 236,
        238, 240, 241, 242, 243, 244
    individual mandate on, 112
    as issue in 2010 election, 29, 256, 260,
        264, 276–77, *277*, 278–79, *278*, *279*,
        280–82, *282*, 283–84, *283*, 297–98
    limited access to, 2, 10, 13, 14, 18, 70
    Obama's plan for, 1, 2, 4, 13–14, 16, 17,
        69–81, 251, 256, 259, 264, 280–82,
        282, 283–84, *283*, 297–98
    public opposition to, 4, 78–79, 82, 204
    "public option" for, 71, 172, 224, 264
    spending cuts in, 76–77
    surtax and, 68, 81
    taxes needed for, 39
    Ted Kennedy's work on, 179
    as unconstitutional, 112–13
    waiting time and, 71–72, 81
    see also doctors
Health Department, U.S., 288
heart valves, *277*

hedge funds, 97
Hegel, Friedrich, 265
Hemings, Sally, 30
Henderson, Fritz, 111
Henderson, Nev., 161
Hendrickson, Mark W., 117
Henry V, 5–6
Heritage Foundation, 63, 64, 112, 113, 128
Hewlett-Packard, 151, 175
Hill, 174
Hill, Baron, *208*, 212
Himes, Jim, *220*, 225
hip replacement, *277*
Hispanics, 264
Hitler, Adolf, 50, 84
Hock, Doug, 160
Hodes, Paul, 146
Hoeven, John, 148, 235
Hoffman, Doug, 232
Holder, Eric, 137, 138, 243
Holland & Hart, 159, 161–62
Holly's Health Mart, 224
Honduras, 15
Hormats, Robert, 125
House Armed Services Committee, 229
House Ethics Committee, 226
House Financial Services Committee, 108,
    125, 229, 232, 239
House of Representatives, U.S.:
    banking scandal in, 169
    health-care bill in, 81
    in 2010 election, 204–45, 249
House Ways and Means Committee, 63,
    250
housing, housing industry, 49, 298
    foreclosures in, 170
Housing and Urban Development
    Department, U.S., 191, 196
Howard Hughes Corp., 161
Hoyer, Steny, 218
HR 4173, 211
Huffington Post, 119
Hurricane Katrina, 180
hybrid cars, *270*
hydrogen, 131
hyperinflation, 53

IBM, 43
Illinois, in 2010 election, 144, 149, 150

Il Trovatore (opera), 254
immigrants, immigration, 18, 33, 184–85, 221, 262, 264
India, 14, *95,* 128, 132
Indiana:
    state pension funds in, 116–17
    in 2010 election, 144, 149
Indiana State Police Pension Fund, 117
Indiana Teachers' Retirement Fund, 117
Indiana University, *269*
Indian tribes, 156–57
Indonesia, 16, *93,* 94, *95,* 99
industrial revolution, 43
IndyMac, 195
inflation, 31, 47–55, 281
    cost-push, 50
    debt, deficits, and, 9, 12, 38, 49–50, 91
    demand-pull, 48
    as ended by eventual recession, 13
    harbingers of, 12–13
    measurement of, 53–54
    price of gold and, 51–52, *51, 52*
    retirement funds hurt by, 47
    tax brackets and, *67, 68*
information-based economy, 43
inheritance tax, *see* death tax
Institute for Quantitative Social Science, 27
insurance, cost of, *277*
    see also health-care reform
insurance companies, 15, 19
interest rates, *86*
    as currently low, 11, 90–91
    on debt, 12, 47, 88
    eventual increase in, 13, 50–51, 56, 85–86
    as forced up by deficit, 9
    as low in early 2000s, 48, 83
    and subprime mortgages, 59, 83
intergenerational transfers, 66–67
International Monetary Fund (IMF), 96, 97–98
    austerity imposed by, 102
    SDIs of, 57–59
    U.S. sovereignty threatened by, 2, 10, 16, 92–93, 99
    U.S voting power in, 98
Internet, 42, 121–22, 295–96, 298–305
interrogations, 19, 140

investment banks, 97
Investor's Business Daily, 77
Iowa City, Wis., *268*
Iran, 2, 96
    atomic bomb sought by, 15, 16, 263
Iraq, 218
Iraq War, 181, 186, 210, 237, 262, 265, 285, 286
Ireland, 57
Israel:
    Gaza blockaded by, 217, 218, 234
    Iran's threat to, 16, 263
    settlements built by, 15
Italy, 27, 93, 95, *95,* 265

Jackson, Jesse, 304
Japan, 27–28, 39, 56, 93, *95,* 264
    dollar under siege by, 58
    exports of, 99
    GDP of, *95*
    U.S. debt held by, 87
Jefferson, Thomas, 29, 30
Jefferson, William, 177
jihad, 135
Johanns, Mike, 80
John Murtha Airport, 268
Johnson, Lyndon, 285
Jones, Van, 186
JPMorgan Chase, 104, *123*
Justice Department, U.S., 137, 243

Kadish, Lawrence, 85–86
Kagen, Steve, *221,* 244
Kanjorski, Paul, *221,* 238–39
Kansas, in 2010 election, 144, 147
Kashkari, Neel, 125
Katyal, Neal, 140
Kelly, Susan, 231
Kennedy, Anthony, 202
Kennedy, John F., 4, 271
Kennedy, Robert, 306, 307
Kennedy, Ted, 179, 180, 250
Kennedy family, 30, 303
Kentucky, in 2010 election, 144, 146–47
Kerry, John, 228, 229, 265, 303
KeyCorp, *104*
Keynesian economics, 271
Kilroy, Mary Jo, *208,* 217
Kirk, Mark, 150

Kirkegaard, Jacob Funk, 42
Kirkpatrick, Ann, *220*, 222–23
Kirschner, Nestor, 93–94
Kirszner, Rebecca, 163
Kissell, Larry, *220*, 234–35
Klukowski, Ken, 115
Korean War, 116
Kosmas, Suzanne, *220*, 226
Kotlikoff, Laurence, 66
Kratovil, Frank, Jr., *208*, 212–13
Kuhl, Randy, 233
Kuwait, 58
Kyoto Protocol, 126

Labor Department, U.S., 42
Labor Statistics, Bureau of, 35, 45
laissez-faire, 97
Lamontagne, Ovide, 146
Lancaster County, Pa., *269*
Landrieu, Mary, 153
Las Vegas, Nev., 161, 166
Las Vegas Review-Journal, 154
Laughlin, Nev., 162–63
layoffs, 28
Lazarus, Emma, 20
Lehman Brothers, 19, 103, 114, 123, 124, 125
Leibowitz, Jon, 121, 122
leisure, 21, 27
lending, 60
Lenin, Vladimir, 28
Levin, Mark, 20
Levine, Arthur S., 76
Lewinsky, Monica, 307
Lewis, C. S., 20
Lewis, Ken, 107
Liberty and Tyranny, 20
Lieberman, Joseph, 71, 177, 180, 251
"limousine liberals," 30–31
Lincoln, Abraham, 29–30, 295
Lincoln, Blanche, 148, 167–75
    campaign contributors to, 168, *168,* 173, *173, 174*
    farm subsidies received by, 174
Lincoln, Thomas, 29
line-item veto, 266
Lionel Sawyer & Collins, 160, 161
Lisbon, Treaty of, 99
living wills, 69

loans:
    FHA's guaranteeing of, 59–60
    Obama's encouragement of, 59, 60–61
lobbyists, 124, 152, 157–58, 159–62, 266
local taxes, 63
Los Angeles Times, 61, 108, 159, 160, 163
Louisiana, 157, 305
    Obama's health-care reform and, *80,* 153
Lowden, Sue, 148
Lula da Silva, Luiz Inácio, 94

McCain, John, 145, 146, 165, 205, 207, 253, 265
    bank regulation increased by, 103
    campaign finance reform bill of, 123
    negative news stories on, 119–20
McDonnell, Bob, 249
McGurn, William, 201–2
McMahon, Linda, 151
McMahon, Mike, *220,* 230
McMahon, Vince, 151
McNerney, Jerry, *220,* 224
McVeigh, Timothy, 134
Madison County, Ill., *269*
Madoff, Bernie, 49
Maffei, Dan, *220, 233*
Maine, *269*
malpractice, 76, 201
mammograms, 14
manufacturing jobs, 10, 12, 14, 16, 37, 40–41, *40,* 47, 126, 128, 129
Marcus, Ruth, 122
marginal tax rate, 63, *67*
Marist Institute for Public Opinion, 185
Markey, Betsy, *208,* 209–10
Mark Twain National Forest, *269*
Marshall, Jim, *220,* 227
Martin, Jim, 118–19
Martinez, Mel, 145
Marx, Karl, 102, 103
Maryland, 305
Massa, Eric, *220,* 233–34
Massachusetts, 146, 249, 250
    Brown's victory in, 143, 198
    Obama's health-care reform and, *80,* 284
    state health care plan in, 71–72
Matheson, Jim, *221,* 242, 254

Medicaid, *86*, 113, 114, 153, 280, 281–82, 284

Medicare, 63, *68*, 70, 79, 80, 86, *86*, 88, 114, 171, 210, 219, *255*, 262, *277*, 278

Medicare Advantage, 82, *277*

Medigap, 153, *277*

Meek, Kendrick, 147

Meier, Ray, 232

Melancon, Charlie, 253

Melloan, George, 88, 90, 91

Mencken, H. L., 182–83

Mexico, *93*, 94, *95*
    GM in, 111

Michigan, 109
    Obama's health-care reform and, *80*

Microsoft, *123*, *268*

Minnick, Walt, *208*, 211

Mississippi, 76, 157, 253–54

Missouri, in 2010 election, 144, 145

Mitchell, Harry, *220*, 221

Mitterrand, François, 28

Mohammed, Khalid Sheikh, 137–38

Mollohan, Alan, *221*, 243, 253

Money Matters, 53

money supply, 11, 13, 38, 49

Mongiardo, Daniel, 146

Montana, Obama's health-care reform and, *80*, 81

Moore, Michael, 133, 302

Moran, Jerry, 147

Morgan Stanley, 104, *104*

mortgage, 256, 270

mortgage-backed securities, 11, 49, 59

mortgage lending, 38, 59–62

mortgages, 171
    renegotiation of terms of, 167, 192–93
    subprime, 59–61, 83, 105, 192, 195

Motors Liquidation Company, 110, 111

Mourdock, Richard, 117

Moveon.org, 16, 302, 303

MSNBC, 120

Murphy, Patrick, *221*, 237–38

Murrah Federal Building, 134

Murray, Patty, 152

Mutual of Omaha, *81*

NAACP, 166

Nagy, Piroska, 96

Napolitano, Andrew P., 114–15, *114*

Napolitano, Janet, 138

National Bureau of Economic Research, 53

national debt, 83–92, 170
    change in, 88–89, *89*
    Democratic support for raising ceiling on, 209, 210, 212, 215, 216, 217, 218, 223, 225, 227, 230, 231, 232, 235, 236, 237, 239, 240, 241, 242, 243, 244
    inflation caused by, 9, 12, 91
    interest on, 12, 91
    as issue in 2010 election, *257*, *258*
    Obama's increase in, 9, 12, 16, 53, 54, 84–92, 280
    as owed to foreigners, 87

National Health Service Corps, 75

nationalism, 28

National Journal, 23

National Mining Association, 160

National Resource Defense Council, 130

National Rifle Association, 183–84

natural gas, 131

NBC, 120

Neal, Joe, 166

Nebraska, Obama's health-care reform and, *81*, 114, 153, 283–84

Nebraska Blue Cross/Blue Shield, *81*, 153

negative campaigns, 286–91

Nelson, Ben, 114, 153, 178

Nelson, Sheffield, 289–90

Netherlands, 96

Nevada, in 2010 election, 144, 148

Nevada State Athletic Commission, 165

"New Colossus, The" (Lazarus), 20

New Economic Policy (NEP), 28

New England Journal of Medicine, 77

New Hampshire, in 2010 election, 144, 146, 147

New Jersey, 249, 250

Newmont Mining Corp., 160

news organizations, government aid for, 121–22
    see also specific news organizations

New York, N.Y., terrorism trial and, 137

New York Observer, 172

New York Post, 140, 183, 199

New York State, 284
    in 2010 election, 144, 151

New York Times, 3, 44, 62, 87, 124, 139–40, 184, 187, 198, 239

Ney, Bob, 236
Nixon, Richard, 271
no-fly list, 139
North American Free Trade Agreement
    (NAFTA), 132, 234, 262
North Dakota:
    Obama's health-care reform and, 81
    in 2010 election, 144, 147, 148
Northern Mariana Islands, 158
Northern Trust, 104
North Korea, 2, 263
North Las Vegas, Nev., 161
Norton, Gale, 157
Norton, Jane, 149
Norway, 96
Notice Pleading Restoration Act (2009),
    201
Nye, Glenn, 208, 218

Obama, Barack:
    abuse of power by, 118–19
    Afghanistan policies of, 200, 261–62,
        284–86, 298
    auto industry ruined by, 38, 267
    bank control desired by, 103–8, 267
    campaign donors of, 123, 123
    as committed socialist, 17, 20–23
    control of banks desired by, 103–9
    debt increased by, 9, 12, 16, 53, 54,
        84–92, 280
    deficit enlarged by, 5, 12, 15, 46, 54,
        91–92, 256, 262, 267, 271, 272, 273,
        274, 275–76, 275, 280
    deficit lies of, 91–92
    European love of, 29
    foreign policy of, 1, 14–15
    Fox News criticized and blackballed by,
        10, 16, 119–22, 125
    G-20 endorsed by, 98
    health-care plan of, 1, 2, 4, 13–14, 16,
        17, 69–81, 251, 256, 264, 267, 280,
        297–98; see also health-care reform
    individualism disdained by, 17–18
    as issue in 2010 election, 255–56,
        258–59, 260–64, 267–68, 268, 269,
        270, 276–86
    Nobel Peace Prize won by, 46
    as post-American president, 92
    "saving jobs" as goal of, 32
    Specter welcomed to Democratic Party
        by, 198
    subprime mortgage market encouraged
        by, 59, 60–61
    taxes raised by, 2, 5, 10, 46, 47, 63–65,
        64, 67, 68–69, 133, 262, 279–84
    in 2008 election, 304–5
    2011 budget proposal of, 67
    unconstitutional positions of, 112–18
    unemployment increased by, 33, 34, 36,
        42, 45, 262, 265, 267, 270–76
    U.S. sovereignty compromised by, 2–3
Office of Management and Budget (OMB),
    85
Ohio, in 2010 election, 144, 145–46
oil, 130, 131
    drilling for, 218
    weakened dollar and, 48
Oklahoma City, Okla., 134
Olson, Ted, 190
O'Neill, John, 303
online gambling, 156
OPEC, 131
Opel, 111
Open Secrets, 123, 223–24
optimism, 33
Oregon, in 2010 election, 144, 151, 152
Organisation for Economic Co-operation
    and Development (OECD), 63
orthopedists, 74
OSHA, 288
Outrage (Morris and McGann), 105, 140,
    211, 243, 266
outsourcing, 110
overtime, 28
Owens, Bill, 220, 231–32

pacemakers, 79, 277
Pacific Investment Management Co., 46
Pacific Northwest National Lab, 130
Paese, Michael, 125
Palin, Sarah, 146
    "death panels" criticized by, 70
Parrish, Steve, 189
part-time work, 44–45
Past Due: The End of Easy Money and the
    Renewal of the American Economy
    (Goldman), 41
Paterson, David, 151, 185

Patterson, Mark, 124
Paul, Rand, 146
Paul, Ron, 146
Paulson, Henry, 103, 104, 124
Pelosi, Nancy, 4, 243–44, 251, 254, *255*
    Democratic support for, 207, 209, 211,
        212, 214, 215, 216, 217, 219, 228, 230,
        231, 234, 235, 240, 242
    ethics and, 177
    high taxes desired by, 30, 63, *64*
    millionaire surtax pushed by, 39
Pennsylvania, in 2010 election, 144, 149,
    150
pessimism, 35, 46
Peters, Garry, *220*, 228
Peterson Institute for International
    Economics, 42
Petraeus, David, 202
Pew Global, 23
Pew Research Center, 119, 120
Phelps, Edmund, 46
Philip Morris, 186–90, 191, 193
Pimco Group, 88
Platt, Ronald, 158
Poland, 2, 15, 96
Polish-Americans, 198–99
political action committees (PACs), *155,*
    156, 157, 160, 164, 178, 233, 252
political ads, *see* television and radio ads
Politico.com, 170
Pomeroy, Earl, *220*, 235
Porter, Jon, 214
Portland, Oreg., *270*
Portman, Rob, 145–46
Post Office, 20, 22
Prasad, Eswar, 55–56
primaries, 4
Primark Decision Economics, 41
privacy issues, 139–40
private sector borrowing, crowding out of,
    89, 90
progressive taxes, 63
Proposition 8, 190
prosthetic limbs, *277*
public option, 71, 172, 224, 264
public schools, 20
publishing, 12
Putin, Vladimir, 15, 263
put options, 195, 196

Qatar, 58
Quality Adjusted Life Years (QALYs),
    69–70

racial profiling, 137, 139
radio ads, *see* television and radio ads
radiologists, 74
Rahall, Nick, *221,* 243–44
Raines, Franklin, 105
Rangel, Charlie, 63, 209, 219, 242, 250,
    254
Rasmussen Poll, 32, 78, 145, 146, 147,
    148, 149, 150, 151, 270, 271, 275, 276,
    279–80, 281
Rather, Dan, 303–4
Reagan, Ronald, 15, 28, 32, 87, 91, 102, 148,
    304
Reagan administration, 53
Reaganomics, 33
RealtyTrac, 170
Reason, 60
rebuttal advertising, 288–90
REC Employee Holiday Fund, 164
recession, 9
reconciliation, 81, 250
Redbrick Partners, 196
redistribution, 2
Regions Financial, *105*
Regula, Ralph, 236
regulations, 2
Reid, Harry, 4, 113, 148, 152–66, 167, 172,
    181, 182, 184, 214, 250, 251, 253, *255*
    civil rights claims of, 166
    earmarks of, 152, 162–64
    ethical issues of, 153, 157–66
    family of, 159–62
    gambling industry and, 156–58
    health-care reform and, 81, 114, 153,
        171, 284
    money for 2010 raised by, 154, *154, 155,*
        156
    "Negro dialect" remark of, 166
    PACs of, *155, 156,* 157, 160, 164, 166
    unpopularity of, 154
Reid, Josh, 160
Reid, Key, 160
Reid, Leif, 160
Reid, Rory, 160, 161
Reid Victory Fund, 166

religion, 22
Rendell, Ed, 290
Republican Party, U.S.:
importance of electing, 11, 16
TARP and, 103
2010 election strategy of, 249–91
2010 possibilities of, 143–52, 204–8
upward mobility allowed by, 61
retail, retailers, 11, 42
retirement pension funds, 47
retirement plans, 37
Revolution Will Not Be Televised, The
(Trippi), 303
Rice, Condoleezza, 181
Riley, Bob, 133
Riza, Shaha, 96
road construction, *270*
robber barons, 20, 31
Rockefeller, Jay, 30
Rogoff, Kenneth S., 46
Romanoff, Andrew, 149
Romney, Mitt, 71–72
Roosevelt, Franklin Delano, 182
Rose Law Firm, 291
Ross, Mike, *220*, 223–24
Rove, Karl, 307
Rubio, Mario, 147
Russia, 2, 16, 58, 93, *93*, 94, 97, 100, 263
GDP of, *95*
Rutnik, Kirsten, *see* Gillibrand, Kirsten
Ryan, Jim, 158

Sabato, Larry, 185
safety net, 21, 24
Sahm, Claudia, 49
salaries, 45
Salazar, John, *220*, 224–25
Salazar, Ken, 224
Samuelson, Paul, 56
Santayana, George, 62
Sarkozy, Nicholas, 97, 101–2
Saudi Arabia, 2, 16, 58, 93, 94, 95, *95*, 99,
100, 218
SAVE Act, 184
Saxena, Puru, 53
schools, 31
Schumer, Chuck, 182, 185
Scozzafava, Dede, 232
Searchlight Leadership Fund, 157

Securities and Exchange Commission, 16,
124
Sedgwick, Robert, 107
Senate, U.S.:
health-care bill in, 81, 171
in 2010 election, 143–204, 249
Senate Agriculture Committee, 173–74
Senate Committee on Energy and Public
Works, 179
Senate Environmental Committee, 175
Senate Ethics Committee, 159–60, 175,
176–77
Senate Finance Committee, *68*
Senate Foreign Relations Committee, 181
September 11, 2001, terrorist attacks of,
133, 134, 137, 167, 186, 265, 307
Sestak, Joe, 200
Shakespeare, William, 5–6
Shapiro, Matthew, 49
Sharia Law, 94
Shauer, Mark, *208*, 213
Shays, Chris, 225
Shea-Porter, Carol, *208*, 215
Sidley Austin LLP, *123*
Simmons, Rob, 151
Sinai, Allen, 36–37, 41
Singapore, 218
Singer, Brown, & Barringer, 166
60 Minutes, 122
Skelton, Ike, *220*, 228–29
slavery, 30
Slemrod, Joel, 49
Sloan, Melanie, 124
Smoot-Hawley tariff (1930), 132
Snow, Tony, 181
socialism, 5, 17, 20–27, 28, 32–33, 46,
102–12, 251
see also financial regulations
Social Security, 39, 54, 86, *86*, 88, 262, 280
see also FICA
Solomon, John, 157, 164
Soros, George, 30, 31, 58, 302
South Africa, 2, 16, 95, *95*, 96, 99
South Dakota, 170
Obama's health-care reform and, *81*
South Korea, *95*
GM in, 111
Soviet Union, 19, 28–29, 32
Space, Zack, *220*, 236

Spain, 56–57, 96
Special Drawing Rights (SDR), 57–59
Specter, Arlen, 150, 197–204
    campaign contributions of, 200–201,
        202, 203, 204
    resignation from Republican Party, 198
    trial lawyers and, 201–2
speculation, 48
Spitzer, Eliot, 184
Spratt, John, *221,* 239–40
stagflation, 48
Stalin, Joseph, 28–29
state holding companies, *101*
state-owned enterprises (SOEs), 111
State Street, 104
state taxes, 63, *278*
steering committee, 118
"Stimulus 2" program, 90, 268, 272
stimulus checks, 49–50
stimulus package, 62, 92
    adjustment postponed by, 43–44
    construction industry ruined by, 38
    deficit increased by, 12, 55, 272
    Democratic support for, 4, 146, 209, 210,
        212–13, 214, 215, 216, 217, 218, 219,
        222, 223, 224, 225, 226, 227, 228, 229,
        230, 231, 232, 234, 235, 236, 237, 238,
        239, 241, 242, 243, 244
    as ineffective on unemployment, 32,
        43, 272
    money printed for, 49
    public disapproval of, 4
    in savings accounts, 49–50
    wasteful spending in, 267–68, *268, 269,
        270*
stock market crash (2008), 9, 171
Stokes, Bruce, 23–24
Storch, Adam, 124
Strauss-Kahn, Dominique, 96
Stubbs, Joseph, 71
student loans, for doctors, 10, 74–76
subprime mortgages, 59–61, 83, 105, 192,
    195
suicide, 25–26
Summers, Larry, 66
SunTrust, *105*
Superfund, *81*
supply-side economics, 58
Supreme Court, U.S., 112, 201, 265

surtax, 39, 67, 68, 81, 280–81
Sweden, 64, 96
swine flu, 31–32
swing voters, 250
Switzerland, 96
Syracuse University, *268*

Taiwan, 96
Taliban, 284
Tanner, John, 253
Tarkanian, Danny, 148
TARP funds, 90, 92
taxes:
    Bush's cuts of, 39, 54–55, 65, 67, *67, 68,*
        102, 226, 281
    capital gains, 47, 54, *67, 68*
    carbon, 10, 14, 41, 131
    death, 2, 65–66, *68*
    deficit and, 5, 15, 39, *67*
    economic growth rekindled by cutting
        of, 46–47
    in Europe, 24
    exemptions on, 68
    future increases in, 39, 56, 62–69
    inflation and, *67, 68*
    and interest on debt, 12
    as issue in 2010 election, 279–82, *282,*
        283–84, *283*
    local, 63
    on middle class, 78
    Obama's raising of, 2, 5, 10, 46, 47, 63–
        65, *64,* 67, 68–69, 133, 262, 279–84
    progressive, 63
    state, 63, *278*
    vicious circle of, 32
    see also FICA
tax evasion, 156
tax havens, 28
Teague, Harry, *208,* 215–16
Tea Party movement, 305–6, 308
Telegraph, 57
television and radio ads, 295–96
    authors' suggestions for, 252–53, *252,*
        254–55, *255,* 256, *257, 258, 262, 263*
terrorism, terrorists, 19, 131
    see also Fort Hood terrorist attack;
        September 11, 2001, terrorist attacks
        of
Terry, Mary Sue, 249

Texans Against Government Waste and Unconstitutional Conduct, 117
Thatcher, Margaret, 28, 102
This Time Is Different: Eight Centuries of Financial Folly (Rogoff and Reinhart), 46
Thompson, Tommy, 150
Tiahrt, Todd, 147
Times (London), 96
Time Warner, *123*
Titus, Dina, *208*, 214
tobacco, 186–90, 191, 193
Today, 138
"too big to fail," 9, 107, 108, 118
Toomey, Pat, 150
tort reform, 76
trade deficit, 88
Transparency International, 94
Treasury Department, U.S., 16, 50, 104, 109
Treasury Inflation Protected Securities (TIPS), 47
Treasury securities, 11, 43, 49, 50, 55, 56, 90
triangulation, 264
Trippi, Joe, 302–3, 304
Troubled Asset Relief Program (TARP), 15–16, 103–4, 106, 107, 119, 125
    as unconstitutional, 114–15, *114, 115*, 117–18
trueslant.com, 172
Truman, Harry, 116
Tsongas, Paul, 304
Turkey, 95, *95*
TV companies, 168
Twitter, 296, 299
tyranny, 20

underemployment rate, 34–35, *35*, 45
unemployment, 9, 33–47, 216, 267, 270
    death tax and, 65–66
    in Europe, 23, 24, 36, *36*
    government spending on, *86*
    as issue in 2010 election, 256, 259, 265, 270–76
    permanent increase in, 11, 16, 35–36, 42, 44–45
    stimulus package's effect on, 32, 43, 272
    underestimation of, 34–35, *35*, 45

Unfit for Command: Swift Boat Veterans Speak Out Against John Kerry (O'Neill), 303
unions, 20, 24, 100, *101*, 133, 262
United Auto Workers, 116, 118
United Nations, dollar attacked by, 56
United States:
    capital flight to, 28
    Chinese exports to, 55, 99, 128
    GDP of, *95*
    happiness in, 24–25
    threatened sovereignty of, 2, 10, 16
UPS, 22
USA Drug, 223
USA Today, 73, 77, 165
US Bancorp, 104
usury, 167, 169–70, 171
Utah, 254
utility companies, 168

vacations, 28
Venezuela, 15, 94, 96, 218, 263
Vermont, 302
    Obama's health-care reform and, *80, 81*
veterans, 20
Veterans Administration, 22
Vietnam War, 285, 303
Village Voice, 183–84, 193
Virginia, 249, 250, 305
Voinovich, George, 145
Volcker, Paul, 11
Vote.com (Morris and McGann), 302

Walberg, Tim, 213
Walker, H. Kenneth, 72
Wallace, Chris, 120
Wall Street Journal, 24, 27, 35, 42, 58, 75–76, 80, 88, 91, 99, 122–23, 136, 153–54, 192–93, 196–97, 201
Walsh, Michael, 180–81
Warner, John, 180
war on terror, *86*, 133–40, 302
warrantless searches, 140
Washington, 305
    in 2010 election, 144, 151, 152
Washington, George, 30
Washington Examiner, 62, 123
Washington Post, 121, 135, 136
Washington State University, *269*

Weimar Germany, 50, 91
welfare, *86*
Wells Fargo, *105*
wheelchairs, *277*
Whitacre, Edward, Jr., 111
White, Frank, 291
Whitman, Christine Todd, 249
Wiens, Tom, 149
Wisconsin, in 2010 election, 144, 149, 150
Wolfowitz, Paul, 96
Woodhill, Louis, 43
work, 26–27
World Bank, 96
World Trade Center, 1993 attack on, 133
    see also September 11, 2001, terrorist
        attacks of

World War I, 91
Wyden, Ron, 152
Wyoming, Obama's health-care reform
        and, *81*

Yale University, 153
Yeltsin, Boris, 93
Yemen, 135, 136
yen, 56, 58
Youngstown Sheet & Tube Company v.
        Sawyer, 116
YouTube, 296, 299, 301–2
yuan, 58

Zimbabwe, 53
Zumbrun, Joshua, 44–45